アメリカ
国際私法・国際取引法
判例研究

松岡 博　Hiroshi Matsuoka

大阪大学出版会

はしがき

　グローバリゼーションの進展に伴って，国際関係私法の中核をしめる国際私法・国際取引法の重要性はますます高まりつつある．わが国でもこれに対応し，「法例」が全面改正され，「法の適用に関する通則法」が制定されるとともに，明文の規定のない国際裁判管轄についても新たな立法作業が続けられている．永年の懸案であったCISGへの加入も平成21年の8月に実現した．
　このような状況の下では，日本と経済社会の様々な面において緊密な交流のある，アメリカ合衆国の国際私法（抵触法）・国際取引法を理解する必要性は極めて高いといえるであろう．とりわけ豊富な判例を有する判例法国であるアメリカについて，これらの分野における主要な判例を研究，教育する必要があることはおそらく異論のないところであろう．
　そこで本書では，アメリカ国際私法・国際取引法の14件の判例を取り上げ，紹介，検討することとした．取り上げた判例は，国際裁判管轄・国際商事仲裁の判例が5件，法選択（準拠法）の判例が6件，域外適用の判例が3件という3部構成となっている．14の判例はいずれもケースブックなどに掲載されているリーディング・ケースを中心に選択した．そのうち，2件の州際事件を除き，他はいずれも国際事件であり，日本との関連の事件も3件をとりあげた．
　いずれの判例も，これを正確に理解するには，原文の英語で読むことが必要と考え，まず，判決の主要部分の英文を左頁に掲げ，その翻訳を右頁にという方法を採用した．見開きにしたのは，英文と訳とを一覧できるようにとの配慮からである．
　つぎに［解説］では，判例を理解するのに必要な関連判例，学説，立法などを説明し，［本件参考文献］では，わが国の日本語で書かれた当該判決の紹介文献を掲げた．また［設問］では，判決を理解するのに必要となるポイントを設問の形という掲げた．判例を読む前後に読んで活用していただきたい．本書が研究者や実務家はもとより，これからアメリカのロースクールへ

留学したいと考えておられる方々にもお役に立てれば望外の喜びである．

　本書で取り上げた判例は，これまで大阪大学，京都大学，帝塚山大学の大学院の授業で取り扱ったものが中心であるが，このような形で公刊することができたのは，なによりも「帝塚山大学国際ビジネス法務塾」に負うところが大きい．法務塾は，平成19年度文部科学省の「社会人学び直しニーズ対応教育プログラム」に採択された取り組みであり，本書はその法務塾の第5期の「外国判例講読」の講義録をそのまま再現したものである．

　本書の公刊は，また多くの方々のご尽力とご協力のたまものである．とりわけ，法務塾で本書の素材となった資料を使って，一緒に「外国判例講読」を教えて頂いた松永詩乃美（大阪経済大学専任講師），片岡雅世（帝塚山大学専任講師），金美善（帝塚山大学助手）の各氏と，本書の厄介な校正の仕事を引き受けて頂いた前田実紀（帝塚山大学大学院博士後期課程），ウジム（田淵電機法務知財部）の両氏に厚く御礼を申し上げたい．また本書の原稿執筆の相当部分は，関西学研都市にある㈶国際高等研究所のフェロー研究室でなされた．すばらしい快適な研究環境を提供して頂いた高等研の関係者の皆様にも感謝したい．最後に本書の企画から編集に至るまで万端にわたってご尽力頂いた大阪大学出版会の岩谷美也子編集長に心からの謝意を表したい．

平成22年3月
奈良の帝塚山大学研究室にて
松　岡　　博

目　次

I　国際裁判管轄・国際商事仲裁

1　対人管轄(1)：Helicopteros Nacionales de Colombia, S.A. v. Hall, 466 U.S. 408 (1984) ─────── 2

【解説】　1　対人管轄（権）
　　　　　2　一般管轄権と特別管轄権
　　　　　3　一般管轄権の基礎：「継続的で組織的な」活動
　　　　　4　反対意見
　　　　　5　一般管轄権の行使に対する制限的立場
　　　　　6　合衆国政府の裁判所の友（amicus curie）としての意見

2　対人管轄(2)：Asahi Metal Industry Co., Ltd. v. Superior Court of California, 480 U.S. 102 (1987) ─────── 24

【解説】　1　対人管轄権革命：*International Shoe* 判決
　　　　　2　「通商の流れ」の理論と *World-Wide Volkswagen* 判決
　　　　　3　2段階テスト：最小限の関連とフェアネス
　　　　　4　最小限の関連
　　　　　5　フェアネス又は相当性
　　　　　6　管轄権拡大法（long arm statute）

3　対人管轄(3)：Miller v. Honda Motor Co., 779 F.2d 769 (1st Cir. 1985) ─────── 54

【解説】　1　*Howse* 判決
　　　　　2　多国籍企業に対する裁判管轄権
　　　　　3　法人格否認が肯定された事例
　　　　　4　アメリカ子会社に対する管轄権

4 合意管轄：The Bremen v. Zapata Off- Shore Co., 407 U.S.1 (1972) ———— 70

　【解説】　1　本件以前の判例状況
　　　　　2　第2リステイトメント第80条
　　　　　3　本判決の法理
　　　　　4　その後の展開：*Carnival Cruise Lines* 判決
　　　　　5　仲裁合意：*Scherk* 判決

5 仲裁適格性：Mitsubishi Motors Corporation v. Soler Chrysler-Plymouth, Inc., 473 U.S. 614 (1985) ———— 100

　【解説】　1　仲裁適格性：証券取引法上の請求と独占禁止法上の請求
　　　　　2　*American Safety* 判決
　　　　　3　*Scherk* 判決
　　　　　4　本件多数意見
　　　　　5　その後の展開
　　　　　6　仲裁適格性と裁判管轄

II　法選択（準拠法）

6 旅客運送契約中の準拠法約款：Siegelman v. Cunard White Star Ltd., 221 F.2d 189 (2d Cir.1955) ———— 132

　【解説】　1　アメリカ国際私法における当事者自治の原則
　　　　　2　第2リステイトメントにおける当事者自治の原則とその制限
　　　　　3　附合契約における準拠法約款の効力
　　　　　4　第2リステイトメントにおける解決
　　　　　5　*Fricke* 判決

7 競業禁止約款の準拠法：Nordson Corp. v. Plasschaert, 674 F.2d 1371 (11th Cir.1982) ———— 164

　【解説】　1　競業禁止約款における法の抵触
　　　　　2　第2リステイトメントにおける当事者自治の原則
　　　　　3　当事者による法選択を否定した判決
　　　　　4　*Barnes* 判決
　　　　　5　競業禁止に関する準拠法約款の効力についてのアメリカ法の傾向

8 代理店契約の準拠法：Southern International Sales Co., Inc. v. Potter & Brumfield Div., 410 F.Supp.1339 (S.D.N.Y.1976) ── 192

【解説】 1 代理店契約と法の抵触
2 抵触法第2リステイトメント第187条第2項b号
3 本件への適用
4 第2リステイトメント第188条
5 *Wood Bros. Homes Inc. v. Walker Adj. Bureau*, 198 Colo. 444, 601 P.2d 1369（1979）．
6 Summary Judgment

9 契約能力の準拠法：Lilienthal v. Kaufman, 239 Or.1, 395 P.2d 543 (1964) ──────── 208

【解説】 1 契約の準拠法
2 利益分析論
3 不法行為事件における利益分析論
4 本件における利益分析論
5 学説の対応

10 生産者責任の準拠法：Tomlin v. Boeing Co., 650 F.2d 1065 (9th Cir. 1981) ──────── 236

【解説】 1 生産物責任における法の抵触
2 生産物責任の準拠法に関する判例の法選択方法論
3 *Reyno v. Piper Aircraft* 判決
4 *Turcotte v. Ford Motor Company* 判決
5 *Johnson v. Spider Staging Corporation* 判決
6 第2リステイトメントの「最も重要な関係」のアプローチ
7 生産物責任の準拠法に関するハーグ条約

11 著作権の準拠法：Itar-Tass Rusian Agency v. Rusian Kurier, Inc., 153 F.3d 82 (2d Cir.1998) ──────── 260

【解説】 1 著作権の準拠法
2 著作権の所有権問題と侵害問題との区別
3 著作権の所有権
4 著作権侵害
5 法選択アプローチか域外適用か
6 ALI原則

v

III 域外適用

12 独占禁止法の域外適用：Timberlane Lumber Co. v. Bank of America N.T.& S.A., 549 F.2d 597 (9th Cir.1976) ———— 288

【解説】
1 American Banana Co. v. United Fruit Co. における属地主義
2 United States v. Aluminum Co. of America, 148 F.2d 416（2d Cir. 1945）における効果理論の採用
3 Timberlane 判決
4 アメリカ対外関係法第3リステイトメント
5 Hartford 判決
6 Empagran 判決

13 商標法の域外適用：Steele v. Bulova Watch Co., 344 U.S. 280 (1952) ———— 318

【解説】
1 商標法の域外適用と属地主義
2 Vanity Fair Mills, Inc. v. T. Eaton Co. 234 F.2d 633（2d Cir. 1956）判決
3 Wells Fargo & Co. v. Wells Fargo Express Co. 556 F.2d 406（9th Cir. 1977）判決
4 McBee v. Delica Co., 417 F.3d 197（1st Cir. 2005）判決

14 証券法の域外適用：Zoelsch v. Arthur Andersen & Co., 824 F.2d 27 (D.C. Cir.1987) ———— 340

【解説】
1 証券取引所法第10条(b)
2 証券法の域外適用における行為テストと効果テスト
3 第2巡回区控訴裁判所の関連判決
4 アメリカ対外関係法第3リステイトメント第416条（証券に関する行為を規律する管轄権）
5 その後の展開

事項索引　368
判例索引　372

I 国際裁判管轄・国際商事仲裁

1 | 対人管轄(1):
Helicopteros Nacionales de Colombia, S.A. v. Hall, 466 U.S. 408 (1984)

JUSTICE BLACKMUN delivered the opinion of the Court.

We granted certiorari in this case to decide whether the Supreme Court of Texas correctly ruled that the contacts of a foreign corporation with the State of Texas were sufficient to allow a Texas state court to assert jurisdiction over the corporation in a cause of action not arising out of or related to the corporation's activities within the State.

I

Petitioner Helicopteros Nacionales de Colombia, S.A. (Helicol), is a Colombian corporation with its principal place of business in the city of Bogota in that country. It is engaged in the business of providing helicopter transportation for oil and construction companies in South America. On January 26, 1976, a helicopter owned by Helicol crashed in Peru. Four United States citizens were among those who lost their lives in the accident. Respondents are the survivors and representatives of the four decedents.

At the time of the crash, respondents' decedents were employed by Consorcio, a Peruvian consortium, and were working on a pipeline in Peru. Consorcio is the alter ego of a joint venture named Williams-Sedco-Horn (WSH). The venture had its headquarters in Houston, Tex. Consorcio had been formed to enable the venturers to enter into a contract with Petro Peru, the Peruvian state-owned oil company. Consorcio was to

> ペルーにおけるヘリコプターの墜落事故に基づく不法行為死亡訴訟において，テキサス州が外国会社（コロンビア会社）に対して対人管轄権を行使することは，合衆国連邦憲法修正第14条の適正手続条項に反するとして，これを認めなかった事例

BLACKMUN 裁判官が法廷意見を言い渡した．

テキサス州と外国法人との関連からみて，テキサス州裁判所が，外国法人に対しその法人の州内における活動から生じたものではなく，又それと関連を有しない訴訟原因に関して管轄権を行使するのに十分であると，テキサス最高裁が判示したことが正しかったかどうかを決定するために，本件においてわれわれは裁量的上訴を認めた．

I 上訴人 Helicopteros Nacionales de Colombia, S.A.（Helicol）は，コロンビア会社であり，その主たる営業所を同国のボゴタ市に有している．この会社は南アメリカにおいて石油及び建設会社のために，ヘリコプター輸送を提供する業務に従事している．1976 年 1 月 26 日，Helicol の所有するヘリコプターがペルーで墜落した．この事故で死亡した者の中に 4 人の米国人が含まれていた．被上訴人は，この 4 人の死者の遺族と代理人である．

墜落の当時，被上訴人の死者たちは，ペルーのコンソーシアムである Consorcio に雇われており，ペルーのパイプラインで働いていた．Consorcio は，Williams-Sedco-Horn（WSH）という名のジョイント・ベンチャーの分身であった．そのベンチャーは，テキサスのヒューストンに本拠を有していた．Consorcio は，ペルー国有の石油会社 Petro Peru とジョイント・ベンチャーが契約することができるように，設立されたものであった．Consorsio

construct a pipeline for Petro Peru running from the interior of Peru westward to the Pacific Ocean. Peruvian law forbade construction of the pipeline by any non-Peruvian entity.

Consorcio/WSH needed helicopters to move personnel, materials, and equipment into and out of the construction area. In 1974, upon request of Consorcio/WSH, the chief executive officer of Helicol, Francisco Restrepo, flew to the United States and conferred in Houston with representatives of the three joint venturers. At that meeting, there was a discussion of prices, availability, working conditions, fuel, supplies, and housing. Restrepo represented that Helicol could have the first helicopter on the job in 15 days. The Consorcio/WSH representatives decided to accept the contract proposed by Restrepo. Helicol began performing before the agreement was formally signed in Peru on November 11, 1974. The contract was written in Spanish on official government stationery and provided that the residence of all the parties would be Lima, Peru. It further stated that controversies arising out of the contract would be submitted to the jurisdiction of Peruvian courts. In addition, it provided that Consorcio/WSH would make payments to Helicol's account with the Bank of America in New York City.

Aside from the negotiation session in Houston between Restrepo and the representatives of Consorcio/WSH, Helicol had other contacts with Texas. During the years 1970-1977, it purchased helicopters (approximately 80% of its fleet), spare parts, and accessories for more than $ 4,000,000 from Bell Helicopter Company in Fort Worth. In that period, Helicol sent prospective pilots to Fort Worth for training and to ferry the aircraft to South America. It also sent management and maintenance personnel to visit Bell Helicopter in Fort Worth during the same period in order to receive "plant familiarization" and for technical consultation. Helicol received into its New York City and Panama City, Fla., bank accounts over $ 5 million in payments from Consorcio/WSH drawn upon

1　対人管轄(1)：Helicopteros Nacionales de Colombia, S.A. v. Hall

は，ペルーの内陸部から西へ太平洋にまで至るパイプラインをペルーのために建設することになっていた．ペルー法は，ペルー法人でないものによるパイプラインの建設を禁止していた．

　Consorcio/WSHは，建設現場への，又はそこからの人員，材料，備品の輸送のためにヘリコプターを必要としていた．1974年に，Consorcio/WSHの要請により，Helicolの最高執行役員Francisco Restrepoは，合衆国に飛行機で行き，ヒューストンで3つの共同企業体の代表者と会合をもった．その会合で，価格，入手可能日，雇用条件，燃料，供給品及び住宅についての議論が行われた．Restrepoは，Helicolが15日以内に最初のヘリコプターを用意できると説明した．Consorcio/WSHは，Restrepoの提案した契約を受け入れることを決定した．Helicolは，契約が正式にペルーで1974年11月11日に署名される以前に，履行を開始した．契約はスペイン語で政府の正式の便せんに書かれ，すべての当事者の居所はペルーのリマとなる旨が規定されていた．さらに，契約から生じる紛争はペルーの裁判所の管轄に服するとの規定があった．それに加えて，Consorcio/WSHは，ニューヨーク市にあるバンク・オブ・アメリカのHelicolの口座に支払うとの条項があった．

　RestrepoとConsorcio/WSHの代表者とのヒューストンでの交渉以外に，Helicolはテキサスと他の関連をもっていた．1970年から1977年にかけて，ホート・ワースにあるBell Helicopter Companyからヘリコプター（自社所有機の約80％），予備の部品，及びアクセサリーを4百万ドル以上購入した．その期間，Helicolは将来のパイロットを訓練するためと，ヘリコプターを南アメリカに運ぶために，ホート・ワースに派遣した．Helicolはまた，同じ期間中，「プラントに習熟させる」ためと技術的な相談のために，管理職と整備要員をホート・ワースにあるBell Helicopterを訪問するために派遣した．Helicolは，ヒューストンのFirst City National Bank振り出しのConsorcio/WSHからの5百万ドルを超える支払いをニューヨーク市とフロリダのパナ

5

First City National Bank of Houston.

Beyond the foregoing, there have been no other business contacts between Helicol and the State of Texas. Helicol never has been authorized to do business in Texas and never has had an agent for the service of process within the State. It never has performed helicopter operations in Texas or sold any product that reached Texas, never solicited business in Texas, never signed any contract in Texas, never had any employee based there, and never recruited an employee in Texas. In addition, Helicol never has owned real or personal property in Texas and never has maintained an office or establishment there. Helicol has maintained no records in Texas and has no shareholders in that State. None of the respondents or their decedents were domiciled in Texas, but all of the decedents were hired in Houston by Consorcio/WSH to work on the Petro Peru pipeline project.

Respondents instituted wrongful-death actions in the District Court of Harris County, Tex., against Consorcio/WSH, Bell Helicopter Company, and Helicol. Helicol filed special appearances and moved to dismiss the actions for lack of *in personam* jurisdiction over it. The motion denied. After a consolidated jury trial, judgment was entered against Helicol on a jury verdict of $1,141,200 in favor of respondents. ......

The Texas Court of Civil Appeals, Houston, First District, reversed the judgment of the District Court, holding that *in personam* jurisdiction over Helicol was lacking. 616 S. W. 2d 247 (Tex. 1981). The Supreme Court of Texas, with three justices dissenting, initially affirmed the judgment of the Court of Civil Appeals. ...... Seven months later, however, on motion for rehearing, the court withdrew its prior opinions and, again with three justices dissenting, reversed the judgment of the intermediate court. 638 S.

1 対人管轄(1)：Helicopteros Nacionales de Colombia, S.A. v. Hall

マ市にある銀行口座に受け入れた．

　以上のほかには，Helicol とテキサス州との間にはその他の事業上のなんらの関連も存在しない．Helicol はテキサスで事業活動を行うことの許可は与えられていなかったし，同州内において訴状の送達を受けるべき代理人を有してもいなかった．テキサスでヘリコプター事業を行わなかったしテキサスに到達するなんらの製品も売らなかったし，テキサスで事業の勧誘をしなかったし，テキサスでいかなる契約をも締結してもいないし，そこで従業員を雇用していないし，テキサスで従業員のリクルートもしていない．加えて，Helicol は，テキサスで不動産や動産も所有していないし，そこで事務所や施設も有していない．Helicol はテキサスになんらの会議資料も保有していないし，同州には株主もいない．被上訴人又はその死者のだれもテキサスに住所を有していない．ただ，死亡した者全員が，Petro Peru のパイプラインで働くために，ヒューストンにおいて Consorcio/WSH に雇用された．

　被上訴人は，テキサスのハリス郡地方裁判所に不法行為死亡訴訟を Consorcio/WSH, Bell Helicopter 社，及び Helicol に対して提起した．Helicol は特別出頭し，自己に対する対人管轄権の欠如を理由に却下の申立をした．申立は却下された．併合された陪審審理の後に，被上訴人勝訴の1,141,200ドルの陪審評決が Helicol に対して下された．……

　テキサスのヒューストン第一地区民事控訴裁判所は，Helicol に対する対人管轄権が欠けていたと判示して，地方裁判所の判決を破棄した．616 S.W.2d 247（Tex.1981）．テキサス最高裁は，3人の裁判官が反対したが，最初は，民事控訴裁判所の判決を支持した．……しかし，裁判所は，7ヶ月後，再審理の申立に基づいて，さきの意見を撤回し，ここでも3人の裁判官が反対したが，控訴裁判所の判決を破棄した．638 S. W. 2d 870（Tex. 1982）．テキサス裁判所が対人管轄権を有していると判断するに際して，テキサス最高裁

W. 2d 870 (Tex.1982). In ruling that the Texas courts had *in personam* jurisdiction, the Texas Supreme Court first held that the State's long-arm statute reaches as far as the Due Process Clause of the Fourteenth Amendment permits. *Id.*, at 872. Thus, the only question remaining for the court to decide was whether it was consistent with the Due Process Clause for Texas courts to assert *in personam* jurisdiction over Helicol. *Ibid.*

II Even when the cause of action does not arise out of or relate to the foreign corporation's activities in the forum State, due process is not offended by a State's subjecting the corporation to its *in personam* jurisdiction when there are sufficient contacts between the State and the foreign corporation. *Perkins* v. *Benguet Consolidated Mining Co.*, 342 U.S. 437 (1952); see *Keeton* v. *Hustler Magazine, Inc.*, 465 U.S. 770, 779 -780 (1984). In *Perkins*, the Court addressed a situation in which state courts had asserted general jurisdiction over a defendant foreign corporation. During the Japanese occupation of the Philippine Islands, the president and general manager of a Philippine mining corporation maintained an office in Ohio from which he conducted activities on behalf of the company. He kept company files and held directors' meetings in the office, carried on correspondence relating to the business, distributed salary checks drawn on two active Ohio bank accounts, engaged an Ohio bank to act as transfer agent, and supervised policies dealing with the rehabilitation of the corporation's properties in the Philippines. In short, the foreign corporation, through its president, "[had] been carrying on in Ohio a continuous and systematic, but limited, part of its general business," and the exercise of general jurisdiction over the Philippine corporation by an Ohio court was "reasonable and just." 342 U.S., at 438, 445.

All parties to the present case concede that respondents' claims against Helicol did not "arise out of," and are not related to, Helicol's activities within Texas. We thus must explore the nature of Helicol's contacts with

は，まず，州の管轄権拡大法は，修正第 14 条の適正手続条項が許容するところまで及ぶと判示した．同上 872 頁．かくして裁判所に決定すべく残された唯一つの問題は，テキサスの裁判所が Helicol に対人管轄権を行使することが適正手続条項に合致するかどうかであるということになった．同上.

II 訴訟原因が法廷地州における外国会社の活動から生じたものでもないし，またそれに関連するものでもない場合であっても，州と外国会社との間に十分な関連が存在するときには，州がその会社を州の対人管轄権に服せしめることは，適正手続条項に違反するものではない．*Perkins v. Benguet Consolidated Mining Co.*, 342 U.S. 437 (1952); *Keeton v. Hustler Magazine, Inc.*, 465 U.S. 770, 779-780 (1984) 参照．*Perkins* 事件においては，当裁判所は，州裁判所が被告である外国会社に対して一般管轄権を行使した場合に直面した．フィリピン諸島が日本によって占領されていた間，フィリピンの鉱業会社の社長・総支配人がオハイオに事務所を有しており，そこで会社のための活動に従事していた．彼はその事務所で会社の書類を保管し，取締役会議を開き，事業に関する通信を続け，2 つの使用されているオハイオの銀行口座から振り出された給料の小切手を配送し，オハイオ銀行を名義書換代理人として活動するために雇用し，さらにフィリピンにある会社の財産の回復を処理する方針を指揮した．要するに，その外国会社は社長を通じて，「オハイオにおいて，限られてはいるが，継続的で，組織的な一般的な事業の一部分を行っていたのであり，」オハイオ裁判所によるフィリピン会社に対する一般管轄権の行使は，「相当で正しい．」342 U.S., at 438,445.

被上訴人の Helicol に対する請求は，Helicol のテキサスにおける活動「から生じた」ものではないし，それに関連するものでもないことを本件の当事者はすべて認めている．Helicol とテキサス州との関連が，*Perkins* 事件にお

the State of Texas to determine whether they constitute the kind of continuous and systematic general business contacts the Court found to exist in *Perkins*. We hold that they do not.

It is undisputed that Helicol does not have a place of business in Texas and never has been licensed to do business in the State. Basically, Helicol's contacts with Texas consisted of sending its chief executive officer to Houston for a contract-negotiation session; accepting into its New York bank account checks drawn on a Houston bank; purchasing helicopters, equipment, and training services from Bell Helicopter for substantial sums; and sending personnel to Bell's facilities in Fort Worth for training.

The one trip to Houston by Helicol's chief executive officer for the purpose of negotiating the transportation-services contract with Consorcio/WSH cannot be described or regarded as a contact of a "continuous and systematic" nature, as *Perkins* described it, see also *International Shoe Co. v. Washington*, 326 U.S., at 320, and thus cannot support an assertion of *in personam* jurisdiction over Helicol by a Texas court. Similarly, Helicol's acceptance from Consorcio/WSH of checks drawn on a Texas bank is of negligible significance for purposes of determining whether Helicol had sufficient contacts in Texas. There is no indication that Helicol ever requested that the checks be drawn on a Texas bank or that there was any negotiation between Helicol and Consorcio/WSH with respect to the location or identity of the bank on which checks would be drawn. Common sense and everyday experience suggest that, absent unusual circumstances, the bank on which a check is drawn is generally of little consequence to the payee and is a matter left to the discretion of the drawer. Such unilateral activity of another party or a third person is not an appropriate consideration when determining whether

1　対人管轄(1)：Helicopteros Nacionales de Colombia, S.A. v. Hall

いてわれわれが存在すると判示したような，継続的で組織的な一般的事業に関連する種類のものであるかどうかを決定するために，Helicolとテキサス州との関連の性質を調べなければならない．われわれはそのようなものではない，と判断する．

　Helicolがテキサスに事業所を有していないこと，また同州内において事業を行う許可を受けたことがないことは争われていない．基本的にHelicolとテキサス州との関連は，その最高執行役員を契約交渉の会議のためヒューストンに派遣したこと，ヒューストンの銀行で振り出された銀行小切手をニューヨークの銀行口座に受け入れたこと，相当額のヘリコプター，備品，及び訓練のサービスをBell Helicopterから購入したことと，フォート・ワースのBellの施設に人員を派遣したことである．

　Helicolの最高執行役員をConsorcio/WSHとの輸送サービス契約の交渉のためにヒューストンに一回派遣したことは，*Perkins*事件が述べるような「継続的で組織的な」性質の関連であるということはできない．*International Shoe Co. v. Washington,* 326 U.S., at 320 をも参照．したがって，テキサス裁判所によるHelicolに対する対人管轄権の行使を支持することはできない．同様に，テキサスの銀行で振り出された小切手をConsorcio/WSHからHelicolが受け取ったことは，Helicolがテキサスにおいて十分な関連を有していたかどうかを決定するためには無視しうるほどの意義しかない．小切手をテキサスの銀行で振り出すようにHelicolが要求したとか，小切手が振り出される銀行の場所や身元について，HelicolとConsorcio/WSHとの間になんらかの交渉があったことは示されていない．小切手の振出銀行は，特別の事情がない限りは，支払いを受ける者にとっては一般にあまり重要ではないし，振出人の裁量に委ねられる事柄であることは，常識と日常的な経験の示すところである．このような他方当事者又は第三者の一方的な活動は，被告が法廷地州と管轄権の行使を正当とするほどの十分な関連を有していたかど

a defendant has sufficient contacts with a forum State to justify an assertion of jurisdiction.

The Texas Supreme Court focused on the purchases and the related training trips in finding contacts sufficient to support an assertion of jurisdiction. We do not agree with that assessment, for the Court's opinion in *Rosenberg Bros. & Co.* v. *Curtis Brown Co.*, 260 U.S. 516 (1923) (Brandeis, J., for a unanimous tribunal), makes clear that purchases and related trips, standing alone, are not a sufficient basis for a State's assertion of jurisdiction. ......

The defendant in *Rosenberg* was a small retailer in Tulsa, Okla., who dealt in men's clothing and furnishings. It never had applied for a license to do business in New York, nor had it at any time authorized suit to be brought against it there. It never had an established place of business in New York and never regularly carried on business in that State. Its only connection with New York was that it purchased from New York wholesalers a large portion of the merchandise sold in its Tulsa store. The purchases sometimes were made by correspondence and sometimes through visits to New York by an officer of the defendant. The Court concluded: "Visits on such business, even if occurring at regular intervals, would not warrant the inference that the corporation was present within the jurisdiction of [New York]." *Id.*, at 518.

This Court in *International Shoe* acknowledged and did not repudiate its holding in *Rosenberg*. See 326 U.S., at 318. In accordance with *Rosenberg*, we hold that mere purchases, even if occurring at regular intervals, are not enough to warrant a State's assertion of *in personam* jurisdiction over a nonresident corporation in a cause of action not related

1　対人管轄(1)：Helicopteros Nacionales de Colombia, S.A. v. Hall

うかを決定するときには，適切な考慮事項ではない．

　テキサスの最高裁判所は，管轄権の行使を支持するのに十分な関連があるかどうかを判断するにあたって，物品の購入とそれに関連する訓練のための出張に焦点を集中した．われわれはその評価に同意することはできない．というのは，*Rosenberg Bros.& Co. v. Curtis Brown Co.*, 260 U.S. 516 (1923)（Brandeis 判事による全員一致の意見）における，当裁判所の意見は，物の購入とそれに関連する出張は，それだけでは州による管轄権の行使にとって十分な基礎ではないことを明確にしているからである．……

　Rosenberg 事件の被告は，オクラハマのタレサの小さな小売業者であり，紳士用衣服と服飾品を扱っている．この小売業者はニューヨークで事業活動の許可を申請しなかったし，いかなる時においても，そこで自己に対して訴訟が提起されることの権限を与えたこともなかった．その業者はまた，ニューヨークに確立した事業所を有していないし，同州において定期的に事業を行ってもいなかった．ニューヨークとの唯一の関連は，ニューヨークの卸売業者からタレサで売る大量の商品を購入したという点にあった．この購入はときには通信によってなされることもあったし，またときには被告の役員がニューヨークを訪問することによってなされることもあった．当裁判所は，「そのような事業に関する訪問は，定期的に行われるものであっても，会社が［ニューヨーク］の管轄権内に所在するという推論を保証するものではない」と結論した．同上 518 頁.

　当裁判所は，*International Shoe* 事件において，*Rosenberg* 事件における上の判示を承認し，拒否しなかった．326 U.S., at 318 参照．*Rosenberg* 事件に従い，われわれは単なる購入はたとえ定期的に行われるものであっても，この購入取引と関連しない訴訟原因に関して，非居住者である会社に対して州が対人管轄権を行使することを認めるには十分ではないと判示する．Helicol

to those purchase transactions. Nor can we conclude that the fact that Helicol sent personnel into Texas for training in connection with the purchase of helicopters and equipment in that State in any way enhanced the nature of Helicol's contacts with Texas. The training was a part of the package of goods and services purchased by Helicol from Bell Helicopter. The brief presence of Helicol employees in Texas for the purpose of attending the training sessions is no more a significant contact than were the trips to New York made by the buyer for the retail store in *Rosenberg.* See also *Kulko* v. *California Superior Court*, 436 U.S., at 93 [1978] (basing California jurisdiction on 3-day and 1-day stopovers in that State "would make a mockery of" due process limitations on assertion of personal jurisdiction).

III We hold that Helicol's contacts with the State of Texas were insufficient to satisfy the requirements of the Due Process Clause of the Fourteenth Amendment. Accordingly, we reverse the judgment of the Supreme Court of Texas.

It is so ordered .

Justice BRENNAN, dissenting.

……

As a foreign corporation that has actively and purposefully engaged in numerous and frequent commercial transactions in the State of Texas, Helicol clearly falls within the category of nonresident defendants that may be subject to that forum's general jurisdiction. Helicol not only purchased helicopters and other equipment in the State for many years, but also sent pilots and management personnel into Texas to be trained in the use of this equipment and to consult with the seller on technical matters. Moreover, negotiations for the contract under which Helicol provided transportation services to the joint venture that employed the

1 対人管轄(1)：Helicopteros Nacionales de Colombia, S.A. v. Hall

がテキサスへ同州におけるヘリコプターとその備品の購入に関連して人員を送ったという事実は，決して Helicol とテキサスとの関連を高めたと結論することはできない．訓練は，Helicol が Bell Helicopter から購入された物品とサービスのパッケージの一部分なのである．訓練活動に出席するためにテキサスに Helicol の社員が短い期間滞在したことは，*Rosenberg* 事件における小売業者のための買い主によるニューヨークへの旅行以上に重要な関連であるとはいえない．*Kulko v. California Superior Court,* 436 U.S., at 93 [1978] をも参照（カルフォルニア州における 3 日と 1 日の一時滞在に同州の管轄権を基礎づけることは，対人管轄権の主張に対する適正手続による制限を「まやかしであると証明するであろう」）．

III　われわれは，Helicol とテキサス州との関連が修正第 14 条の適正手続条項の要件を充足するには不十分であると判断する．したがってテキサス最高裁の判決を破棄する．

以上のように判決する．

BRENNAN 裁判官の反対意見
……

Helicol は，テキサス州において積極的かつ意図的に無数の，頻繁な商業活動に従事した外国法人として，明らかに法廷地の一般管轄権に服する非居住被告の範疇に入る．Helicol は長年にわたって州内でヘリコプター及びその他の備品を購入しただけでなく，パイロットと管理職員をこの装備の使用の訓練のため，及び売主と技術的な事項について相談するために，テキサスに派遣した．さらに，被上訴人の死者を雇用した共同企業体に Helicol が輸送サービスを行うことを定めた契約の交渉がテキサスで行われた．これらを総合して考えると，これらの関連は，Helicol がテキサスにおける事業取引

respondents' decedents also took place in the State of Texas. Taken together, these contacts demonstrate that Helicol obtained numerous benefits from its transaction of business in Texas. In turn, it is eminently fair and reasonable to expect Helicol to face the obligations that attach to its participation in such commercial transactions. Accordingly, on the basis of continuous commercial contacts with the forum, I would conclude that the Due Process Clause allows the State of Texas to assert general jurisdiction over petitioner Helicol.

The Court also fails to distinguish the legal principles that controlled our prior decisions in *Perkins* and *Rosenberg*. In particular, the contacts between petitioner Helicol and the State of Texas, unlike the contacts between the defendant and the forum in each of those cases, are significantly related to the cause of action alleged in the original suit filed by the respondents. Accordingly, in my view, it is both fair and reasonable for the Texas courts to assert specific jurisdiction over Helicol in this case.

By asserting that the present case does not implicate the specific jurisdiction of the Texas courts, see *ante*, the Court necessarily removes its decision from the reality of the actual facts presented for our consideration. Moreover, the Court refuses to consider any distinction between contacts that are "related to" the underlying cause of action and contacts that "give rise" to the underlying cause of action. In my view, however, there is a substantial difference between these two standards for asserting specific jurisdiction. Thus, although I agree that the respondents' cause of action did not formally "arise out of" specific activities initiated by Helicol in the State of Texas, I believe that the wrongful-death claim filed by the respondents is significantly related to the undisputed contacts between Helicol and the forum. On that basis, I would conclude that the Due Process Clause allows the Texas courts to assert specific jurisdiction over this particular action.

1　対人管轄(1)：Helicopteros Nacionales de Colombia, S.A. v. Hall

から多くの利益を得ていることを示している．その見返りとして，Helicolがそのような商業取引に従事したことに付着する債務に直面することを要求することは，明らかに公正であり，相当でもある．したがって法廷地との継続的な商業的関連を基礎に，適正手続条項はテキサス州が上訴人Helicolに一般管轄権を行使することを許容するものと判断する．

　裁判所はまた，*Perkins*事件と*Rosenberg*事件における，われわれのさきの判決を支配した法原則を区別することに失敗した．とくに上訴人Helicolとテキサス州との関連が，これらの事件における被告と法廷地の関連とは異なり，被上訴人によって提起されたもとの訴訟において主張されている訴訟原因と密接に関連している．したがって私の見解では，本件においてテキサス裁判所がHelicolに対して特別管轄権を行使するのは，公平であり，また相当でもある．

　裁判所は，本件がテキサス裁判所の特別管轄権の問題を含んでいないと主張することによって，*前記参照*，われわれの検討のために提起されている実際の事実が有している現実性をその判断から奪う結果になっている．さらに裁判所は，基礎となっている訴訟原因に「関係する」関連と，基礎となっている訴訟原因を「生ぜしめる」関連とを区別することを拒否している．しかしながら，私の考えでは，特別管轄権を行使する2つの基準の間には実質的な差異が存在する．したがって私は，被上訴人の訴訟原因が，テキサスにおいてHelicolが開始した特定の活動「から生じ」たものではないことには同意するが，被上訴人が提起した不法死亡による請求権が，Helicolと法廷地との間の疑問の余地のない関連に密接に関係していると確信する．それに基づいて，私は適正手続条項は，テキサスの裁判所が本件訴訟に特別管轄権を行使することを許容すると結論する．

......

　Limiting the specific jurisdiction of a forum to cases in which the cause of action formally arose out of the defendant's contacts with the State would subject constitutional standards under the Due Process Clause to the vagaries of the substantive law or pleading requirements of each State. For example, the complaint filed against Helicol in this case alleged negligence based on pilot error. Even though the pilot was trained in Texas, the Court assumes that the Texas courts may not assert jurisdiction over the suit because the cause of action "did not 'arise out of,' and [is] not related to," that training. See *ante*, at 415. If, however, the applicable substantive law required that negligent training of the pilot was a necessary element of a cause of action for pilot error, or if the respondents had simply added an allegation of negligence in the training provided for the Helicol pilot, then presumably the Court would concede that the specific jurisdiction of the Texas courts was applicable.

......

【解　説】

　本件は，ペルーにおけるヘリコプターの墜落事故に基づく不法行為死亡訴訟において，テキサス州がコロンビア会社に対して対人管轄権を行使することは，合衆国連邦憲法修正第14条の適正手続条項に反するとして，これを認めなかった事例である．

1　対人管轄（権）

　本件では，テキサス州がコロンビア会社に対して対人管轄権を行使することが合衆国連邦憲法修正第14条の適正手続条項（Due Process Clause）に反するかどうかが問題となった．

1　対人管轄(1)：Helicopteros Nacionales de Colombia, S.A. v. Hall

……
　法廷地の特別管轄権の行使を，訴訟原因が被告と当該州との関連から形式的に生じる事件に制限することは，適正手続条項のもとでの憲法上の基準を各州の実質法や答答手続要件の気まぐれに服せしめることになる．たとえば本件申立において Helicol に対して，パイロットのミスに基づく過失責任が主張されたとしよう．パイロットがテキサスで訓練されたとしても，裁判所は，テキサスの裁判所が，訴訟原因はその訓練から「から生じた」または「関係しない」から，その訴訟に管轄権を行使してはならないと考えている．前掲 415 頁参照．しかし，もし適用される実質法がパイロットの訓練の過失がパイロットのミスの訴訟原因の必要な要素であることを要求しているとすれば，又は被上訴人が単に Helicol のパイロットに提供した訓練の過失の主張を付加したとすれば，そのときは裁判所がたぶんテキサス裁判所の特別管轄権の行使を容認したであろう．
……

　対人管轄権（personal or *in personam* jurisdiction）とは，裁判所が州際・国際事件において被告に対して有効に判決を下すことができる権限をいう．人的（裁判）管轄権ということもある．対人管轄権の基礎としては，伝統的には，自然人については，被告が，法廷地で令状の送達を受けたこと，法廷地にドミサイルを有すること，管轄権の行使に同意したこと，法人については，法廷地で設立されたこと，事業活動を行っていること，管轄権の行使に同意したことがあげられる．
　対人管轄権は，裁判管轄権（judicial Jurisdiction）の 1 つで，他に物的管轄権，準対物管轄権がある．これらの点については，ウィリアム・M・リッチマン＝ウィリアム・L・レイノルズ著（松岡・吉川・高杉・北坂訳）『アメリカ抵触法（上巻）』（レキシスネキシスジャパン，2008）4-5 頁参照．

2 一般管轄権と特別管轄権

本件では，対人管轄のうち，いわゆる一般管轄権の有無が問題となっている．一般管轄権（general jurisdiction）とは，本件に即していえば，外国法人に対しその法人の「州内における活動から生じたものではなく，又それと関連を有しない訴訟原因に関して」，裁判所が行使する管轄権のことである．わが国における普通裁判籍にほぼ対応するといってよい．

これに対して特別管轄権（specific jurisdiction）は，被告の州内における活動から生じたか又はそれに関連する訴訟原因に基づいて，州が行使する管轄権を意味する．アメリカにおける一般管轄権と特別管轄権の区別は，最初に次の論文によって提唱された．von Mehren & Trautman, *Jurisdiction to Adjudicate: Suggested Analysis*, 79 Harv. L. Rev. 1121（1966）．一般管轄権と特別管轄権について簡単には，リッチマン＝レイノルズ・前掲173-176頁参照．

3 一般管轄権の基礎：「継続的で組織的な」活動

本件法廷意見は，まず，一般論として，訴訟原因が法廷地州における外国会社の活動から生じたものでもないし，又それに関連するものでもない場合であっても，法廷地州と外国会社との間に十分な関連が存在するときには，州がその会社を州の対人管轄権に服せしめることは，連邦憲法の適正手続条項に違反するものではない，とする．

その上で，本件におけるテキサスと外国会社との関連は，一般管轄権の基礎としては不十分である，と判断した．その際，法廷地との十分な関連があるかどうかの基準は，外国法人の法廷地内における関連が「継続的で組織的な」性質のものであるかどうかである．これは判旨も引用する *Perkins v. Benguet Consolidated Mining Co.*, 342 U.S.437（1952）が採用した基準である．なお抵触法第2リステイトメントでは，「継続的かつ実質的」という表現が用いられている．Restatement, Second, Conflict of Laws, §35, comment b（1971）．第2リステイトメント研究会訳「〈邦訳〉アメリカ抵触法第二リステイトメント㈢」民商法雑誌74巻1号153頁（1976）［川又良也］参照．

1 対人管轄(1)：Helicopteros Nacionales de Colombia, S.A. v. Hall

テキサス州最高裁は，本件においてテキサスにおける物品の購入とそれに関連する出張がテキサスの管轄権を行使するのに十分な関連がある，と判断した．しかし本件連邦最高裁の法廷意見は，これを否定し，物品の購入とそれに関連する出張は，*Perkins* 判決のいう「継続的で組織的な」ものではなく，それだけではテキサスによる一般管轄権の行使にとって十分な基礎ではないと結論した．

4 反対意見

これに対して，Brennan 裁判官の反対意見は，Helicol は長年にわたって州内でヘリコプターと備品を購入しただけでなく，パイロットと管理職員をこの装備の使用の訓練等のために，テキサスに派遣したこと，さらに，Helicol が輸送サービスを行うことを定めた契約の交渉がテキサスで行われたことなどを総合して考えると，テキサス州が Helicol に一般管轄権を行使することは許される，と判断する．

さらに，反対意見は，本件において提起された不法死亡による請求権は，Helicol と法廷地と活動に密接に関連しているから，テキサスが特別管轄権を行使することが許されると判断する点においても，法廷意見と相違する．

学説でも法廷意見の結論に反対する見解がある．たとえば，リッチマン＝レイノルズ・前掲 83-86 頁参照．

5 一般管轄権の行使に対する制限的立場

一般管轄権に関する連邦最高裁の指針を示す判決としては，本件と *Perkins* 判決の域を超えるものはほとんどないといわれる．リッチマン＝レイノルズ 176 頁．本件法廷意見は，州外法人とくに外国法人に対する一般管轄権の行使を厳しく制限する立場をとった．このような観点からすると，法人に対する一般管轄権の行使が認められるのは，法廷地州において，法人が設立されたか，主たる営業所を有するか，又は営業許可を有する場合に限られるのではないかとの指摘がある．Russel Weintraub, International Litigation and Arbitration, 6（3rd ed. 2001）．

I 国際裁判管轄・国際商事仲裁

　ところが，アメリカの裁判所の判決の中には，本件法廷意見の立場とは異なり，依然として法廷地州における，ごく僅かな活動を根拠に一般管轄権を基礎づけようとするものがある．たとえば，*United Rope Distributors, Inc. v. Kimbely Line*, 785 F. Supp. 446（S.D.N.Y.1992）では，貨物の紛失の訴訟において，法廷地の銀行で実質的にすべての所得を受け取り，また実質的にはすべての費用の支払いをするという形で法廷地の銀行を利用することを根拠とする，船舶の所有者に対する一般管轄権の行使が支持された．

6　合衆国政府の裁判所の友（amicus curie）としての意見

　合衆国政府は，本件において法廷の友（amicus curie 法廷助言者ともいう．裁判所に係属する社会的に影響力の強い事件などについて，裁判所に第三者として意見を提出する者をいう．）として，アミカス・ブリーフ（意見書）を提出し，その中で，もし単にアメリカで製品を購入しただけで，外国企業をアメリカ裁判所の管轄権に服させるのに十分であると判断されるならば，外国企業はアメリカ製品を購入しなくなるだろうから，アメリカ企業の世界市場における競争力は悪影響を受けるであろう，と主張した．法廷意見は直接にはこの点に言及していないが，結果的にはこの合衆国政府の見解を受け入れていることになる．

【本件参考文献】

野村美明・阪大法学49巻3・4号385-389頁（1999）．

ウィリアム・M・リッチマン＝ウィリアム・L・レイノルズ著（松岡・吉川・高杉・北坂訳）『アメリカ抵触法（上巻）』（レキシスネキシスジャパン，2008）81-86, 173-176頁．

坂本正光『アメリカ法における人的管轄権の展開』（九州大学出版会，1990）50-54頁．

1　対人管轄(1)：Helicopteros Nacionales de Colombia, S.A. v. Hall

【設　問】

1　本件の主要な争点はなにか．また本件を例にとって，アメリカ法における対人管轄とはどのようなものかを説明せよ．
2　本件の事実の概要を述べよ．
　　原告（被上訴人）はどこの国の国籍を有するか，どこに居住しているか．被告（上訴人）は誰か．どこの国の会社か．どのような事業をどこで営んでいるか．事故はどこの国で発生したか．法廷地（裁判が行われた地）はどこか．
3　原告はどのような請求を求めたのか．これに対する被告の抗弁はなにか．
4　テキサス州の地方裁判所，控訴裁判所，最高裁判所の判決の結論を述べよ．
5　連邦最高裁の結論はどうか．*Perkins* 事件の結論と論理と比較せよ．
6　裁判所の主要な判旨（判決理由）を要約せよ．
7　連邦最高裁の判旨の外国法人に対する管轄権に関する一般論はどのようなものか．
　　また，判旨は本件を一般管轄権の問題と捉えているか．一般管轄権とはどのようなものか．
8　テキサス州最高裁は，コロンビア会社 Helicol に対する管轄権を肯定するにあたって，どのようなテキサスとの関連を重要と考えたか．また，これに対する連邦最高裁の立場はどうか．
9　連邦最高裁の判旨は，テキサスとの間にどのような関連が存在し，どのような関連が存在しないといっているか．
10　反対意見は，どのような点で多数意見と異なるか．
11　合衆国政府のアミカス・ブリーフ（意見書）について説明せよ．
12　要するに本件はどのような判決か．また本件の結論，理由づけに賛成か．

2 | 対人管轄(2):
Asahi Metal Industry Co., Ltd.
v. Superior Court of Califonia,
480 U.S. 102 (1987)

JUSTICE O'CONNOR announced the judgment of the Court and delivered the unanimous opinion of the Court with respect to Part I, the opinion of the Court with respect to Part II-B, in which THE CHIEF JUSTICE, JUSTICE BRENNAN, JUSTICE WHITE, JUSTICE MARSHALL, JUSTICE BLACKMUN, JUSTICE POWELL, and JUSTICE STEVENS join, and an opinion with respect to Parts II-A and III, in which THE CHIEF JUSTICE, JUSTICE POWELL, and JUSTICE SCALIA join.

This case presents the question whether the mere awareness on the part of a foreign defendant that the components it manufactured, sold, and delivered outside the United States would reach the forum State in the stream of commerce constitutes "minimum contacts" between the defendant and the forum State such that the exercise of jurisdiction "does not offend 'traditional notions of fair play and substantial justice.'" *International Shoe Co.* v. *Washington*, 326 U.S. 310, 316 (1945), quoting *Milliken* v. *Meyer*, 311 U.S. 457, 463 (1940).

I

On September 23, 1978, on Interstate Highway 80 in Solano County, California, Gary Zurcher lost control of his Honda motorcycle and collided with a tractor. Zurcher was severely injured, and his passenger and wife, Ruth Ann Moreno, was killed. In September 1979, Zurcher filed a product liability action in the Superior Court of the State

カルフォルニアで発生した事故について，タイヤチューブを製造した台湾会社による，チューブの部品製造メーカーである日本会社に対する製造物責任の求償訴訟において，カルフォルニア州裁判所が日本会社に対して対人管轄権を行使することは，適正手続条項に違反するとされた事例

O'CONNOR 裁判官が裁判所の判決を発表し，第Ⅰ部について裁判所の全員一致意見を言い渡した．第Ⅱ部のBに関する裁判所の意見については，主席裁判官，BRENNAN 裁判官，WHITE 裁判官，MARSHALL 裁判官，BLACKMUN 裁判官，POWELL 裁判官，STEVENS 裁判官が同調し，第Ⅱ部のAと第Ⅲ部については，主席裁判官，POWELL 裁判官，SCALIA 裁判官が同調した．

本件は，外国の被告が，合衆国外で製造，販売，引渡しをした部品が通商の流れに従い法廷地州に到達するであろうことを単に知っていただけで，被告と法廷地州との「最小限の関連」を構成し，管轄権の行使が「『フェアプレイと実質的正義という伝統的な観念』を侵害しない」ものであるかという問題を提起している．*International Shoe Co. v. Washington*, 326 U.S. 310, 316（1945），*Milliken v. Meyer*, 311 U.S. 457, 463（1940）を引用.

Ⅰ　1978年9月23日カルフォルニアのサロナ郡のインターステイト・ハイウエイ80で，Gary Zurcher がホンダのオートバイのコントロールを失い，トラクターと衝突した．Zurcher は，重傷を負い，同乗していた妻 Ruth Ann Moreno は死亡した．1979年9月，Zurcher は，サロナ郡のカルフォルニア州上位裁判所に製造物責任訴訟を提起した．Zurcher は，1978

of California in and for the County of Solano. Zurcher alleged that the 1978 accident was caused by a sudden loss of air and an explosion in the rear tire of the motorcycle, and alleged that the motorcycle tire, tube, and sealant were defective. Zurcher's complaint named, *inter alia*, Cheng Shin Rubber Industrial Co., Ltd. (Cheng Shin), the Taiwanese manufacturer of the tube. Cheng Shin in turn filed a cross-complaint seeking indemnification from its codefendants and from petitioner, Asahi Metal Industry Co., Ltd. (Asahi), the manufacturer of the tube's valve assembly. Zurcher's claims against Cheng Shin and the other defendants were eventually settled and dismissed, leaving only Cheng Shin's indemnity action against Asahi.

California's long-arm statute authorizes the exercise of jurisdiction "on any basis not inconsistent with the Constitution of this state or of the United States." Cal. Civ. Proc. Code Ann. §410.10 (West 1973). Asahi moved to quash Cheng Shin's service of summons, arguing the State could not exert jurisdiction over it consistent with the Due Process Clause of the Fourteenth Amendment.

In relation to the motion, the following information was submitted by Asahi and Cheng Shin. Asahi is a Japanese corporation. It manufactures tire valve assemblies in Japan and sells the assemblies to Cheng Shin, and to several other tire manufacturers, for use as components in finished tire tubes. Asahi's sales to Cheng Shin took place in Taiwan. The shipments from Asahi to Cheng Shin were sent from Japan to Taiwan. Cheng Shin bought and incorporated into its tire tubes 150,000 Asahi valve assemblies in 1978; 500,000 in 1979; 500,000 in 1980; 100,000 in 1981; and 100,000 in 1982. Sales to Cheng Shin accounted for 1.24 percent of Asahi's income in 1981 and 0.44 percent in 1982. Cheng Shin alleged that approximately 20 percent of its sales in the United States are in California. Cheng Shin purchases valve assemblies from other suppliers as

2 対人管轄(2)：Asahi Metal Industry Co., Ltd. v. Superior Court

年の事故はオートバイの後輪が突然空気がなくなり，爆発したために発生したと主張し，オートバイのタイヤ，チューブ，シーラントに欠陥があったと主張した．Zurcher の訴状は，とりわけ台湾のチューブ製造者 Cheng Shin Rubber Industrial Co., Ltd.（Cheng Shin）を名指しした．これに対して Cheng Shin は，共同被告と，チューブのバルブの部品の製造者である，上訴人 Asahi Metal Industry Co., Ltd.（Asahi）からの賠償を求める交差訴状を提出した．Zurcher の Cheng Shin 及び他の被告に対する請求は，のちに和解，却下され，Cheng Shin の Asahi に対する求償訴訟だけが残った．

カルフォルニアの管轄権拡大法は，「当州と合衆国の憲法に反しない限りどのような基礎に基づく」管轄権の行使をも認めている．Cal. Civ. Proc.Code Ann. §410.10（West 1973）．Asahi は，同州は修正第14条の適正手続条項に従えば，自社に対する管轄権を行使することはできないと主張して，Cheng Shin による召喚状の送達を無効とするように申し立てた．

この申立に関連して，Asahi と Cheng Shin から次のような情報が提出された．Asahi は，日本会社であり，日本でタイヤ・バルブの部品を製造し，その部品を Cheng Shin その他のいくつかのタイヤ製造業者に完成タイヤ・チューブの部品として使用するために売却している．Asahi の Cheng Shin への販売は台湾で行われた．Asahi から Cheng Shin への船荷は日本から台湾に送られた．Cheng Shin は1978年には Asahi の150,000個，1979年には500,000個，1980年には500,000個，1981年は100,000個，1982年は100,000個のバブル部品を買い，自己のタイヤ・チューブに装着した．Cheng Shin への販売は，1981年には Asahi の収入の1.24%，1982年には0.44%を占める．Cheng Shin は自社の合衆国における販売の約20%がカルフォルニアであると主張する．Cheng Shin はバルブの部品を他の供給業者からも

well, and sells finished tubes throughout the world.

In 1983 an attorney for Cheng Shin conducted an informal examination of the valve stems of the tire tubes sold in one cycle store in Solano County. The attorney declared that of the approximately 115 tire tubes in the store, 97 were purportedly manufactured in Japan or Taiwan, and of those 97, 21 valve stems were marked with the circled letter "A", apparently Asahi's trademark. Of the 21 Asahi valve stems, 12 were incorporated into Cheng Shin tire tubes. The store contained 41 other Cheng Shin tubes that incorporated the valve assemblies of other manufacturers. An affidavit of a manager of Cheng Shin whose duties included the purchasing of component parts stated: "'In discussions with Asahi regarding the purchase of valve stem assemblies the fact that my Company sells tubes throughout the world and specifically the United States has been discussed. I am informed and believe that Asahi was fully aware that valve stem assemblies sold to my Company and to others would end up throughout the United States and in California.'" 39 Cal. 3d 35, 48, n.4, 702 P.2d 543, 549-550, n.4 (1985). An affidavit of the president of Asahi, on the other hand, declared that Asahi "'has never contemplated that its limited sales of tire valves to Cheng Shing in Taiwan would subject it to lawsuits in California.'" *Ibid.* The record does not include any contract between Cheng Shin and Asahi.

Primarily on the basis of the above information, the Superior Court denied the motion to quash summons, stating: "Asahi obviously does business on an international scale. It is not unreasonable that they defend claims of defect in their product on an international scale."

The Court of Appeal of the State of California issued a peremptory writ of mandate commanding the Superior Court to quash service of summons. The court concluded that "it would be unreasonable to require Asahi to

購入しており，世界中にチューブの完成品を販売している．

 1983 年に Cheng Shin の弁護士はサロナ郡のあるサイクル・ストアで売られているタイヤ・チューブのバルブ軸の非公式な検査を実施した．弁護士の主張するところによれば，その店で売られているバルブ軸約 115 のうち，97 が日本または台湾で製造され，これらの 97 のうち，21 が明らかに Asahi の商標である，「A」の円形の印がついていた．21 の Asahi のバルブ軸のうち，12 が Cheng Shin のタイヤ・チューブに装着されていた．その店には，その他の製造者のバルブ部品を装着した 41 のその他の Cheng Shin のチューブがあった．構成部品の購入の任務をも担当する Cheng Shin のマネージャーの宣誓供述書には，「バルブ軸部品の購入に関する商談の際に，当社が世界中，とりわけ合衆国にチューブを販売しているという事実は，議論された．Asahi は，当社に売られたバルブ軸部品が合衆国とカルフォルニアに到達するであろうことを十分に知っていたと確信する．」39 Cal. 3d 35, 48 n.4, 702 P.2d 543, 549-550, n.4（1985），と述べている．これに対して，Asahi の社長の宣誓供述書は，Asahi が「台湾における Cheng Shin へのタイヤ・バルブの限られた量の販売がカルフォルニアにおける訴訟に服することになるとは思いもしなかった」（同上）と述べている．記録には Asahi と Cheng Shin の契約は全く含まれていない．

 主として上の情報に基づいて，上位裁判所は，「Asahi は明らかに国際的な事業を営んでおり，国際的な規模でのその製造物の欠陥に関する請求について防御するのは不当ではない」と述べて，召喚状を無効とする申立を認めなかった．

 カルフォルニア州控訴裁判所は，上位裁判所に召喚状の送達を無効とすることを命じる職務執行令状を発行した．裁判所は，「Asahi に，自社の部品が含まれている製品がカルフォルニアを含む全世界で売られるであろうという，

respond in California solely on the basis of ultimately realized foreseeability that the product into which its component was embodied would be sold all over the world including California."

The Supreme Court of the State of California reversed and discharged the writ issued by the Court of Appeal. 39 Cal. 3d 35, 702 P.2d 543 (1985). The court observed: "Asahi has no offices, property or agents in California. It solicits no business in California and has made no direct sales [in California]." *Id.*, at 48, 702 P.2d, at 549. Moreover, "Asahi did not design or control the system of distribution that carried its valve assemblies into California." *Id.*, at 49, 702 P. 2d, at 549. Nevertheless, the court found the exercise of jurisdiction over Asahi to be consistent with the Due Process Clause. It concluded that Asahi knew that some of the valve assemblies sold to Cheng Shin would be incorporated into tire tubes sold in California, and that Asahi benefited indirectly from the sale in California of products incorporating its components. The court considered Asahi's intentional act of placing its components into the stream of commerce——that is, by delivering the components to Cheng Shin in Taiwan——coupled with Asahi's awareness that some of the components would eventually find their way into California, sufficient to form the basis for state court jurisdiction under the Due Process Clause.

We granted certiorari, and now reverse.

II

A ......

Applying the principle that minimum contacts must be based on an act of the defendant, the Court in *World-Wide Volkswagen Corp.* v. *Woodson*, 444 U.S. 286 (1980), rejected the assertion that a *consumer's* unilateral act of bringing the defendant's product into the forum State was a sufficient constitutional basis for personal jurisdiction over the defendant.

2 対人管轄(2)：Asahi Metal Industry Co., Ltd. v. Superior Court

最後になって現実のものとなる予見可能性のみに基づいて，カルフォルニアでの応訴を強制することは不当である」と結論した．

　カルフォルニア州最高裁判所は，破棄して控訴審の発行した令状を取り消した．39 Cal. 3d 35, 702 P.2d 543（1985）．裁判所は，「Asahi はカルフォルニアに事務所も財産も代理人も有していない．カルフォルニアで事業の勧誘も行っていないし，直接の販売も［カルフォルニアで］行っていない」と述べた．Id., at 48, 702 P.2d, at 549. さらに，「Asahi はそのバルブ部品をカルフォルニアまで運んだ販売システムを設計，支配していない」．Id., at 49, 702 P.2d, at 549. それにもかかわらず，裁判所は Asahi に対する管轄権の行使が適正手続条項に合致すると判断した．裁判所は，Asahi が Cheng Shin に売られたバルブ部品のいくつかがカルフォルニアで売られるタイヤ・チューブに組み込まれることを知っており，Asahi がその部品を装着した製品のカルフォルニアにおける販売から利益を得ていたと結論した．裁判所は，Asahi がその部品を通商の流れに意図的に置いたという行為――つまり台湾において Cheng Shin にその部品を引き渡すこと――により，同時に Asahi がその部品のいくつかは，やがてカルフォルニアにたどり着くであろうことを知っていたことをもあわせると，適正手続条項上，州裁判所の管轄権の行使に対する十分な基礎を提供すると考えた．

　われわれは裁量的上訴を認めた．そして破棄する．

II　A……

　最小限の関連は，被告の行為に根拠を置くものでなければならないという原則を適用して，当裁判所は，*World-Wide Volkswagen Corp. v. Woodson,* 444 U.S. 286（1980）判決において，被告の製品を法廷地州に持ち込んだという*消費者の一方的な行為*が，被告に対する対人管轄権に対する十分な憲法上の基礎であるという主張を退けた．

......

Since *World-Wide Volkswagen,* lower courts have been confronted with cases in which the defendant acted by placing a product in the stream of commerce, and the stream eventually swept defendant's product into the forum State, but the defendant did nothing else to purposefully avail itself of the market in the forum State. Some courts have understood the Due Process Clause, as interpreted in *World-Wide Volkswagen,* to allow an exercise of personal jurisdiction to be based on no more than the defendant's act of placing the product in the stream of commerce. Other courts have understood the Due Process Clause and the above-quoted language in *World-Wide Volkswagen* to require the action of the defendant to be more purposefully directed at the forum State than the mere act of placing a product in the stream of commerce.

The reasoning of the Supreme Court of California in the present case illustrates the former interpretation of *World-Wide Volkswagen.* The Supreme Court of California held that, because the stream of commerce eventually brought some valves Asahi sold Cheng Shin into California, Asahi's awareness that its valves would be sold in California was sufficient to permit California to exercise jurisdiction over Asahi consistent with the requirements of the Due Process Clause. The Supreme Court of California's position was consistent with those courts that have held that mere foreseeability or awareness was a constitutionally sufficient basis for personal jurisdiction if the defendant's product made its way into the forum State while still in the stream of commerce. See *Bean Dredging Corp.* v. *Dredge Technology Corp.,* 744 F.2d 1081 (CA5 1984); *Hendrick* v. *Daiko Shoji Co.,* 715 F.2d 1355 (CA9 1983).

Other courts, however, have understood the Due Process Clause to require something more than that the defendant was aware of its product's entry into the forum State through the stream of commerce in order for

2 対人管轄(2)：Asahi Metal Industry Co., Ltd. v. Superior Court

……

　World-Wide Volkswagen 判決以来，下級審裁判所は次のような事件に直面した．すなわち，被告が通商の流れに製品を置くことによって行為し，その流れがついには被告の製品を法廷地州に運んだが，被告は法廷地州の市場を意図的に利用する行為をそれ以外にはなにもしなかったという事件である．いくつかの裁判所は，*World-Wide Volkswagen* 事件で解釈されたように，適正手続条項は，対人管轄権の行使を被告がその製品を通商の流れに置くという行為だけで，基礎づけられることを許容するものと理解した．他の裁判所は，適正手続条項とさきに引用した *World-Wide Volkswagen* 事件における文言を，通商の流れに商品を置くという単なる行為以上のより意図的に法廷地州に向けられた行為を必要とすると理解した．

　本件におけるカルフォルニア最高裁判所の推論は *World-Wide Volkswagen* 事件の前者の解釈の例である．カルフォルニア最高裁判所は，通商の流れがついには Asahi が Cheng Shin に売ったいくつかのバルブをカルフォルニアに運んだのだから，Asahi がそのバルブがカルフォルニアで売られるであろうことを知っていたことは，適正手続に合致して，カルフォルニアが Asahi に対して管轄権を行使することを許容するに十分であると判示した．カルフォルニア最高裁の立場は，被告の製品が通商の流れにある間に法廷地州に到達した場合には，単なる予見可能性又は知っていたということだけで，憲法上，対人管轄権を行使する十分な基礎があるというこれらの裁判所と一致する．*Bean Dredging Corp. v. Dredge Technology Corp.*, 744 F.2d 1081 (CA5 1984); *Hedrick v. Daiko Shoji Co.*, 715 F.2d 1355 (CA9 1983) 参照．

　しかしながら他の裁判所は，被告がその製品が通商の流れに沿って法廷地州に入ったことを知っていたこと以上のなにかが，州が被告に対して管轄権を行使するためには必要であると理解してきた．たとえば，本件において州

the State to exert jurisdiction over the defendant. In the present case, for example, the State Court of Appeal did not read the Due Process Clause, as interpreted by *World-Wide Volkswagen*, to allow "mere foreseeability that the product will enter the forum state [to] be enough by itself to establish jurisdiction over the distributor and retailer." ...... In *Humble* v. *Toyota Motor Co.*, 727 F.2d 709 (CA8 1984), an injured car passenger brought suit against Arakawa Auto Body Company, a Japanese corporation that manufactured car seats for Toyota. Arakawa did no business in the United States; it had no office, affiliate, subsidiary, or agent in the United States; it manufactured its component parts outside the United States and delivered them to Toyota Motor Company in Japan. The Court of Appeals, adopting the reasoning of the District Court in that case, noted that although it "does not doubt that Arakawa could have foreseen that its product would find its way into the United States," it would be "manifestly unjust" to require Arakawa to defend itself in the United States. *Id.*, at 710-711, quoting 578 F. Supp. 530, 533 (ND Iowa 1982). See also *Hutson* v. *Fehr Bros., Inc.*, 584 F.2d 833 (CA8 1978); see generally *Max Daetwyler Corp.* v. *R. Meyer*, 762 F.2d 290, 299 (CA3 1985) ....

We now find this latter position to be consonant with the requirements of due process. The "substantial connection," *Burger King*, [Corp. v. Rudzewicz] 471 U.S., at 475; *McGee*, 355 U.S., at 223 [1957], between the defendant and the forum State necessary for a finding of minimum contacts must come about by *an action of a the defendant purposefully directed toward the forum State. Burger King, supra,* at 471 U.S., at 475; *Keeton* v. *Hustler Magazine, Inc.*, 465 U.S. 770, 774 (1984). The placement of a product into the stream of commerce, without more, is not an act of the defendant purposefully directed toward the forum State. Additional conduct of the defendant may indicate an intent or purpose to serve the market in the forum State, for example, designing the product for the market in the forum State, advertising in the forum State, estab-

控訴審は，修正手続条項が，*World-Wide Volkswagen* 事件において解釈されたように，「製品が法廷地州に入ることを単に知っていたことがそれだけで販売店や小売業者に対する管轄権を樹立するのに十分である」ことを許容するものとは理解しなかった．…… *Humble v. Toyota Motor Co.*, 727 F.2d 709（CA8 1984）において，負傷した自動車の同乗者が，Toyota のために自動車シートを製造した日本会社 Arakawa Auto Body Company に対して訴訟を提起した．Arakawa は，合衆国において事業活動を行っていないし，事務所，関連会社，子会社，代理人を合衆国に有していない．また会社はその構成部品を合衆国外で製造し，それらを Toyota Motor Company に日本で引き渡した．控訴審はその事件の地方裁判所の推論を採用し，「Arakawa が，その製品が合衆国へ入ることは予見しえたことは疑いない」けれども，Arakawa に合衆国で防御することを要求することは「明らかに不当」であろう，と指摘した．*Id.*, at 710-711, 578 F. Supp. 530, 533（ND Iowa 1982）を引用．*Hutson* v. *Fehr Bros., Inc.*, 584 F.2d 833（CA8 1978）；一般的には，*Max Daetwyler Corp.* v. *R. Meyer*, 762 F.2d 290, 299（CA3 1985）を参照……

　われわれはこの後者の立場が適正手続の要請に合致するものと判断する．最小限の関連の判断にとって必要とされる被告と法廷地州との間の「実質的な関連」，*Burger King*,［Corp. v. Rudzewicz］471 U.S., at 475; *McGee*, 355 U.S., at 223 [1957] は，*法廷地州に意図的に向けられた被告の行為によって生じるものでなければならない*．前掲 *Burger King*, at 471 U.S., at 476; *Keeton* v. *Hustler Magazine, Inc.*, 465 U.S. 770, 774（1984）．通商の流れに製品を置くこと，それだけでは意図的に法廷地州に向けられた被告の行為ではない．付加的な被告の行為，たとえば法廷地州の市場用に製品を設計すること，法廷地州における広告，法廷地州の顧客に対する定期的な助言を提供するルートを設定すること，又は法廷地州における販売代理店としてつとめることに同意したディストリビューターを通じて製品を市場に出すこ

lishing channels for providing regular advice to customers in the forum State, or marketing the product through a distributor who has agreed to serve as the sales agent in the forum State. But a defendant's awareness that the stream of commerce may or will sweep the product into the forum State does not convert the mere act of placing the product into the stream into an act purposefully directed toward the forum State.

Assuming, *arguendo*, that respondents have established Asahi's awareness that some of the valves sold to Cheng Shin would be incorporated into tire tubes sold in California, respondents have not demonstrated any action by Asahi to purposefully avail itself of the California market. Asahi does not do business in California. It has no office, agents, employees, or property in California. It does not advertise or otherwise solicit business in California. It did not create, control, or employ the distribution system that brought its valves to California. There is no evidence that Asahi designed its product in anticipation of sales in California. On the basis of these facts, the exertion of personal jurisdiction over Asahi by the Superior Court of California exceeds the limits of due process.

II B

The strictures of the Due Process Clause forbid a state court from exercising personal jurisdiction over Asahi under circumstances that would offend "'traditional notions of fair play and substantial justice.'" *International Shoe Co.* v. *Washington*, 326 U.S., at 316, quoting *Milliken* v. *Meyer*, 311 U.S., at 463.

We have previously explained that the determination of the reasonableness of the exercise of jurisdiction in each case will depend on an evaluation of several factors. A court must consider the burden on the defendant,

とは，法廷地州の市場を利用しようとする意図又は目的を示すものであろう．しかし，被告が通商の流れに沿って製品が法廷地州に到達するかもしれない又は到達するであろうことを知っていたことは，流れに製品を置いたという単なる行為を法廷地州に意図的に向けられた行為へと転換するわけではない．

　Cheng Shin に売られたバルブのいくつかがカルフォルニアで売られるチューブに組み込まれるであろうことを被告が知っていたことをかりに被上訴人が立証したとしても，上訴人 Asahi がカルフォルニアの市場を意図的に利用する行為をしたということを証明したことにはならない．Asahi はカルフォルニアで事業活動を行っていない．事務所も代理人も従業員も財産もカルフォルニアに有していない．Asahi はカルフォルニアで広告をしていないし，事業の勧誘も行っていない．Asahi はそのバルブをカルフォルニアに持ち込んだ流通システムを創設，支配又は使用もしていない．Asahi がカルフォルニアでの販売を予想してその製品を設計したという証拠は存在しない．これらの事実を基礎にすれば，カルフォルニア上位裁判所が Asahi に対して対人管轄権を行使したことは適正手続の制限を越えている．

II B

　適正手続条項による制限は，州の裁判所が「フェアプレイと実質的正義という伝統的観念」*International Shoe Co. v. Washington,* 326 U.S., at 316, *Milliken* v. *Meyer,* 311 U.S., at 463 を引用．に反するような状況下で，Asahi に対して対人的管轄権を行使することを禁じている．

　われわれがさきに説明したように，それぞれの事件において管轄権の行使が正当であるかどうかの決定は，複数の要素をどのように評価するかにかかっている．裁判所は被告の負担，法廷地州の利益，原告が救済を受ける利益

the interests of the forum State, and the plaintiff's interest in obtaining relief. It must also weigh in its determination "the interstate judicial system's interest in obtaining the most efficient resolution of controversies; and the shared interest of the several States in furthering fundamental substantive social policies." *World-Wide Volkswagen*, 444 U.S., at 292 (citations omitted).

A consideration of these factors in the present case clearly reveals the unreasonableness of the assertion of jurisdiction over Asahi, even apart from the question of the placement of goods in the stream of commerce.

Certainly the burden on the defendant in this case is severe. Asahi has been commanded by the Supreme Court of California not only to traverse the distance between Asahi's headquarters in Japan and the Superior Court of California in and for the County of Solano, but also to submit its dispute with Cheng Shin to a foreign nation's judicial system. The unique burdens placed upon one who must defend oneself in a foreign legal system should have significant weight in assessing the reasonableness of stretching the long arm of personal jurisdiction over national borders.

When minimum contacts have been established, often the interests of the plaintiff and the forum in the exercise of jurisdiction will justify even the serious burdens placed on the alien defendant. In the present case, however, the interests of the plaintiff and the forum in California's assertion of jurisdiction over Asahi are slight. All that remains is a claim for indemnification asserted by Cheng Shin, a Tawainese corporation, against Asahi. The transaction on which the indemnification claim is based took place in Taiwan; Asahi's components were shipped from Japan to Taiwan. Cheng Shin has not demonstrated that it is more convenient for it to litigate its indemnification claim against Asahi in California rather than in

を考慮しなければならない．裁判所はまた，その決定にあたっては，「紛争の最も効率的な解決を得ることに対する州際間の裁判所のシステムの利益と，さらには基本的実質的社会政策を促進することに対して複数の州が共有する利益」をも考慮しなければならない．*World-Wide Volkswagen*, 444 U.S., at 292（脚注略）．

　本件においてこれらの要素を考慮すると，Asahi に対する管轄権の行使が，通商の流れに商品を置いたことの問題を別としても，明らかに相当でないことを示している．

　本件における被告の負担は明らかに重い．Asahi は，カルフォルニアの最高裁判所により，日本の Asahi の本社とサロナ郡のカルフォルニア上位裁判所間の距離を行き来することを命じられただけでなく，Cheng Shin との紛争を外国の裁判所システムに服することをも命じられた．外国の法体系のもとで防御しなければならない者に課せられる独特の負担は，国境を越えて対人管轄権を長い手のように，拡張することが相当であるかどうかを評価するに際して重要なウエイトが置かれるべきである．

　最小限の関連が立証されたときには，原告の利益と，管轄権を行使することに対して法廷地が有する利益によって，外国人被告に対してさえも重大な負担を課することが正当化されるであろう．しかしながら，本件の場合には，原告の利益と Asahi にカルフォルニアが管轄権を行使することに対して法廷地が有する利益はとるに足らないものである．台湾会社の Cheng Shin が Asahi に対して主張している求償訴訟だけが残っているにすぎない．求償請求の基礎となっている取引は台湾で発生し，Asahi の部品は日本から台湾へ船積みされた．Cheng Shin は，Asahi に対する求償請求を台湾や日本で提起するよりもカルフォルニアで提起する方がより便宜であることを証明しては

Taiwan or Japan.

Because the plaintiff is not a California resident, California's legitimate interests in the dispute have considerably diminished. The Supreme Court of California argued that the State had an interest in "protecting its consumers by ensuring that foreign manufacturers comply with the state's safety standards." 39 Cal. 3d, at 49, 702 P. 2d, at 550. The State Supreme Court's definition of California's interest, however, was overly broad. The dispute between Cheng Shin and Asahi is primarily about indemnification rather than safety standards. Moreover, it is not at all clear at this point that California law should govern the question whether a Japanese corporation should indemnify a Taiwanese corporation on the basis of a sale made in Taiwan and a shipment of goods from Japan to Taiwan. *Phillips Petroleum Co. v. Shutts*, 472 U.S. 797, 821-822 (1985); *Allstate Insurance Co. v. Hague*, 449 U.S. 302, 312-313 (1981). The possibility of being haled into a California court as a result of an accident involving Asahi's components undoubtedly creates an additional deterrent to the manufacture of unsafe components; however, similar pressures will be placed on Asahi by the purchasers of its components as long as those who use Asahi components in their final products, and sell those products in California, are subject to the application of California tort law.

World-Wide Volkswagen also admonished courts to take into consideration the interests of the "several States," in addition to the forum State, in the efficient judicial resolution of the dispute and the advancement of substantive policies. In the present case, this advice calls for a court to consider the procedural and substantive policies of other *nations* whose interests are affected by the assertion of jurisdiction by the California court. The procedural and substantive interests of other nations in a state court's assertion of jurisdiction over an alien defendant will differ from case to case. In every case, however, those interests, as well as the Federal Government's interest in its foreign relations policies, will be best

2 対人管轄(2)：Asahi Metal Industry Co., Ltd. v. Superior Court

いない．

　原告はカルフォルニアの住民ではないから，紛争に対してカルフォルニアが有する正当な利益は相当に小さくなる．カルフォルニア最高裁判所は，同州が「外国の製造者に同州の安全基準を遵守させることによって自州の消費者を保護する」利益を有すると主張した．39 Cal. 3d, at 49, 702 P. 2d, at 550. しかしながら，州最高裁判所によるカルフォルニアの利益の定義は，明らかに広すぎる．Cheng Shin と Asahi 間の紛争は，主として安全基準というよりは求償に関するものである．さらに日本会社が台湾会社に対して，台湾でなされた販売と日本から台湾への船積みに基づく損失を補償すべきかどうかという問題にカルフォルニア法が適用されるかどうかは，この時点では少しも明らかではない．*Phillips Petroleum Co.* v. *Shutts*, 472 U.S. 797, 821-822（1985）; *Allstate Insurance Co.* v. *Hague*, 449 U.S. 302, 312-313（1981）．Asahi の部品に関する事故の結果としてカルフォルニアの裁判所に呼び出されるという可能性があることは，安全でない部品の製造者に対して付加的な抑止力を与えることは確かである．しかしながら同様の圧力は，Asahi の部品をその最終の製品に使用し，これらの製品をカルフォルニアで販売する者がカルフォルニアの不法行為法の適用に服する限りにおいて，その部品の購入者によって Asahi に対して課せられるであろう．

　World-Wide Volkswagen 判決はまた，紛争の効率的な司法解決と実質的法目的の促進において，法廷地州だけでなく，「複数の州の利益」を考慮すべきことを裁判所に警告した．本件においては，この忠告はカルフォルニア裁判所の管轄権の行使によってその利益が影響を受ける他の*国家*の手続的，実質的法目的を考慮すべきことを裁判所に要求する．州裁判所による外国人被告に対する管轄権の行使における他の国家の手続的，実質的利益は事件毎に異なるであろう．しかしながら，これらの利益は，政府の外交関係の政策における連邦の利益と同様，あらゆる事件において，特定の事件における管轄権の行使の相当性の注意深い探求と，外国人被告の重い負担は，原告又は法廷

served by a careful inquiry into the reasonableness of the assertion of jurisdiction in the particular case, and an unwillingness to find the serious burdens on an alien defendant outweighed by minimal interests on the part of the plaintiff or the forum State. "Great care and reserve should be exercised when extending our notions of personal jurisdiction into the international field." *United States* v. *First National City Bank*, 379 U.S. 378, 404 (1965) (Harlan, J., dissenting). See Born, Reflections on Judicial Jurisdiction in International Cases, to be published in 17 Ga. J. Int'l & Comp. L. 1 (1987).

Considering the international context, the heavy burden on the alien defendant, and the slight interests of the plaintiff and the forum State, the exercise of personal jurisdiction by a California court over Asahi in this instance would be unreasonable and unfair.

III Because the facts of this case do not establish minimum contacts such that the exercise of personal jurisdiction is consistent with fair play and substantial justice, the judgment of the Supreme Court of California is reversed, and the case is remanded for further proceedings not inconsistent with this opinion.

It is so ordered.

JUSTICE BRENNAN, with whom JUSTICE WHITE, JUSTICE MARSHALL, and JUSTICE BLACKMUN join, concurring in part and concurring in the judgment.

I do not agree with the interpretation in Part II-A of the stream-of-commerce theory, nor with the conclusion that Asahi did not "purposely avail itself of the California market." *Ante*, at 112. I do agree, however,

地の側における僅かな利益によって凌駕されると簡単に判断しないことによって，最もよく達成される．「対人管轄権に関するわれわれの観念を国際的な分野にまで拡張するときには，非常な注意と慎重さが行使されるべきである．」 *United States v. First National City Bank*, 379 U.S. 378, 404（1965）（Harlan 裁判官の反対意見）．Born, Reflections on Judicial Jurisdiction in International Cases, to be published in 17 Ga. J. Int'l & Comp. L. 1（1987）参照．

　国際的なコンテキスト，外国人被告に対する重い負担及び原告と法廷地利益が僅かなことを考慮すると，本件における Asahi に対するカルフォルニア裁判所による管轄権の行使は相当ではなく，また公正でもないであろう．

III　本件の事実は，最小限の関連を立証するものではなく，したがって管轄権の行使がフェアプレイと実質的正義に合致しないから，カルフォルニア最高裁判所の判決は破棄され，この意見と矛盾しないように，さらなる手続のために差し戻す．

　以上のように判決する．

　BRENNAN 裁判官の一部補足及び判決に補足意見．WHITE 裁判官，MARSHALL 裁判官，BLACKMUN 裁判官が同調．

　私は，通商の流れ理論の第 II 部の A における解釈にも，また Asahi が「カルフォルニアの市場を意図的に利用し」なかったという結論にも同意しない，前掲 112 頁．しかしながら，本件における Asahi に対する対人管轄権の行使

with the Court's conclusion in Part II-B that the exercise of personal jurisdiction over Asahi in this case would not comport with "fair play and substantial justice," *International Shoe Co. v. Washington*, 326 U.S. 310, 320 (1945). This is one of those rare cases in which "minimum requirements inherent in the concept of 'fair play and substantial justice' ...... defeat the reasonableness of jurisdiction even [though] the defendant has purposefully engaged in forum activities." *Burger King Corp. v. Rudzewicz*, 471 U.S. 462, 477-478 (1985). I therefore join Parts I and II-B of the Court's opinion, and write separately to explain my disagreement with Part II-A.

Part II-A states that "a defendant's awareness that the stream of commerce may or will sweep the product into the forum State does not convert the mere act of placing the product into the stream into an act purposefully directed toward the forum State." Under this view, a plaintiff would be required to show "[additional] conduct" directed toward the forum before finding the exercise of jurisdiction over the defendant to be consistent with the Due Process Clause. I see no need for such a showing, however. The stream of commerce refers not to unpredictable currents or eddies, but to the regular and anticipated flow of products from manufacture to distribution to retail sale. As long as a participant in this process is aware that the final product is being marketed in the forum State, the possibility of a lawsuit there cannot come as a surprise. Nor will the litigation present a burden for which there is no corresponding benefit. A defendant who has placed goods in the stream of commerce benefits economically from the retail sale of the final product in the forum State, and indirectly benefits from the State's laws that regulate and facilitate commercial activity. These benefits accrue regardless of whether that participant directly conducts business in the forum State, or engages in additional conduct directed toward that State. Accordingly, most courts and commentators have found that jurisdiction premised on the placement

が「フェアプレイと実質的正義」に合致しないであろうという裁判所の第Ⅱ部Bの結論には賛成である.*International Shoe Co.* v. *Washington*, 326 U.S. 310, 320 (1945). これは,「『フェアプレイと実質的正義』という観念に固有の最小限の要求が,……被告が意図的に法廷地の活動に従事した場合であった [としても], 管轄権が相当であると認められない, 稀な場合の1つである.」

Burger King Corp. v. *Rudzewicz*, 471 U.S. 462, 477-478 (1985). したがって私は裁判所意見の第Ⅰ部と第Ⅱ部のBには賛成し, 第Ⅱ部のAに対する反対の意見を書く.

第Ⅱ部のAは,「被告が通商の流れに沿って製品が法廷地州に到達するかもしれない又は到達するであろうことを知っていたことは, 流れに製品を置いたという単なる行為を法廷地州に意図的に向けられた行為へと転換するわけではない.」と述べている. この見解によれば, 原告は, 被告に対する管轄権の行使が適正手続条項に合致していると判断されるより先に, 法廷地に向けられた「[付加的な] 行動」を示すことが要求されるであろう. しかしながら私はこのような立証が必要だとは思わない. 通商の流れといわれているものは, 予見することのできない渦や傍流ではなく, 製造者から小売りまでの流通に至る, 製品の正規で, 予期することのできる流れなのである. このプロセスにおいてある参加者が最終製品が法廷地州において市場に出されていることを知っている限り, そこでの訴訟の可能性は不意打ちではない. また, そこでの訴訟が, それに対応する利益を伴わない負担を課すものでもないであろう. 通商の流れに製品を置いた被告は, 法廷地州における最終製品の小売りから経済的に利益を享受しており, 商業活動を規制し, 促進するその州の法から間接的に利益を得ているのである. これらの利益はその参加者が法廷地州において直接に事業活動を行うかにかかわりなく生じるものである. したがってほとんどの裁判所と学者は通商の流れに製品を置いたことに基づく管轄権は適正手続条項に合致し, 追加的な行為の立証を必要としないと判

of a product into the stream of commerce is consistent with the Due Process Clause, and have not required a showing of additional conduct.

The endorsement in Part II-A of what appears to be the minority view among Federal Courts of Appeals represents a marked retreat from the analysis in *World-Wide Volkswagen* v. *Woodson*, 444 U.S. 286 (1980).

......
JUSTICE STEVENS, with whom JUSTICE WHITE and JUSTICE BLACKMUN join, concurring in part and concurring in the judgment.

The judgment of the Supreme Court of California should be reversed for the reasons stated in Part II-B of the Court's opinion. While I join Parts I and II-B, I do not join Part II-A for two reasons. First, it is not necessary to the Court's decision. An examination of minimum contacts is not always necessary to determine whether a state court's assertion of personal jurisdiction is constitutional. See *Burger King Corp.* v. *Rudzewicz*, 471 U.S. 462, 476-478 (1985). Part II-B establishes, after considering the factors set forth in *World-Wide Volkswagen Corp.* v. *Woodson*, 444 U.S. 286, 292 (1980), that California's exercise of jurisdiction over Asahi in this case would be "unreasonable and unfair." This finding alone requires reversal; this case fits within the rule that "minimum requirements inherent in the concept of 'fair play and substantial justice' may defeat the reasonableness of jurisdiction even if the defendant has purposefully engaged in forum activities." *Burger King*, 471 U.S., at 477-478 (quoting *International Shoe Co.* v. *Washington*, 326 U.S. 310, 320 (1945)). Accordingly, I see no reason in this case for the plurality to articulate "purposeful direction" or any other test as the nexus between an act of a defendant and the forum State that is necessary to establish minimum contacts.

2 対人管轄(2)：Asahi Metal Industry Co., Ltd. v. Superior Court

断してきたのである．

　連邦控訴裁判所間で少数意見と考えられる見解を第Ⅱ部のAにおいて支持することは，*World-Wide Volkswagen v. Woodson*, 444 U.S. 286（1980）における分析からの明白な退却を意味するものである．

……

　STEVENS 裁判官の一部補足及び判決に補足意見．WHITE 裁判官と BLACKMUN 裁判官が同調．

　カルフォルニアの最高裁判所の判決は，法廷意見の第Ⅱ部のBで述べられた理由で破棄されるべきである．私は第Ⅰ部と第Ⅱ部のBには同調するけれども，第Ⅱ部のAには2つの理由から同調しない．第1に，それは裁判所の決定にとって必要ではない．最小限の関連の検討は，州の裁判所による対人管轄権の行使が合憲であるかどうかを決定するために必ずしもつねに必要なものではない．*Burger King Corp. v. Rudzewicz*, 471 U.S. 462, 476-478（1985）参照．第Ⅱ部のBは，*World-Wide Volkswagen Corp. v. Woodson*, 444 U.S. 286, 292（1980）において示された要素を考慮した後に，本件におけるAsahi に対するカルフォルニアによる管轄権の行使は，「不当で，不公正」であろうと確証する．この判断だけで破棄されるべきである．この事件は「『フェアプレイと実質的正義』という観念に固有の最小限の要求が，被告が意図的に法廷地の活動に従事した場合であったとしても，管轄権が相当であると認められない」というルールに当てはまる事件である．*Burger King*, 471 U.S., at 477-478（*International Shoe Co. v. Washington*, 326 U.S. 310, 320（1945）を引用）．したがって，本件において多数意見が最小限の関連を確立するのに必要な被告の行為と法廷地州との関係として，「意図的に向けられたこと」又はその他のテストを明確にしようとする理由を見出すことはできない．

Second, even assuming that the test ought to be formulated here, Part II-A misapplies it to the facts of this case. ...... Whether or not [Asahi's] this conduct rises to the level of purposeful availment requires a constitutional determination that is affected by the volume, the value, and the hazardous character of the components. In most circumstances I would be inclined to conclude that a regular course of dealing that results in deliveries of over 100,000 units annually over a period of several years would constitute "purposeful availment" even though the item delivered to the forum State was a standard product marketed throughout the world. ......

【解　説】

　本件は，カルフォルニアで発生した事故について，タイヤチューブを製造した台湾会社から，チューブの部品製造メーカーである日本会社に対して提起された製造物責任の求償訴訟において，カルフォルニア州裁判所が日本会社に対して対人管轄権を行使することは，適正手続条項に違反するとされた事例である．連邦最高裁の対人管轄権の行使に関する指導的先例の1つである．

　日本会社 Asahi に対するカルフォルニア州裁判所の対人管轄権の行使が憲法に違反するとされた事例であり，管轄権の行使に制限的な傾向を示す判決といえる．

1　対人管轄権革命：*International Shoe* 判決

　International Shoe Co. v. Washington, 326 U.S. 310（1945）判決は，被告に対する州内での令状の送達や被告の所在を対人管轄権の必須の要件とする伝統的理論を全面的に変更した連邦最高裁の画期的判決である．連邦最高

第 2 に，かりにそのようなテストがここで公式化されるべきだと仮定しても，第 II 部の A はそれを本件の事実に誤って適用している．………［Asahi の］行為が意図的な利用のレベルに達しているかどうかは，部品の量，値段，危険の性質によって影響を受ける憲法上の決定が必要とされる問題である．数年間にわたる期間中，毎年 100,000 個以上の引渡しをもたらす定期的な取引は，たとえ法廷地州に引き渡された品目が世界中を市場とする標準的な製品であったとしても，ほとんどの状況下では，「意図的な利用」となる，と私は結論したい．
……

裁は，この事件で，伝統的な管轄権のフレームワークに変革をもたらした判決において，「伝統的なフェアプレイと実質的正義の観念」に抵触しない程度の被告と法廷地との最小限の関連が認められる限り，州裁判所が法廷地州内に存在していない被告に対して裁判管轄権を行使しても，憲法上の適正手続に違反しないと判断した．*International Shoe* 判決を中心とした管轄権革命については，リッチマン＝レイノルズ（松岡・吉川・高杉・北坂訳）『アメリカ抵触法（上巻）』51-63 頁参照．また *International Shoe* 事件については，山本敬三・英米判例百選 I 公法 94-95 頁（1978），坂本正光『アメリカ法における人的管轄権の展開』43-52 頁（九州大学出版会，1990），坂本正光・英米判例百選（第 3 版）162-63 頁（1996），川又良也「米国連邦裁判所の外国会社に対する管轄権について」（『商事法の解釈と展望』所収 611-612 頁（1984））参照．

2 「通商の流れ」の理論と *World-Wide Volkswagen* 判決

連邦最高裁は，その後，*World-Wide Volkswagen v. Woodson*, 444 U.S. 286, 292（1980）において，不法行為・製造物責任訴訟における管轄権に関

する「通商の流れ」の理論について，法廷地州の消費者によって購入されることを予想して，製品を通商の流れにおいた企業に対する裁判管轄権の行使は，適正手続に違反しないとの一般論を展開しながらも，ニューヨークで同州の住民に販売された自動車がオクラホマで事故を起こしたという偶然の事情だけから，被告と法廷地州との関連を認めることはできないとして，結果的には被告に対する管轄権の行使を否定した．

通商の流れの理論については，リッチマン＝レイノルズ・前掲182頁参照．

また，*World-Wide Volkswagen*事件については，野村美明・阪大法学126号116-124頁（1983），リッチマン＝レイノルズ・前掲67-71頁（2008）参照．

3　2段階テスト：最小限の関連とフェアネス

本件O'Connor裁判官による意見は，法廷地と被告との最小限の関連（判旨ⅡA）と，フェアプレイと実質的正義（判旨ⅡB）という二段階テストにより，管轄権の行使は，適正手続に反するとした．

しかしその射程距離をあまり広く読むのは問題であり，限定的に読む必要がある．判旨ⅡAの部分をどう読むかいかんによる．

4　最小限の関連

本件判旨ⅡAは，被告と法廷地との最小限の関連があるかどうかのテストにおいて，制限的な通商の流れの理論をとり，被告が製品を通商の流れに乗せただけでは被告に対する管轄権の行使には不十分であるとする．単に製品を通商の流れに置くという以上のなにか付加的な行為を必要とすべきであるとした上で，本件ではその付加的な行為がないと判断する．

しかしこの部分については，4人の裁判官（O'Connor, Rehnquist, Powell, Scalia）の賛成しかない点に注意する必要がある（これに対して，製品を通商の流れに置いたという認識があれば十分であるとする，4人の反対意見がある）．また，その後の判決でも，判旨ⅡAを最高裁の意見としてどこまで尊重するかは意見が分かれている．したがって，判旨ⅡAの立場は，有力ではあるが，これ

で流れが決まったというわけではない.

ⅡAと同じ立場から, 日本会社（トヨタの部品メーカー）に対する損害発生地の管轄を否定した判決としては, 判旨も引用する *Humble v. Toyota Motor Co.*, 727 F.2d 709（CA 81984）がある.

これに対して, *Deutsch v. West Coast Machinery Co.*, 80 Wash. 2d 707（1972）は, 同じ製造物責任の求償訴訟において, 本判決と異なり, 日本会社（関西鉄工）に対する事故発生地の米国ワシントン州裁判所の管轄を認めた事例である. なお, この事件と関連する日本における訴訟として, 大阪地判昭和52・12・22判タ361号127頁がある. また, *Hedric v. Daiko Shoji Co.*, 715 F.2d 1355（9th Cir.1983）, modified 733 F.2d 1335（9th Cir. 1984）も *Deutsch* 事件と同趣旨の判決である（O'Connorの意見はこの判決の立場に反対する）.

本判決後の簡潔な状況については, Russel J. Weintraub, International Litigation and Arbitlation 14-15（3rd ed. 2001）.

5 フェアネス又は相当性

本件においては, 判旨ⅡBがとくに重要である. カルフォルニアの管轄権の行使が, フェアプレイと実質的正義の観点からみて, 相当であるかどうかを判断し, これを否定した. この部分については, Scalia裁判官を除く8人の裁判官が賛成している.

法廷意見は, まず, 相当性の判断において考慮すべき要素として, ①被告の負担, ②法廷地州の利益, ③便宜な法廷地における原告の利益, ④紛争の最も効率的な解決を得ることに対する州際間の裁判所のシステムの利益, ⑤基本的な実質的社会政策を促進することに対して複数の州が共有する利益を列挙する. この5つの要素についての説明, 分析については, リッチマン＝レイノルズ・前掲187-196頁参照.

本件では, 法廷意見によると, Asahiは, 外国企業であり, 日本とカルフォルニアを往復しなければならないだけでなく, 外国の裁判システムに服さなくてはならず, その負担が重いこと, これに対して, 本件が求償訴訟であ

って，Cheng Shin が台湾企業であり，カルフォルニアの住民ではないから，原告の利益，法廷地の利益が僅かである，との点が強調されている．この点からいってもとくに本件が求償訴訟である点が重視されていることがわかる．また，本件が州際事件ではなく，被告が日本企業であり，国際訴訟である点が考慮されている点も注目される．

なお，判旨ⅡBに批判的な見解としては，リッチマン＝レイノルズ前掲101-102頁がある．これによると，O'Conner 裁判官による通商の流れの理論の再構成は，きわめて厄介であるとして，次のように批判する．同裁判官の意見が優勢になったら，消費者はアメリカの裁判所で外国会社を訴えることができなくなり，アメリカの消費者からアメリカの法廷地を奪うことになるだろう．同裁判官の意見について言いうる最上のことは，それが法でないということであると．

6 管轄権拡大法 (long arm statute)

ロング・アーム法ともいう．*International Shoe* 判決により，州の対人管轄権の範囲が従来考えられていたより広いものであることが認められたため，各州が新たな立法により管轄権の範囲を拡張した．この法律を管轄権拡大法又はロング・アーム法という．この点について詳しくは，リッチマン＝レイノルズ・前掲145-163頁参照．

【本件参考文献】

孝橋宏・アメリカ法［1988］160頁．
藤田康弘『日米国際訴訟の実務と論点』127-141頁（日本評論社，1998）．
野村美明・阪大法学49巻3・4号393-398頁（1999）．
リッチマン＝レイノルズ著（松岡・吉川・高杉・北坂訳）『アメリカ抵触法（上巻）』（レキシスネキシスジャパン，2008）95-103頁．
坂本正光『アメリカ法における人的管轄権の展開』（九州大学出版会，1990）89-97頁．

2 対人管轄(2)：Asahi Metal Industry Co., Ltd. v. Superior Court

【設　問】

1　本件の主要な争点はなにか．
2　本件の事実の概要を述べよ．事件と当事者に関するカルフォルニア，日本，台湾の関連を整理せよ．
3　Asahi は当初から被告として訴えられたか．どのような経緯で訴訟に巻き込まれたか．
4　カルフォルニア州最高裁判所の判決の結論を述べよ．
5　連邦最高裁の結論はどうか．
　　また，*International Shoe* 事件，その後の管轄権拡大法の制定，*World-Wide Volkswagen* 事件について説明せよ．
6　O'Connor 裁判官の意見をとくに2段階テスト（ⅡA（最小限の関連），ⅡB（reasonableness））を中心に要約せよ．
7　本判決における裁判官の意見構成について整理せよ．
8　最小限関連テスト及び製造物責任における「通商の流れの理論」について説明せよ．
9　フェアプレイと実質的正義（管轄権行使の合理性）テストについて説明し，最小限テストとの関係を説明せよ．
10　本件が求償訴訟であることは，どのような意味をもつか．
11　本件判旨から，日本会社が米国での訴訟への対応策を考えよ．
12　要するに本件はどのような判決か．また本件の結論，理由づけに賛成か．

3 | 対人管轄(3):
Miller v. Honda Motor Co., 779 F.2d 769 (1st Cir. 1985)

TORRUELLA, Circuit Judge.

The issue presented by this case is whether we will expand the reach of our recent decision in *Howse v. Zimmer Manufacturing Co., Inc.*, 757 F.2d 448 (1st Cir. 1985), a case involving the service of process requirements of Mass. Gen. Laws Ann. ch. 223 §38, for the purpose of permitting the acquisition of *in personam* jurisdiction over a foreign corporation which lacks any direct contacts with this jurisdiction. Because we believe that *Howse* delineates the outer limits of what is permitted by the due process clause, we reject the invitation proffered by appellants and affirm the district court's decision to the effect that *in personam* jurisdiction is lacking over defendant/appellee Honda Motor Co., Ltd. (Honda). Since jurisdictional controversies are so fact-dependent, we commence with a summary of the relevant particulars.

Plaintiffs/appellants Marion and Donald Miller (Miller) are residents of Massachusetts. In February, 1980, the Millers, while vacationing in Bermuda, rented a Honda PC 50 moped from Smatt's Cycle Livery, Ltd. (Smatt), a Bermudian enterprise. Mrs. Miller had an accident while using the vehicle, sustaining serious injuries which resulted in a quadriplegic condition. She will, in all probability, be confined to a bed or wheelchair the rest of her life, totally dependent on others for all aspects of her care, even for breathing, for which she requires the use of a respirator.

日本企業ホンダのモペットが英領バーミューダで事故を起こし，重傷を負ったマサチューセッツ住民がマサチューセッツ連邦地裁に提起した製造物責任訴訟において，マサチューセッツ裁判所のホンダに対する対人管轄権が否認された事例

　TORRUELLA 巡回区控訴審裁判官
　本件で提起されている争点は，この法域［マサチューセッツ］となんらの直接の関連を有しない外国法人に対する対人管轄権の取得を可能とするために，Mass. Gen. Laws Ann. ch. 223 §38 が規定する訴状の送達の要件に関する *Howse v. Zimmer Manufacturing Co., Inc.*, 757 F.2d 448（1st Cir. 1985）事件における最近のわれわれの決定が，その適用される範囲を拡大すべきか，という問題である．*Howse* 事件が適正手続条項によって許容される外側の境界を画していると考えるから，控訴人によって主張されている要請を退け，被告・被控訴人 Honda Motor Co., Ltd.（Honda）に対する対人管轄権を欠いていたとする地方裁判所の判断を支持する．管轄に関する争いは，事実によって大きく左右されるから，関連する事実関係の要約から始める．

　原告・控訴人 Marion and Donald Miller（Miller）は，マサチューセッツの住民である．1980 年 2 月，Miller 夫妻は，バーミューダで休暇中，Honda の原付モペット PC50 をバーミューダ企業である Smatt's Cycle Livery, Ltd.（Smatt）から借りた．Miller 夫人が車両を使用中に事故に遭遇し，重傷を負い，その結果，四肢麻痺の状態になった．彼女は，ほぼ確実に，残りの人生をベッドと車いすでの生活を余儀なくされ，その看護のすべての面において他人に依存するほかなく，呼吸することさえ人工呼吸装置の使用を必要とする．

The vehicle in question was manufactured for Honda, a Japanese company, by another company located in Taiwan, Koyo Kogyo Co., Ltd. (Koyo). Honda had the moped shipped to Bermuda via Asia and South America. There it was sold to Honda Livery, Ltd. (Honda Bermuda), a Bermuda corporation. Honda Bermuda then sold it to Smatt's who, as indicated, was the owner of the moped when the accident occurred.

The Millers brought a products liability suit against Honda in the United States District Court for the District of Massachusetts. The suit was dismissed, the court ruling that the facts were insufficient to justify an assertion of personal jurisdiction over Honda.

The record is uncontroverted that Honda-manufactured vehicles, and other products are sold in Massachusetts by authorized dealers who purchase them from a California corporation, American Honda Motor Co., Inc. (American Honda). American Honda is a wholly-owned subsidiary of Honda. Honda, however, conducts no direct business activities in Massachusetts and has no offices, bank accounts nor employees located therein. Nor has it entered into any franchise or distributorship agreements in Massachusetts or with any business entity located in that state. There is not even any allegation that Honda's employees have ever visited Massachusetts.

The record is uncontradicted that Honda's direct involvement with goods destined for the North American market ends dockside in Japan with the sale of these goods to Honda American, which is the company that sells to the Massachusetts dealers. American Honda is also the company that has contacts with Massachusetts normally associated with the granting of *in personam* jurisdiction over a foreign corporation. It is not, however, a party defendant in this suit. We surmise that the reason for

3 対人管轄(3)：Miller v. Honda Motor Co.

問題の車は日本会社 Honda のために台湾に所在する別の会社 Koyo Kogyo Co., Ltd. (Koyo) によって製造された．Honda は，そのモペットをアジア，南アメリカ経由でバーミューダに船積みした．そこでモペットはバーミューダ会社である Honda Livery, Ltd. (Honda Bermuda) に売られた．それから Honda Burmuda はモペットをさきに述べたように，事故発生当時にそのモペットの所有者である Smatt's に販売した．

Miller 夫妻は，Honda に対してマサチューセッツ地区合衆国地方裁判所に製造物訴訟を提起した．裁判所は，本件事実の下では，Honda に対する対人管轄権の主張を正当化するには不十分であると判示し，訴訟は却下された．

Honda 製造の車両とその他の製品がカルフォルニア会社である American Honda Motor Co., Inc. (American Honda) から，それらの製品を購入する権限あるデイーラーによって，マサチューセッツで販売されていることについては記録から争いはない．American Honda は，Honda の完全所有の子会社である．しかしながら，Honda はマサチューセッツで直接の事業活動を行っていないし，そこで事務所も銀行口座も従業員も有していない．Honda はフランチャイズやディストリビューター契約をマサチューセッツにおいて又は同州に所在する事業体と締結したこともない．Honda の従業員がマサチューセッツをかつて訪問したことがあるという主張さえもない．

北米市場に向けられた商品と Honda との直接のかかわりは，American Honda に対するこれらの商品の販売により，日本の波止場で終わることは記録から議論の余地がなく，マサチューセッツのディーラーに販売した会社は American Honda なのである．American Honda はまた，州外会社に対する対人管轄権を認めることと通常は結びつくマサチューセッツとの関連を有している．しかしながら，American Honda は，本件訴訟において当事者たる被告ではない．その理由は，American Honda はバーミューダとなんらの関

this is that American Honda has no Bermuda connection, and more importantly, because American Honda cannot be charged with the manufacturing defects, having had no apparent intervention with that end of the business. The Millers rely on *Howse v. Zimmer Manufacturing Co., Inc.*, *supra*, in their attempt to acquire Massachusetts jurisdiction over Honda. Unfortunately, as indicated, that case is not applicable.

Howse, although extremely liberal in allowing the assumption of jurisdiction, is clearly distinguishable from the present situation. Howse, a Massachusetts resident, suffered a broken hip while in Spain. He underwent surgery in a United States naval hospital in that country during which a "nail and plate" implant, allegedly manufactured by Zimmer, was inserted into his hip. Upon his return to the United States, Howse sued Zimmer in Massachusetts, alleging that the fracture improperly healed due to defects in the implant. Zimmer, a Delaware corporation with its principal place of business in Indiana, had none of the contacts which are traditionally thought to establish personal jurisdiction under §38. As in the present case, Zimmer was neither registered in, nor did it have a traditional type of agent in the Massachusetts. It manufactured no products there nor did it have an office, bank accounts, nor employees located there. It had not entered into franchises or distributorship agreements in Massachusetts. Its products were sold in Massachusetts exclusively by a representative, Docherty Associates, Inc., which did business under the name Zimmer Docherty Associates. The district court found that there was no personal jurisdiction over Zimmer. We reversed.

Two important distinguishing features appear in *Howse* that are absent in the present situation, however. First, Zimmer engaged in a systematic pattern of activities in Massachusetts closely approximating the regular conduct of domestic enterprises:

To us most significantly, Zimmer is "always" sending representatives

3　対人管轄(3)：Miller v. Honda Motor Co.

連はなく，さらに重要なことには，American Honda がその取引にはなんら関与していなかったから，製造上の欠陥についての責任を問えなかったからである．Miller 夫妻は，Honda への管轄権を獲得しようとして，前掲 *Howse v. Zimmer Manufacturing Co., Inc.* 事件に依拠する．不幸なことに，さきに指摘したように，その事件は適用されない．

　Howse 事件は，管轄権の取得を認めることにきわめて寛大であるけれども，本件の状況とは明らかに異なっている．マサチューセッツの住民である Howse は，スペインにいる間に腰部を骨折した．彼はその国の米国海軍病院で手術を受け，その間に Zimmer により製造されたと主張されている「鋲とプレート」の移植片が彼の腰部に埋め込まれた．合衆国に帰ってから，Howse はマサチューセッツで Zimmer に訴えを提起し，移植片の欠陥により，骨折がうまく治癒しなかったと主張した．主たる営業地をインディアナに有するデラウエア法人である Zimmer は，第 38 条において伝統的に対人管轄権が取得されるものと考えられる関連をなんら有してはいなかった．本件と同様に，Zimmer はマサチューセッツにおいて登録されていないし，伝統的なタイプの代理人を有してもいなかった．事務所も銀行口座も駐在する従業員もそこには有していなかった．マサチューセッツでフランチャイズ契約もディストビューター契約も締結しなかった．その製品はマサチューセッツでは，Zimmer Docherty Associates という名で事業を営んでいる Docherty Associates Inc. という代理人によって専属的に販売されていた．地方裁判所は Zimmer に対人管轄権は存在しないと判示した．われわれは破棄した．

　しかしながら，本件の状況には存在しないが，*Howse* 事件には存在する 2 つの重要な区別しうる特徴がある．第 1 に，Zimmer は，マサチューセッツにおいて州内会社の正規の行動に密接に近い，組織的な活動のパターンに従事していた．
　　われわれにとって，最も重要なのは，Zimmer が「つねに」新製品と

to Massachusetts to confer with surgeons concerning the development of new products and specific need products. We think this pattern of extensive instate activities removes Zimmer from the category of defendant encountered in *Caso* ...... While the case is close, the fact that Zimmer representatives are constantly in and out of Massachusetts in order to deal directly with customers, coupled with the sizeable sales volume and other factors removes this from the "mere solicitation" and "solicitation plus" category......

Howse, supra at 452-453, (emphasis supplied) (footnote omitted).

Second, we noted, that payments for the products sold in Massachusetts was always made directly to Zimmer in Indiana, even when the Massachusetts dealer, Zimmer Docherty Associates, filled the order from his in-state inventory.

Both of these factors are missing from the present situation. This is not to say, of course, that the mere absence of these conditions, if other traditionally relevant indicia are present, would by themselves defeat jurisdiction. As previously indicated, these controversies are highly fact-specific and all evidence must be carefully weighed and evaluated before concluding whether or not there is jurisdiction. What is clear from the record is that permitting the acquisition of *in personam* jurisdiction over Honda in this case would offend all notions of fair play and due process. See *World-Wide Volkswagen Corp. v. Woodson*, 444 U.S. 286, 62 L. Ed. 2d 490, 100 S. Ct. 559 (1980); *International Shoe Co. v. Washington*, 326 U.S. 310, 90 L. Ed. 95, 66 S. Ct. 154 (1945). In the present case Zimmer's equivalent is American Honda, not Honda. Honda is one step further removed than Zimmer, a gap which, at least under the circumstances before us, can not be bridged.

3 対人管轄(3)：Miller v. Honda Motor Co.

特別需要の製品の開発に関して外科医と会合するために，代表者をマサチューセッツに送っていたということである．この広汎な州内での活動のパターンが Zimmer を Caso 事件において遭遇した被告の範疇から排除する……．事件は微妙であるが，Zimmer が代表者をマサチューセッツの内外に顧客と取引するために絶えず送っていたという事実は，相当の販売量と他の要因とをあわせ考えると，「単なる勧誘」及び「勧誘プラス」という範疇からこれを除去する……．

Howse，前掲452-453頁（「かっこ」は追加）（脚注略）．

第2に，マサチューセッツの販売店 Zimmer Docherty Associates が，その州内にある在庫品から注文を出したときには，マサチューセッツで売られた製品の支払いは，つねにインディアナにある Zimmer に対して直接なされた．

これらの要素の双方ともが本件の状況には存在しない．このことはもとより，これらの条件が存在しなければそれだけで，もし他の伝統的に関連のある徴候が存在しても，管轄権を欠くであろうということを意味するものではない．さきに指摘したように，これらの紛争は，大きく事実によって左右されるから，すべての証拠は，管轄権があるかどうかを結論する前に，注意深く秤量され，評価されなければならない．本件における Honda に対する*対人管轄権の取得*を認めることは，フェアプレイと適正手続のあらゆる観念に違反するであろうことは，記録から明らかである．*World-Wide Volkswagen Corp. v. Woodson*, 444 U.S. 286, 62 L. Ed. 2d 490, 100 S. Ct. 559（1980）; *International Shoe Co. v. Washington*, 326 U.S. 310, 90 L. Ed. 95, 66 S. Ct. 154（1945）参照．本件において Zimmer に相当するのは，American Honda であり，Honda ではない．Honda は，Zimmer より，さらにワンステップ離れたところにあり，少なくとも本件の状況の下では，そのギャップは埋められえない．

Appellants make one additional claim as an alternate ground for finding jurisdiction. They urge that we apply the doctrine of corporate disregard and find that American Honda is in fact an agent of its Japanese parent. The Supreme Judicial Court of Massachusetts has stated that the fiction of corporate separateness should be disregarded only:

 a) when there is active and direct participation by the representatives of one corporation, apparently exercising some form of pervasive control in the activities of another, and there is *some fraudulent or injurious consequence of the intercorporate relationship*, or b) when there is a confused intermingling of activity of two or more corporations engaged in a common enterprise with *substantial disregard of the separate nature of the corporate entities*, or *serious ambiguity* about the manner and capacity in which various corporations and their respective representatives are acting.

My Bread Baking Co. v. Cumberland Farms Inc., 353 Mass. 614, 619, 233 N.E.2d 748, 752 (1968). (Emphasis ours). See also *Westcott Construction Corp. v. Cumberland Const. Co., Inc.*, 3 Mass. App. Ct. 294, 297-98, 328 N.E.2d 522, 525 (1975); *Willis v. American Permac, Inc.*, 541 F. Supp. 118, 122 (D. Mass. 1982).

The district court found that the affairs of Honda and American Honda were not so intertwined as to demonstrate that the two corporations are, in reality, a single entity subject to the application of the doctrine in question. The evidence in the record supports this conclusion.

Although there is common membership on the board of directors by two officers, the day to day operational decisions of each company are made by separate groups of corporate officers. Of the twenty-four officers and directors at Honda, only one is from American Honda, its president,

控訴人は管轄権を認めるべきもう1つの理由として，1つの付加的な請求をしている．控訴人が主張するのは，われわれが法人格否認の法理を採用し，American Honda が実際には日本の親会社の代理人であると判示すべきという点にある．マサチューセッツの最高裁判所は，法人格の分離の擬制は次の場合においてのみ無視されるべきと述べてきた．

　　a）一方の法人の代表者による積極的で直接的な参加が存在し，他の法人の活動に対してなんらかの形の*浸透的な支配*を明らかに行使し，かつ法人間の関係のなんらかの*詐欺的又は有害な結果*が存在しているとき，又はb）共同の事業に従事する複数の法人の活動に*法人格の独立的性質の実質的な無視を伴う混乱した混同*，又は異なった法人とその代表者が行動している方法と資格に関して*重大な曖昧さ*が存在しているとき．

My Bread Baking Co. v. Cumberland Farms Inc., 353 Mass. 614, 619, 233 N.E.2d 748, 752 (1968)．(強調はわれわれのもの)．*Westcott Construction Corp. v. Cumberland Const. Co., Inc.*, 3 Mass. App. Ct. 294, 297-98, 328 N.E.2d 522, 525 (1975); *Willis v. American Permac, Inc.*, 541 F. Supp. 118, 122 (D. Mass. 1982) 参照．

　地方裁判所は，Honda と American Honda との業務は，2つの法人が現実において問題の法理が適用される単一の法主体であることを指し示すほどには，密接に結びついていない，と判示した．記録にある証拠はこの結論を支持している．

　取締役会には2人の共通の構成員がいるけれども，それぞれの会社の日常の業務の決定は，別のグループの会社役員によって行われている．Honda の24人の役員，取締役のうち，社長1人だけが American Honda からであり，その関与は日本での取締役会への出席に限られている．14人の American

and his involvement is limited to attending board meetings in Japan. Of fourteen directors and officers of American Honda, the chairman of the board is also the executive vice-president of Honda, but he has no involvement in running the operations of American Honda and receives reports when he visits American Honda in California for meetings. At those meetings, only the affairs of American Honda are discussed. Honda reimburses American Honda for warranty repairs. It also charged American Honda interest for delayed payments. American Honda controls its own advertising and marketing schemes, and the types of goods it feels are appropriate for the American market. Last, but not least, American Honda maintains a completely separate system for personnel management, financial planning, and real estate planning.

Appellants' argument primarily rests on equity. Mrs. Miller's severe physical limitations preclude her traveling to Bermuda to litigate this action there; it would present no significant burden for Honda to litigate in Massachusetts. Such an argument, although emotive, cannot deter us from being fair to *all* parties. It would be contrary to long established legal doctrine to apply the corporate disregard doctrine to the relationship between Honda and American Honda. Even where there is a common control of a group of separate corporations engaged in a single enterprise, failure to meet the criteria established in *My Bread Baking Co., supra*, will defeat any attempt to pierce the corporate veil. See *NCR Credit Corporation v. Underground Camera, Inc.*, 581 F. Supp. 609, 612 (D. Mass. 1984). After all, there is nothing fraudulent or against public policy in limiting one's liability by the appropriate use of corporate insulation. While sympathetic to the appellants' tragedy, we cannot find any legal basis for assumption of *in personam* jurisdiction over Honda. For these reasons the decision of the district court is

Affirmed.

Hondaの役員,取締役のうち,取締役会の議長はまた,Hondaの執行副社長であるが,彼はAmerican Hondaの業務の遂行には関与していないし,会合のためにカルフォルニアにあるAmerican Hondaを訪問するときに報告を受けるにすぎない.これらの会合において,American Hondaの業務のみが討議される.Hondaは,American Hondaに対して,修繕保証の補填を行う.Hondaは,また支払い遅延に対する利息をAmerican Hondaに課した.American Hondaは,自身の宣伝及び市場計画,さらにアメリカ市場で適切と考える商品のタイプがなにかについて,コントロールしている.最後に,しかし,それは価値が最小というわけではないが,American Hondaは人事管理,財政計画及び不動産計画のために,完全に独立したシステムを維持している.

　上訴人の議論は主としてエクイティに立脚している.Miller夫人の厳しい身体的障害は彼女がバーミューダに行き,そこで本件訴訟を提起するために旅行することを阻んでいる.Hondaがマサチューセッツで訴訟を提起することにはなんら重大な負担を課するものではないであろう.このような議論は,感情に訴えるものではあるが,われわれがすべての当事者に公平であることを妨げるものではない.HondaとAmerican Hondaとの間に法人格否認の法理を適用することは,長く確立した法原則に反するものである.単一の事業に従事する独立した法人のグループの共通のコントロールが存在する場合であっても,前掲 *My Bread Baking Co.* 事件において確立された基準に適合しないことは,法人のベールを剥がすいかなる試みをも失敗に終わらせるであろう.*NCR Credit Corporation v. Underground Camera, Inc.*, 581 F. Supp. 609, 612（D. Mass. 1984）参照.結局のところ,法人格の分離を適切に利用することによって,自己の責任を制限することには,なんら詐欺的なところや公序に反することはない.上訴人の悲劇に対しては同情するが,Hondaに対する対人管轄権の行使に対するなんら合法的な根拠をわれわれは見出すことはできない.これらの理由により,地方裁判所の判決は
　支持される.

I　国際裁判管轄・国際商事仲裁

【解　説】

　本件は，日本企業ホンダのモペットが英領バーミューダで事故を起こし，重傷を負ったマサチューセッツ住民がマサチューセッツ連邦地裁に提起した製造物責任訴訟において，マサチューセッツ裁判所の日本会社ホンダに対する対人管轄権が否認された事例である．

1　*Howse* 判決

　まず裁判所は，州外会社に対する管轄権の取得を寛大に認めた先例である *Howse* 事件と本件を区別し，本件の事実関係の下では，ホンダに対する管轄権の行使を認めることは，フェアプレイと適正手続のあらゆる観念に違反することは明らかであるとしてこれを認めなかった．

2　多国籍企業に対する裁判管轄権

　次に本件は，多国籍企業に対する法人格否認の法理の適用が問題となった事例として注目される．

　子会社に管轄権が認められるからといって，親会社に対する管轄権が認められるわけではない．その逆も同様である．しかし子会社が別個独立して法的に存在していることが虚構であるといえるほど，親会社が子会社を支配しているとすれば，裁判所は，管轄権の目的からいっても子会社の「法人格を否認」し，子会社の法廷地との関連を親会社に帰することができる．この点については，ウィリアム・M・リッチマン＝ウィリアム・L・レイノルズ（23頁）著（松岡・吉川・高杉・北坂訳）『アメリカ抵触法（上巻）』（レキシスネキシスジャパン，2008）143-144 頁参照．なお，抵触法第 2 リステイトメントも同様の立場を採用する．Restatement, Second, Conflict of Laws, §52, comment b (1971). 第 2 リステイトメント研究会訳「〈邦訳〉アメリカ抵触法第二リステイトメント(4)」民商法雑誌 74 巻 2 号 156-157 頁（1976）［西賢，三浦正人担当］参照．

　本件では，裁判所は，親会社日本ホンダと子会社米国ホンダとの間には，

単一の法主体と認めるほどに緊密な関係はなく，法人格否認の法理は適用されないとし，日本会社である親会社ホンダに対する対人管轄権の行使を否認した．

同様に，*Jazini v. Nissan Motor Co.*, 148 F.3d 181（2d Cir.1998）も，ニューヨーク住民が，イランで日産車を運転中に衝突して負傷し，ニューヨークの連邦地方裁判所に，日本会社日産が完全所有子会社である米国日産の活動を根拠にニューヨークの管轄権に服するとして，訴訟を提起した事例である．連邦地裁が管轄権が欠けているという理由で申立を却下した．控訴審も原告は，管轄権の問題に関してディスカバリィを認めるに必要な事実を立証しなかったとして控訴を棄却した．

アメリカにおける多国籍企業に対する管轄権については，田中美穂『多国籍企業の法規制と責任』15-28頁（大阪大学出版会，2005）参照．

3 法人格否認が肯定された事例

これに対して，*Bulova Watch Co., Inc. v. K. Hattori & Co.*, 508 F. Supp. 1322（1981）は，日本の親会社に対する管轄権の行使を肯定した事例である．

4 アメリカ子会社に対する管轄権

本件は，親会社に対する管轄権の行使は否認したが，American Hondaに対する管轄権は，傍論ながら肯定した．

【設　問】

1　本件の主要な争点はなにか．
2　本件の事実の概要を述べよ．事件と当事者に関するマサチューセッツ，日本，英領バーミューダの関連を整理せよ．
3　判旨の結論を要約せよ．
4　*Howse* 判決はどのような判決か．本件との異同はどうか．判旨はこの事件をどのように読んだか．
5　本件におけるホンダに対する管轄権の取得を認めることは，フェアプレイと適正手続のあらゆる観念に違反するとの判旨についてどう思うか．
6　法人格否認の法理とはどのようなものか．
7　法人格否認の法理の本件への適用について説明し，論評せよ．
8　*Nissan Motor Co.* 事件を紹介し，本件と比較せよ．
9　本件は要約するとどのような判決か．
10　本件の結論，理由づけに賛成か．

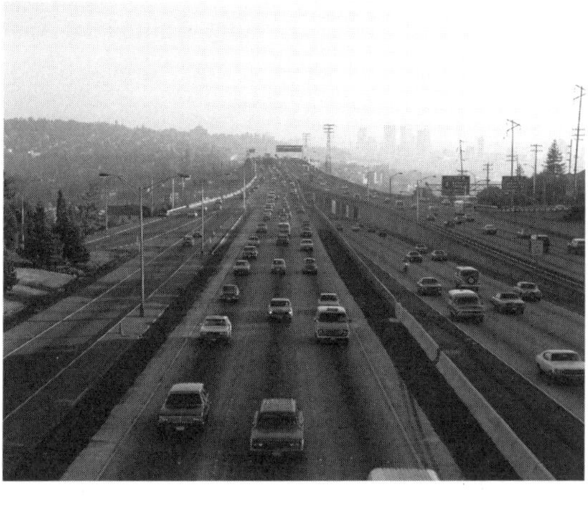

4 合意管轄：
The Bremen v. Zapata Off-Shore Co., 407 U.S.1 (1972)

CHIEF JUSTICE BURGER delivered the opinion of the Court.

We granted certiorari to review a judgment of the United States Court of Appeals for the Fifth Circuit declining to enforce a forum-selection clause governing disputes arising under an international towage contract between petitioners and respondent. The circuits have differed in their approach to such clauses. For the reasons stated hereafter, we vacate the judgment of the Court of Appeals.

In November 1967, respondent Zapata, a Houston-based American corporation, contracted with petitioner Unterweser, a German corporation, to tow Zapata's ocean-going, self-elevating drilling rig *Chaparral* from Louisiana to a point off Ravenna, Italy, in the Adriatic Sea, where Zapata had agreed to drill certain wells.

Zapata had solicited bids for the towage, and several companies including Unterweser had responded. Unterweser was the low bidder and Zapata requested it to submit a contract, which it did. The contract submitted by Unterweser contained the following provision, which is at issue in this case:

"Any dispute arising must be treated before the London Court of Justice."

In addition the contract contained two clauses purporting to exculpate Unterweser from liability for damages to the towed barge.

After reviewing the contract and making several changes, but without

ドイツ会社と米国会社との間に締結された国際曳航契約中のロンドンの裁判所を専属管轄裁判所とする法廷地選択条項が原則として有効とされた事例

BURGER 首席裁判官が法廷意見を言い渡した.
　われわれは，上訴人と被上訴人との間の国際的曳航契約から生じる紛争を規律する法廷地選択条項を執行することを否定した合衆国第5巡回区控訴裁判所の判決を再審理するために，裁量的上訴を認めた．かかる条項に対するアプローチにおいて巡回区控訴裁判所間で意見が異なってきた．われわれは，以下に述べる理由により，控訴審裁判所の判決を取り消す．

　1967年11月に，ヒューストンに本拠を置く被上訴人である米国法人 Zapata は，上訴人であるドイツ法人 Unterweser との間に，Zapata の外洋航行用の自動持ち上げ掘削船 *Chaparral* 号をルイジアナからアドリア海にあるイタリーのラヴェナ沖のある地点まで曳航する契約を締結した．そこで Zapata は，鉱泉を掘削する合意をしていた．
　Zapata は，曳航のための入札を要請し，Unterweser を含む数社が入札に応じた．Unterweser が低価格の入札者であり，Zapata は契約書を提出するよう求め，それが提出された．Unterweser により提出された契約には，本件で争われている，次の条項が含まれていた.
　　「発生するすべての紛争は，ロンドン裁判所で処理されなければならない.」
　さらに契約には，曳航の目的物に生じた損害について Unterweser の免責を意図した2つの条項が含まれていた．
　契約を再検討し，いくつかの修正を加えた後に，しかし法廷地選択条項と

any alteration in the forum-selection or exculpatory clauses, a Zapata vice president executed the contract and forwarded it to Unterweser in Germany, where Unterweser accepted the changes, and the contract became effective.

On January 5, 1968, Unterweser's deep sea tug *Bremen* departed Venice, Louisiana, with the *Chaparral* in tow bound for Italy. On January 9, while the flotilla was in international waters in the middle of the Gulf of Mexico, a severe storm arose. The sharp roll of the *Chaparral* in Gulf waters caused its elevator legs, which had been raised for the voyage, to break off and fall into the sea, seriously damaging the *Chaparral*. In this emergency situation Zapata instructed the *Bremen* to tow its damaged rig to Tampa, Florida, the nearest port of refuge.

On January 12, Zapata, ignoring its contract promise to litigate "any dispute arising" in the English courts, commenced a suit in admiralty in the United States District Court at Tampa, seeking $3,500,000 damages against Unterweser *in personam* and the *Bremen in rem*, alleging negligent towage and breach of contract. Unterweser responded by invoking the forum clause of the towage contract, and moved to dismiss for lack of jurisdiction or on *forum non conveniens* grounds, or in the alternative to stay the action pending submission of the dispute to the "London Court of Justice." Shortly thereafter, in February, before the District Court had ruled on its motion to stay or dismiss the United States action, Unterweser commenced an action against Zapata seeking damages for breach of the towage contract in the High Court of Justice in London, as the contract provided. Zapata appeared in that court to contest jurisdiction, but its challenge was rejected, the English courts holding that the contractual forum provision conferred jurisdiction.

In the meantime, Unterweser was faced with a dilemma in the pending action in the United States court at Tampa. The six-month period for filing action to limit its liability to Zapata and other potential claimants

免責条項には修正を加えずに，Zapata の副社長は契約書に署名し，それをドイツの Unterweser に送り，そこで Unterweser はその修正を受け入れ，契約は有効となった．

　1968年1月5日に，Unterweser の深海タグボート Bremen 号は，Chaparral 号を曳航してイタリーに向けて，ルイジアナのヴェニスを出発した．1月9日，船隊がメキシコ湾中央の国際水域において，激しい嵐が発生した．湾水域における激しい Chaparral 号の横揺れによって，航海中揚げられていた昇降機の脚がぷっつり折れて，海中に落ち，Chaparral 号に著しい損傷を与えた．この緊急事態において Zapata は，Bremen 号に最も近い避難港である，フロリダのタンパに損傷した掘削船を曳航するよう指示した．

　1月12日，Zapata は，「発生するすべての紛争」を英国裁判所において提起するという契約約束を無視して，タンパの連邦地方裁判所に Unterweser に対して*対人的に*，Bremen 号に対して*対物的に*，曳航上の過失と契約違反を理由とする350万ドルの損害賠償を請求する海事訴訟を提起した．Unterweser は，曳航契約中の法廷地選択条項を援用し，管轄権の欠如又はフォーラム・ノン・コンヴェニエンスを理由に却下するか，又は選択的に「ロンドン裁判所」への紛争の付託の間，訴訟停止することの申立を行った．その後すぐ，2月に，地裁が合衆国での訴訟を停止又は却下する申立についての判示をする前に，Unterweser が Zapata に対して，契約に定めるロンドンの高等法院に曳航契約違反に対する損害賠償を求める訴訟を開始した．Zapata は同裁判所に管轄権を争うために出頭したが，英国裁判所は契約中の法廷地条項が管轄権を付与したと判示して，その主張は拒否された．

　その間，Unterweser は，タンパの合衆国裁判所に係属している訴訟においてジレンマに直面していた．Zapata と他の潜在的請求者に対する自らの責任を制限する訴訟を提起する6ヶ月の期間が消滅しようとしていた．しかしタ

was about to expire, but the United States District Court in Tampa had not yet ruled on Unterweser's motion to dismiss or stay Zapata's action. On July 2, 1968, confronted with difficult alternatives, Unterweser filed an action to limit its liability in the District Court in Tampa. That court entered the customary injunction against proceedings outside the limitation court, and Zapata refilled its initial claim in the limitation action.

It was only at this juncture, on July 29, after the six-month period for filing the limitation action had run, that the District Court denied Unterweser's January motion to dismiss or stay Zapata's initial action. In denying the motion, that court relied on the prior decision of the Court of Appeals in *Carbon Black Export, Inc.* v. *The Monrosa*, 254 F.2d 297 (CA5 1958), cert. dismissed, 359 U.S. 180 (1959). In that case the Court of Appeals had held a forum-selection clause unenforceable, reiterating the traditional view of many American courts that "agreements in advance of controversy whose object is to oust the jurisdiction of the courts are contrary to public policy and will not be enforced." 254 F.2d, at 300-301. Apparently concluding that it was bound by the *Carbon Black* case, the District Court gave the forum-selection clause little, if any, weight. Instead, the court treated the motion to dismiss under normal *forum non conveniens* doctrine applicable in the absence of such a clause, citing *Gulf Oil Corp.* v. *Gilbert*, 330 U.S. 501 (1947). Under that doctrine "unless the balance is strongly in favor of the defendant, the plaintiff's choice of forum should rarely be disturbed." *Id.,* at 508. The District Court concluded: "The balance of conveniences here is not strongly in favor of [Unterweser] and [Zapata's] choice of forum should not be disturbed."

Thereafter, on January 21, 1969, the District Court denied another motion by Unterweser to stay the limitation action pending determination of the controversy in the High Court of Justice in London and granted

4　合意管轄：The Bremen v. Zapata Off-Shore Co.

ンパの合衆国地裁は，Zapata の訴訟を停止又は却下する Unterweser の申立に関する判断をまだ下してはいなかった．1968 年 7 月 2 日，困難な選択に直面して，Unterweser は，タンパの地方裁判所にその責任を制限する訴訟を提起した．同裁判所は，制限裁判所以外での訴訟手続に対する通例の差止め命令を出した．そして Zapata は，制限訴訟における自らの最初の請求を再び提出した．

　この時点ではじめて，7 月 29 日に，制限訴訟を提起する 6 ヶ月が経過した後になって，地方裁判所は，Zapata の当初の訴訟を停止又は却下する Unterweser の 1 月の申立を否認した．申立を否認するにあたって，同裁判所が依拠したのは，*Carbon Black Export, Inc. v. The Monrosa*, 254 F.2d 297 (CA5 1958), cert. dismissed, 359 U.S. 180 (1959) における巡回区控訴裁判所の以前の決定であった．その事件において同巡回区控訴裁判所は，多くのアメリカ裁判所の伝統的な見解「合意の目的が裁判所の管轄権を奪い取ることにある紛争に関する事前の合意は，公序に反し，執行されないであろう．」254 F.2d, at 300-301 を繰り返して，法選択条項を執行できないと判示した．明らかに *Carbon Black* 判決によって拘束されると推断して，地方裁判所は法廷地選択条項に，かりにあるとしても僅かなウエイトしか与えなかった．その代わりに同裁判所は，*Gulf Oil Corp. v. Gilbert*, 330 U.S. 501 (1947) を引用して，そのような条項がない場合に適用される通常のフォーラム・ノン・コンヴェニエンスの法理の下でその申立を処理した．その原則の下では，「バランスが著しく被告に有利でない限りは，原告の法廷地選択がめったに妨げられるべきでない．」同上 508 頁．地方裁判所は，「便宜性のバランスは，著しく［Unterweser］に有利でないから，［Zapata の］法廷地の選択は妨げられるべきではない」と結論した．

　その後，1969 年 1 月 21 日に，地方裁判所は，ロンドンの高等法院に紛争の決定係属中の制限訴訟を，停止すべきことを求める Unterweser による他の申立を否認し，Unterwese がさらにロンドンの裁判所で訴訟を起こすこと

Zapata's motion to restrain Unterweser from litigating further in the London court. The District Judge ruled that, having taken jurisdiction in the limitation proceeding, he had jurisdiction to determine all matters relating to the controversy. He ruled that Unterweser should be required to "do equity" by refraining from also litigating the controversy in the London court, not only for the reasons he had previously stated for denying Unterweser's first motion to stay Zapata's action, but also because Unterweser had invoked the United States court's jurisdiction to obtain the benefit of the Limitation Act.

On appeal, a divided panel of the Court of Appeals affirmed, and on rehearing *en banc* the panel opinion was adopted, with six of the 14 *en banc* judges dissenting. As had the District Court, the majority rested on the *Carbon Black* decision, concluding that "'at the very least'" that case stood for the proposition that a forum-selection clause "'will not be enforced unless the selected state would provide a more convenient forum than the state in which suit is brought.'" From that premise the Court of Appeals proceeded to conclude that, apart from the forum-selection clause, the District Court did not abuse its discretion in refusing to decline jurisdiction on the basis of *forum non conveniens*. It noted that (1) the flotilla never "escaped the Fifth Circuit's mare nostrum, and the casualty occurred in close proximity to the district court"; (2) a considerable number of potential witnesses, including Zapata crewmen, resided in the Gulf Coast area; (3) preparation for the voyage and inspection and repair work had been performed in the Gulf area; (4) the testimony of the *Bremen* crew was available by way of deposition; (5) England had no interest in or contact with the controversy other than the forum-selection clause. The Court of Appeals majority further noted that Zapata was a United States citizen and "the discretion of the district court to remand the case to a foreign forum was consequently limited" ──especially since it appeared likely that the English courts would enforce the exculpatory clauses. In the Court of Appeals' view, enforcement of such clauses would

4　合意管轄：The Bremen v. Zapata Off- Shore Co.

を禁止するZapataの申立を認めた．地方裁判所裁判官は，制限訴訟手続に管轄権を行使し，紛争に関するすべての事項を決定する管轄権を有すると判示した．同裁判官は，UnterweserによるZapataの訴訟を停止する最初の申立を否認するために同裁判官が述べた理由だけでなく，Unterweserが制限法の利益を受けようとして合衆国の管轄権を援用したことのために，Unterweserがさらにロンドンの裁判所に紛争を提起することを控えることによって，「エクイティに従う」ことを要求されると判示した．

　控訴では，控訴審裁判所の意見は分かれたが，上訴を棄却した．そして*大法廷の再審理では大法廷で*14人中6人の裁判官の反対意見付きで，上訴を棄却した．地裁と同様に，多数意見は，*Carbon Black*判決に依拠して，「少なくとも」同事件は，法廷地選択条項は「選択された国が訴訟が提起された国よりもいっそう便宜な法廷地でない限りは執行されないであろう」という立場にたっていると結論した．そのような前提から，控訴審裁判所は，法廷地選択条項の問題を離れて考えても，フォーラム・ノン・コンヴィニエンスに基づいて管轄権を否認することを拒否したことによって地裁がその裁量権を濫用しなかったと結論するに至った．裁判所は次のように指摘した．(1)船隊は，「決して第5巡回区の領海から離れ」なかったし，「事故は地裁にきわめて近い場所で起こった」，(2)Zapata社の乗組員を含め証人となりうる者の多くがメキシコ湾域に居住している，(3)航海の準備，検査及び修理の作業がメキシコ湾域で行われた，(4)*Bremen*号乗組員の証言は，宣誓供述調書により入手できる，(5)英国は，法廷地選択条項以外には，本件紛争になんらの利益も関連をも有していない．控訴審の多数意見は次のように指摘する．すなわち，さらに，Zapataは，合衆国市民であり，「事件を外国の法廷に送り返すという地裁の裁量権は，その結果として制限される．」——それは，とくに英国裁判所が免責条項を執行するであろうと思われたからである．控訴審の見解では，そのような条項の執行は，*Bisso v. Inland Waterways Corp.*, 349 U.S.85（1955）と，*Dixilyn Drilling Corp.* v. *Crescent Towing & Salvage*

be contrary to public policy in American courts under *Bisso* v. *Inland Waterways Corp.*, 349 U.S. 85 (1955), and *Dixilyn Drilling Corp.* v. *Crescent Towing & Salvage Co.*, 372 U.S. 697 (1963). Therefore, "the district court was entitled to consider that remanding Zapata to a foreign forum, with no practical contact with the controversy, could raise a bar to recovery by a United States citizen which its own convenient courts would not countenance."

We hold, with the six dissenting members of the Court of Appeals, that far too little weight and effect were given to the forum clause in resolving this controversy. For at least two decades we have witnessed an expansion of overseas commercial activities by business enterprises based in the United States. The barrier of distance that once tended to confine a business concern to a modest territory no longer does so. Here we see an American company with special expertise contracting with a foreign company to tow a complex machine thousands of miles across seas and oceans. The expansion of American business and industry will hardly be encouraged if, notwithstanding solemn contracts, we insist on a parochial concept that all disputes must be resolved under our laws and in our courts. Absent a contract forum, the considerations relied on by the Court of Appeals would be persuasive reasons for holding an American forum convenient in the traditional sense, but in an era of expanding world trade and commerce, the absolute aspects of the doctrine of the *Carbon Black* case have little place and would be a heavy hand indeed on the future development of international commercial dealings by Americans. We cannot have trade and commerce in world markets and international waters exclusively on our terms, governed by our laws, and resolved in our courts.

Forum-selection clauses have historically not been favored by American courts. Many courts, federal and state, have declined to enforce

4 合意管轄：The Bremen v. Zapata Off-Shore Co.

Co., 372 U.S. 697（1963）の下では，アメリカの裁判所においては公序に反するであろう．それゆえに，「紛争となんらの実際的な関連もない外国の法廷に Zapata を送り返すことは，それ自身の便利な裁判所が支援しない合衆国市民による損害賠償に対する障害を引き起こしうると地裁は考えることができたのである．」

　われわれは，控訴審の 6 人の反対意見のメンバーと同じく，本件紛争を解決するにあたって，あまりに僅かのウエイトと効果しか法廷地選択条項に与えられていないと判断する．少なくともここ 20 年間，われわれは米国に本拠を置く企業が海外の商業活動を積極的に拡大していくことを目のあたりにしてきた．かつては事業関心を控え目に領域内に限定しがちであった距離的障害は，いまや存在しない．本件では，専門知識を有する米国企業が外国企業と大洋を横切って数千マイルも複雑な機械を曳航する契約を締結しているのを問題としている．厳粛な契約が存在しているにもかかわらず，もしわれわれがすべての紛争はアメリカの法によりアメリカの裁判所で解決されなければならないという，偏狭な地域主義の観念に固執するとすれば，アメリカの事業と産業の拡大は，どうみても促進されることにはならないであろう．契約された法廷地が存在しない場合には，控訴審裁判所が依拠した考慮事項は，伝統的な意味における便利なアメリカの裁判所を支持する説得力のある理由となるであろうが，しかし世界貿易と通商の拡大の時代においては，*Carbon Black* 判決理論の無制約的な側面は，ほとんど重要な位置をもたず，アメリカ人による国際的な通商取引の将来的な発展に対する重い障害となるであろう．世界市場と国際的な水域における貿易と通商を，われわれの法によって規律され，われわれの裁判所で解決される，われわれの条件のみに基礎づけさせることはできない．

　法廷地選択条項は，歴史的にみるとアメリカの裁判所であまりいい評価を受けてこなかった．連邦及び州の多くの裁判所は，この条項が「公序に反す

such clauses on the ground that they were "contrary to public policy," or that their effect was to "oust the jurisdiction" of the court. Although this view apparently still has considerable acceptance, other courts are tending to adopt a more hospitable attitude toward forum-selection clauses. This view, advanced in the well-reasoned dissenting opinion in the instant case, is that such clauses are prima facie valid and should be enforced unless enforcement is shown by the resisting party to be "unreasonable" under the circumstances. We believe this is the correct doctrine to be followed by federal district courts sitting in admiralty. It is merely the other side of the proposition recognized by this Court in *National Equipment Rental, Ltd. v. Szukhent*, 375 U.S. 311 (1964), holding that in federal courts a party may validly consent to be sued in a jurisdiction where he cannot be found for service of process through contractual designation of an "agent" for receipt of process in that jurisdiction. In so holding, the Court stated:

> "It is settled ... that parties to a contract may agree in advance to submit to the jurisdiction of a given court, to permit notice to be served by the opposing party, or even to waive notice altogether." *Id.*, at 315-316.

This approach is substantially that followed in other common-law countries including England. It is the view advanced by noted scholars and that adopted by the Restatement of the Conflict of Laws. It accords with ancient concepts of freedom of contract and reflects an appreciation of the expanding horizons of American contractors who seek business in all parts of the world. Not surprisingly, foreign businessmen prefer, as do we, to have disputes resolved in their own courts, but if that choice is not available, then in a neutral forum with expertise in the subject matter. Plainly, the courts of England meet the standards of neutrality and long experience in admiralty litigation. The choice of that forum was made in an arm's-length negotiation by experienced and sophisticated businessmen, and absent some compelling and countervailing reason it should be honored by the parties and enforced by the courts.

4 合意管轄：The Bremen v. Zapata Off-Shore Co.

る」との理由で，またはその効果が裁判所の「管轄権を奪い取る」ものであるという理由でこの条項を否定してきた．この見解は今日でもなおかなりの支持を得ているけれども，他の裁判所は法廷地選択条項にもっと好意的な態度を採用しようとしている．この見解は，本件におけるよく理由づけられた反対意見において展開されているものであるが，そのような条項は原則として有効であり，反対当事者によって当該状況の下で「不相当」であると証明されるのでない限り，執行されるべきであるというものである．われわれの信じるところでは，この見解こそ海事事件を担当する連邦地裁が従うべき正しい理論である．これは，*National Equipment Rental, Ltd. v. Szukhent*, 375 U.S. 311（1964）において当裁判所が承認した立場のもう1つ別の側面であり，連邦裁判所において当事者は，彼がその法域において訴状を受け取るための「代理人」を契約上指定することを通じて，その者が訴状の送達のために所在しない法域において訴えられることを有効に同意することができると判示した．そう判示するにあたって，当裁判所は次のように述べた．

>「契約当事者は，通知が反対当事者によって送達され，または通知を全く放棄することさえできるように，前もって特定の裁判所に管轄権に服することを合意することができることは……確立されている．」同上315-316頁．

このアプローチは，英国を含めた他のコモンロー諸国において行われているのと実質的には同じものである．それは著名な学者が主張する見解であり，抵触法リステイトメントが採用するものでもある．それは古くからの契約自由の原則という考え方に合致し，世界のあらゆる地域にわたって事業を追求するアメリカ契約者の活動範囲の拡大を正しく認識することを意味している．驚くべきことではないが，外国のビジネスマンは，われわれと同様に，自国の裁判所で紛争が解決されることを好む．しかしその選択が得られないときは，その問題に専門知識をもった中立的な法廷地において解決されることを好むものである．明らかに英国の裁判所は中立性と海事関係訴訟における永い経験という基準に適合する．その法廷地の選択は，経験があり，洗練されたビジネスマンによって市場ベースでの交渉においてなされたものであり，

The argument that such clauses are improper because they tend to "oust" a court of jurisdiction is hardly more than a vestigial legal fiction. It appears to rest at core on historical judicial resistance to any attempt to reduce the power and business of a particular court and has little place in an era when all courts are overloaded and when businesses once essentially local now operate in world markets. It reflects something of a provincial attitude regarding the fairness of other tribunals. No one seriously contends in this case that the forum-selection clause "ousted" the District Court of jurisdiction over Zapata's action. The threshold question is whether that court should have exercised its jurisdiction to do more than give effect to the legitimate expectations of the parties, manifested in their freely negotiated agreement, by specifically enforcing the forum clause.

There are compelling reasons why a freely negotiated private international agreement, unaffected by fraud, undue influence, or overweening bargaining power, such as that involved here, should be given full effect. In this case, for example, we are concerned with a far from routine transaction between companies of two different nations contemplating the tow of an extremely costly piece of equipment from Louisiana across the Gulf of Mexico and the Atlantic Ocean, through the Mediterranean Sea to its final destination in the Adriatic Sea. In the course of its voyage, it was to traverse the waters of many jurisdictions. The *Chaparral* could have been damaged at any point along the route, and there were countless possible ports of refuge. That the accident occurred in the Gulf of Mexico and the barge was towed to Tampa in an emergency were mere fortuities. It cannot be doubted for a moment that the parties sought to provide for a neutral forum for the resolution of any disputes arising during the tow.

4 合意管轄：The Bremen v. Zapata Off-Shore Co.

なんらかの説得力のある，反対の理由がない限り，当事者によって尊重され，裁判所によって執行されるべきである．

　そのような条項は，裁判所の管轄権を「奪い取ろ」うとするものであるから，不適切であるという議論は，法的フィクションの痕跡以外のなにものでもない．それは特定の裁判所の権限と業務を限定しようとするいかなる試みに対しても向けられた裁判所の歴史上の抵抗に主として基づくものであり，すべての裁判所が負担過剰で，かつては本質的に地域的だったビジネスがいまや世界市場において事業活動する時代には，ほとんど存在価値を有していない．それは他の裁判所の公正さに対するなにか偏狭な態度を反映している．本件においてその法廷地選択条項が Zapata の訴訟に対する地方裁判所の管轄権を「奪い取った」とは誰も本気に主張しないであろう．はじめに取り組むべき問題は，裁判所が法廷地条項を明確に執行することにより，当事者の自由に交渉された合意に明らかに示された当事者の正当な期待を実現する以上のことをなすために管轄権を行使すべきであったかどうかである．

　本件のように，詐欺，不当威圧又は圧倒的な交渉力によって影響を受けていない，自由に交渉された私的な国際的合意が完全に有効と認められるべき納得できる十分な理由がある．本件においては，たとえば，きわめて高価な装備を，ルイジアナからメキシコ湾と大西洋を横断し，地中海を通って，アドリア海にある最終の目的地まで曳航することを意図する，2つの異なった国の会社間の非日常的な取引が問題となっている．その航海中，多くの法域の領水を横断することになっていた．*Chaparral* 号は，ルートのどの地点でも損傷を被ることがあり得たし，避難することができる港も数え切れないほどあった．事故がメキシコ湾で発生し，積荷が緊急時にタンパに曳航されたのは単なる偶然であった．当事者が曳航中に生じるすべての紛争の解決のために中立的な法廷地を定めようとしたことはいささかも疑いの余地もない．もし訴訟が事故が発生するかもしれないどの法廷地においても維持されるとすれば，又はもし *Bremen* 号か Unterweser がたまたま所在するかもしれな

Manifestly much uncertainty and possibly great inconvenience to both parties could arise if a suit could be maintained in any jurisdiction in which an accident might occur or if jurisdiction were left to any place where the *Bremen* or Unterweser might happen to be found. The elimination of all such uncertainties by agreeing in advance on a forum acceptable to both parties is an indispensable element in international trade, commerce, and contracting. There is strong evidence that the forum clause was a vital part of the agreement, and it would be unrealistic to think that the parties did not conduct their negotiations, including fixing the monetary terms, with the consequences of the forum clause figuring prominently in their calculations. Under these circumstances, as Justice Karminski reasoned in sustaining jurisdiction over Zapata in the High Court of Justice, "the force of an agreement for litigation in this country, freely entered into between two competent parties, seems to me to be very powerful."

Thus, in the light of present-day commercial realities and expanding international trade we conclude that the forum clause should control absent a strong showing that it should be set aside. Although their opinions are not altogether explicit, it seems reasonably clear that the District Court and the Court of Appeals placed the burden on Unterweser to show that London would be a more convenient forum than Tampa, although the contract expressly resolved that issue. The correct approach would have been to enforce the forum clause specifically unless Zapata could clearly show that enforcement would be unreasonable and unjust, or that the clause was invalid for such reasons as fraud or overreaching. Accordingly, the case must be remanded for reconsideration.

We note, however, that there is nothing in the record presently before us that would support a refusal to enforce the forum clause. The Court of Appeals suggested that enforcement would be contrary to the public policy of the forum under *Bisso v. Inland Waterways Corp.*, 349 U.S. 85

いどこにおいても管轄権が認められるとすれば，両当事者にとって非常な不確実性と多分非常な不便が生じるであろうことは明らかである．そのようなすべての不確実性を，両当事者にとって受け入れられる法廷地を前もって合意することによって除去しようとすることは，国際的な貿易，通商及び契約にとって欠くことのできない要因である．法廷地条項が合意のきわめて重要な部分であるという強い証拠がある．当事者が金銭的な条件を定めることを含めて，彼らの事前の計画の中に法廷地条項の結果を考慮して，交渉を行わなかったと考えるのは非現実的である．このような状況の下においては，高等法院のKarminski裁判官がZapataに対する管轄権を指示するにあたって理由づけたように，「2つの権限のある当事者間で自由に締結されたこの国の訴訟を定めた合意の拘束力は私にとっては大変強力であると思われる．」

　かくして今日における通商の現実と国際貿易の拡大を考慮すると，われわれは，無効とすべき強力な状況がない限り，法廷地条項は支配すると結論する．地方裁判所と控訴裁判所の意見はそれほど明確ではないが，彼らがロンドンがタンパよりももっと便利な法廷地であることをUnterweserに立証する責任を課したことは合理的にみて明らかであると思われる．もっとも契約がその争点を明確に解決していたのであるが．正しいアプローチは，Zapataがその条項の執行が不相当で正しくないか，又はその条項が詐欺又は圧倒的な交渉力の差違のような理由で有効でないということを明らかに証明するのでない限り，法廷地条項を執行することであったろう．したがって事件は再検討のために差し戻さなければならない．

　しかしながら，現に面前にある記録には，法廷地条項の執行を拒否することを支持するものはなにも存在しないことを指摘しておく．控訴審裁判所は，*Bisso v. Inland Waterways Corp.*, 349 U.S. 85（1955）に基づき，その条項の執行は法廷地の公序に反すると考えた．というのは，*Chaparral*号に対

(1955), because of the prospect that the English courts would enforce the clauses of the towage contract purporting to exculpate Unterweser from liability for damages to the *Chaparral*. A contractual choice-of-forum clause should be held unenforceable if enforcement would contravene a strong public policy of the forum in which suit is brought, whether declared by statute or by judicial decision. See, *e. g.*, *Boyd* v. *Grand Trunk W. R. Co.*, 338 U.S. 263 (1949). It is clear, however, that whatever the proper scope of the policy expressed in *Bisso*, it does not reach this case. *Bisso* rested on considerations with respect to the towage business strictly in American waters, and those considerations are not controlling in an international commercial agreement.......

Courts have also suggested that a forum clause, even though it is freely bargained for and contravenes no important public policy of the forum, may nevertheless be "unreasonable" and unenforceable if the chosen forum is *seriously* inconvenient for the trial of the action. Of course, where it can be said with reasonable assurance that at the time they entered the contract, the parties to a freely negotiated private international commercial agreement contemplated the claimed inconvenience, it is difficult to see why any such claim of inconvenience should be heard to render the forum clause unenforceable. We are not here dealing with an agreement between two Americans to resolve their essentially local disputes in a remote alien forum. In such a case, the serious inconvenience of the contractual forum to one or both of the parties might carry greater weight in determining the reasonableness of the forum clause. The remoteness of the forum might suggest that the agreement was an adhesive one, or that the parties did not have the particular controversy in mind when they made their agreement; yet even there the party claiming should bear a heavy burden of proof. Similarly, selection of a remote forum to apply differing foreign law to an essentially American controversy might contravene an important public policy of the forum. For example, so long as *Bisso* governs American courts with respect to the

するUnterweserの損害賠償責任を免責しようとする曳航契約中の条項を英国裁判所が執行するであろうと予測したからである．契約上の法廷地選択条項は，その執行が訴訟が提起された法廷地の強い公序に反する場合には，それが制定法によるものであろうと，裁判所の判決により宣言されたものであろうと，執行できないと判断されるべきである．たとえば，*Boyd v. Grand Trunk W. R. Co.*, 338 U.S. 263（1949）参照．しかしながら，*Bisso* 判決において宣言されている法目的の適切な範囲がどのようなものであろうとも，それは本件には妥当しないことは明らかである．アメリカの領水内に厳格に限られた曳航ビジネスに関する政策考慮に基づく *Bisso* 判決とこれらの政策考慮は，国際的商業合意においては機能していない．……

　裁判所はまた，法廷地条項はたとえそれが自由に交渉され，法廷地の重要な公序になんら反しないものであったとしても，選択された法廷地が訴訟の審理にとって著しく不便であるときは，「不相当」であり，執行することはできない，と示唆している．もちろん，当事者が契約を締結した当時，自由に交渉された私的な国際的商業合意の当事者が，主張されているような不便を考慮したと相当の確実性をもっていうことができる場合には，そのような不便がどのようなものであれ，法廷地条項を執行できないとする説得力のある理由を見出すことは困難である．われわれは，遠く離れた外国の法廷地において，本質的に地域的な紛争を解決するために，2人のアメリカ人同士の合意を扱っているのではない．そのような事件では，当事者の一方又は双方にとって契約上の法廷地の著しい不便は，法廷地条項の相当性を決定するに際して，大きなウエイトを有するであろう．法廷地が遠隔の地にあることは，合意が附合的なものであるか，又は当事者が合意を締結したときに，特定の紛争を念頭においていなかったことを意味するかもしれない．しかしそのような場合でも，請求当事者が重い立証責任を負うべきである．同様に，本質的にアメリカの紛争に外国の異なった法を適用することとなる，遠く隔たった法廷地の選定は，法廷地の重要な公序に反することになるかもしれない．たとえば，*Bisso* 判決がアメリカ領水内の曳航ビジネスに関してアメリカ裁

towage business in American waters, it would quite arguably be improper to permit an American tower to avoid that policy by providing a foreign forum for resolution of his disputes with an American towee.

This case, however, involves a freely negotiated international commercial transaction between a German and an American corporation for towage of a vessel from the Gulf of Mexico to the Adriatic Sea. As noted, selection of a London forum was clearly a reasonable effort to bring vital certainty to this international transaction and to provide a neutral forum experienced and capable in the resolution of admiralty litigation. Whatever "inconvenience" Zapata would suffer by being forced to litigate in the contractual forum as it agreed to do was clearly foreseeable at the time of contracting. In such circumstances it should be incumbent on the party seeking to escape his contract to show that trial in the contractual forum will be so gravely difficult and inconvenient that he will for all practical purposes be deprived of his day in court. Absent that, there is no basis for concluding that it would be unfair, unjust, or unreasonable to hold that party to his bargain.

……

Vacated and remanded.

MR. JUSTICE DOUGLAS, dissenting.

……

Respondent is a citizen of this country. Moreover, if it were remitted to the English court, its substantive rights would be adversely affected. Exculpatory provisions in the towage control provide (1) that petitioners, the masters and the crews "are not responsible for defaults and/or errors in the navigation of the tow" and (2) that "damages suffered by the towed object are in any case for account of its Owners."

4 合意管轄：The Bremen v. Zapata Off-Shore Co.

判所を支配している限り，アメリカの曳航者がそのアメリカの被曳航者との紛争の解決のために外国の法廷地を定めることによってその法目的を回避することを求めることは，おそらく適当ではないであろう．

　しかしながら本件は，ドイツとアメリカの会社がメキシコ湾からアドリア海まで船舶の曳航のために，自由に交渉された国際的な商業取引に関するものである．さきに指摘したように，ロンドン法廷地の選択は，この国際取引にきわめて重大な確実性を確保し，海事訴訟の解決に経験のある，有能な中立的法廷地を提供するための明らかに合理的な試みである．Zapata が合意した契約上の法廷地で訴訟を遂行することを強いられることによって，どのような「不便」を被むることになろうとも，それは契約締結時に明らかに予測可能であった．そのような場合において，契約上の法廷地における審理が著しく困難で不便であり，その結果，彼があらゆる目的からみて裁判所における審理の機会を奪われるということを立証する責任は，その契約から逃れようと求めている当事者に課せられている．それがない限り，その当事者を彼の契約に拘束することが不公正であるとか，正当でないとか，不相当であると結論する根拠は存在しない．
……

破棄差戻

DOUGLAS 裁判官の反対意見
……
　被上訴人は，この国の市民である．さらに英国の裁判所に事件が送付されたならば，その実体的権利は不利にとり扱われるであろう．曳航管理における免責条項は，(1)上訴人，船長及び乗組員は，「曳航航海における過失及び又は瑕疵に対して責任を負わず」，(2)「曳航の目的物が被った損害にはいかなる場合であってもその所有者の責任である」と規定する．

89

Under our decision in *Dixilyn Drilling Corp* v. *Crescent Towing & Salvage Co.*, 372 U.S. 697, 698, "a contract which exempts the tower from liability for its own negligence" is not enforceable, though there is evidence in the present record that it is enforceable in England. That policy was first announced in *Bisso* v. *Inland Waterways Corp.*, 349 U.S. 85; and followed in *Boston Metals Co.* v. *The Winding Gulf*, 349 U.S. 122; *Dixilyn, supra*;……. Although the casualty occurred on the high seas, the *Bisso* doctrine is nonetheless applicable……..

Moreover, the casualty occurred close to the District Court, a number of potential witnesses, including respondent's crewmen, reside in that area, and the inspection and repair work were done there. The testimony of the tower's crewmen, residing in Germany, is already available by way of depositions taken in the proceedings.

All in all, the District Court judge exercised his discretion wisely in enjoining petitioners from pursuing the litigation in England.

I would affirm the judgment below.

【解 説】

　本件は，ドイツ会社と米国会社との間に締結された国際曳航契約中のロンドンの裁判所を専属管轄裁判所とする法廷地選択条項が原則として有効とされた事例である．

1 本件以前の判例状況

　合衆国の裁判所は，一般的には法廷地選択条項に効力を与えることを拒否してきた．この立場は，1934年の抵触法リステイトメントによって支持された．

当裁判所の判決である*Dixilyn Drilling Corp v. Crescent Towing & Salvage Co.*, 372 U.S. 697, 698 では,「曳航者自身の過失から生じる責任を曳航者から免除する契約は」執行できない,と判示する.これに対して本件の記録では英国法では執行可能であるとの十分な証拠がある.その法目的は最初に,*Bisso v. Inland Waterways Corp.*, 349 U.S. 85 において宣言され,*Boston Metals Co. v. The Winding Gulf*, 349 U.S. 122; 前掲 *Dixilyn* 判決において追随された.……事故は公海で発生したけれども,*Bisso* 判決の法理がそれにもかかわらず適用される.……

さらに事故は地裁の近くで発生し,多くの証人となる可能性のある者は,上訴人の乗組員を含めて,その地域に居住している.そして検査と修理作業はそこで行われた.ドイツにいる曳航者の乗組員の証言はすでに手続中にとられた証言録取によって利用可能である.

地裁の裁判官は,概してその裁量権を賢明に行使し,上訴人が英国での訴訟の遂行を禁止した.

私は原審判決を支持する.

裁判所が法廷地選択条項を執行することを始めた画期的な判決は,1955年の第2巡回区控訴裁判所の *Wm. H. Muller & Co. v. Swedish American Line Ltd.*, 224 F.2d 806 (2d Cir.1955) であった(本判決については,川又良也「船荷証券における裁判管轄約款」海法会誌復刊9号9頁以下(1962)参照).*Muller* 判決で裁判所が強調したのは,法廷地選択条項は管轄権を奪うことはできないが,裁判所が合意管轄が特定の状況の下で不合理でないと判断した場合には,裁判所は適切に管轄権の行使を拒否し,当事者が合意した法廷地へ訴訟を追いやることができるという点であった.このテストは,法廷地選択条項が合理的であるかどうかということと,これを立証する責任は原告にあるという

ものであった.この立場の変化は,1971年の抵触法第2リステイトメント80条に採用された.

2　第2リステイトメント第80条

抵触法第2リステイトメント第80条は次のように規定する.

「訴訟地に関する当事者の合意は,州の管轄権を奪うことはできない.しかしながら,そのような合意は不公正又は不合理(unfair or unreasonable)でない限り,効力を与えられる.」

その根拠は,第80条に付せられた注釈a(comment a)で概略次のように説明されている.

私人は管轄権のルールを変更することはできない.私人は契約によって邦の有する管轄権を奪うことはできない.しかしこのことは,契約から生じるすべての訴訟が特定の邦のみにおいて提起されるべきとする契約中の条項になんらのウエイトも与えられないことを意味するものではない.そのような条項は訴訟が当事者にとって便利な(convinient)法廷地で提起されることを確保しようとする当事者の企てを表している.裁判所は,自らが不適切な法廷地であると判断するならば,当然に訴訟を受理しようとしないであろう.そして訴訟が契約中に指定された以外の地において提起されたという事実は,その法廷地が不適切なものであり,裁判所がその裁量により訴訟を受理することを拒否すべきと判断する十分な理由を与えることになる.しかしながら,そのような条項はもしもそれが,不平等な交渉力の行き過ぎた又は不公正な使用の結果であるか,又は当事者によって選択された法廷地が特定の訴訟の審理にとって著しく不便である場合には,無視されるであろう.これに対してこのような条項は,そうすることが公正で,合理的である場合には,有効とされ,訴訟は却下されるであろう(Restatement, Second, Conflict of laws, § 80, comment a (1971)).なお,この第80条のブラック・レターは後に改正され,「州の管轄権を奪うことはできない,しかしながら」の部分は,削除された.

他方,*Muller*判決以後も,依然として法廷地選択条項に否定的な判決もあ

り，その典型的な例が，控訴審判決が依拠した第 5 巡回区控訴裁判所の *Carbon Black* 判決と *Indussa Corp., v. S.S. Ranborg,* 377 F.2d 200（2d Cir. 1967）であった．連邦最高裁は本件でこれに決着をつけた．

3 本判決の法理

　本判決ではどのような法理が確立されたといえるであろうか．その点を判旨に沿って整理してみよう（曽野和明・アメリカ法［1976］279 頁参照）．

　本判決は，法廷地選択条項は，原則として有効であり，反対当事者によって当該状況の下で「不相当」であると証明されるのでない限り，執行されるべきであるとの立場を採用した．つまり，本件のように法廷地の選択が，経験があり，洗練されたビジネスマンによって市場ベースで自由に交渉された場合には，なんらかの説得力のある，反対の理由がない限り，当事者によって尊重され，裁判所によって執行されるべきであるとする．

　法廷地条項を原則として有効とする根拠としては，まず，契約自由の原則に合致することがあげられる．そしてたとえ原告が合意した契約上の法廷地で訴訟を遂行することを強いられることによって，不便を被ることになろうとも，それは契約締結時に明らかに予測可能であったということができる．

　また，すべての紛争はアメリカの法によりアメリカの裁判所で解決されなければならないという，偏狭な地域主義の観念に固執するとすれば，アメリカの事業と産業の拡大は，促進されない．世界市場と国際的な水域における貿易と通商を，われわれの法によって規律され，われわれの裁判所で解決されるべきものと考えるべきでない．そうすることはいまや，世界中にわたって事業を追求するアメリカ契約者の活動範囲の拡大を正しく認識しているとはいえない．

　さらにビジネスマンは，問題に専門知識をもった中立的な法廷地において解決されることを好むものである．本件では明らかに英国の裁判所は中立性と海事関係訴訟における永い経験という基準に適合する．

　以上のように考えると，法廷地選択条項は原則として有効であり，執行すべきであるということになる．

しかし原告が法廷地条項の執行が不相当で正しくないか，又は法廷地条項が詐欺又は圧倒的な交渉力の差違のような理由で有効でないことを明らかに証明する場合はこの限りではない．さらに法廷地条項はたとえそれが自由に交渉され，法廷地の重要な公序になんら反しないものであったとしても，選択された法廷地が訴訟の審理にとって著しく不便であるときにも「不相当」であり，執行することはできない．

4 その後の展開：*Carnival Cruise Lines* 判決

連邦最高裁は，1991年の *Carnival Cruise Lines, Inc. v. Shute*, 499 U.S 585（1991）において，性質的には合衆国内の州際事件であるが，法廷地選択条項の *The Bremen* 判決の理論を再確認した．

裁判所は，フロリダ州の裁判所を専属管轄裁判所とする法廷地選択条項をその附合契約的性質，不公平で不平等な当事者間の地位と利害関係及び司法的救済に対する弱い当事者の権利の侵害にもかかわらず，有効と認めた．以下にはこの判決の抄訳を掲げておく．

Blackman 裁判官が判決を言い渡した．

本件海事事件においてわれわれは，合衆国第9巡回区控訴裁判所が，上訴人 Carnival Cruise Lines Inc. により被上訴人 Eulala　Shute と Russel Shute に対して発行された切符に含まれている法廷地条項の執行を拒否したことが正しかったかどうかを主として検討する．

I Shute 一家は，ワシントンのアーリントンの旅行代理店を通じて，上訴人の船舶である Tropicale 号での7日間のクルーズ航海切符を購入した．被上訴人は運賃を代理店に支払い，その支払いはフロリダのマイアミにある上訴人へと送られた．その後，上訴人は，切符を作成し，ワシントンの被上訴人に送った．それぞれの切符の表紙の左の下のコーナーには，次の警告があった．

「最終頁にある契約条件に従うことを条件として

重要：契約を読んでください．──最後の1，2，3頁」4月15日それぞれのチケットの「契約1頁」には次のように記されている．
……

3．(a)乗客としてここに記されている者による本契約の承諾は，それぞれの者によるこの航海切符のすべての文言と条件の承諾と合意であると判断されるものとする．
……

8．本契約に関連又は付随して生じるすべての紛争と事態はどのようなものであれ，いかなる他の州又は国の裁判所をも排除して，合衆国のフロリダ州に所在する裁判所に提起されるべきものと，乗客と運送人により又はその間で合意される．
……

最後に引用したパラグラフが本件で争われている法廷地選択条項である．

II　被上訴人らは，カルフォルニアのロサンゼルスでTropicale号に乗船した．船はプエルトバラータ，メキシコを航海し，ロサンゼルスに帰った．船がメキシコ沿岸沖の国際領水にある間に，被上訴人Eulala Shuteが船の調理室（galley）のガイド付きツアーの間にデッキのマットで滑ったときに負傷した．被上訴人らは，ワシントン西部地区連邦地裁に上訴人に対して訴訟を提起し，Shute夫人の負傷は，Carnival Cruise Linesとその従業員の過失によって引き起こされたと主張した．

上訴人は，略式判決の申立をし，被上訴人の切符中の法廷地選択条項により，Shuteは上訴人に対する訴訟をフロリダ州の裁判所に提起しなければならないと主張した．……地裁は申立を認めた．……控訴審裁判所が破棄した．
……

III　まずはじめに，われわれの検討の範囲を指摘しておく．第1に本件は海事事件であり，連邦法がわれわれの検討する法廷地選択条項の効力の問題を規律する．……第2にわれわれは，被上訴人が航海契約に入る前に

法廷地選択条項について十分な通知を受けていたかどうかの問題には立ち入らない．被上訴人は法廷地選択条項を知っていたことを実質的に認めている．

このコンテキストの下で，被上訴人は法廷地選択条項の効力の執行が認められるべきではないと主張する．その理由は，この条項は，*The Bremen* 判決における当裁判所の判示（teaching）に反し，交渉の所産ではなかったし，その執行は被上訴人から裁判所における審理の機会を奪う結果をもたらすからである．

IV

A

上訴人と被上訴人はともに当裁判所の *The Bremen* 判決の意見が本件を規律することを強く主張し，両サイドとも同意見の広範囲にわたる表現の中に自己の立場に対する十分な支持を見出そうとしている．この一見すると矛盾することが生じたのは，本件と *The Bremen* 判決間の鍵となっている事実関係の相違，つまり，*The Bremen* 判決の一般原則を本件の事実に自動的，単純に適用することを排除する相違から大部分は引き出されたものである．
……

被上訴人が —— 又は他のどのようなクルーズの乗客も —— 通常の商業上の切符中の法廷地選択条項の文言について上訴人と交渉をするだろうと想定するのは完全に不合理であろう．このような種類の切符は，ひな形契約であり，その文言は交渉の対象とはならず，切符の個々の購入は，クルーズ・ラインと同等の交渉力を有していないだろうことは常識の教えるところである．控訴審の分析は，個々の契約が作成されたビジネス・コンテキストにおける重大な相違を無視することによって，*The Bremen* 判決における当裁判所の判旨をいくぶん，歪曲したように思われる．

本件において問題となっている法廷地選択条項の相当性を評価するに際しては，*The Bremen* 判決の分析を，ひな形旅客契約の現実を考慮するためにいっそう精緻なものにしなければならない．まず第1に，われわれは交渉されていない法廷地選択条項はそれが交渉の対象となっていないというだけの理由で，決して執行されえないという控訴審の決定を採用しない．この種の

ひな形契約中に合理的な法廷地条項を挿入することは，いくつかの理由で許容されてしかるべきであろう．すなわち，まず第1に，クルーズ・ラインは，訴訟が提起される可能性のある場所を制限する特別の利益を有している．というのは，クルーズ船は典型的に多くの場所からの乗客を運んでいるから，クルーズでの事故によっていくつかの異なった法廷地で訴訟に引き込まれることは起こりそうにないとはいえない．加えて，紛争解決のための事前の法廷地を決めておく条項は，混乱を消散させ，……訴訟当事者に正しい法廷地を決定するための口頭審理前の申立の時間と費用を節約させるとともに，これらの申立を決定するために費やされるべき司法的資源を保存するという健全な効果を有する．最後に，当然のことながら，本件で問題となっているような法廷地条項を含む切符を購入する乗客は，訴えられるかもしれない法廷地を制限することによってクルーズ・ラインが受ける節約を反映した運賃の削減という形で利益を享受している．
……

　ひな形旅行契約中に含まれた法廷地選択条項が基本的な公正さについての司法審査に服するということは強調するに値する．本件においては，クルーズの乗客が正当な請求を行うことを阻止する手段として，紛争が解決されるべき法廷地として，上訴人がフロリダを指定したことを示すものはなにもない．そのような悪意の動機があると考えることは，次の2つの事実から間違いであることが示されている．すなわち，上訴人はフロリダにその主たる営業所を有しており，そのクルーズの多くがフロリダの港から出発し，そこに帰って行くという事実である．同様に上訴人が詐欺又は欺瞞により，法廷地条項に対する被上訴人の同意を獲得したという証拠も存在しない．最後に，被上訴人は法廷地条項の通知を受けていたから，なんらの罰を受けることなく，契約を拒否する選択権を有していたであろう．したがって，本件においては，控訴審裁判所は法廷地選択条項を執行することを拒否した点で誤っていたと結論する．
……

V 控訴審の判決は破棄される．
以上のように判決する．

　以上が *Carnival Cruise Lines* 判決の法廷意見の抄訳である．この判決に対しては，学説からの批判が強い．たとえば，多数意見のあげる3つの理由は根拠としては弱いとの批判がある．すなわち，複数の法廷地での訴訟の提起は，クルーズラインの力を弱体化させるわけではないし，その危険に対して保険をかけ，価格で調整することもできる．また管轄の争いで審理前の費用のかかることは確かであるが，法廷地条項がその解決策とはならない．というのはその条項の有効性は，最小限関連公式という微妙で捉えにくく，事実依存型の基準によってテストされるからである．最後に法廷地条項による費用の削減が料金の削減となり，本当に乗客に還元されるかはもっと慎重な検討を必要するとの見解がある．W. Richman & W. Reynolds, Understanding Conflict of Laws（3rd ed. 2002), at 79-80. リッチマン＝レイノルズ著（松岡・吉川・高杉・北坂訳『アメリカ抵触法（上巻）』（レキシスネキシスジャパン，2008) 132 頁．

　Carnival Cruise Lines 判決の評釈としては，Patric J. Borchers, *Forum Selection Agreements in the Federal Courts After Carnival Cruise: A Proposal For Congressional Reform,* 67 Wash. L. Rev.55（1992); Linda S. Mullenix, *Another Easy Case, Some More Bad Law: Carnival Cruise Lines and Contractual Personal Jurisdiction,* 27 Tex. Int'l L. J. 324（1992).

5　仲裁合意：*Scherk* 判決

　連邦最高裁は，*Scherk v. Alberto-Culver Co.*, 417 U.S. 506（1974) において，米国会社によるドイツ人に対する証券取引法に基づく損害賠償請求について，パリの国際商業会議所の仲裁によるとの仲裁条項に基づいて，国際事件であることを理由の1つとして，その仲裁適格性を肯定し，国内事件で証券取引法上の請求について仲裁適格性を否認した *Wilko* 判決の論理には従わなかった．*Scherk* 判決については，曽野和明・アメリカ法267頁以下（1976）参照．

【本件参考文献】

曽野和明・アメリカ法［1976］272-280頁.

リッチマン＝レイノルズ著（松岡・吉川・高杉・北坂訳『アメリカ抵触法（上巻）』
（レキシスネキシスジャパン，2008）130-131頁.

【設　問】

1　本件の主要な争点はなにか.
　　また，本件の契約中に挿入された法廷地選択条項はどのようなものであったか.
2　事実の概要を説明し，事件と当事者に関するアメリカ，ドイツなどとの関連を整理せよ.
3　第1審・原審・本件判決の結論はどうか.
4　本件判旨を要約せよ.
　　本件判旨によれば，法廷地選択条項が有効となる要件を整理せよ.
5　本件判旨によれば，どのような場合に法廷地選択条項の効力は否定されるか.
6　契約中の免責条項が英国法上有効であるということが，本件の解決にどのような影響を与えているといえようか.
7　Douglas裁判官の反対意見について説明せよ.
8　本件のような法廷地選択条項について，アメリカの裁判所は当初，一般的にどのような態度をとっていたか.
9　抵触法第2リステイトメント第80条の規定を説明し，本件判旨と比較せよ.
　　またその後の改訂について説明せよ.
10　本件は要約するとどのような判決か．その結論，理論構成に賛成か.
11　1991年の最高裁のCarnival Cruise Lines判決を紹介せよ.

5 | 仲裁適格性：
Mitsubishi Motors Corporation v. Soler Chrysler-Plymouth, Inc., 473 U.S. 614 (1985)

JUSTICE BLACKMUN delivered the opinion of the Court.

The principal question presented by these cases is the arbitrability, pursuant to the Federal Arbitration Act, 9 U. S. C. §1 *et seq.*, and the Convention on the Recognition and Enforcement of Foreign Arbitral Awards (Convention), [1970] 21 U.S.T. 2517, T.I.A.S. No. 6997, of claims arising under the Sherman Act, 15 U. S. C. §1 *et seq.*, and encompassed within a valid arbitration clause in an agreement embodying an international commercial transaction.

I

Petitioner-cross-respondent Mitsubishi Motors Corporation (Mitsubishi) is a Japanese corporation which manufactures automobiles and has its principal place of business in Tokyo, Japan. Mitsubishi is the product of a joint venture between, on the one hand, Chrysler International, S.A. (CISA), a Swiss corporation registered in Geneva and wholly owned by Chrysler Corporation and, on the other, Mitsubishi Heavy Inc., a Japanese corporation. The aim of the joint venture was the distribution through Chrysler dealers outside the continental United States of vehicles manufactured by Mitsubishi and bearing Chrysler and Mitsubishi trademarks. Respondent-cross-petitioner Soler Chrysler-Plymouth, Inc. (Soler), is a Puerto Rico corporation with its principal place of business in Pueblo Viejo, Guaynabo, Puerto Rico.

On October 31, 1979, Soler entered into a Distributor Agreement with CISA which provided for the sale by Soler of Mitsubishi-manufactured

国際販売契約中に挿入された仲裁条項中に含まれると解釈された独占禁止法から生じる請求について，その仲裁適格性が肯定された事例

BLACKMUN 裁判官が法廷意見を言い渡した．

これらの事件で提起されている主要な問題は，連邦仲裁法 9 U.S.C.§1 以下及び外国仲裁判断の承認及び執行に関する条約（条約）［1970］21 U.S. T. 2517, T.I.A.S. No.6997 によれば，シャーマン法 15 U.S.C. §1 以下から生じ，国際商取引に関する合意中の有効な仲裁条項に含まれた請求権が仲裁適格性を有するかである．

I 上訴人・反訴被上訴人 Mitsubishi Motors Corporation（Mitsubishi）は，自動車を製造し，主たる営業所を日本の東京に有する日本会社である．Mitsubishi は，一方ではジュネーブで登録され，Chrysler Corporation により完全に所有されたスイス会社である Chrysler International, S.A.（CISA）と，他方では日本会社の Mitsubishi Heavy Inc. との間のジョイント・ベンチャーの所産である．このジョイント・ベンチャーの目的は，Mitsubishi により製造され，Mitsubishi と Chrysler の商標をつけた自動車を合衆国本土外で Chrysler のディーラーを通じて販売することであった．被上訴人・反訴上訴人 Soler Chrysler-Plymouth, Inc.（Soler）は，プエルトリコの Pueblo Viejo, Guaynabo に主たる営業所を有するプエルトリコ会社である．

1979 年 10 月 31 日，Soler は CISA との間に，Mitsubishi の製造した自動車をサンジュアン首都圏を含む指定地域における Soler による販売を定めた

vehicles within a designated area, including metropolitan San Juan. On the same date, CISA, Soler, and Mitsubishi entered into a Sales Procedure Agreement (Sales Agreement) which, referring to the Distributor Agreement, provided for the direct sale of Mitsubishi products to Soler and governed the terms and conditions of such sales. *Id.*, at 42. Paragraph VI of the Sales Agreement, labeled "Arbitration of Certain Matters," provides:

"All disputes, controversies or differences which may arise between [Mitsubishi] and [Soler] out of or in relation to Articles I-B through V of this Agreement or for the breach thereof, shall be finally settled by arbitration in Japan in accordance with the rules and regulations of the Japan Commercial Arbitration Association."
......

Soler ran into serious difficulties in meeting the expected sales volume, and by the spring of 1981 it felt itself compelled to request that Mitsubishi delay or cancel shipment of several orders. About the same time, Soler attempted to arrange for the transshipment of a quantity of its vehicles for sale in the continental United States and Latin America. Mitsubishi and CISA, however, refused permission for any such diversion, citing a variety of reasons, and no vehicles were transshipped. Attempts to work out these difficulties failed. Mitsubishi eventually withheld shipment of 966 vehicles, apparently representing orders placed for May, June, and July 1981 production, responsibility for which Soler disclaimed in February 1982.

The following month, Mitsubishi brought an action against Soler in the United States District Court for the District of Puerto Rico under the Federal Arbitration Act and the Convention. Mitsubishi sought an order, pursuant to 9 U. S. C. §§4 and 201, to compel arbitration in accord with paragraph VI of the Sales Agreement. Shortly after filing the complaint,

5　仲裁適格性：Mitsubishi Motors Corporation v. Soler Chrysler-Plymouth, Inc.

ディストリビューター契約を締結した．同日，CISA，Soler と Mitsubishi は，売買手続契約（売買契約）を締結した．その契約はディストリビューターに言及し，Mitsubishi 製品の Soler への直接販売を規定し，かかる売買の約定と条件を決めた．同上 42 頁．売買契約のパラグラフ 6 は，「一定事項の仲裁」と題され，次のように定める．

　「この契約の第 I 条 B から第 V 条まで又はそれに関連して又はその違反のために生じる［Mitsubishi］と［Soler］間のすべての紛争，争い又は相違は，日本商事仲裁協会の規則及び規制に従って日本において仲裁により最終的に解決されるものとする．」
……

Soler は，期待された販売量に達するのに重大な困難に陥り，1981 年の春までには，Mitsubishi に対して注文のいくつかを遅らすか，キャンセルすることを要求せざるを得ないと感じた．これとほぼ同じ時期に，Soler は，その多量の自動車を合衆国本土とラテンアメリカへの販売のために積み替えを手配しようとした．しかしながら，Mitsubishi と CISA は，いろんな理由をあげてこのような積み替えの許可を拒絶し，自動車の積み替えは行われなかった．これらの困難を打開しようとする試みは失敗した．Mitsubishi は最終的に 1981 年製品の 5 月，6 月，7 月向けに出された注文に該当するとみられる 966 台の自動車の船積みを取りやめた．Soler は，1982 年 2 月にそれに対する責任を否認した．

翌月，Mitsubishi は連邦仲裁法と条約に基づいて，プエルトリコ地区の合衆国地方裁判所に Soler に対する訴訟を提起した．Mitsubishi は，9 U.S.C §§4 及び 201 により，販売契約パラグラフ 6 に従って，仲裁に服することの命令を求めた．申立をしたしばらく後に，Mitsubishi は日本商事仲裁協会に対して仲裁を求める申請を行った．

Mitsubishi filed a request for arbitration before the Japan Commercial Arbitration Association.

Soler denied the allegations and counterclaimed against both Mitsubishi and CISA. It alleged numerous breaches by Mitsubishi of the Sales Agreement, raised a pair of defamation claims, and asserted causes of action under the Sherman Act, 15 U. S. C. §1 *et seq.*; the federal Automobile Dealers' Day in Court Act, 70 Stat. 1125, 15 U. S. C. §1221 *et seq.*; the Puerto Rico competition statute, P.R. Laws Ann., Tit. 10, §257 *et seq.* (1976); and the Puerto Rico Dealers' Contracts Act, P.R. Laws Ann., Tit. 10, §278 *et seq.* (1976 and Supp. 1983). In the counterclaim premised on the Sherman Act, Soler alleged that Mitsubishi and CISA had conspired to divide markets in restraint of trade. To effectuate the plan, according to Soler, Mitsubishi had refused to permit Soler to resell to buyers in North, Central, or South America vehicles it had obligated itself to purchase from Mitsubishi; had refused to ship ordered vehicles or the parts, such as heaters and defoggers, that would be necessary to permit Soler to make its vehicles suitable for resale outside Puerto Rico; and had coercively attempted to replace Soler and its other Puerto Rico distributors with a wholly owned subsidiary which would serve as the exclusive Mitsubishi distributor in Puerto Rico. ……

After a hearing, the District Court ordered Mitsubishi and Soler to arbitrate each of the issues raised in the complaint and in all the counterclaims save two and a portion of a third. With regard to the federal antitrust issues, it recognized that the Courts of Appeals, following *American Safety Equipment Corp.* v. *J. P. Maguire & Co.*, 391 F.2d 821 (CA2 1968), uniformly had held that the rights conferred by the antitrust laws were "'of a character inappropriate for enforcement by arbitration,'" quoting *Wilko* v. *Swan*, 201 F.2d 439, 444 (CA2 1953), rev'd, 346 U.S. 427 (1953). The District Court held, however, that the international char-

5　仲裁適格性：Mitsubishi Motors Corporation v. Soler Chrysler-Plymouth, Inc.

　Solerは，その主張を否認し，MitsubishiとCISAに対して反訴を提起した．Solerは，Mitsubishiによる販売契約の無数の違反を主張し，名誉毀損請求を提起し，そしてシャーマン法 15 U.S.C.§1 以下．; the federal Automobile Dealers' Day in Court Act, 70 Stat.1125, 15 U.S.C. §1221 以下；the Puerto Rico competition statute, P.R. Laws Ann., Tit 10 257 以下（1976）；及び the Puerto Rico Dealers' Contracts Act, P.R. Laws Ann., Tit. 10, §278 以下（1976 及び Supp.1983）に基づく訴訟原因を主張した．シャーマン法に基づく反訴において，Solerは，MitsubishiとCISAが取引を制限する市場分割の共同謀議を行ったと主張した．Solerによれば，Mitsubishiはその計画を実行するために，SolerがMitsubishiから購入することを義務づけた自動車を北，中央又は南アメリカのバイヤーに再販売することをSolerに許容することを拒否した．また，注文された自動車及びヒーターや霜取り器のような部品，それらはSolerがプエルトリコの範囲外での再販売に自動車を適合させることを可能にするのに必要なものであるが，それらを船積みすることを拒否し，そしてSolerその他のプエルトリコのディストリビューターをプエルトリコにおけるMitsubishiの専属的ディストリビューターに強制的にとって換えようと試みた．……

　審問の後に，地方裁判所は，MitsubishiとSolerに対して，訴状及びすべての反訴請求において提起された個々の争点について，2つの争点と3番の争点の一部を除いて，仲裁に付すべきことを命じた．連邦独占禁止法の争点に関しては，巡回区控訴裁判所が一致して，*Wilko v. Swan*, 201 F.2d 439, 444（CA2 1953), rev'd, 346 U. S. 427（1953）を引用して，*American Safety Equipment Corp. v. J. P. Maguire & Co.*, 391 F.2d 821（CA2 1968）に従い，独占禁止法によって付与された権利は「仲裁による執行に適切ではない性質のものである」と判断してきたことを地方裁判所は認めた．

acter of the Mitsubishi-Soler undertaking required enforcement of the agreement to arbitrate even as to the antitrust claims. It relied on *Scherk* v. *Alberto-Culver Co.*, 417 U.S. 506, 515-520 (1974), in which this Court ordered arbitration, pursuant to a provision embodied in an international agreement, of a claim arising under the Securities Exchange Act of 1934 notwithstanding its assumption, *arguendo*, that *Wilko*, which held nonarbitrable claims arising under the Securities Act of 1933, also would bar arbitration of a 1934 Act claim arising in a domestic context.

The United States Court of Appeals for the First Circuit affirmed in part and reversed in part. 723 F.2d 155 (1983). It first rejected Soler's argument that Puerto Rico law precluded enforcement of an agreement obligating a local dealer to arbitrate controversies outside Puerto Rico. It also rejected Soler's suggestion that it could not have intended to arbitrate statutory claims not mentioned in the arbitration agreement. Assessing arbitrability "on an allegation-by-allegation basis," *id.*, at 159, the court then read the arbitration clause to encompass virtually all the claims arising under the various statutes, including all those arising under the Sherman Act.

Finally, after endorsing the doctrine of *American Safety*, precluding arbitration of antitrust claims, the Court of Appeals concluded that neither this Court's decision in *Scherk* nor the Convention required abandonment of that doctrine in the face of an international transaction. 723 F.2d, at 164-168. Accordingly, it reversed the judgment of the District Court insofar as it had ordered submission of "Soler's antitrust claims" to arbitration. Affirming the remainder of the judgment, the court directed the District Court to consider in the first instance how the parallel judicial and arbitral proceedings should go forward.

We granted certiorari primarily to consider whether an American court

5 仲裁適格性：Mitsubishi Motors Corporation v. Soler Chrysler-Plymouth, Inc.

しかしながら，地方裁判所は Mitsubishi-Soler の事業の国際的性格から，独占禁止法上の請求に関しても，仲裁合意の執行を要求すると判示した．地方裁判所は，*Scherk v. Alberto-Culver Co.*, 417 U.S. 506, 515-520（1974）に依拠したこの事件で当裁判所は国際契約中に含まれた条項に従い，1934年の証券取引所法下で生じる請求を仲裁に付すべきことを命じた．1933年証券取引法の下で生じた請求を仲裁不適格と判示した *Wilko* 事件が，仮に内国的コンテキストで生じる1934年法上の請求についても仲裁を禁止するであろう，という裁判所の推測にもかかわらず，そう命じたのである．

合衆国第1巡回区控訴裁判所は，原判決の一部を支持し，一部を破棄した．723 F.2d 155（1983）．まず同裁判所は，地域のディラーにプエルトリコ以外の地で紛争を仲裁に付することを義務づける合意の執行をプエルトリコ法が排除するという Soler の主張を排斥した．裁判所はまた，仲裁契約で言及されていない制定法上の請求を仲裁に付するということを意図しえなかったという Soler の主張をも認めなかった．「個々の主張ごとに」同上159頁，仲裁適格性を判断して，それから裁判所は仲裁条項がシャーマン法から生じるすべてのものを含む様々な制定法から生じるすべての請求を文字通り含むものと解釈した．

最後に，独占禁止法に関する請求についての仲裁を排除した *American Safety* 事件の法理を支持した後に，控訴審裁判所は当裁判所の *Scherk* 事件における決定と条約のいずれもが国際取引であるにもかかわらず，この法理の適用を放棄することを要求するものではないと結論した．723 F.2d, at 164-168．したがって裁判所は，「Soler の独占禁止法の請求」を仲裁に服することを地方裁判所が命じた限りにおいて，地方裁判所の判決を破棄した．判決の残りの部分を維持して，裁判所は第1審で，裁判と仲裁の並行手続をどのように進めるべきかを考慮することを地方裁判所に命じた．

独占禁止法上の請求を仲裁により解決する合意を，その合意が国際取引か

should enforce an agreement to resolve antitrust claims by arbitration when that agreement arises from an international transaction.

II At the outset, we address the contention raised in Soler's cross-petition that the arbitration clause at issue may not be read to encompass the statutory counterclaims stated in its answer to the complaint. ……Soler reasons that, because it falls within the class for whose benefit the federal and local antitrust laws and dealers' Acts were passed, but the arbitration clause at issue does not mention these statutes or statutes in general, the clause cannot be read to contemplate arbitration of these statutory claims.

We do not agree, for we find no warrant in the Arbitration Act for implying in every contract within its ken a presumption against arbitration of statutory claims. The Act's centerpiece provision makes a written agreement to arbitrate "in any maritime transaction or a contract evidencing a transaction involving commerce…… valid, irrevocable, and enforceable, save upon such grounds as exist at law or in equity for the revocation of any contract." 9 U. S. C. §2. The "liberal federal policy favoring arbitration agreements," *Moses H. Cone Memorial Hospital* v. *Mercury Construction Corp.*, 460 U.S. 1, 24 (1983), manifested by this provision and the Act as a whole, is at bottom a policy guaranteeing the enforcement of private contractual arrangements…….* * * "The Arbitration Act establishes that, as a matter of federal law, any doubts concerning the scope of arbitrable issues should be resolved in favor of arbitration, whether the problem at hand is the construction of the contract language itself or an allegation of waiver, delay, or a like defense to arbitrability." *Moses H. Cone Memorial Hospital*, 460 U.S., at 24-25.

……

In sum, the Court of Appeals correctly conducted a two-step inquiry,

5 仲裁適格性：Mitsubishi Motors Corporation v. Soler Chrysler-Plymouth, Inc.

ら生じるときにおいて，アメリカの裁判所が執行すべきかどうかを主として考慮するために，われわれは裁量的上訴を認めた．

II　まずはじめに，Solerの交差申立で提起されている主張，すなわち，本件仲裁条項は訴状の答弁において述べられた制定法上の反訴請求を含むものと読んではならないという主張を検討する．……Solerが根拠とするのは，Solorは連邦及び州の独占禁止法とディラーズ法がその者の利益のために制定された対象の範疇に入るが，本件仲裁条項がこれらの制定法又は制定法一般になんら言及していないから，仲裁条項はこれらの制定法上の請求の仲裁を考慮していると読むことはできないという点にある．

われわれは同意することができない．というのは，仲裁法中にはその範囲内にあるすべての契約において，制定法上の請求について仲裁に不利な推定を暗示するような根拠はなんら見出しえないからである．その法律の主要な規定は，「すべての海事取引又は商事に関する取引を明示する契約中にある」書面による仲裁合意を「契約の取消のために法上，又はエクイテイ上認められている理由に基づく場合を除いては，……有効で，取り消すことができず，又は執行可能である」としている．9 U. S. C. §2. この規定とその法全体によって明らかにされている「仲裁合意を尊重するという自由な連邦の政策」*Moses H. Cone Memorial Hospital v. Mercury Construction Corp.*, 460 U.S. 1, 24（1983）は，根本的には，私的な契約取り決めの執行を保証する政策である…．＊＊＊「連邦法の問題として仲裁可能な争点の適用範囲に関するすべての疑問は，提起されている問題が，契約文言それ自体の解釈であろうと，放棄や遅滞の主張又は仲裁適格性の抗弁であろうと，仲裁に有利なように解決されるべきことを仲裁法は明らかにしている．」*Moses H. Cone Memorial Hospital*, 460 U.S., at 24-25.

……

要するに，控訴審は二段階の検討を正しく行った．最初は，仲裁に付する

first determining whether the parties' agreement to arbitrate reached the statutory issues, and then, upon finding it did, considering whether legal constraints external to the parties' agreement foreclosed the arbitration of those claims. We endorse its rejection of Soler's proposed rule of arbitration-clause construction.

III We now turn to consider whether Soler's antitrust claims are nonarbitrable even though it has agreed to arbitrate them. In holding that they are not, the Court of Appeals followed the decision of the Second Circuit in *American Safety Equipment Corp. v. J. P. Maguire & Co.*, 391 F.2d 821 (1968). Notwithstanding the absence of any explicit support for such an exception in either the Sherman Act or the Federal Arbitration Act, the Second Circuit there reasoned that "the pervasive public interest in enforcement of the antitrust laws, and the nature of the claims that arise in such cases, combine to make...... antitrust claims....... inappropriate for arbitration." *Id.*, at 827-828. We find it unnecessary to assess the legitimacy of the *American Safety* doctrine as applied to agreements to arbitrate arising from domestic transactions. As in *Scherk v. Alberto-Culver Co.*, 417 U.S. 506 (1974), we conclude that concerns of international comity, respect for the capacities of foreign and transnational tribunals, and sensitivity to the need of the international commercial system for predictability in the resolution of disputes require that we enforce the parties' agreement, even assuming that a contrary result would be forthcoming in a domestic context.

......

The Bremen and *Scherk* establish a strong presumption in favor of enforcement of freely negotiated contractual choice-of-forum provisions. Here, as in *Scherk*, that presumption is reinforced by the emphatic federal policy in favor of arbitral dispute resolution. And at least since this Nation's accession in 1970 to the Convention, see [1970] 21 U.S.T. 2517, T.I.A.S. 6997, and the implementation of the Convention in the same year

という当事者の合意が制定法上の争点に及ぶかどうかを決定し，そしてそれから，その判断に基づき，当事者の外部に存在する法的制限がこれらの請求についての仲裁を禁ずるかどうかを考慮した．われわれは，Solerの提起した仲裁条項の解釈原則を同裁判所が拒絶したことを支持する．

III 次に今度は，Solerの独占禁止法上の請求が，それが仲裁に付することを合意したとしても，仲裁不適格であるかどうかを検討する．仲裁に付することができないと判示するにあたって，控訴審は第2巡回区控訴裁判所の*American Safety Equipment Corp. v. J. P. Manguire & Co.*, 391 F.2d 821 (1968) の判断に従った．シャーマン法にも仲裁法のいずれにも，そのような例外を支持する明文の規定がないにもかかわらず，第2巡回区裁判所はそこで「独占禁止法上の執行に対する広汎な公的利益とそのような事件において生じる請求の性質とが結びついて，……独占禁止法上の請求を……仲裁に不適格にする」同上827-828頁という理由を述べた．われわれは，国内取引から生じる仲裁合意に適用される*American Safety*法理の正当性を評価することは必要がないと判断する．*Scherk v. Alberto-Culver Co.*, 417 U. S. 506 (1974) 事件におけるように，国際礼譲の関心，外国及び超国家的な法廷の権限に対する尊重と，紛争解決における予見可能性に対する国際的な商事システムの必要性への配慮が，国内的なコンテキストでは逆の結果が起こりうると考えても，われわれが当事者の合意を執行すべきことを要求するものであると結論する．
……

*The Bremen*事件と*Scherk*事件は，自由に交渉された法廷選択条項の執行に有利な強い推定を確立した．ここでも，*Scherk*事件と同様に，この推定は仲裁による紛争解決を有利に扱う確固たる連邦の政策によって補強されている．そして少なくともこの国が条約に1970年に加盟したことと，[1970] 21 U.S. T.2 517, T.I.A.S. 6997参照，同年の連邦仲裁法の改正による条約の実施以来，その連邦の政策は，国際通商の分野において特別の効力をもって適

by amendment of the Federal Arbitration Act, that federal policy applies with special force in the field of international commerce. Thus, we must weigh the concerns of *American Safety* against a strong belief in the efficacy of arbitral procedures for the resolution of international commercial disputes and an equal commitment to the enforcement of freely negotiated choice-of-forum clauses.

At the outset, we confess to some skepticism of certain aspects of the *American Safety* doctrine. As distilled by the First Circuit, 723 F.2d, at 162, the doctrine comprises four ingredients. First, private parties play a pivotal role in aiding governmental enforcement of the antitrust laws by means of the private action for treble damages. Second, "the strong possibility that contracts which generate antitrust disputes may be contracts of adhesion militates against automatic forum determination by contract." Third, antitrust issues, prone to complication, require sophisticated legal and economic analysis, and thus are "ill-adapted to strengths of the arbitral process, *i.e.*, expedition, minimal requirements of written rationale, simplicity, resort to basic concepts of common sense and simple equity." Finally, just as "issues of war and peace are too important to be vested in the generals,... decisions as to antitrust regulation of business are too important to be lodged in arbitrators chosen from the business community ——particularly those from a foreign community that has had no experience with or exposure to our law and values." See *American Safety*, 391 F.2d, at 826-827.

Initially, we find the second concern unjustified. The mere appearance of an antitrust dispute does not alone warrant invalidation of the selected forum on the undemonstrated assumption that the arbitration clause is tainted. A party resisting arbitration of course may attack directly the validity of the agreement to arbitrate. See *Prima Paint Corp. v. Flood & Conklin Mfg. Co.*, 388 U.S. 395 (1967). Moreover, the party may attempt

5 仲裁適格性：Mitsubishi Motors Corporation v. Soler Chrysler-Plymouth, Inc.

用される．このようにして，われわれは，国際商事紛争の解決のための仲裁手続の有効性に対する強い信念と自由に交渉された法選択条項の執行に対応する責任に対して，*American Safety* 事件に対する強い関心とを秤量しなければならない．

まずはじめにわれわれは，*American Safety* 法理のある側面に若干の疑念をもっていることを告白する．第1巡回区控訴裁判所が要約したように，723 F.2d, at 162, この理論は4つの構成部分からなっている．第1に，3倍賠償金の私訴の手段により，政府による独占禁止法の執行を補助する点において私的当事者が中心的な役割を果たしている．第2に，「独占禁止紛争を引き起こす契約は附合契約であるかもしれないという可能性は，契約による自動的な法廷地の決定に不利に作用する．」第3に，複雑になりがちな独占禁止法上の争点は，洗練した法的，経済的分析を必要とし，かくして「仲裁手続の長所，つまり，迅速，書面による理由を最小限にしか必要としないこと，簡潔，常識と単純なエクイティという基本的な観念に依存するという長所に適合しない．」最後に，「戦争と平和の問題が，将軍に委ねるには重要に過ぎる」ように，…「事業の独占禁止規制に関する決定は，企業社会から選ばれた仲裁人，——とりわけわれわれの法と価値に経験がなく，それに直面することのない外国社会からの人々に委ねるには重要に過ぎる．」*American Safety*, 391 F.2d, at 826-827 参照．

最初に第2の懸念は正当化することはできないと判断する．独占禁止法に関する紛争が附合契約であるという単なる外観だけから，仲裁条項が腐敗したものであるという，立証されていない推論に基づいて，選択された法廷を無効とすることは認められない．仲裁条項に抵抗する当事者は，もとより仲裁合意の有効性を直接攻撃することができる．*Prima Paint Corp. v. Flood & Conklin Mfg. Co.*, 388 U.S. 395（1967）参照．さらに，当事者は法廷地

to make a showing that would warrant setting aside the forum-selection clause——that the agreement was "[affected] by fraud, undue influence, or overweening bargaining power"; that "enforcement would be unreasonable and unjust"; or that proceedings "in the contractual forum will be so gravely difficult and inconvenient that [the resisting party] will for all practical purposes be deprived of his day in court." *The Bremen*, 407 U.S., at 12, 15, 18. But absent such a showing——and none was attempted here——there is no basis for assuming the forum inadequate or its selection unfair.

Next, potential complexity should not suffice to ward off arbitration. We might well have some doubt that even the courts following *American Safety* subscribe fully to the view that antitrust matters are inherently insusceptible to resolution by arbitration, as these same courts have agreed that an undertaking to arbitrate antitrust claims entered into *after* the dispute arises is acceptable. And the vertical restraints which most frequently give birth to antitrust claims covered by an arbitration agreement will not often occasion the monstrous proceedings that have given antitrust litigation an image of intractability. In any event, adaptability and access to expertise are hallmarks of arbitration. The anticipated subject matter of the dispute may be taken into account when the arbitrators are appointed, and arbitral rules typically provide for the participation of experts either employed by the parties or appointed by the tribunal. Moreover, it is often a judgment that streamlined proceedings and expeditious results will best serve their needs that causes parties to agree to arbitrate their disputes; it is typically a desire to keep the effort and expense required to resolve a dispute within manageable bounds that prompts them mutually to forgo access to judicial remedies. In sum, the factor of potential complexity alone does not persuade us that an arbitral tribunal could not properly handle an antitrust matter.

5 仲裁適格性：Mitsubishi Motors Corporation v. Soler Chrysler-Plymouth, Inc.

選択条項の無効を正当化するような立証をすること，——つまり合意は「詐欺，不当威圧又は圧倒的な交渉力により［影響を受けた］」こと，「執行は不当で正しくない」，又は「契約された法廷地における」手続が「非常に複雑で不便であり，［抵抗している当事者が］あらゆる実際的目的からみて裁判所における機会を奪われている」*The Bremen,* 407 U.S. at, 12, 15, 18 ことを当事者は立証しようと試みることができる．しかし，そのような立証がない限りは，——そして本件ではなにも試みられていない——法廷地が不適切であるか，その選択が不公正であると推定するなんらの根拠も存在しない．

次に潜在的な複雑さは，仲裁を排除するのに十分ではない．*American Safety* 事件に従う裁判所でさえも，独占禁止法に関する事項が本来的に仲裁による解決に適さないという見解に完全に賛成しているというには若干の疑念がある．というのは，これらの同じ裁判所が紛争が生じてから後に締結された独占禁止法に関する請求について仲裁するという合意は許されることについては一致しているからである．そして仲裁合意によってカバーされる独占禁止法に関する請求を最も頻繁に生ぜしめる垂直的制限は，独占禁止法訴訟に対して処理の難しいというイメージを与えてきた途方もなく複雑な手続をそれほど引き起こすことはない．いずれにしても適応性と専門家へのアクセスの容易なことは，仲裁の顕著な特徴である．紛争の予期可能な対象は，仲裁人が選任されるときに考慮することができるものであり，また仲裁規則は典型的には当事者によって採用されるか，法廷によって任命されるかのいずれかにより専門家の参加を定めている．さらに当事者にその紛争を仲裁に付することを合意させるのは，しばしば簡潔な手続と迅速な結果が当事者のニーズに最もよくかなうであろうという判断なのである．また彼らに裁判所の救済へのアクセスを互いになしですませようとするのは，典型的には，紛争を解決するのに要求される努力と費用を処理可能な範囲に保とうとする欲求なのである．要するに，潜在的な複雑さの要素は，それだけでは，仲裁廷が独占禁止法事項を適切に処理しえないということをわれわれに説得することはできない．

For similar reasons, we also reject the proposition that an arbitration panel will pose too great a danger of innate hostility to the constraints on business conduct that antitrust law imposes. International arbitrators frequently are drawn from the legal as well as the business community; where the dispute has an important legal component, the parties and the arbitral body with whose assistance they have agreed to settle their dispute can be expected to select arbitrators accordingly. We decline to indulge the presumption that the parties and arbitral body conducting a proceeding will be unable or unwilling to retain competent, conscientious, and impartial arbitrators.

We are left, then, with the core of the *American Safety* doctrine —— the fundamental importance to American democratic capitalism of the regime of the antitrust laws. ...... Without doubt, the private cause of action plays a central role in enforcing this regime. ...... As the Court of Appeals pointed out:

"A claim under the antitrust laws is not merely a private matter. The Sherman Act is designed to promote the national interest in a competitive economy; thus, the plaintiff asserting his rights under the Act has been likened to a private attorney-general who protects the public's interest." 723 F.2d, at 168, quoting *American Safety*, 391 F.2d, at 826.

The treble-damages provision wielded by the private litigant is a chief tool in the antitrust enforcement scheme, posing a crucial deterrent to potential violators. ......

The importance of the private damages remedy, however, does not compel the conclusion that it may not be sought outside an American court.

......

There is no reason to assume at the outset of the dispute that interna-

5 仲裁適格性：Mitsubishi Motors Corporation v. Soler Chrysler-Plymouth, Inc.

　同様の理由により，われわれはまた仲裁廷が，独占禁止法が課している事業活動への制限に対する生来の敵意というあまりに大きな危険をもたらすものであるという立場をも拒否する．国際仲裁人はしばしば実業界からと同様に，法曹界からも選任される．紛争が重要な法的問題を含んでいるときは，当事者及び当事者が紛争の解決の支援を合意した仲裁機関が仲裁人をそれに応じて選任することを期待することができる．当事者及び手続を進める仲裁機関が適任で，良心的かつ公平な仲裁人を選べないとか，又はその気がないという推論に陥ることをわれわれは拒否する．

　そこで，残されたのは，*American Safety* 原則の中核にあるもの，すなわち，独占禁止法の制度が，米国の民主的資本主義にとって基本的な重要性を有するという問題である．……私的な訴訟原因がこの制度を実施する上で，中心的な役割を果たしていることは疑問の余地がない．……控訴審が次のように指摘している．

　　「独占禁止法に基づく請求は，単なる私的な事柄ではない．シャーマン法は，競争的な経済における国家的な利益を促進するために立案された．かくしてその法律に基づいてその権利を主張する原告は，公的利益を保護する，私的な検事総長にたとえられてきた．」723 F.2d, at168, *American Safety*, 391 F.2d, at 826 を引用．

私人である訴訟当事者によって行使される3倍賠償の規定は，独占禁止法の執行スキームにおける主要な手段であり，想定される侵害者に対する厳しい抑止力を有している．……
　しかしながら，民事上の賠償金の救済の重要性は，その救済がアメリカの裁判所以外のところに求めてはならないという結論を強要するものではない．……

　議論の最初に，国際仲裁は適切なメカニズムを提供しないであろうと考え

tional arbitration will not provide an adequate mechanism. To be sure, the international arbitral tribunal owes no prior allegiance to the legal norms of particular states; hence, it has no direct obligation to vindicate their statutory dictates. The tribunal, however, is bound to effectuate the intentions of the parties. Where the parties have agreed that the arbitral body is to decide a defined set of claims which includes, as in these cases, those arising from the application of American antitrust law, the tribunal therefore should be bound to decide that dispute in accord with the national law giving rise to the claim. Cf. *Wilko* v. *Swan*, 346 U.S., at 433-434. And so long as the prospective litigant effectively may vindicate its statutory cause of action in the arbitral forum, the statute will continue to serve both its remedial and deterrent function.

Having permitted the arbitration to go forward, the national courts of the United States will have the opportunity at the award-enforcement stage to ensure that the legitimate interest in the enforcement of the antitrust laws has been addressed. The Convention reserves to each signatory country the right to refuse enforcement of an award where the "recognition or enforcement of the award would be contrary to the public policy of that country." Art. V(2)(b), 21 U.S.T., at 2520. …… While the efficacy of the arbitral process requires that substantive review at the award-enforcement stage remain minimal, it would not require intrusive inquiry to ascertain that the tribunal took cognizance of the antitrust claims and actually decided them.

As international trade has expanded in recent decades, so too has the use of international arbitration to resolve disputes arising in the course of that trade. The controversies that international arbitral institutions are called upon to resolve have increased in diversity as well as in complexity. Yet the potential of these tribunals for efficient disposition of legal disagreements arising from commercial relations has not yet been

5 仲裁適格性：Mitsubishi Motors Corporation v. Soler Chrysler-Plymouth, Inc.

る理由は存在しない．たしかに国際仲裁廷は，特定の国家の法的規範に対してなんらの優先的な忠誠心を負ってはいない．したがって法廷は特定の国家の制定法上の指令を正当と認める直接の義務は負ってはいない．しかしながら，法廷は当事者の意思を実現させる義務はある．これらの事件におけるように，仲裁法廷がアメリカの独占禁止法の適用から生じる請求を含む，一定の範囲の請求を決定すべきことを当事者が同意した場合には，法廷はその請求を生ぜしめた国家法に従って紛争を解決しなければならない．Cf. *Wilko v. Swan*, 346 U.S., at 433-434. そして予想される訴訟当事者が仲裁法廷において効果的にその制定法上の訴訟原因を立証しうる限りにおいて，その制定法はその救済的及び阻止的機能の双方を果たし続けるであろう．

仲裁を進めることを認めたとしても，合衆国の国家裁判所は判断の執行段階において独占禁止法の執行における正当な利益が保護されるべきことを確保する機会をもつ．条約は，各署名国に「判断の承認及び執行が，その国の公の秩序に反する」Art.V (2)(b), 21 U.S.T., at 2520……場合には，判断の執行を拒否する権限を留保している．仲裁手続の効率性からすると，判断の執行段階における実質的な審査は最小限に留めることが要求されるものではあるが，法廷が独占禁止法上の請求を考慮し，実際にそれらを決定したことを確認することが，それほど差し出がましい調査をなすべきことを要求するものではないであろう．

国際貿易が近年拡大したのに応じて，国際貿易から生じる紛争を解決するために国際仲裁を利用することもまた拡大した．国際仲裁機関が解決することを要請される紛争は多様性と複雑性を増している．しかしこれらの法廷が，商業関係から生じる法的不一致の効率的な処理に対して有する可能性は，いまだ検証されてはいない．もしもこれらの仲裁機関が国際的法秩序の中核的地位を占めるべきものとすれば，国家裁判所は，「仲裁に対する裁判所の古い

tested. If they are to take a central place in the international legal order, national courts will need to "shake off the old judicial hostility to arbitration," *Kulukundis Shipping Co.* v. *Amtorg Trading Corp.*, 126 F.2d 978, 985 (CA2 1942), and also their customary and understandable unwillingness to cede jurisdiction of a claim arising under domestic law to a foreign or transnational tribunal. To this extent, at least, it will be necessary for national courts to subordinate domestic notions of arbitrability to the international policy favoring commercial arbitration. See *Scherk, supra.*

Accordingly, we "require this representative of the American business community to honor its bargain," *Alberto-Culver Co.* v. *Scherk*, 484 F.2d 611, 620 (CA7 1973) (Stevens, J., dissenting), by holding this agreement to arbitrate "[enforceable] ... in accord with the explicit provisions of the Arbitration Act." *Scherk*, 417 U.S., at 520. The judgment of the Court of Appeals is affirmed in part and reversed in part, and the cases are remanded for further proceedings consistent with this opinion.

JUSTICE POWELL took no part in the decision of these cases.

JUSTICE STEVENS, with whom JUSTICE BRENNAN joins, and with whom JUSTICE MARSHALL joins except as to Part II, dissenting.
......

In my opinion, (1) a fair construction of the language in the arbitration clause in the parties' contract does not encompass a claim that auto manufacturers entered into a conspiracy in violation of the antitrust laws; (2) an arbitration clause should not normally be construed to cover a statutory remedy that it does not expressly identify; (3) Congress did not intend §2 of the Federal Arbitration Act to apply to antitrust claims; and (4) Congress did not intend the Convention on the Recognition and Enforcement of Foreign Arbitral Awards to apply to disputes that are not covered by the Federal Arbitration Act.

5 仲裁適格性：Mitsubishi Motors Corporation v. Soler Chrysler-Plymouth, Inc.

敵意を断ち切り」, *Kulukundis Shipping Co. v. Amtorg Trading Corp.*, 126 F.2d 978, 985（CA2 1942）また，国内法から生じた請求権の管轄権を外国又は超国家的法廷に委ねることを嫌悪する裁判所の慣習的で理解しうる傾向を断ち切る必要があろう．少なくともその限りで，国家裁判所は仲裁適格性に関する国内的な考え方を商事仲裁を優遇する国際的政策に従属させることが必要である．前掲 *Scherk* 判決参照.

したがってわれわれは，この仲裁合意が「仲裁法の明示の規定に従って……［執行される］と判示することによって，*Alberto-Culver Co. v. Scherk*, 484 F.2d 611, 620（CA7 1973）(Stevens 裁判官の反対意見)，このアメリカの実業界の代表がその約束を尊重することを要求する．」*Scherk*, 417 U. S., at 520. 控訴審裁判所の判決は一部支持，一部破棄し，事件をこの意見に合致するようさらなる手続のために差し戻す．

POWELL 裁判官は，これらの事件の決定に参加しなかった．

STEVENS 裁判官の反対意見，BRENNAN 裁判官が同調，MARSHALL 裁判官が第Ⅱ部以外は同調．
……

私見によれば，(1)当事者の契約中の仲裁条項の文言を公正に解釈すると，自動車製造者が独占禁止法に違反して共同謀議を行ったという請求はそこに含まれていない．(2)仲裁条項は，それが明示に確認していない制定法上の救済を含んでいる，と通常は解釈されるべきではない．(3)連邦仲裁法2条が独占禁止法に関する請求に適用されるとは連邦議会は考えていなかった．(4)外国仲裁判断の承認及び執行に関する条約が連邦仲裁法がカバーしていない紛争に適用されるとは連邦議会は考えてはいなかった．

I International Comity

It is clear then that the international obligations of the United States permit us to honor Congress' commitment to the exclusive resolution of antitrust disputes in the federal courts. The Court today refuses to do so, offering only vague concerns for comity among nations. The courts of other nations, on the other hand, have applied the exception provided in the Convention, and refused to enforce agreements to arbitrate specific subject matters of concern to them.

It may be that the subject-matter exception to the Convention ought to be reserved——as a matter of domestic law——for matters of the greatest public interest which involve concerns that are shared by other nations. The Sherman Act's commitment to free competitive markets is among our most important civil policies. This commitment, shared by other nations which are signatory to the Convention, is hardly the sort of parochial concern that we should decline to enforce in the interest of international comity. Indeed, the branch of Government entrusted with the conduct of political relations with foreign governments has informed us that the "United States' determination that federal antitrust claims are nonarbitrable under the Convention ... is not likely to result in either surprise or recrimination on the part of other signatories to the Convention." Brief for United States as *Amicus Curiae* 30.
……

The Court's repeated incantation of the high ideals of "international arbitration" creates the impression that this case involves the fate of an institution designed to implement a formula for world peace. But just as it is improper to subordinate the public interest in enforcement of antitrust policy to the private interest in resolving commercial disputes, so is it

5　仲裁適格性：Mitsubishi Motors Corporation v. Soler Chrysler-Plymouth, Inc.

I　国際礼譲

　合衆国の国際的な義務は，独占禁止法に関する紛争の専属的な解決を連邦裁判所に委ねることをわれわれに許容していることは明らかである．本日，当裁判所は，国家間の礼譲に対する漠然とした関心を提示して，そうすることを拒否した．他方，他の国の裁判所は条約に規定された例外を適用し，それらの国にとって特別の関心のある事項に関する仲裁合意を実行することを拒否した．

　条約の例外事項は──国内法の問題として──他の国家によって共有されている関心事に関連する最大の公的利益に関する事項について，留保されるべきであろう．競争的な市場に対するシャーマン法の責任は，われわれの最も重要な民事上の政策である．条約の加盟国によって共有されているこの責任は，国際礼譲の利益のために執行を拒否するべき自国中心的な関心事の類ではない．外国政府との政治的関係の行動に責任を有する政府の機関がわれわれに知らせるところによると，「連邦独占禁止法に関する請求が条約上仲裁に適さないという，合衆国の決定は，…条約の他の締約国の側に驚きも非難をも引き起こさないであろう」法廷の友としての合衆国のブリーフ（意見書）30頁．
……

　「国際仲裁」の高い理想に対する当裁判所の繰り返し唱えられる呪文は，本件が世界平和に対する信条を実行することを目的として設立された機構の運命にかかわっているかのごとき印象を作り出している．しかし，独占禁止法に関する政策の執行に対する公的利益を商業的な紛争を解決する私的な利益に従属させるのが適当でないのと同じように，世界統合のヴィジョンがこの

equally unwise to allow a vision of world unity to distort the importance of the selection of the proper forum for resolving this dispute. Like any other mechanism for resolving controversies, international arbitration will only succeed if it is realistically limited to tasks it is capable of performing well —— the prompt and inexpensive resolution of essentially contractual disputes between commercial partners. As for matters involving the political passions and the fundamental interests of nations, even the multilateral convention adopted under the auspices of the United Nations recognizes that private international arbitration is incapable of achieving satisfactory results.

In my opinion, the elected representatives of the American people would not have us dispatch an American citizen to a foreign land in search of an uncertain remedy for the violation of a public right that is protected by the Sherman Act. This is especially so when there has been no genuine bargaining over the terms of the submission, and the arbitration remedy provided has not even the most elementary guarantees of fair process. Consideration of a fully developed record by a jury, instructed in the law by a federal judge, and subject to appellate review, is a surer guide to the competitive character of a commercial practice than the practically unreviewable judgment of a private arbitrator.

Unlike the Congress that enacted the Sherman Act in 1890, the Court today does not seem to appreciate the value of economic freedom. I respectfully dissent.

5　仲裁適格性：Mitsubishi Motors Corporation v. Soler Chrysler-Plymouth, Inc.

紛争を解決するための適切な法廷地の選択の重要性を歪曲することを強要することもまた賢明なことではない．紛争を解決する他のメカニズムと同じように，国際仲裁が唯一成功しうるのは，国際仲裁がよく果たすことのできる任務——つまり商業上のパートナー間の本質的に契約上の紛争の迅速で低廉な解決に国際仲裁が現実的に限定される場合であろう．政治的信念と国家の基本的な利益を含む事項に関する限りでは，国際連合の支援により採択された多国間条約でさえも，私的な国際商事仲裁が満足のいく結果を達成することができないことを認識しているのである．

　私見によれば，アメリカの国民の選ばれた代表者は，シャーマン法によって保護される公的権利の侵害に対してアメリカ市民を不確かな救済を求めて外国に送らせはしないであろう．このことはとりわけ，［仲裁］付託条件に対する真正な交渉力がなく，定められている仲裁の救済が公正な手続の最も初歩的な保証さえ有してないときはそうである．十分に明らかにされた記録の陪審員による考慮，連邦裁判所判事による法に関する説示，上級審での再審査は，実際的には仲裁人の再審不能の判断よりも，取引実務の競争的性質に対してより確実な指針となる．

　1890年シャーマン法を制定した議会と異なり，本日の裁判所は自由経済の価値を十分に認識していないように思われる．私は丁重に反対する．

【解　説】

　本件は，国際売買契約中に挿入された仲裁条項中に含まれると解釈された独占禁止法から生じる請求について，その仲裁適格性が肯定された事例である．

1　仲裁適格性：証券取引法上の請求と独占禁止法上の請求

　本件で主として問題となっているのは，独禁法上の請求について，仲裁で解決できるかという仲裁適格性の問題である．

　アメリカの連邦仲裁法では，仲裁の対象となる紛争又は権利についてなんらの制限を設けていない．しかし，特別の公益的理由のある場合には，私人の権利に関するものであっても，仲裁に適さないとされてきた領域がある（高桑・アメリカ法514頁（1986））．

　まず，証券取引法上の権利に関する仲裁については，連邦最高裁判所は，*Wilko v. Swan*, 346 U.S. 427（1953）において，証券法上の紛争は仲裁に適しないとして，仲裁適格性を否定した．また，独占禁止法上の権利についても，第2巡回区控訴裁判所の*American Safety Equipment Corp. v. J. P. Manguire & Co.*, 391 F.2d 821（2d Cir. 1968）が，本件判旨で説明されているような理由により，その仲裁適格性を否定した．両者は，いずれも本件と異なり，国内事件である．

2　American Safety 判決

　上掲*American Safety*判決では，ライセンシーがライセンサーに宣言判決を求める訴訟を提起し，ライセンス契約が違法であり，最初から無効であり，ロイヤルティの義務は生じなかったと主張した．その理由はライセンス契約中のある条項がシャーマン法に違反したものだからである．これに対して，ライセンサーのロイヤルティ権利者の譲受人がライセンス契約上の仲裁条項を援用した．ライセンシーはその後，譲受人に対して別の宣言判決を求める訴訟を提起し，ライセンシーによって開始された仲裁手続に対する差止めを求めた．ライセンシーは，合衆国仲裁法に基づいてすべての争点につき，仲

裁が係属している間，宣言判決訴訟を停止する申立をした．ニューヨーク南部地区連邦地裁は宣言判決訴訟を停止する中間命令を出して，ライセンシーに仲裁に進むよう指示した．ライセンシーが上訴した．

第2巡回区控訴裁判所は独占禁止法上の請求は仲裁に不適格であると判示し，さらなる手続のために差し戻した．判旨は，「独占禁止法上の請求は単なる私的な事項ではない．シャーマン法は，競争的な経済における国家利益を促進することを企図したものである．したがって同法に基づいてその権利を主張する原告は，公的利益を保護する私的な司法長官になぞられてきた」と指摘している．

3　*Scherk*判決

ところが，証券取引法に関しては，連邦最高裁は，国際事件である*Scherk v. Alberto-Culver Co.*, 417 U.S. 506 (1974) において，米国会社によるドイツ人に対する証券取引法に基づく損害賠償請求について，パリの国際商業会議所の仲裁によるとの仲裁条項に基づいて，国際事件であることを理由の1つとして，その仲裁適格性を肯定し，*Wilko*判決の論理には従わなかった．*Scherk*判決については，曽野和明・アメリカ法267頁以下（1976）参照．

4　本件多数意見

本件*Mitsubishi*判決の多数意見も，少なくとも国際取引については，独占禁止法上の請求について仲裁により解決できること，つまり仲裁適格性を肯定した．証券取引法に関して仲裁適格性を肯定した*Scherk*判決と同じ立場をとる．多数意見は，*American Safety*判決が独占禁止法上の請求について仲裁適格性を否認する根拠としてあげた4つの理由をそれぞれ否定し，少なくとも国際事件については仲裁適格性を認めた．

これに対して反対意見は，*American Safety*事件の判決とほぼ同様の理由により，国際事件であっても，外国における仲裁判断に委ねるべき理由はないとしている．

5 その後の展開

本件以後は，内国事件における独占禁止法上の請求についても，仲裁適格性を認める判決が出ている．たとえば，*Kotam Electronics v. JBL Consumer Products, Inc.*, 93 F.3d 724（11th Cir.1996）, cert. denied 519 U.S. 1110（1997）は，本件 *Mitubishi* 判決に照らすと，その推論の多くは，国内の独占禁止法に関する紛争にも適用できるとし，*American Safety* 法理は，もはや追随されるべきではないとしている．Russell J. Weitraub, Internatinal Litigation and Arbitration, 85（3rd ed.2001）．

また，本件の影響の下で，下級審裁判所の中には，公法上の請求がなされた場合であっても，国際的な仲裁条項の執行を認める傾向がある．たとえば，RICO（事業への犯罪組織等の浸透の取り締まりに関する法律）に基づく請求について，仲裁を命じる事例として，*Genesco v. Kakiuchi & Co.*, 825 F.2d 840（2d Cir. 1987）がある．

6 仲裁適格性と裁判管轄

日本会社の立場からすると，米国裁判所が日本会社に対して管轄権を有する場合であっても，仲裁条項があれば，独占禁止法上の請求に関する場合であっても，米国裁判所の管轄権の行使を排除することができる．その意味で，仲裁適格性を広く認めるということは，外国会社に対する米国裁判所の管轄権行使を制限することを認めることになろう．

【本件参考文献】

高桑昭・アメリカ法 510-17 頁（1986）．
上野典子・国際商事法務 12 巻 5 号 352-53 頁（1984）．
野木林忠邦・国際商事法務 12 巻 8 号 606-607 頁（1984）．
金子＝田村・公正取引 422 号 11 頁（1985）．
大隈一武『国際商事仲裁の理論と実務』84 頁以下（中央経済社，1995）．

5 仲裁適格性：Mitsubishi Motors Corporation v. Soler Chrysler-Plymouth, Inc.

【設 問】

1 本件の主要な争点はなにか．また，本件の契約中に挿入された仲裁条項はどのようなものであったか．
2 事実の概要を説明し，事件と当事者に関するアメリカ，日本，スイス，プエルトリコとの関連を整理せよ．
3 仲裁適格性とはどのようなものか．またこの点に関するSolerの主張，地裁，控訴審の判旨を紹介せよ．
4 *American Safety* 事件とはどのような判決か．
5 法廷意見の主要な部分を要約せよ．
6 法廷意見は，*American Safety* 事件をどのように読んだか．
7 *The Bremen* 判決（401 U.S. 1（1972）前掲本書4判決），*Scherk* 判決（417 U.S. 506（1974））はどのような判決か．これらの判決は，本件判決にどのような意味をもつか．
8 Stevens裁判官の反対意見を要約せよ．法廷意見との重要な差異はなにか．
9 仲裁適格性と裁判管轄の関係について説明せよ．
10 本件はどのような判決か．また本件の結論，理由づけに賛成か．

Ⅱ 法選択（準拠法）

6 旅客運送契約中の準拠法約款：
Siegelman v. Cunard White Star Ltd., 221 F.2d 189 (2d Cir.1955)

HARLAN, Circuit Judge

　Plaintiff, in his own right and as administrator of his wife's estate, brings this action to recover for injuries suffered by his wife on the defendant's vessel, the R.M.S. Queen Elizabeth. The action was begun in a New York state court on December 14, 1951, and removed on diversity grounds to the federal district court for the Southern District of New York on January 3, 1952, the requisite jurisdictional amount being present.

　On September 9, 1949, the Compass Travel Bureau, Inc., Cunard's New York agent, issued to Mr. and Mrs. Elias Siegelman document describing itself as a 'Contract Ticket.' ......

　On September 24, 1949, when the Queen Elizabeth had been at sea four days, Mrs. Siegelman was injured. While she was seated in a dining room chair, she and the chair were overthrown. Her chair was alleged to be the only one in the dining room which was not bolted to the floor. Upon returning to New York, the Siegelmans retained an attorney to prosecute their claim against Cunard. On August 31, 1950, after Cunard's doctor had examined Mrs. Siegelman, Cunard offered $800, the approximate amount of medical expenses stated to have been incurred by the plaintiff and his wife, in settlement of the claim. This offer was made to the Siegelmans' lawyer over the telephone by Swaine, a claim agent of Cunard. Noticing that the ticket required suits for bodily injury to be brought within a year of the injury, and that the injury had occurred

米国のニューヨーク州住民が英国の船会社との間に締結したニューヨーク＝シェルブール（フランス）間の国際旅客運送契約中に指定された英国法が事故の出訴期限の放棄に関する問題について適用された事例

HARLAN 巡回裁判官

　原告は，自身の権利において，かつ妻の遺産の管理人として，ニューヨークからシェルブールまでの航海の途中で妻が被告の船舶である R.M.S. クイーンエリザベス号の船上で被った傷害の損害賠償を求める訴訟を提起した．訴訟は，1951 年 12 月 14 日にニューヨーク州裁判所で始まり，州籍の相違により，1952 年 1 月 3 日にニューヨーク南部地区連邦地裁に移送された．管轄権のために必要な訴額は存在している．

　1949 年 9 月 9 日，Cunard のニューヨーク代理人である Compass Travel Bureau, Inc. は，Elias Siegelman 夫妻に「契約切符」と書かれた書類を発行した．……

　1949 年 9 月 24 日，クイーン・エリザベス号が 4 日間の航海中，Siegelman 夫人が傷害を被った．夫人が食堂の椅子に座っていたとき，彼女とその椅子がひっくり返った．食堂の中で彼女の椅子だけがフロアーにボルトで締められていなかったと主張されている．ニューヨークに帰って，Siegelman 夫妻は，Cunard に対する請求を実行するために弁護士を雇った．1950 年 8 月 31 日，Cunard は，Cunard の医師が Siegelman 夫人を診察した後，クレームの示談金として 800 ドルの申込をした．その額は原告とその妻が被ったと述べられていた医療費とほぼ同じであった．この申込は，Cunard の代理人である Swaine から Siegelman の弁護士に電話でなされた．弁護士は，人身傷害の訴訟は，傷害後 1 年以内に提起すべきことを切符が要求していることと，傷害がほぼ 1 年近く前に発生したことに気づいて，依頼人の権利を守るため

133

barely less than a year ago, the lawyer asked Swaine whether it would be necessary to begin suit in order to protect his clients' rights. Swaine is said to have stated that no suit was necessary, that the filing of an action would be futile in view of the prospect of early settlement, and that Cunard's offer would stand open.

Subsequently Mrs. Siegelman died. Then, on January 4, 1951, Cunard withdrew its offer, which had not yet been accepted, stating that it could not be tendered to any one other than the injured party.

On December 14, 1951, this suit was begun, claiming on behalf of the deceased damages for pain and medical expenses, and on behalf of her husband, damages for other medical expenses and for loss of consort. Cunard denied legal responsibility for the accident, and set up as a further defense the plaintiff's failure to bring the action within a year of the date the injury was suffered.

In January, 1953, the defendant moved to dismiss the action on the latter ground. Treating the motion as one for summary judgment, and having received affidavits from the attorneys and from the plaintiff, the court found the issues for the defendant, and dismissed the complaint.

On this appeal appellant asserts that Cunard is barred from using the period of limitation as a defense, because of Swaine's statement that suit was unnecessary. The provisions of the 'Contract Ticket' relevant to the appeal are as follows:

'10. ...... No suit, action or proceeding against the Company or the ship, or the Agents of either, shall be maintainable for loss of life of or bodily injury to any passenger unless...... (b) ...... the suit, action or proceeding is commenced within one year from the day when the death or injury occurred.

'11. The price of passage hereunder has been fixed partly with reference to the liability assumed by the Company as defined by this

に Cunard に対する訴訟を提起する必要があるかどうかを Swaine に聞いた．Swaine は，早期に合意が成立する見込みがあるから，訴状の提出は不要であり，Cunard の申込はそのまま撤回されずに維持されるだろうと答えたといわれている．

　その後，Siegelman 夫人が死亡した．それから，1951 年 1 月 4 日に，Cunard は，まだ承諾されていなかった申込を撤回し，申込は負傷した当事者以外の者に対してなされたものではないと述べた．

　1951 年 12 月 14 日，本件訴訟が始まり，死者に対しては慰謝料と医療費，夫に対してはその他の医療費と慰謝料が主張された．Cunard は，事故の法的責任を否認するとともに，さらに原告が傷害を被ってから 1 年以内に訴訟を提起しなかったことを抗弁として主張した．

　1953 年 1 月に，被告は後者を理由に訴訟を却下する申立をした．この申立を略式判決を求めるものとして扱い，弁護士と原告から宣誓供述書を受け取った後に，裁判所は被告勝訴の判断をし，申立を却下した．

　本件上訴において上訴人は，Cunard が訴訟の提起は必要ないと Swaine が言ったのだから，抗弁として出訴期限の経過を利用することはできない，と主張している．本件上訴に関連する「契約切符」の条項は以下のとおりである：

　「10. ……乗客に対する生命の喪失又は人身傷害に基づく，会社，船舶又その代理人に対する訴え，訴訟又は手続は，……(b)……訴え，訴訟又は手続が死亡又は傷害の日の 1 年以内に提起したものでない限り，維持することはできないものとする．

　「11. 以下の旅行価格は，この契約により会社が引き受ける責任に関して部分的に固定されるものとし，他の又は異なった責任を創設する合

contract, and no agreement, alteration or amendment creating any other or different liability shall be valid unless made in writing and signed for the Company by its Chief Agent at the port of embarkation.

　　'20. All questions arising on this contract ticket shall be decided according to English Law with reference to which this contract is made.'

　Before reaching the merits of the plaintiff's claim, we must deal with a number of preliminary questions: (1) Are federal or state choice-of-law rules to be applied here? (2) What is the applicable choice-of-law rule of the proper authority? (3) If the applicable choice-of-law rule points to the use of English law, what difference is made by the facts that English law was not pleaded or proved below, and that the plaintiff made no attempt to supply affidavits of experts on English law, after the trial Judge had offered him an opportunity to do so?

I ……

Ⅱ　Our next question is: under the federal choice-of-law rule, what law governs the issues here? We are not concerned with the law applicable to the accident. Instead we must decide what law applies to the validity and interpretation of certain provisions of the 'Contract Ticket,' and to the effect of Swaine's conduct upon Cunard's right to resort to the one-year limitation period in the contract.

　The ticket stipulated that 'All questions arising on this contract ticket

意，改訂又は変更は，乗船港の主たる代理人により，会社のために署名した文書によるのでなければ，有効ではないものとする．

「20．この契約切符から生じるすべての問題はこの契約がそれにしたがって締結される英国法により決定されるべきものとする．」

　原告の請求の適否に立ち入る前に，われわれは多くの予備的な問題を処理しなければならない．つまり，(1)本件で適用されるのは連邦の法選択規則か，それとも州のものか．(2)適切な権限ある機関の本件に適用される法選択規則とはどのようなものか．(3)適用される法選択規則が英国法を適用すべきことを指示するとすれば，原審では英国法が主張も立証もされなかったという事実と，事実審裁判官が原告にそうする機会を与えた後に，原告が英国法に関する専門家の宣誓供述書を提供しようとしなかったという事実との間にどのような違いがあるか．

I　［裁判所は，本件請求は，公海上で侵害が生じた不法行為ではないから，*Erie R. R. Co. v. Tompkins* 判決から生じる原則には服さないと判示する．したがって州ではなく，連邦の法選択規則が適用されることになるとする．］（訳者注）

II　われわれの次の問題は，連邦の法選択規則によれば，どの法が本件の争点に適用されるかである．われわれは事故に対して適用される法を問題としているのではない．そうではなく，われわれは，どの法が，「契約切符」の一定の条項の解釈，有効性及び Swaine のとった行動が契約中の1年の出訴期限を援用する Cunard の権利に対して有する効果の問題に適用されるかを決定しなければならないのである．

　切符は，「この契約切符から生じるすべての問題はこの契約がそれに従って

shall be decided according to English Law with reference to which this contract is made.' Considering, as we do, the ticket to be a contract —— see Foster v. Cunard White Star, 2 Cir., 1941, 121 F.2d 12 —— the provision that English law should govern must be taken to represent the intention of both parties. Therefore, this provision, if effective under the federal choice-of-law rule, renders English law applicable here, even though, absent the provision, some other law would govern under the applicable federal conflicts rule......

......[S]ince we cannot assume that the parties' choice of law will always foreclose the court from applying another law, our question is whether the contract provision here should have the effect, under federal conflicts rules, of making the English law applicable to the particular questions posed by this case. While this question may appear on the surface to be purely one of conflict of laws, we think it also involves interpretation of the contract. For it is not altogether free from doubt what is meant by the stipulation that 'All questions arising on this contract ticket shall be decided according to English Law......

......

Three questions as to the scope of this provision arise under its language. First, are questions to be decided by the 'whole' English law, including its conflicts rules, or just by the substantive English law? That is, are questions to be decided according to the law of England, or instead, as an English court might decide them, applying where appropriate the law of some other country?

We think the provision must be read as referring to the substantive law alone, for surely the major purpose of including the provision in the ticket was to assure Cunard of a uniform result in any litigation no matter where the ticket was issued or where the litigation arose, and this result might

締結される英国法により決定されるべきものとする」と規定している．本件切符を契約と考えるならば，われわれはそうするのだが，── Foster v. Cunard White Star, 2 Cir., 1941, 121 F.2d 12 参照 ── 英国法が適用されるという条項は，両当事者の意思を表明するものと解されねばならない．したがってこの条項が連邦の法選択規則上有効であれば，その条項がなければどこか他の法が連邦の抵触規則によれば適用される場合であっても，本件では英国法が適用されることになる……

……当事者の法選択が存在すれば，つねに裁判所が他の法を適用することを排除されると考えることはできないから，問題は，本件の契約条項が，連邦抵触規則上，本件で提起された特定の問題に対して英国法が適用されるとする効果を有するかどうかである．この問題は，表面上は，純粋に抵触法上の問題であるとみえるかもしれないが，それはまた，契約の解釈にも関連するものであると思われる．というのは，「この契約切符から生じるすべての問題は英国法により決定されるべきものとする……」という条項が意味するものがなにかは，完全に疑問の余地がないわけではないからである……
……

　この条項の範囲について文言上，3つの問題が生じる．第1に問題は，抵触法を含む「全」英国法によって決定されるべきか，それとも英国の実質法によって決定されるべきか．すなわち，問題は英国法に従って決定されるべきか，それとも英国の裁判所が問題を決定するのと同じように，適切な場合にはどこか他の国の法を適用しなければならないかどうか．

　この条項は実質法のみを指定したものと読まれなければならないと考える．というのは，たしかにこの条項を切符中に含めた主要な目的は，切符がどこで発行されようと，訴訟がどこで提起されようと，Cunard にどの訴訟においても統一的な結果を保証することにあり，そしてこの結果は英国の「全」

not obtain if the 'whole' law of England were referred to. Second, does the provision intend that questions of validity of the contract and its provisions, as well as questions of interpretation, are to be governed by English law? The language of the clause, covering 'all question,' indicates that validity as well as interpretation is embraced. Third, is the recital meant to require the application of English law to the question of what conduct may amount to a waiver of its provisions? Although the wording of the clause——relating to questions arising 'on' the contract ——may indicate that such a question was not meant to be covered, it appears unnatural to hold that all questions of validity and interpretation were intended to be governed by English law but that this question was not. We therefore consider that the question of what conduct was sufficient to operate as a waiver of the ticket's provisions was also meant to be determined by English law.

We now come to the inquiry as to the extent to which this provision, so construed, is to be given effect in deciding the particular issues before us. Those issues are: (1) Is the one-year limitation period provided in the contract for the bringing of suits valid? (2) Does Swaine's conduct prevent Cunard from using the period as a defense? and (3) How is this matter affected by the clause requiring alterations of the contract to be in writing? It appears not to be contested that the ticket should be treated as a contract and that failure to bring the action within the contract limitation period would be a defense under English law——see Jones v. Oceanic Steam Navigation Co., (1924) 2 K.B. 730, but since the same result would follow under American law——see 46 U.S.C.A. §183(b); Scheibel v. Agwilines, Inc., 2 Cir., 1946, 156 F.2d 636——we need not decide whether English law is applicable to the first of these issues. As to the second and third issues——where English and American law may differ ——in the view which we take of the case, we need really only deal with applicability of English law to the second issue——via., whether Swaine's conduct prevents Cunard from using the one-year limitations provision as

6 旅客運送契約中の準拠法約款：Siegelman v. Cunard White Star Ltd.

法が指定されているとすれば，確保されないからである．第2に，本条項は，契約の解釈の問題のみならず，契約とその条項の有効性の問題も英国法によるべきことを意図しているであろうか．「すべての問題」という本条項の文言は，解釈だけでなく，有効性もそれに含まれていることを示している．第3に，その記述は，どのような行為が本条項の放棄となるかという問題への英国法の適用を要求することを意味するのか．条項の——契約「から」生じる問題に関してとの——文言からはそのような問題はカバーされていないといえるかもしれないけれども，契約の有効性と解釈に関するすべての問題は英国法によると意図されていたが，この問題はそうでないと判断するのは不自然であると思われる．したがってどのような行為が切符の条項の放棄として，機能するに十分であるかの問題もまた英国法により決定されることを意味すると考える．

さてこれからわれわれは，そのように解釈された本条項がわれわれの前に提起された特定の争点を決定するに際して，有効と認められる限度に関する審理に取りかかる．これらの争点とは，(1)訴訟の提起に関し，契約中に規定された1年の出訴期限は有効か．(2) Swaine の行為は，Cunard が抗弁としてその期限を利用することを妨げるか．(3)このことは，契約の変更を書面にすべきことを要求する条項によって，どのように影響を受けるかである．切符が契約として扱われることと，契約の制限期間内に訴訟を提起しないことが英国法上抗弁となることは争われていない．——Jones v. Oceanic Steam Navigation Co., (1924) 2 K.B. 730 参照．しかし米国法によっても同じ結果となろう——46 U.S.C.A. §183 (b)；Scheibel v. Agwilines, Inc., 2 Cir. 1946, 156 F.2d 636 参照——われわれは，英国法がこれらの争点の最初のものに適用されるかどうかを決定する必要はない．第2，第3の争点に関しては，——英国法と米国法が異なるかもしれない——われわれの扱う事件のことを考えると，われわれは，第2の争点に対する英国法の適用のみを扱う必要がある——つまり，Swaine の行為は，Cunard が抗弁として1年の出訴期

a defense——although in light of what we say below we think that English law would clearly control the third issue——viz., the effect of the 'alterations' clause.

As we have said, we construe the contract as establishing the intention of the parties that English law should govern both the interpretation and validity of its terms. And we think it clear that the federal conflicts rule will give effect to the parties' intention that English law is to be applied to the interpretation of the contract. Stipulating the governing law for this purpose is much like stipulating that words of the contract have the meanings given in a particular dictionary. See Cheatham, Goodrich, Griswold, & Reese, Cases on Conflict of Laws 461 (1951). On the other hand, there is much doubt that parties can stipulate the law by which the validity of their contract is to be judged. Beale, Conflict of Laws §332.2 (1935). To permit parties to stipulate the law which should govern the validity of their agreement would afford them an artificial device for avoiding the policies of the state which would otherwise regulate the permissibility of their agreement. It may also be said that to give effect to the parties' stipulation would permit them to do a legislative act, for they rather than the governing law would be making their agreement into an enforceable obligation. And it may be further argued that since courts have not always been ready to give effect to the parties' stipulation, no real uniformity is achieved by following their wishes. See Beale, op. cit. supra, at page 1085.

Here, of course, the question is neither one of interpretation nor one of validity, but instead involves the circumstances under which parties may be said to have partially rescinded their agreements or to be barred from enforcing them. The question is, however, more closely akin to a question of validity. Nevertheless, we see no harm in letting the parties' intention control. See Hal Roach Studios, Inc., v. Film Classics, 2 Cir., 1946, 156

6 旅客運送契約中の準拠法約款：Siegelman v. Cunard White Star Ltd.

限を利用することを妨げるか——これに対し以下にわれわれが述べるところに照らせば，英国法が明らかに第3の争点——つまり，「変更」条項の効力をも規律すると考える．

さきに述べたように，われわれは，本件契約を英国法が契約の条項の有効性と解釈の双方に適用されるべきであるという当事者の意思を証明するものとして，解釈する．そして連邦抵触法規則は，英国法が契約の解釈に適用されるべきとの当事者の意思を有効と認めることは明らかであると考える．この目的のために準拠法を合意で定めることは，契約中の言葉が特定の辞書において与えられている意味を有していると合意で定めることとほとんど同じである．Cheatham, Goodrich, Griswold, & Reese, Cases on Conflict of Laws 461 (1951) 参照．他方，契約の有効性が判断されるべき法を当事者が合意により定めることができるかについては，大いに疑問がある．Beale, Conflict of Laws §332.2 (1935). 当事者にその合意を規律すべき法を指定することを許すことは，さもなければ彼らの合意を規律すべき州の政策を回避する恣意的な手段を当事者に付与することになるであろう．また，当事者の合意に効力を認めることは，当事者に立法的行為をなすことを許すことになるといわれることがある．というのは当事者の合意を強制力のある義務へと転換させるのは，準拠法ではなく，当事者だからである．そしてさらに，裁判所は当事者の合意をつねに有効なものと認めるとは限らないから，当事者の希望に従うことによって，現実の統一性が確保されるとは限らないといわれるかもしれない．Beale, 前掲1085頁参照．

もちろん，本件において問題となっているのは，有効性の問題でもないし，解釈の問題でもない．そうではなくてむしろ問題は，当事者がその合意を部分的に取り消した又は合意を実行することを禁じられる，といわれる状況にかかわるものなのである．しかしながら，この問題は有効性の問題により密接に類似している．それにもかかわらず，当事者の意思が支配することを認めることに不都合があるとは，われわれは思わない．Hal Roach Studios, Inc.,

F.2d 596, 598; Duskin v. Pennsylvania-Central Airlines Corp., 6 Cir., 1948, 167 F.2d 727, 729-730; Note, Commercial Security and Uniformity through Express Stipulations in Contracts as to Governing Law, 62 Harv. L.Rev. 647 (1949). Instead of viewing the parties as usurping the legislative function, it seems more realistic to regard them as relieving the courts of the problem of resolving a question of conflict of laws. Their course might be expected to reduce litigation, and is to be commended as much as good draftsmanship which relieves courts of problems of resolving ambiguities. To say that there may be no reduction in litigation because courts may not honor the provision is to reason backwards. A tendency toward certainty in commercial transactions should be encouraged by the courts. Furthermore, in England, where much of the litigation on these contracts might be expected to arise, the parties' stipulation would probably be respected. Vita Food Products, Inc. v. Unus Shipping Co., Ltd., (1939) A.C. 277 (P.C.) (similar provision in bill of lading given effect; construed, however, as referring to England's whole law, including its conflicts rules).

Where the law of the parties' intention has been permitted to govern the validity of contracts, it has often been said (1) that the choice of law must be bona fide, and (2) that the law chosen must be that of a jurisdiction having some relation to the agreement, generally either the place of making or the place of performance. The second of these conditions is obviously satisfied here.

The fact that a conflicts question is presented in the absence of a stipulation is some indication that the first condition is also satisfied. Furthermore, there does not appear to be an attempt here to evade American policy. We have no statute indicating a policy contrary to England's on this subject. Cf. New York Life Insurance Co. v. Cravens, 1900, 178 U.S. 389, 20 S.Ct. 962, 44 L.Ed. 1116. And there is no suggestion that English law is oppressive to passengers. We regard the primary purpose of making English law govern here as being not to substitute

v. Film Classics, 2 Cir., 1946, 156 F.2d 596, 598; Duskin v. Pennsylvania-Central Airlines Corp., 6 Cir., 1948, 167 F.2d 727, 729-730; Note, Commercial Security and Uniformity through Express Stipulations in Contracts as to Governing Law, 62 Harv.L.Rev. 647（1949）参照．当事者が立法的機能を奪っているとみるのではなく，抵触法問題を解決するという問題から裁判所を解放するものととらえることの方がより現実的であると思われる．そのやり方が訴訟を減少させることが期待され，曖昧なことを解決する問題から裁判所を解放する優れた起草者の技法として推奨されるべきである．裁判所が条項を尊重しないかもしれないから訴訟が減少することはあり得ないということは，誤った推論である．商取引の確実性に対する傾向は，裁判所により推進されるべきである．さらにこれらの契約から生じる訴訟の多くが提起されるかもしれない英国においては，当事者の指定は多分有効なものとして尊重されるであろう．Vita Food Products, Inc. v. Unus Shipping Co., Ltd.,（1939）A.C. 277（P.C.）（船荷証券における同様の条項が有効と認められた．しかし，抵触法を含む英国法全体を指すものと解釈された）．

　当事者の意図した法が契約の有効性を支配することを許容された場合に，(1)法選択は善意でなければならないこと，(2)選択された法は，合意となんらかの関係，一般的には締結地か，履行地のどちらかの関係を有する法域の法でなければならない，としばしばいわれてきた．本件ではこれらの要件の2番目は，明らかに満たされている．

　指定のない場合における抵触法問題が提起されているという事実は，第1の要件もまた満たされていることをいくぶんかは示唆している．さらに米国の政策を回避しようとする試みは本件では存在しないようにみえる．この問題に関する英国の政策に反するような政策を示唆するような制定法は存在しない．Cf. New York Life Insurance Co. v. Cravens, 1900, 178 U.S. 389, 20 S. Ct. 962, 44 L.Ed. 1116. そして英国法が乗客に抑圧的であるということはなんら示されていない．本件において英国法を支配させる主要な目的は，米国の政策の代わりに英国の政策を置き換えるというのではなく，むしろ一方

English for American policies, but rather on the one hand, to achieve uniformity of result, which is often hailed as the chief objective of the conflict of laws, and on the other hand, to simplify administration of the contracts in question. Cunard's employees need be trained in only one set of legal rules.

This is not to suggest that English and American policies on this subject are identical. Any difference in law reflects some difference in policy. Consequently, to the extent English and American policies may differ on this question, we would consider that the parties may choose to have the English policies apply. But we express no opinion on what result would follow if we had stronger policies at stake, or if the parties had attempted a feined rather than a genuine solution of the conflicts problem.

III We must next decide whether it is within our competence to apply English law, which was neither pleaded nor proved below.

......

IV Finally we come to the substantive question whether Swaine's conduct prevents Cunard from successfully invoking the contractual limitation period as a defense.

......

では，抵触法の主要な目的としてしばしば歓迎される結果の統一性を達成し，他方では，問題となっている契約の執行を容易化することにある，と考える．Cunardの従業員は，ただ一組の法規則のみによって訓練される必要がある．

このことはこの問題に関する英国と米国の政策が同一であることを意味するのではない．法におけるなんらかの相違は，政策におけるなんらかの相違を反映している．したがって，この問題に関して英国と米国の政策が異なる限りにおいて，当事者は英国の政策が適用されることを選択したものと，われわれは考える．しかし，もしもわれわれのもっと強い政策が危うくなったとすれば，又は当事者が抵触法問題の純粋な解決よりも偽装された解決を試みた場合に，どのような結果になるかについては，われわれはなんらの意見をも表明しない．

III　われわれは，次に原審で主張も立証もされなかった英国法を適用することがわれわれの権限内にあるかどうかを決定しなければならない．
　［裁判所は，英国法の内容が地裁の裁判官が理解したものではないことを立証するのは原告であり，そうすることは原告に許容されている，と判示する．］（訳者注）
……

IV　最後にSwaineの行動によって，Cunardが抗弁として契約上の出訴期限をうまく主張することができるかどうかという実質的な問題にわれわれは直面する．
……
　［裁判所は，英国法上，かりにSwaineが出訴期限を放棄する権限を与えられていたとしても，放棄も禁反言も存在しないと判示した．英国法は，禁反言を主張するためには，単に意思の不実表示ではなく，明示の約束と事実の不実表示を要求している．最後にSwaineの行動がかりに出訴期限を中断し

Affirmed.

FRANK, Circuit Judge (dissenting).

This case presents an important question relative to the rights of American passengers travelling from American ports on English vessels. Here a ticket, covering a voyage from New York to Cherbourg, was purchased by an American in New York. ...... The injury to the passenger occurred on the high seas on September 24, 1949. This suit was brought on December 14, 1951. The statute of limitations had not then run. But the district court granted a summary judgment, dismissing the suit, on the ground that clause 10 of the passenger's ticket provided that no suit should be commenced except within one year. The plaintiff's undisputed affidavit showed that, in New York, on August 31, 1949, about three weeks before the year expired, defendant's claim agent, in connection with an offer of settlement made by him to the passenger, told the latter's lawyer that it would not be necessary to file suit within the year. On January 4, 1951, after the year had elapsed, defendant withdrew the settlement offer.

Disregarding for the moment clause 20 of the ticket (referring to 'English law'), I think it clear that, under federal and New York decisions, the defendant waived (or is estopped to assert) the one-year provision (clause 10) and thereby completely abandoned it.

My colleagues, in holding that there was no waiver or estoppel, rely principally on that English decision and on clause 20 which reads: 'All questions arising on this contract ticket shall be decided according to English Law with reference to which this contract is made.'

I think this clause does not import 'English law' concerning a waiver after the injury occurred. For, at best, as my colleagues apparently

6　旅客運送契約中の準拠法約款：Siegelman v. Cunard White Star Ltd.

たとしても，Cunard が申込を撤回したときから，出訴期限は再び開始したのであるから，訴訟は禁止されるとした．〕（訳者注）

上訴棄却

FRANK 巡回裁判官（反対意見）
　本件は英国の船舶で米国の港から旅行する米国乗客の権利に関する重要な問題を提起する．本件ではニューヨークからシェルブールまでの航海をカバーする切符は，米国人によりニューヨークで購入された．……乗客に対する傷害は 1949 年 9 月 24 日に公海で発生した．本件訴訟は，1951 年 12 月 14 日に提起された．当時はまだ出訴期限法の期間は満了していなかった．しかし地方裁判所は，乗船切符の 10 条が訴訟は 1 年以内でない限り開始されるべきでないと規定していることを理由に，訴えを却下し，略式判決を認めた．争いのない原告の宣誓供述書によれば，1949 年 8 月 31 日にニューヨークで出訴期限が消滅する 3 週間前に被告のクレーム代理人が乗客に対する彼の和解の申込に関連して，乗客の弁護士にその年度内に訴訟を提起することは不要であると告げた．1951 年 1 月 4 日に年度が経過した後になって，被告は和解の申込を撤回した．

　（「英国法」を指定する）切符の 20 条をしばらく無視するとすれば，連邦及びニューヨークの判決によれば，被告が 1 年条項（10 条）を放棄した（又は主張することを禁反言により禁止される）こと，そしてそれによりそれを完全に断念したことは明らかであると思われる．
　私の同僚たちは，放棄も禁反言も存在しないと判示するにあたって，英国の判決と「契約から生じるすべての問題は，この契約がそれに従って締結された英国法により決定されるべきものとする」と書いてある 20 条に主として依拠する．
　私の考えるところでは，この条項は事故が発生した後の放棄の問題に関し

concede, the words 'on this contract' are ambiguous, i.e., do not (to say the least) unambiguously cover the post-injury conduct, in New York, of defendant's claim agent.

Because the contract was made in New York, for a journey beginning in New York, the usual rule is that its provisions must be interpreted according to New York 'law', or by the 'maritime law' which, as previously noted, must (absent decisions on the subject) be learned from federal 'law' as to internal transactions. ......

Surely, in interpreting that ambiguous provision, we should not look to English decisions. Thus to consult 'English law,' in interpreting an American contract ambiguously referring to 'English law,' would indeed be a pulling-yourself-up-by-your-own-bootstraps device. Especially is this true here, since the interpretation of a clause in a contract like this involves an important internal public policy. For, since the document was a fixed printed form prepared by defendant and tendered to the passenger, clause 20, under New York and federal decisions, must be construed most strongly against defendant.

This rule is given special emphasis when, as here, the contract contains a multitude of complicated provisions relative to a subject matter with which the tendering party is peculiarly familiar and the other party is not. See, e.g., Gaunt v. John Hancock Life Ins. Co., supra ...... There is an added fact, not here controlling but surely not to be ignored: The provisions of the ticket are printed in small type and in a crowded way. While they are not wholly illegible, they are difficult to read, as any one will discover who tries reading them. (One can be sure that the steamship company does not thus print its advertisements addressed to prospective passengers.)
......

て「英国法」を導入するものではない．せいぜいのところ，私の同僚が認めるように,「この契約から」という言葉は曖昧であり，つまり，被告のクレーム代理人の，ニューヨークにおける時効発生後の行為を（ごく控え目にいっても）明確にカバーするものではないからである．

　契約はニューヨークで始まる旅行のためにニューヨークで締結されたのであるから，通常の規則はその条項がニューヨーク「法」又はさきに指摘したように，（その点についての判決がない場合には）国内取引に関する連邦「法」から突き止められるべき「海事法」に従って解釈されなければならない．……
　その曖昧な条項を解釈するにあたって，英国法をみるべきではないことは明らかである．かくして「英国法」に曖昧に言及する米国契約を解釈するに際して，「英国法」を参照することは，実際には自分の靴のつまみ皮で自分を引っ張り上げるようなやり方である．とくにこのことは本件に当てはまる．というのは本件のような契約中の条項の解釈は，重要な国内的公序にかかわるからである．文書は被告によって準備された固定した印刷方式で乗客に交付されたのであるから，20条は，ニューヨークと連邦の判決によれば被告に最も厳しく不利に解釈さなければならない．

　この原則は，本件のように契約が交付する当事者にはとくによく知られており，他方の当事者にはそうでない事項についての多数の複雑な条項を含んでいるときはとくに強調されるべきである．たとえば，前掲 Gaunt v. John Hancock Life Ins. Co., ……参照．さらに本件では決定的ではないが，無視することのできない付加的な事実がある．すなわち，切符の条項は小さな字体で，ぎっしりと印刷されている．それらは全く読めないというわけではないが，誰かがそれを読もうと試みる人を見つけたとしても，それを読むのは困難である．（船会社は乗客となるべき人向けの宣伝にこのように印刷しないのは確かであろう.）
……

I call attention to another factor which, while unnecessary to my conclusion, I think supports it: The ticket is what has been called a 'contract of adhesion' or a 'take-it-or-leave-it' contract. In such a standardized or massproduction agreement, with one-sided control of its terms, when the one party has no real bargaining power, the usual contract rules, based on the idea of 'freedom of contract,' cannot be applied rationally. For such a contract is 'sold not bought.' The one party dictates its provisions; the other has no more choice in fixing those terms than he has about the weather. The insurance policy cases are outstanding examples, but there are many others. Our courts, in particular contexts, have, in effect, nullified many provisions of such agreements, if unfair to the weaker party who must take-or-leave. Often our courts have done so by rather strained constructions of seemingly unambiguous language or by other indirect or 'back-door' methods. Referring to such decisions, several brilliant commentators have suggested that the courts forthrightly adopt a general doctrine which calls for refusal to enforce directly ─ i.e., without recourse to such indirect devices ─ highly unfair provisions of all so-called 'contracts of adhesion' where there was no possibility of real bargaining. These writers urge that some decisions, in cases where this point of view was not presented to, or considered by, the courts should not now be deemed controlling. Their position is that of Holmes and Corbin, i.e., that the courts will do justice better by forthrightly, not obliquely, articulating important doctrines of public policy. The commentators on 'adhesion' contracts do not at all suggest that all standardized contracts be stricken down, for they recognize that such contracts often serve a highly useful purpose where the parties are not markedly unequal in bargaining power (as in many 'commercial' contracts).

私の結論に不必要ではあるが，結論を支持すると思われる，もう1つ別の要素に注意を喚起したい．切符は，いわゆる「附合契約」又は「甘受するか止めにするか」といわれる契約である．このような条件が一方的にコントロールされ，標準化された，又は大量的な合意において，当事者の一方がなんら現実の交渉力を有しない場合には，「契約自由の原則」の観念に基づく通常の契約規則が適用されるとするのは合理的ではない．なぜならそのような契約は，「買われるのではなく，売られるのである」．一方当事者が契約の条項を決定する．他方の当事者はこの条項の決定に何の選択権をも有しないのは，彼が天候についてなんらの選択権をも有しないのと同様である．保険証券がその顕著な例であるが，ほかに多くのものがある．われわれの裁判所は，特定のコンテキストの下で，このような契約の多くの条項が甘受するか，止めにするかしなければならない弱い当事者にとって不公正な場合には，実際にはそれを無効と判示してきた．裁判所はしばしば，みたところ明白な言葉を不自然に解釈したり，あるいは他の間接的ないしは「裏口」操作により，そうしてきた．これらの判決に依拠しつつ，若干の優れた学者は現実的な交渉の可能性が全くなかった場合には，裁判所は率直にすべての「附合契約」の非常に不公正な条項を直接的に——つまり，前述のような間接的操作に頼ることなく——，その履行を拒否すべきことを示唆してきた．これらの学者は，裁判所にこのような観点が提示されていないか，考慮されていない判決は，いまや支配的なものと考えるべきでないと強く主張している．彼らの立場は，HolmesやCorbinの立場，つまり，裁判所は遠回しにではなく，率直に，公序にかかわる重要な理論をはっきりと表現することによって正義を行おうとする立場なのである．「附合」契約に関して，これらのコメンテイターは，決してすべての標準契約を取り消すべきだというわけではない．というのは，このような契約がしばしば当事者がその交渉力において顕著に不平等でない場合には（多くの「商業的」契約のように），非常に有益な目的に奉仕するものであることを彼らは認めているからである．

All this has special pertinence hare: A party, like the passenger here, having no real choice about the matter, cannot in fairness be said to have joined in a 'choice of law' merely because the carrier has inserted a provision that some particular foreign 'law' shall govern; therefore it would seem that that party should not be bound by such a provision. I shall not elaborate this point, since it is amply discussed in a recent excellent article, Ehrenzweig, 'Adhesion Contracts in The Conflict of Laws,' 53 Col. L. Rev. (1953) 1072, where most of the authorities are cited and considered.

I grant that, in this context, I am stressing the need to do justice in particular instances. I do so unashamedly. For it is generally agreed that the decisions of conflict-of-laws cases by mechanized rules, without regard to particularized justice, cannot be defended on the ground that they have promoted certainty and uniformity, since such results have not been thus achieved. Several wise commentators have urged that the element of justice should have a dominating influence. ......

6 旅客運送契約中の準拠法約款：Siegelman v. Cunard White Star Ltd.

　以上のことすべては，本件ではとくによく当てはまる．本件の乗客のような当事者は，事柄について全く現実の選択権をもたず，単に運送人がどこかある特定の外国「法」が規律すべきであるという条項を挿入したという理由で，「法選択」に参加したとは公平にみていえない．したがって，この当事者はこのような条項によって拘束されるべきではないと思われる．この点は，Ehrenzweig, Adhesion Contracts in The Conflict of Laws 53 Col. L. Rev（1953）1072, という優れた論文において詳細に論じられているので，私は検討を差し控える．そこではほとんどの典拠が引用され，検討されている．

　この点に関連して，私は個々の事案において正義を行う必要性を強調していることを認める．私は恥じることなくそうする．というのは，個々の事案に即した正義を考慮しない機械的な規則による抵触法事件の決定は，それが確実性と統一性を促進するという理由では，そのような結果は達成されないがゆえに，正当化されるものではないからである．正義という要因が決定的な影響力をもつべきことは，幾人かの賢明な学者の主張するところである．
……

　[Frank 裁判官の反対意見の結論部分は，多数意見が放棄による禁反言に関する英国法を誤って解釈していると論じている．なお，附合契約に関する議論に加えて，Frank 判事は多数意見に対して次の理由からも反対している．①多数意見によって解釈されている英国法はアメリカの公序に反する．②約款 20 条の解釈，すなわち放棄の問題はこの条項の範囲外である．③アメリカ法が放棄の問題を支配する．④反致により英国の抵触法規則が適用され，これによればアメリカ法が適用される．⑤多数意見による英国実質法の解釈は正しくない．]（訳者注）

Ⅱ　法選択（準拠法）

【解　説】

　本件は，米国のニューヨーク州住民が英国の船会社との間に締結したニューヨーク＝シェルブール（フランス）間の国際旅客運送契約中に指定された英国法が事故の出訴期限の放棄に関する問題について適用されるとした事例である．

1　アメリカ国際私法における当事者自治の原則
　本件は，1955年の比較的古い判決であるが，契約の準拠法として，当事者自治を認めた判決のリーディングケースとして有名である．Richman & Reynolds, Understanding Conflict of Laws,（3rd ed. 2002）at 224-225. 多くのケースブックでも取り上げられている．たとえば，Currie, Kay & Kramer, Conflict of Laws,（6th ed. 2001）at 98-101; Hay, Weintraub & Borchers, Conflict of Laws（11th ed. 2000), at 479-486 ； Lowenfeld, Conflict of Laws: Federal, and International Perspective, 259-270（2d ed.1998）など．
　1934年の第1リステイトメントは，契約の準拠法として，主として契約締結地法主義を採用し，当事者による準拠法の指定を認めていなかった．第1リステイトメントの報告者であったBeale教授も，当事者による指定は，本来適用されるべき法の適用を回避する手段を当事者に与えることになるばかりでなく，当事者に立法的行為をなすことを許すことになるとして，これを否定していた．これに対して，近時は，確実性・予見可能性の確保，当事者の正当な期待の保護，国際・州際取引の安全，実質法における契約自由の原則を根拠に当事者自治の原則を肯定する立場が有力となった．この点について詳しくは，松岡博『アメリカ国際私法の基礎理論』1-41頁（大阪大学出版会，2007）参照．

2　第2リステイトメントにおける当事者自治の原則とその制限
　1971年の第2リステイトメント第187条も本件と同様，当事者自治の原則を採用する．問題となるのは，当事者の意思が契約の準拠法を決定するこ

とを認めた場合において，これにどのような制限を設けるかである．この点については，第2リステイトメント第187条第2項が重要であるが，この点は次の *Nordson* 判決と *Southern International* 判決で取り上げることにしたい．

3　附合契約における準拠法約款の効力

　本件はまた，附合契約における当事者自治を否定する少数意見でも有名である．

　多数意見は乗船切符を契約と考え，その準拠法約款に規定された英国法が権利の放棄の問題を支配することを承認した．多数意見によれば，当事者自治承認の根拠は多面的であるが，強調されているのは統一性の確保であろう．つまり，当事者自治の妥当性の根拠として，第2リステイトメントや学説が主として確実性，予見可能性の確保と当事者の正当な期待の保護をあげるのと比べると，旅客運送契約が大量契約であり，したがって統一的な計画と計算に基づく事業遂行のために，統一性の確保が重要であるという指摘が重要であろう．切符中にこの条項を含ませる主要な目的は，切符がどこで発行され，訴訟がどこで提起されたとしても船会社にどの訴訟においても統一ある結果を確保せしめるにあり，「Cunard の従業員は，ただ一組の法規則のみによって訓練される必要がある」．

　多数意見が，本件の旅客運送契約に対して普通の契約と同様に，当事者自治の原則が依然として妥当するものとしたのに対して，Frank 裁判官の反対意見は，本件のような附合契約に対しては契約自由の原則の観念に基づく通常の契約規則が適用されるべきではなく，別個の取扱いが必要であったと主張する．

　少数意見によれば，本件の乗客は保険契約の申込人と同様，準拠法の決定に現実の選択権をもたず，契約における準拠法の指定は当事者双方の相互の合意によりなされたのではなく，優越当事者である船会社により一方的に挿入されたものであるから，乗客は公正にみて法選択に参加したとはいえず，したがって，この法選択条項に拘束されないとする．従来の判例の立場が，

附合契約における法選択条項を無効と判示するにしても，公序その他の間接的操作を通じてなされたのに対して，少数意見はそのような間接的操作に頼ることなく，不平等な交渉力を有する当事者間で優越当事者により一方的に起案された法選択条項は，契約の自由を欠くがゆえに，無効であるという一層明確な立場を採用した．その意味できわめて画期的なものであり，附合契約における当事者自治の妥当性を否定する学説，判例の有力な典拠として援用される．

もっとも多数意見が附合契約においてつねに当事者自治を承認することを意味するのではない．多数意見は当事者自治に対する制限として，当事者の法選択は善意でなければならないとし，英国法の内容は抑圧的（oppressive）でないから英国法の指定は無効ではないと判示している．したがって，指定された法律の内容が乗客にとってきわめて不利で苛酷なときは，準拠法約款の効力が否定される余地はある．したがって，多数意見と反対意見の対立は，本件において，英国法を適用することが乗客に苛酷な，不公正な結果を招来するかどうかについての判断の差違にあるといえる．

4　第2リステイトメントにおける解決

抵触法第2リステイトメントは，附合契約については第187条注釈bで次のようにいう．

　　不正（impropriety）又は錯誤　　法選択条項は，他の契約条項と同様に，契約中にその条項を挿入することに対する当事者一方の同意が不実表示，強迫，不当威圧又は錯誤によって得られたのであれば，有効とはなしえないであろうとする．法廷地が考慮するかもしれないもう1つの要素は法選択条項が「附合」契約，すなわち優位当事者によって一方的に起案され，その条項について約定する現実の機会を有しない劣位の当事者に「甘受するか止めにするか」（take-it-or-leave-it）の基礎の上に呈示される契約のうちに含まれているかどうかである．このような契約は通常印刷方式で準備され，かつ少くともその条項中あるものは極小の印刷字体になっていることが多い．各種の乗車券及び保険証券が普通の事例である．この種の契約に含まれている法選択条項は

通常は尊重される．それにもかかわらず，裁判所はこの契約を慎重に吟味する．そして，万一，法選択条項の適用が附合契約加入者に実質上不公正の結果となるならば，裁判所はこの条項の適用を拒むだろう．Restatement Second Conflict of Laws, §187, comment b（1971）．

このように第2リステイトメントにおいては，附合契約における準拠法約款は通常有効である．報告者Reese教授によれば，附合契約中の法選択は無条件に無効であると述べることは賢明でないと考えられた．その理由はこの種の契約はアメリカで広く利用されており，弁護士と訴訟依頼人の時間と費用を節約する有用な方法であるためであると説明される．Reese, *Discussion of Major Areas of Choice of Law*, REQUIL DES COURS, 1964-I, 315 at 371. しかし，不公正の可能性はつねに存在するから，準拠法約款の適用が顧客に実質上不公正の結果となる場合にはその効力を否定されることになる．

5 *Fricke* 判決

次に附合契約に関する注目すべき判決として，2年後のニューヨーク連邦南部地裁の *Fricke v. Isbrandtsen Co.* 151 F. Supp. 465（S.D.N.Y.1957）がある．この判決では，被告船会社による略式判決の申立に関して，ドイツで発行された切符に規定されたアメリカ法の適用を指定する条項の効力が否定された．

原告は英語を解しないドイツ国民で，被告船会社からドイツでアメリカ合衆国への回遊の乗船切符を購入した．切符は英語で書かれ，1年の出訴期限条項と合衆国法を指定する法選択条項を含んでいた．ドイツへの帰国の航海中，原告が負傷し，訴訟は事故の2年後に提起された．

被告が1年の出訴期限を理由に原告の請求を却下する略式判決を申し立てたのに対して，原告は契約条項における合衆国法の指定にもかかわらず，ドイツ法が支配し，同法によれば1年の禁止には効力が与えられないと主張した．裁判所は次のように判示して，合衆国法の指定を無効とした．

本契約に合衆国の法律が適用されるとすれば，原告の請求は禁止されるから，本件の争点は契約を支配するのは合衆国法かどうかである．通常，連邦

Ⅱ　法選択（準拠法）

　裁判所は,「連結点の集中」又は「重心の発見」により契約準拠法を決定する．当事者が準拠法を指定した場合には当事者の期待はその選択を認めることにより，最もよく効力を与えられる．しかし，裁判所の調査は契約条項に限定されない．私人による選定は，裁判所による準拠法決定における重要な要素ではあるが，1つの要素であるにすぎない．多くの要素の考慮は，本件の場合とくに適切である．

　本件のようなタイプの契約は当事者の要求が相互に調整される対等な交渉力の結果として成立するわけではない．むしろ，標準約款が甘受するか，止めにするかという形で乗客に押しつけられる．解釈の統一を確保し，無効の判決を避けるために，この種の契約にはしばしば法選択条項が含まれている．このような条項は Siegelman 判決では効力が認められたが，同事件では契約の締結に関するすべての事項が合衆国で発生したから，裁判所は法選択に関して，アメリカの契約観念を自由に適用できると考えた．しかし本件では切符の販売に関するすべての事項はドイツで発生した．原告がなんらかの法律に思い及んだとすれば，ドイツ法が支配すると感じたであろう．多分ドイツ法は原告のような地位にある当事者に保護を与えるだろう．このような保護は強力な国家的政策となろう．連邦抵触法は多くの重要な連結点の存する外国主権のこのような態度を容認すべきものと思われる．当事者は自ら法選択を規定することによって予見可能性と統一性を追求することは排除されるべきではないけれども，この種の一方的に課せられた規定は履行を主張する当事者が契約内容に無知な他方当事者にその内容を知らせているのでない限り，履行されるべきではない．たとえば，もし原告がドイツ語の写しを与えられ，その規定を理解していれば合衆国法の指定が原告を拘束するであろう．

　裁判所は，このように切符中の合衆国法の指定の効力を否定し，被告による略式判決の申立を却下した．本件で合衆国法を指定する準拠法約款の効力が否定されたのは次の理由によるものと思われる．まず契約準拠法は契約の重心の発見によりなされるが，本件ではこの契約の重心がアメリカ合衆国ではなく，ドイツにあるとされたことである．契約の重心が存在する国を決定するにあたって，当事者による明示の法選択が存在する場合にはこの当事者

6 旅客運送契約中の準拠法約款：Siegelman v. Cunard White Star Ltd.

の法選択は，裁判所による準拠法決定の重要な要素であるにしても，単なる1つの要素にすぎない．しかも附合契約における準拠法約款は対等の交渉力をもたない劣位の当事者に対して一方的に課せられるのであるから，顧客にその内容を知らせるのでない限り，裁判所による準拠法決定の要因としてはほとんど意味をもたないとされる．このように判旨は，附合契約に対してその特殊性を考慮し，当事者の法選択が契約の準拠法決定にとって占めるウエイトを通常の契約よりは軽くみるという立場を採用した．第2に，原告であるドイツ人乗客を保護しようとするドイツの強力な国家的政策が強調されている．このことから，約款に規定された法律の適用が原告を不利にし，不公正な結果を招来するときは，準拠法約款の効力を否定するとの立場に本件判旨がたつと解釈することも可能であろう．

しかし，本件においても準拠法約款の効力が乗客を拘束する可能性は全面的に否定されているわけではない．まず，本件において契約の重心の存在するドイツの法律が規定されていたとすれば，その有効性は疑いの余地はない．さらに判旨が，「原告がドイツ語の写しを与えられ，その規定を理解していれば，合衆国法の指定が原告を拘束するであろう．」と述べているところからすれば，乗客が内容について注意を受け，理解したときは，契約の重心の存在しない国の法を指定する準拠法約款の効力が承認される余地がある．しかしこの場合でも，乗客がその内容について注意を受け，理解したとすれば，乗客の側に法選択の現実性ありとして直ちに準拠法約款が有効とされると解することは妥当ではないであろう．つまり本件は，合衆国が事案に最も密接な関連を有しないにしても，相当程度に密接な関連を有している場合であることを無視することはできないのである．したがって，準拠法約款に指定された法の国が，契約と実質的な関連を有し，かつ，顧客による選択の現実性が存在する限りでは，その準拠法約款の効力が承認される可能性が高いであろう．

重心理論を採用するその他の判決については，松岡博『国際取引と国際私法』（晃洋書房，1993）255-62頁以下参照．

Ⅱ　法選択（準拠法）

【本件参考文献】

松岡博『国際取引と国際私法』（晃洋書房，1993）235頁以下，とくに246-255頁．

【設　問】

1　本件の主要な争点はなにか．その点に関する英国法と米国法はどのように異なるか．
2　事実と当事者がニューヨーク，英国，フランスに対して有する関連を整理せよ．
3　原告の請求はどのようなものか．被告の考えられる反論はどのようなものか．
4　事実審の結論はどうか．その理由は？
5　多数意見は，契約の有効性の問題についてどこの国の法が適用されると考えているか．多数意見は，上の根拠をどのように考えているか．第2リステイトメント第187条の根拠（松岡博『アメリカ国際私法の基礎理論』（大阪大学出版会，2007）26-28頁）と比較せよ．
6　当事者の意思が契約の有効性の準拠法を決定することを認めた場合において，判旨のいう当事者による準拠法の指定が有効とされる2つの要件とはどのようなものか．
7　多数意見は，本件の争点に関する英国法をどのように理解し，適用しているか
8　附合契約とはどのようなものか．附合契約における準拠法約款の効力についてのFrank裁判官の反対意見を要約せよ．
9　契約中の合衆国法の指定が附合契約であることを理由に無効とされたFricke判決を紹介せよ．
10　附合契約に関する第2リステイトメント第187条注釈bを説明せよ．
11　本件はどのような判決か．また本件の結論，理由づけに賛成か．

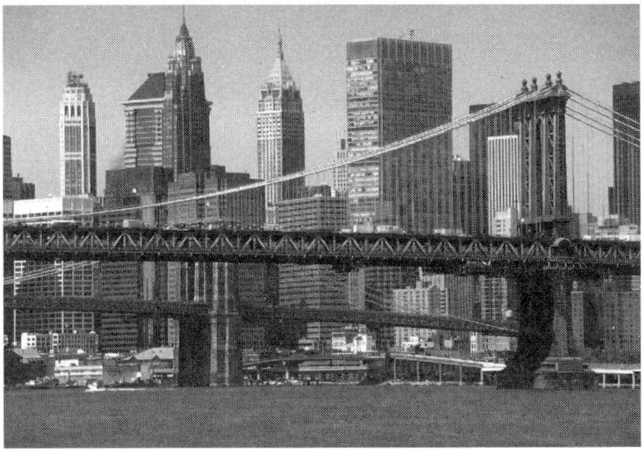

7 競業禁止約款の準拠法：
Nordson Corp. v. Plasschaert, 674 F.2d 1371 (11th Cir.1982)

GODBOLD, Chief Judge:

In this diversity action the District Court, N.D. Ga., issued a preliminary injunction enjoining Joseph Plasschaert, a former employee of Nordson Corporation, from using or disclosing confidential information concerning Nordson's processes and products. The court ordered Plasschaert to return to Nordson all records of confidential information in his possession. It further enjoined him from engaging in any work until May 15, 1982 involving: (1) research, development or engineering relating to hot-melt application equipment, (2) the promotion or sale of hot-melt application equipment in the United States, Canada, and Western Europe, or (3) situations in which loyal fulfillment of his duties and responsibilities would inherently call upon him to reveal or otherwise to use proprietary or confidential information or trade secrets acquired from Nordson or relating to Nordson's activities.

Plasschaert appeals, and we affirm.

I Nordson, an Ohio corporation headquartered in Amherst, Ohio, is the world's leading manufacturer of application equipment for hot-melt adhesives. Plasschaert, a Dutch subject, was employed in 1972 to serve as an area sales manager of hot-melt adhesive equipment in southern Holland. In 1975 he transferred to Brussels, Belgium, to become marketing coordinator of the European market, and there in 1977 he was promoted to marketing manager. In November 1978 Nordson transferred Plasschaert to its Norcross, Georgia, Packaging and Assembly Division office as a marketing specialist-product assembly. In this capacity he was

雇用契約中の準拠法約款に指定された雇用者の本拠地法であるオハイオ州法を適用し，オランダ人従業員との間に締結された競業禁止約款の効力を承認した事例

GODBOLD 首席裁判官

州籍の相違に基づく本件訴訟において，ジョージア北部地区地方裁判所は，Nordson Corporation の元従業員である Joseph Plasschaert が Nordson の製法と製品に関する秘密情報を使用，開示することを禁じる暫定的差止命令を出した．同裁判所はさらに，Plasschaert が Nordson に彼の所有するすべての秘密情報の記録を返還することをも命じた．さらに 1982 年の 5 月 15 日まで次の事項に関するすべての業務に彼が従事することを禁止した．(1)熱可塑性接着剤使用装置に関する研究，開発又はエンジニアリング，(2)合衆国，カナダ，西ヨーロッパにおける熱可塑性接着剤使用装置の販売促進又は販売，(3)彼がその義務と責任を忠実に果たせば，もともと Nordson から獲得したか，又は Nordson の活動に関連した財産，秘密情報又はトレード・シークレットを開示するか，使用することにならざるを得ないような業務．

Plasschaert が上訴し，われわれは上訴を棄却する．

I Nordson は，オハイオのアマーストに本拠を有するオハイオ会社であり，熱可塑性接着剤使用装置の世界的な指導メーカーである．Plasschaert は，オランダ国民であり，南オランダにおける熱可塑性接着剤装置の地区セールス・マネージャーとして 1972 年に雇用された．1975 年に彼は，ベルギーのブラッセルに転勤になり，ヨーロッパ市場のマーケティング・コーディネーターとなり，そこで 1977 年にマーケティング・マネージャーに昇進した．1978 年 11 月に Nordson は，Plasschaert をジョージアのノークロスにある同社の梱包・組立事業部門事務所に製品組立マーケティング・スペシャ

to ascertain new uses for hot-melt equipment but was not to sell or engineer the products.

In connection with this last transfer Plasschaert executed an "Employee Agreement" on November 15, 1978, in Doraville, Georgia, which contained the following excerpts:

I am employed or desire to be employed by Nordson in a capacity in which I may receive or contribute to confidential information. In consideration of such employment or continued employment, and in consideration of being given access to confidential information, I agree to the following:

1. In this agreement:
* * * * * * *
b. Confidential Information means ......

2. Except as required in my duties to Nordson, I will never, either during my employment by Nordson or thereafter, use or disclose any Confidential Information as defined above. Upon termination of my employment with Nordson, all records of Confidential Information including copies thereof in my possession, whether prepared by me or others, will be left with Nordson.
* * * * * * *
4. I promise that during my employment and for a period of two (2) years immediately following the termination of my employment with Nordson or for such part of the two (2) years as may be found lawful, I will not, either as principal, agent, consultant, employee, or otherwise, engage in any work involving any of the following:

a. Research, development or engineering relating to items similar to or competitive with the products I have been assigned to work on or the products I actually do work on at Nordson;

b. The promotion and/or sale of any similar product in direct competition with the line of Nordson which I have promoted and/or

リストとして転勤させた．この立場で，彼は熱可塑性装置の新しい使用法を確認することになっていたが，製品を販売したり，設計することにはなっていなかった．

この最後の転勤に関連して，ジョージアのドラビルにおいて Plasschaert は1978 年 11 月 15 日に「従業員契約」を締結したが，そこには以下に抜粋するところが含まれていた．

　秘密情報を私が受け取り又は貢献することとなるかもしれない立場で，私は Nordson によって雇用されるか，又は雇用されることを希望します．そのような雇用又は雇用継続の対価として，そして秘密情報へのアクセスの機会が与えられることの対価として，私は以下のことに同意します．
　1．この合意文書において：
* * * * * *
　b．秘密情報とは，……を意味する．
　2．Nordson に対する私の義務として要求される場合を除き，Nordson による雇用期間中又その終了後も上に定義されたいかなる秘密情報も私は決して使用又は開示しません．Nordson との雇用終了にあたっては，秘密情報のすべての記録は，私の所有するそのコピーも含めて，私が準備したものであるかどうかにかかわりなく，Nordson のもとに置いていきます．
* * * * * *
　4．私の雇用中及び Nordson との雇用終了後の直近の 2 年間又は適法とされる 2 年の期間内は，本人，代理人，コンサルタント，従業員その他のいかなるものとしてであれ，次に掲げるものに関する業務には，私が従事しないことを約束します．
　a．私が業務担当を割り当てられた製品又は Nordson で実際に仕事を担当した製品と類似又は競合する品目に関する研究，開発又はエンジニアリング；

sold in the same territory or any part thereof during any part of the two-year period immediately preceding the termination of my employment with Nordson;

c. Situations in which the loyal fulfillment of my duties and responsibilities would inherently call upon me to reveal or otherwise to use proprietary or confidential information or trade secrets acquired while at Nordson and relating to Nordson activities.

If I am unable to obtain employment consistent with my abilities and education within one month after termination of my employment with Nordson, because of provisions of this paragraph, such provisions shall thereafter continue to bind me only as long as Nordson shall make payments to me equal to three fourths of my monthly base pay at termination (exclusive of extra compensation, bonus or employee benefits) for each month of such employment, commencing with the second month after termination of my employment with Nordson.

* * * * * *

5. It has been explained to me and I agree that because Nordson has various divisions throughout the country and the world, these obligations will be interpreted and construed in accordance with the laws of the State of Ohio so that everyone will be treated fairly should disputes ever arise.

Plasschaert became disenchanted with his prospects with Nordson and in late 1979 made plans to return to Europe to compete against Nordson. To this end he contacted Peter Dittberner, head of Dittberner, Gmbh, a German competitor of Nordson, in an effort to become a distributor of its hot-melt application equipment. No agreement was reached at that time. In February 1980 Plasschaert incorporated Ranier Corporation. In late April or early May 1980 he prepared the Ranier Plan, a document containing a variety of information on the hot-melt equipment market in general and on Nordson's business in particular. Plasschaert took the

b．Nordsonの系列と直接競合するすべての類似する製品を，私が販売促進し，及び／又は，販売したと同じ地域又はそのどの部分においてもNordsonとの私の雇用終了直近の2年間のうちどの期間内においても，販売促進及び／又は販売すること；

c．私がその義務と責任を忠実に果たせば，もともとNordsonにいる間に獲得し，Nordsonの活動に関連した財産，秘密情報又はトレード・シークレットを開示するか，使用することにならざるを得ないような業務．

もし私が，本パラグラフの条項のために，Nordsonとの雇用の終了後1ヶ月以内に私の能力と教育にふさわしい雇用を獲得できなかったときは，これらの条項はその後も継続して，私を拘束します．ただし，Nordsonが私に終了時の私の月額の基本給（特別報酬，ボーナスまたは従業員給付金を除く）の4分の3の額を，Nordsonとの雇用の終了後の次の月から始めて，その雇用の期間中毎月支払うときに限ります．

＊　＊　＊　＊　＊　＊

5．Nordsonが合衆国と世界中に多数の事業所を有しているために，紛争が発生した場合にすべての者が公平に取り扱われるように，これらの義務はオハイオ州法によって解釈されるという説明を私は受けて，それに合意します．

Plasschaertは，自己の将来の見通しについてNordsonに幻滅を感じて，1979年の終わり頃にはヨーロッパに帰って，Nordsonと競業する計画を作成した．この目的を達成するために，彼は，Nordsonのドイツの競争相手であるDittberner社のトップであるPeter Dittbernerとコンタクトをとり，その熱可塑性装置のディストリビューターになろうとした．そのときは合意は成立しなかった．1980年2月にPlasschaertは，Ranier Corporationを設立した．1980年4月の終わりか，5月の初めに，彼は，熱可塑性装置市場一般と，とくにNordsonの業務に関する情報を含む文書Ranier Planを準備した．

Ranier Plan to Europe in early May and showed at least two pages of it to Peter Dittberner during one of two meetings in which Plasschaert again sought to become a distributor for Dittberner's hot-melt equipment. Again no firm agreement was reached. During this trip Plasschaert obtained financing for his new business and arranged to move his family back to Europe.

Nordson found out about the Ranier Plan because, on this same trip to Europe, Plasschaert showed the plan to a fellow Nordson employee who photocopied and gave it to his superiors who forwarded it to Nordson's management in Ohio. Plasschaert resigned May 12. Nordson filed suit May 14 against Plasschaert and Ranier Corporation alleging that they violated Nordson's common law protection of trade secrets, that Plasschaert breached the employee agreement with regard to disclosure of confidential information and the covenant not to compete, and that Plasschaert engaged in unfair competition with Nordson by his alleged attempt to solicit Nordson employees to join Ranier through use of the Ranier Plan.

The Georgia district judge analyzed this case with care and precision. He recognized that if he applied Georgia principles concerning covenants not to compete Plasschaert's covenant would be unenforceable because two of the subparagraphs contained no limitations on their territorial scope. However, Nordson and Plasschaert specified in paragraph 5 of the agreement that their obligations under the contract would be governed by Ohio law. The court found that under Georgia's conflict of laws rules Georgia would honor this choice by the parties of Ohio law as controlling. Then, applying the law of Ohio, which will enforce a covenant not to compete to the extent necessary to protect the employer's legitimate interests, the court declined to limit the injunction to only one line of hot-melt equipment, limited the geographical scope of the injunction to Western Europe, the United States and Canada (while refusing to limit it to only

Plasschaert は，5月の初めに Ranier Plan をもってヨーロッパに行き，Plasschaert が再び Dittberner の熱可塑性装置のディストリビューターになろうとして求めた2回の会合の1つにおいて，少なくとも2頁を Peter Dittberner に示した．このときも確たる合意は成立しなかった．Plasschaert はこの出張中に彼のビジネスに対する融資を獲得し，家族をヨーロッパに移住させる手配をした．

Nordson は Ranier Plan のことを察知した．というのは，Plasschaert がこのヨーロッパへの出張中にこのプランを同僚の Nordson 従業員に示したが，その者がそれをコピーし，上司に渡し，その上司がオハイオの Nordson の経営陣に送ったからである．Plasschaert は，5月12日に辞職した．5月14日に Nordson は，Plasschaert と Ranier Corporation に対して訴訟を提起し，被告らは Nordson のトレード・シークレットのコモンロー上の保護を侵害し，Plasschaert が秘密情報の不開示と競業禁止約款に関する従業員契約に違反し，さらに Plasschaert が，Nordson の従業員を Ranier plan の使用を通じて Ranier に加わるよう勧誘しようと試みることによって Nordson との，不正競争に従事していると主張した．

　ジョージア地方裁判所の裁判官は本件を注意深く，正確に分析した．裁判官は，競業禁止約款に関するジョージアの原則を適用すれば，Plasschaert の約款が執行できないことは認めた．というのは2つのサブパラグラフがその地理的範囲になんらの制限を設けていなかったからである．しかしながら，Nordson と Plasschaert とは契約のパラグラフ5において彼らの契約上の債務は，オハイオ法によって規律されると規定していた．ジョージアの抵触法規則によれば，ジョージアがこの当事者のオハイオ法の選択を有効なものとして尊重するであろうと地裁は判断した．それから，競業禁止約款を使用者の正当な利益を保護するに必要な限度に限って執行するとするオハイオ法を適用し，裁判所は差止命令を1つの熱可塑性接着剤装置に制限することを拒否し，差止の地理的範囲を西ヨーロッパ，合衆国とカナダに制限し（合衆国のみに制限するようにとの Plasschaert の主張を拒否して），そして継続補償

the United States as Plasschaert urged), and reformed the continued compensation provision upwardly to reflect the higher cost of living in Belgium, where Plasschaert intended to (and did) return. Also, the court upheld without modification a contract provision prohibiting the use or disclosure of confidential information as defined in the agreement.

Plasschaert challenges the district court's decision to apply Ohio law rather than Georgia law and also challenges the district court's enjoining him from selling all hot-melt equipment and from competing against Nordson in Western Europe. We affirm the district court.

II Plasschaert asserts that despite the provision for governance by Ohio law the district court sitting in Georgia must as a matter of Georgia public policy apply Georgia law. As a federal court in a diversity case we must follow Georgia conflict of laws rules. Klaxon Co. v. Stentor Electric Manufacturing Co., 313 U.S. 487, 61 S. Ct. 1020, 85 L. Ed. 1477 (1941). Absent the choice of law provision in the agreement Georgia courts would not enforce this covenant not to compete, see, e.g., Puritan/Churchill Chemical Co., 245 Ga. 334, 265 S.E.2d 16 (1980); Howard Schultz & Assoc. v. Broniec, 239 Ga. 181, 236 S.E.2d 265 (1977). Even when the contract provides for a choice of law under which the covenant would be enforceable, Georgia may elect not to enforce it. See, e.g., Dothan Aviation Corp. v. Miller, 620 F.2d 504 (5th Cir. 1980); Nasco, Inc. v. Gimbert, 239 Ga. 675, 238 S.E.2d 368 (1977).

Though our analysis is somewhat different from that of the district court, we consider essentially the same factors that it examined, and we agree with the district judge that under the facts of this case a Georgia court would honor the parties' choice of law and apply Ohio law.

条項を Plasschaert が帰ろうとしていた（そして現にそうした）ベルギーでの高い生活費を考慮して，上方に修正した．さらに裁判所は，契約中に定義された秘密情報の使用又は開示を禁じる契約条項を修正なしで有効と認めた．

　Plasschaert は，裁判所がジョージア法ではなく，オハイオ法が適用されると判断したこと，及び地裁が西ヨーロッパにおいてすべての熱可塑性接着剤装置の販売と原告との競業を禁止したことに異議を唱えて上訴した．われわれは，地裁の判断を支持する．

II 　Plasschaert は，オハイオ法を指定する条項があっても，ジョージアに所在する連邦地裁はジョージアの公序にかかわる事項として，ジョージア法を適用しなければならないと主張する．州籍の相違に基づく事件においては，連邦裁判所はジョージアの抵触法規則に従わなくてはならない．Klaxon Co. v. Stentor Electric Manufacturing Co., 313 U.S. 487, 61 S. Ct. 1020, 85 L. Ed. 1477 (1941). 契約中に法選択条項のない場合には，ジョージアの裁判所は本件の競業禁止約款を執行しないであろう．たとえば，Puritan/Churchill Chemical Co., 245 Ga. 334, 265 S.E.2d 16 (1980); Howard Schultz & Assoc. v. Broniec, 239 Ga. 181, 236 S.E.2d 265 (1977) 参照．契約中に法選択条項があり，その法によればこの約款が執行できる場合であっても，ジョージアはそれを執行しないことを選択するかもしれない．たとえば，Dothan Aviation Corp. v. Miller, 620 F.2d 504 (5th Cir. 1980); Nasco, Inc. v. Gimbert, 239 Ga. 675, 238 S.E.2d 368 (1977) 参照．

　われわれの分析は，地裁のそれとはいくぶん異なるけれども，本質的には地裁が検討したと同じ要素を考慮する．そして本件事実の下ではジョージア裁判所は当事者の法選択を尊重し，オハイオ法を適用するであろうという点で地裁の裁判官の意見に同意する．

Like the Georgia Supreme Court in Gimbert, we look to the Restatement (Second) of Conflict of Laws §187(2) (1971) to see if Georgia will honor the state law chosen by the parties:

(2) The law of the State chosen by the parties to govern their contractual rights and duties will be applied, even if the particular issue is one which the parties could not have resolved by an explicit provision in their agreement directed to that issue, unless either

(a) the chosen state has no substantial relationship to the parties or the transaction and there is no other reasonable basis for the parties' choice, or

(b) application of the law of the chosen state would be contrary to a fundamental policy of a state which has a materially greater interest than the chosen state in the determination of the particular issue and which, under the rule of §188 (Law Governing in Absence of Effective Choice by the Parties), would be the state of the applicable law in the absence of an effective choice of law by the parties.

Therefore, Georgia will honor the choice of law provision unless there was no reasonable basis for the parties' choice or unless the provision is "contrary to a fundamental policy of a state which has a materially greater interest than the chosen state." Since Nordson is an Ohio corporation headquartered in Ohio, there is a reasonable basis for choosing Ohio law. The provision, however, is contrary to the fundamental Georgia policy against restraints of competition, see Ga. Code Ann. §§2-1409, 20-504. Thus the controlling determination is whether Georgia has a materially greater interest than Ohio in this issue. We hold that it does not.

If the parties have not chosen the law of a state to govern their contract, a court deciding which state law applies must consider contacts with the relevant states, the parties' expectations, the policies of the individual states, and the basic policy underlying the field of law. See, e.g.,

7 競業禁止約款の準拠法：Nordson Corp. v. Plasschaert

　Gimbert 判決でジョージア最高裁判所がしたと同様に，われわれは，ジョージアが当事者により選択された法を適用するかを検討するには，抵触法第2リステイトメント第187条第2項（1971）を参照する．すなわち，

　　(2)　当事者の契約上の権利及び義務を規律するために当事者により選択された邦の法は，問題となっている争点が，その争点に関する当事者の合意における明示の条項により，当事者が約定できなかったものである場合においても，これを適用する．但し，次のいずれかの場合はこの限りでない．

　　(a)　選択された邦が当事者又は取引となんら実質的な関係を有せず，かつ当事者の選択につきほかに相当な根拠がないとき，又は

　　(b)　選択された邦の法の適用が，問題となっている争点の決定につき選択された邦よりも著しく大きな利害関係を有する邦であって，かつ第188条の規則（当事者による有効な選択のない場合の準拠法）によれば当事者による有効な法選択のない場合に準拠法邦となるべき邦の基本的法目的に反するとき．

したがって，ジョージアは，当事者による法選択に対する相当な根拠が存在しないか，又は約款が「選択された邦よりも実質的により大きな利益を有する邦の基本的法目的に反する」のでなければ，準拠法約款を有効とするであろう．Nordson はオハイオに主たる営業所を有するオハイオ会社であるから，オハイオ法を選択する相当な根拠がある．しかし約款は，競争の制限を禁止するジョージアの基本的法目的に反する．Ga. Code Ann. §§2-1409, 20-504 参照．したがって決定的な問題は，ジョージアがこの争点についてオハイオよりも実質的により大きな利益を有するかどうかである．われわれは有しないと判断する．

　当事者が契約を規律すべき邦の法を選択しなかった場合には，どの邦の法が適用されるかを決定する裁判所は，関係する邦との関連，当事者の期待，個々の邦の法目的とその法分野の基礎にある法目的を考慮しなければならない．たとえば，Restatement（Second）of Conflicts §§6(2), 188(2)（1971）

II 法選択（準拠法）

Restatement (Second) of Conflicts §§6(2), 188(2) (1971). If the parties have chosen an applicable law the court must balance these same factors, and the interests of another state must be materially greater than those of the chosen state to override the parties' choice of law. Each case must be analyzed on its own facts. There are no simple directives in a case as close as this one, where there are Georgia cases involving fundamental Georgia policy that apply Georgia law despite the parties' choice of law and other Georgia cases that apply a foreign law even though the parties did not choose a specific state law. Compare Nasco, Inc. v. Gimbert, 239 Ga. 675, 238 S.E.2d 368 (1977), with Commercial Credit Plan, Inc. v. Parker, 152 Ga.App. 409, 263 S.E.2d 220 (1979).

The facts favor honoring the parties' choice of law. Nordson is an international corporation. Plasschaert worked for Nordson in the Netherlands, in Belgium, and in Georgia. Although Plasschaert signed the agreement in Georgia, his signing there, like the bringing of this suit there, was more "an accident of time and geography than through any reason giving rise to a substantial state interest in the litigation." Nordson Corp. v. Plasschaert, No. 80-7855, at 13 (N.D.Ga. Sept. 12, 1980). He had just arrived from Belgium. Most of the negotiations and preparation for the transfer were conducted while Plasschaert was still in Belgium. The agreement implies that Plasschaert might be transferred to different territories during his employment, and it states explicitly that Plasschaert would not compete in any territory in which he worked for Nordson during any part of the two-year period immediately preceding his termination. Thus, the place of performance of the covenant not to compete is Western Europe as well as Georgia. Moreover, both parties are primarily concerned with the agreement's effect in Western Europe because, although Plasschaert worked in Georgia for most of the last two years of his employment, he was already setting up his European business when he quit Nordson. Finally, Plasschaert's domicile, residence, and citizenship are

7　競業禁止約款の準拠法：Nordson Corp. v. Plasschaert

参照．当事者が準拠法を選択した場合，裁判所はこれらの同じ要素と，他邦の利益が選択された邦の利益よりも，当事者の法選択を凌駕するほどまで実質的にみて大きいかをどうかを比較考慮しなければならない．個々の事件は，それぞれその事件固有の事実を基礎にして分析されなければならない．本件と近似した事件での単純な指針は存在しない．ジョージアの事件には，当事者による法選択があるにもかかわらずジョージア法を適用するジョージアの基本的法目的に関する事件があるが，他方，当事者が特定の州の法を選択しなかった場合であっても，他州の法を適用するジョージアの別の判決もあるからである．Nasco, Inc. v. Gimbert, 239 Ga. 675, 238 S.E.2d 368（1977）と Commercial Credit Plan, Inc. v. Parker, 152 Ga. App. 409, 263 S.E.2d 220（1979）とを比較せよ．

　本件の事実関係は，当事者の法選択にとって有利である．Nordson は国際的企業である．Plasschaert は Nordson のためにオランダ，ベルギー，ジョージアで働いた．Plasschaert はジョージアで契約に署名したけれども，そこで彼が署名したことは，本件訴訟のジョージアでの提起と同様に，「訴訟に対する州の実質的な利益をもたらすなんらかの理由となるというよりも時期と場所の偶然」であった．Nordson Corp. v. Plasschaert, No. 80-7855, at 13（N. D. Ga. Sept. 12, 1980）．彼は丁度ベルギーから到着したばかりであり，転勤の交渉と準備の大部分は Plasschaert がベルギー滞在中に行われた．契約から推測すると，Plasschaert は別の地域に転勤になるかも知れず，また，Plasschaert は Nordson のために働いたどの地域においても雇用関係終了後2年間は，競業しない旨が明示に言及されている．かくして競業禁止の履行地は，西ヨーロッパとジョージアである．さらに両当事者は主として，西ヨーロッパにおける合意の効果に関心があった．というのは，Plasschaert は，その雇用の最後の2年間のほとんどはジョージアで働いていたけれども，彼はすでに Nordson の下を去るときには，ヨーロッパでの事業を起こしていたからである．最後に Plasschaert の住所，居所，市民籍はジョージアよりも西ヨーロッパにより深く根ざしている．したがって Plasschaert の牽連関係は，

Ⅱ　法選択（準拠法）

more rooted in Western Europe than in Georgia. Plasschaert's contacts, therefore, are at least as closely related to Western Europe, particularly Belgium, as to Georgia.

　　Georgia emerges from this analysis as the state where Plasschaert and Nordson carried out a substantial part of the contract performance, but in the sequence of events leading up to the signing of the agreement and the relationship between Nordson and Plasschaert after Plasschaert resigned, Georgia interests are all but nonexistent. Neither party expected Plasschaert to spend his career in Georgia, and he was expected to move as needed in the company's business. If Plasschaert had remained with Nordson, Ohio would have had continuing contacts regardless of where he worked. When the employment relationship ended Plasschaert almost immediately returned to Belgium to live in Brussels, the same city he left to come to Georgia.
　　Because each state (Georgia, Ohio, Belgium, and the Netherlands) has an interest in this dispute and because the employment relationship touched each of these states and to a large extent transcended political borders, no state has a "materially greater interest" in the controversy than any other state. Therefore, each state, including Georgia, should defer to the parties' choice of law if that choice has a reasonable basis, and this one does. Moreover, Georgia has even less of an interest in the controversy than its contacts suggest since the injunction would apply mainly to Plasschaert's activities in Western Europe, not in Georgia.

　　Despite the disperse contacts in this case a Georgia court still might refuse to enforce the provision under Ohio law if it finds it "particularly distasteful" to do so……. The terms of this restriction are reasonable, however. Georgia's concern is that the restraint might cause undue injury to the employee or unreasonable injury to the public in general. …… The provision in paragraph 4c of the agreement for continued compensation

178

ジョージアと同じく，少なくとも西ヨーロッパ，とくにベルギーと密接に関連している．

　以上の分析からみると，ジョージアは，NordsonとPlasschaertが契約履行の実質的部分を行った州ではあるが，契約の署名に至るまでの一連の出来事とPlasschaertが辞めた後のNordsonとPlasschaertの関係では，ジョージアの利益はほとんど存在しないに等しい．どちらの当事者もPlasschaertがジョージアでその生涯を過ごすとは思わなかったし，また会社の仕事で必要なときは，転勤するものと考えられていた．PlasschaertがNordsonの下に留まっていたとすれば，オハイオは彼の働く場所のいかんにかかわらず，継続的な関連をもっていたであろう．雇用関係が終わるとほとんどすぐに，Plasschaertは彼がジョージアにくる前に住んでいた都市であるブラッセルに住むために，ベルギーに帰った．
　いずれの州又は国（ジョージア，オハイオ，ベルギー，オランダ）も本件に利害関係をもち，雇用関係はいずれの州又は国にも関連があり，政治的な境界をこえているがゆえに，どの州又は国も他の州又は国よりも事件に「実質的により大きな利益」をもっていない．したがってジョージアを含めて，いずれの州又は国も当事者の法選択が相当な根拠を有する場合には（本件はそうである），その選択に従うべきである．さらにジョージアは，差止が主としてPlasschaertのジョージアではなく，西ヨーロッパの活動に適用されるのであるから，その関連が示唆するよりも事件に少しの利益しか有しない．

　本件との散らばった関連しか有しないにもかかわらず，それでもジョージアの裁判所は，そうすることが「とくに嫌悪すべきもの」と判断すれば，オハイオ法に基づく条項を執行することを拒否するかもしれない．……しかし本件における制限条件は，合理的なものである．ジョージアの関心は，その制限が被用者又は一般社会に不当な損害を引き起こすかどうかにある．……契約中のパラグラフ4cにおける，Plasschaertの給料の4分の3に相当する

equal to three fourths of Plasschaert's pay, especially as adjusted upwardly by the trial judge as permitted under Ohio law,....., alleviates any concern a court may have about his personal well being. Injury to the Georgia public is minimal, if any, since Plasschaert intended to compete mainly in Europe. Moreover, both Georgia and Ohio favor the freedom of parties to contract, both states acknowledge an employer's right to safeguard his confidential information, and both recognize that in protecting its legitimate interests the employer must burden the employee as little as possible. ...... Thus, a Georgia court would not find it "particularly distasteful" to enforce the agreement.

III Plasschaert also contends that there was insufficient evidence for the district court to enjoin him from the selling of all hot-melt equipment and from competing in the geographic areas set forth in the court's order.
......

The findings of fact ...... are not clearly erroneous. ...... Moreover, since under Ohio's reasonableness test, ... a trial judge exercises broad discretion in granting relief under the covenant, it was well within the judge's discretion to include all hot-melt equipment in his injunction.

The trial court also did not err in enjoining Plasschaert from competing in Western Europe as well as the United States and Canada. An employer wanting to protect confidential information is not necessarily compensated adequately by damages for injury caused by breach of confidence, so the employer may prefer a covenant not to compete to prevent the damage from occurring. In the abstract, most confidential information is worthy of protection without geographic limitation because once divulged the information or the fruits of the information quickly can pass to competitors anywhere in the world. See Blake, Employee Agreements Not to Compete, 73 Harv. L. Rev. 625, 667-84 (1960). As a practical matter, however, geographical limits often can be set. Ohio law permits a district

7　競業禁止約款の準拠法：Nordson Corp. v. Plasschaert

継続的補償を定める規定，それはオハイオ法により許容されるとして事実審裁判官により上向けに調整されているが，……その規定は裁判所が彼の個人的な福祉について有するどのような関心をも軽減することになる．ジョージアの社会に対する損害は，たとえあるにしても微少である．というのは，Plasschaert は主としてヨーロッパで競業することを意図していたからである．さらにジョージアとオハイオはともに，当事者の契約の自由を尊重し，両州は使用者の秘密情報を防御する権利を承認し，両者は使用者がその正当な利益を保護するに際して，従業員への負担をできる限り小さくしなければならないことを認めている．……したがってジョージアの裁判所は，その合意を執行することを「とくに嫌悪すべきもの」とは判断しないであろう．

III　Plasschaert はまた，裁判所が彼にすべての熱可塑性装置の販売を禁止し，裁判所の命令において定めた地理的領域において競業することを禁止するための十分な証拠は存在しないと主張する．
……

　裁判所による事実の認定は……明らかに誤っているというわけではない．……さらにオハイオの相当性のテストの下では……事実審裁判所の裁判官は，約款中の救済を認めるに際して広い裁量権を行使できるから，その差止命令の中にすべての熱可塑性装置を包含させることは十分に裁判官の裁量の範囲内にある．

　事実審裁判所はまた，合衆国とカナダと同様に，西ヨーロッパにおいて競業することを Plasschaert に差止命令を発した点で，誤ってはいなかった．秘密情報を防御しようとする使用者は，秘密開示の違反により生じた損害に対する損害賠償金によっては，必ずしも適切な補償を受けられるとは限らない．発生する損害を防止することよりも競業禁止約款を使用者は好むのである．理論的には，ほとんどの秘密情報は，地理的な制限なしに保護を受ける価値がある．というのは，ひとたび漏洩されると，情報又はその情報の果実は，世界中どこにおいても競争相手にすぐに伝わるからである．Blake, Employee Agreements Not to Compete, 73 Harv. L. Rev. 625, 667-84（1960）参照．

court to expand or restrict the area affected to achieve a fair and equitable solution. Raimonde, supra. The trial court rejected both Nordson's request that the injunction be given worldwide scope and Plasschaert's request that the injunction be limited to the United States and issued the injunction to encompass Western Europe, Canada and the United States.

Limiting the countries as it did was a reasonable solution under the circumstances. The hot-melt adhesive market is a specialized, international market. Plasschaert was willing to use confidential information he acquired to further his European operations, and had already disclosed such information in his attempt to secure a distributorship and in his discussions with a fellow employee in Europe. There is ample evidence that Plasschaert assembled confidential information specifically to aid his future business in Europe. Under Ohio law as set out in Raimonde, 42 Ohio St.2d at 26, 325 N.E.2d at 548, the district court properly enjoined Plasschaert from competing against Nordson in Western Europe as well as in the United States and Canada.

AFFIRMED.

【解　説】

　本件は，雇用契約中の準拠法約款に指定された雇用者の本拠地法である，オハイオ州法を適用し，オランダ人との間に締結された競業禁止約款の効力を承認した事例である．

　本件では競業禁止約款（covenant not to compete）の効力の準拠法が主として問題となっている．競業禁止約款とは，労働者の競業行為（とくに離職後の）を禁止する特約．たとえば，同種事業の別会社の設立，同業他社へ就職し，

しかしながら実際問題としては，地理的な制限はしばしば設定可能である．オハイオ法は，公正で公平な解決に到達するために，割り当てる領域を拡大したり，制限することを地方裁判所に許容している．前掲 Raimonde 事件．事実審裁判所は，差止命令は世界中のすべての地域にわたって与えられるべきとの Nordson の要求と，命令は合衆国に限るべきだとの Plasschaert の要求をともに拒絶して，西ヨーロッパ，カナダと合衆国を含む差止命令を出した．

　本件の事情の下では，そのように国を制限することは合理的な解決であった．熱可塑性装置の市場は専門化された国際的市場である．Plasschaert は，自ら取得した秘密情報をヨーロッパの事業活動を推進するために積極的に利用し，そのような情報を，販売権を取得しようとした試みの中で，またヨーロッパにおける同僚従業員との会話において，すでに開示していた．Plasschaert がとくにヨーロッパにおける彼の将来の事業を助けるために秘密情報を集めていたという十分な証拠がある．Raimonde, 42 Ohio St. 2d at 26, 325 N.E. 2d at 548 において述べられたオハイオ法に基づいて，地方裁判所が Plasschaert に対して合衆国とカナダと同様，西ヨーロッパにおいて，Nordson と競業することを禁止したのは適切であった．

　上訴棄却

顧客を奪う行為，同業他社に就職し，技術的秘密などを提供する行為などを禁止する特約をいう．なお，本件では秘密保持約款についても問題となっているが，ここでは主として競業禁止約款に絞って説明する．

1　競業禁止約款における法の抵触

　競業禁止約款についての各国法は，会社の企業秘密の保護を重視して，競業禁止約款に比較的寛容な立場を採用するか，それとも労働者の職業選択の自由，生存権の尊重を重視して，特約に厳格な立場を採用するかという，基

本的な考え方の相違を反映して対立する．

　アメリカでは，州により異なるが，一般的にはコモンローの原則，すなわち，特約は相当であれば，有効で，強行できるというルールが継受されたといわれる．競業禁止約款が相当であるかは，雇用者の保護に値する営業上の権利，労働者の職業選択の自由，生存の権利，市場の競争原理を保とうとする公益などの要素を考慮して判断される．しかし，この相当性の原則を採用する州の間でもその具体的な適用の結果は多様であり，しかもいくつかの州は，制定法により，競業禁止約款は原則として無効とするところもある．そこで法の抵触が生じ，本件のような準拠法決定の必要がある．

2　第2リステイトメントにおける当事者自治の原則

　本件は，競業禁止約款について契約中に当事者が準拠法を指定した場合には，その当事者が指定した法を適用するという，いわゆる当事者自治の原則が承認された事例である．

　本件は，最近の多くの判例と同様に第2リステイトメント第187条第2項bを採用し，契約中の準拠法約款に指定された雇用者の本拠地法であるオハイオ州法を適用して，オランダ人との間に締結された競業禁止約款の効力を承認した．その際，競業禁止約款における競業の制限がジョージアの基本的な法目的であることは認められたが，ジョージアがオハイオよりも大きな利益を有するとは認められなかった．つまりジョージアが従業員の当時の居住地であり，労務の給付地であったにもかかわらず，オハイオよりも大きな利益を有するとされなかった．その理由は，従業員がオランダ人であり，ジョージアよりも西ヨーロッパにより密接な関連を有していると判断されたことにある．

3　当事者による法選択を否定した判決

　本件とは異なり，準拠法約款に指定された法の適用が否定された判決の典型的な例として，たとえば，*Blalock v. Perfect Subscription Co.*, 458 F. Supp. 123（1978）がある．

7　競業禁止約款の準拠法：Nordson Corp. v. Plasschaert

　この事件の原告はアラバマの住民で，アラバマの連邦地裁にデラウェア法人に対して，雑誌のセールスマンとして被告のためになした役務に基づく損害賠償の請求を求める訴訟を提起した．原告は被告とのフランチャイズ契約により，南アラバマと北西フロリダの地域を割り当てられていた．契約中には，契約中及び契約終了後120日間の競業を禁止する約款と，契約はペンシルベニア法が適用されるとの約款があった．被告の抗弁は，原告が辞職すると通告した後，しばらくして被告の競争会社に就職したのであるから，この120日間の競業禁止約款に違反したという点にあった．

　ペンシルベニア法によれば，独立した契約者間では競業禁止約款は有効であった．そこで競業禁止約款の有効性の準拠法の決定が問題となった．裁判所は第2リステイトメントに従い，当事者の選択したペンシルベニア法ではなく，アラバマ法が適用されると判示した．

　①　本件に適用される準拠法はなにか．被告の契約締結時の本店所在地はペンシルベニアであるから，同州は契約と当事者の双方に対してなんらかの関係を有している．アラバマ法によれば，当事者は契約がそのような外国又は他州の法律により規律されるべきことを規定することは完全に適切なことである．したがって当裁判所は準拠法約款は強行されるべきであり，ペンシルベニア法が本件の契約の解釈に適用されると考える．

　②　本件における重要な争点は，契約中の競業禁止約款の有効性である．ペンシルベニア法によれば本件約款が有効である．これに対して，アラバマ法は，「何人に対してであれ，適法な職業，商売又はビジネスに従事することを制限するすべての契約は，その限りで無効である」と規定し，競業禁止約款は，独立契約者間のものであっても，アラバマ法上無効である．したがって問題は，ペンシルベニア法により契約を有効とするか，アラバマ法により契約を無効とするかである．

　③　この点についてのアラバマの先例はなく，抵触法第2リステイトメントの第187条に依拠するのが適切である．リステイトメント第187条第2項bは，明らかに裁判所が競業禁止約款の強行を拒否すべきことを要求している．というのはこの条項は制定法に示されたアラバマの公序に反するもので

あり，またアラバマ法が契約によるペンシルベニア法の選択がなければ適用される法律であり，制定法における同州の政策の表明は基本的な法目的であり，アラバマ州はペンシルベニア州よりもこの争点を決定するのに実質的にみてより大きな利益を有する．

Blalock 判決は，第2リステイトメント第187条第2項bを適用して，当事者の選択したペンシルベニア法の適用を否認した典型的な判決の1つである．裁判所は，(a)アラバマが法選択のなかった場合に適用すべき法律の州であり，(b)競業禁止約款の強行可能性を拒否することは同州の基本的法目的であり，(c)最後にアラバマは，選択されたペンシルベニアよりも問題となっている争点を決定するのにより大きな利益を有している，として準拠法約款の効力を否認したのである．本件の詳細については，松岡博『アメリカ国際私法の基礎理論』（大阪大学出版会，2007）64頁以下を参照．

4　*Barnes* 判決

Barnes Group, Inc. v. C & C Product, Inc., 716 F.2d 1023（4th Cir. 1983）も注目すべき判決である．

原告会社Xはコネティカットに主たる営業所を有するデラウェア法人である．Aは，Xの1部門であり，オハイオに主たる営業所を有している．Aは車や機械の修繕のためのボールトやナットなどを全国的規模で独立契約者を通じて販売している．この独立契約者とAとの契約には契約終了後2年間は類似の商品を販売しないとの競業禁止約款と，この契約は「オハイオ州の法律に従って解釈されるべきものとする」との準拠法約款が含まれていた．6人のセールスマンがAの下を去り，Aの競争会社であり，オハイオ法人である被告Yと契約し，Aとの約款に違反してAの前の顧客に販売を始めた．これらのセールスマンのうち，3人はアラバマ，他の3人はそれぞれ，メリーランド，ルイジアナ，サウスカロライナの住民であった．Aは，これらのセールスマンとYとの取引がAの標準契約に含まれた競業禁止約款に対する不法な侵害となると主張して，Yに対して訴訟を提起した．裁判所が約款に指定されたオハイオ法を適用して，制限約款はAの正当な営業利益を守るため

の合理的な方法であるとして，原告勝訴の判決を下したのに対して，Yが上訴した．

第4巡回区控訴裁判所の多数意見は，競業禁止約款の準拠法について，競業禁止約款はアラバマでは無効であるから，契約はオハイオ法により解釈されるという規定はアラバマの基本的法目的に違反し，アラバマのセールスマンの競業禁止約款にオハイオ法を適用したのは誤りであったと判示した．

*Barnes*判決も第2リステイトメントの方法論に従った判決である．裁判所は，競業禁止約款に関する当事者によるオハイオ法の指定は，アラバマのセールスマンについてのみその強行可能性を否認し，他の3つの州のセールスマンについては肯定した．その意味で部分的に準拠法指定約款の有効性を否認した判決といえるであろう．

第2リステイトメント第187条第2項bの適用に際して，アラバマと他の3つの州とは，①いずれも選択のない場合に適用される法律の州であり，②当事者により選択されたオハイオよりも大きな利害関係を有しているという点では同じであるが，③競業禁止約款の禁止の法目的が選択された法の適用を排除すべきとするほどに，「基本的法目的」であるかどうかという点で異なり，この点が決め手となった．多数意見によれば，オハイオと他の3つの州の法律の差は単に程度の差が存在するにすぎないから，オハイオ法の適用はこれらの州の基本的法目的に反しないとされた（この事件の詳細についても松岡・前掲基礎理論68-72頁参照）．

5 競業禁止に関する準拠法約款の効力についてのアメリカ法の傾向

本件*Nordson*判決を含めて，この点に関する検討を行ったところに従ってその概要を紹介する（松岡・前掲基礎理論75-81頁）．

① 法選択理論としての第2リステイトメントの重要性

まず，法選択方法論としては，第2リステイトメントの重要性を指摘する必要があろう．この点は最近における国際私法の他の分野における傾向とも一致する．多くの判例は当事者自治の原則とその制限を定めた第2リステイトメント第187条を適用して，競業禁止約款について，準拠法約款に指定さ

れた法律の適用を問題とする．

② 当事者による法選択はどこまで尊重されるのか

準拠法約款において当事者によって選択された法は，雇用者の法，すなわち，その主たる事務所の所在地法であることが多い．そして選択された法は雇用者に有利な内容である．その理由としては，準拠法の選択に指導的な役割を果たすのが雇用者であるから，雇用者に有利な法が選択されるのが通常であるということのほか，選択された法の適用が被用者に有利なときは，雇用者は敢えて訴訟で争うことはしないであろう，という点にも求めることができようか．

いずれにしても一般論としては当事者の法選択は，原則としては尊重される．この点は第2リステイトメント第187条や最近の準拠法約款に関するアメリカ判例の一般的傾向である．しかし，競業禁止約款の分野の判例では，法選択が尊重された事例は必ずしも多くはなく，むしろ結果的には否定されることが多い．

当事者による法選択を認めた本件 *Nordson* 判決も Plasschaert とジョージアとの関連が希薄であり，単に一時的な労務給付地，居住地に過ぎず，彼がオランダ国民で，退職後直ちにベルギーで仕事を始めたという特殊な事情が存在した．また，国際事件であり，州際事件とは異なり，アメリカ企業の先端技術を外国人労働者から防衛しなければならないとの認識が判決の結論に影響を及ぼしているかもしれない．

③ どのような場合に当事者による法選択は否定されるか

どのような場合に当事者の指定した法律の適用が排除されるか．その理論的な枠組みを提供するのが，第2リステイトメント第187条第2項bの規定であり，多くの判例が依拠するのもこの規定である．これによると，当事者によって選択された法の適用が排除されるのは，選択された邦の法の適用が，問題となっている争点の決定につき選択された邦よりも著しく大きな利害関係を有する邦であって，かつ第188条の規則によれば当事者による有効な法選択のない場合に準拠法邦となるべき邦の基本的法目的に反するときである．

この要件は，(a)当事者の法選択を排除してその適用が問題となっている州

又は国が，当事者による有効な法選択がなかった場合に適用されるべき法の州又は国であること，(b)その州が問題となっている争点の決定について選択された州又は国よりも著しく大きな利害関係を有する州又は国であること，(c)選択された州又は国の法の適用が，その州又は国の基本的法目的に反することの3つに分けて論じるのが適切であると考えられる．

④　当事者による有効な法選択がなかった場合の準拠法

明示の法選択のない場合の準拠法をどのように決定するかの一般原則は，第2リステイトメント第188条が規定するところである．まず，その第1項は，契約についての争点に関する当事者の権利及び義務は，第6条の原則に従い，その争点との関連で取引及び当事者と最も重要な関係を有する邦の法により，これを定めると規定する．ついで第2項は，当事者による有効な選択のない場合において第6条の原則に従って争点に適用すべき法を決定するにあたり斟酌すべき連結素には次のものが含まれるとして，契約の締結地，契約の交渉地，履行地，契約の目的物の所在地，当事者の住所，居所，国籍，法人の場合はその設立地，当事者の事業所の所在地を列挙する．そして，上に掲げる連結素は個々の争点との関連でその各々が有する重要性の程度に応じてその軽重を判定すべきものと定める．最後に3項は，契約の交渉地と履行地が同一の邦にあるときは，通常はこの邦の法を適用する，ただし第189条-第199条及び第203条に別段の定めのある場合はこの限りでないと規定する．

競業禁止約款にこれを当てはめると，労務給付地で（それは同時に禁止される競業行為の行われる場所であることが多い）であり，かつそれが従業員の住所地又は居住地であるときは，それが一時的な場合を除けば，通常はその法が，当事者による有効な法選択のなかった場合に適用されるべき法の州又は国となるといえるのではなかろうか．とくにその法が労働者に有利なときはそうである．

⑤　法選択がない場合に準拠法州又は国となるべき州又は国が著しく大きな利害関係を有すること

準拠法約款に指定された法の適用を否認するには，法選択のない場合に準

Ⅱ 法選択（準拠法）

拠法州又は国となるべき地が，問題となっている争点の決定について選択された州又は国よりも著しく大きな利害関係を有することも必要である．これを決定するためには，選択された法の地にどれだけ重要な連結点が集中しているかということと，同時に，法選択がない場合に準拠法州又は国となる地にどれだけ他の連結点が集中しているかが，ともに重要な要素となる．

判例において問題となるのは，雇用者の主たる事務所の所在地（選択された法の地であり，その法は雇用者に有利）対 労務給付地（競業行為地）であり，かつ被用者の居住地（その法は被用者に有利），という図式である．多くの裁判例は，労務の給付地であり，被用者の住所地である州が，競業禁止約款の強行を否認することによって自州の被用者を保護する利益の大きさを強調する．

これに対して，競業禁止約款により自州の企業を保護する利益を強調し，雇用者の労務給付地と居住地州の利益がより大きいとはいえないと判示するのは，むしろ例外的な場合である．また本件 Nordson 判決において，ジョージアにおける従業員の居住が一時的であることが，同州がより大きな利害関係を有する州であると認められなかった重要な要因であるというべきである．

⑥ 「基本的法目的」とは何か

ある法域における競業の禁止が，その「基本的法目的」であるかどうかも重要な論点である．準拠法約款に指定された法の適用を否認し，競業禁止約款を強行できないとした判決の多くはこれを肯定する．その場合，競業禁止約款が相当であるかどうかを問わずに，原則的に禁止する制定法を有しているときは，とくにそうである．それは，「基本的法目的は……優位な交渉力を威圧的に用いることから人を保護することを目的とする制定法に含まれることがある．保険会社に対して個々の被保険者が有する権利に関する制定法は，この種の例である」という第2リステイトメント第187条注釈gの説明にまさしく対応するものであると考えられる．

【本件参考文献】

松岡博『アメリカ国際私法の基礎理論』（大阪大学出版会，2007）49頁以下．

7 競業禁止約款の準拠法：Nordson Corp. v. Plasschaert

【設　問】

1　本件の主要な争点はなにか．競業禁止約款とはどのようなものか．この点に関するアメリカ各州の法はどのように対立しているか．本件ではどうか．

2　ジョージア，オハイオ，オランダ，ベルギーが事件と当事者に対して有する関連を整理せよ．

3　本件の裁判所の結論と判旨の主要な部分を紹介せよ．

4　判旨の依拠する契約の準拠法に関する第2リステイトメント第187条の規定を説明せよ．

5　第2リステイトメント第187条第2項bの規定を適用するにあたって問題となる点について説明せよ．

6　準拠法約款に指定された法の適用を否定した*Blalock*判決を紹介せよ．

7　*Barnes*判決を紹介せよ．

8　本件はどのような判決か．また本件の結論，理由づけに賛成か．

9　競業禁止約款の効力の準拠法についてのアメリカ法の傾向を総括せよ．

10　法の適用に関する通則法の規定によれば，本件はどうなるか．

8 代理店契約の準拠法：
Southern International Sales Co., Inc. v. Potter & Brumfield Div., 410 F.Supp.1339 (S.D.N.Y.1976)

EDWARD WEINFELD, District Judge.

This motion for summary judgment requires the court to pass upon the binding effect of a stipulation of the parties as to the law governing the interpretation of their contract.

Defendant Potter & Brumfield is an Indiana-based manufacturer of electrical products. Plaintiff Southern International is a Puerto Rican corporation. By agreement dated April 2, 1969, plaintiff became defendant's exclusive sales representative for Puerto Rico and adjacent United States islands. The agreement provided, among other things, that either party could terminate it "for any reason whatsoever" upon thirty days' notice, and that it "shall be interpreted in accordance with the laws of the State of Indiana." On December 21, 1971, Potter & Brumfield notified Southern International that the contract would be terminated as of February 20, 1972. Southern claims that it had performed "outstandingly" and that the termination was motivated by defendant's purpose to capitalize on the contacts Southern had developed by dealing directly with them.

In September 1972, Southern brought this diversity action, claiming that the termination violated the Puerto Rican Dealers' Contracts Act, which provides in pertinent part:

"Notwithstanding the existence in a dealer's contract of a clause reserving to the parties the unilateral right to terminate the existing relationship, no principal or grantor may directly or indirectly perform

米国インディアナ会社とプエルトリコ会社との間に締結された代理店契約において，契約に指定されたインディアナ法（契約の一方的終了は有効とする）の適用を否定し，正当事由のない限り，契約の一方的終了を禁止するプエルトリコ法が適用されるとした事例

EDWARD WEINFELD 地方裁判所裁判官

本件の略式判決の申立は，当事者の契約の解釈を規律する法に関する当事者の約定の拘束力についての判断を裁判所に要求している．

被告 Potter & Brumfield は，インディアナに本拠を有する電気製品の生産会社である．原告 Southern International は，プエルトリコ会社である．1969年4月2日付けの契約により，原告は被告のプエルトリコ及び合衆国の周辺諸島の専属的販売代理店となった．契約にはいずれの当事者も30日の通知で「その理由のいかんを問わず」契約を終了することができること，及び契約は「インディアナ州法により解釈するものとする」との条項が含まれていた．1971年12月21日に Potter & Brumfield は，Southern International に対して契約を1972年2月20日に終了させるとの通知をした．Southern は，「顕著に」履行を果たしてきたこと，終了は Southern が築きあげてきた取引先をそれらとの直接取引によって利用しようという被告の目的に動機づけられていると主張する．

1972年9月に Southern は，州籍の相違に基づく本件訴訟を提起し，契約終了はプエルトリコの代理店契約法に違反すると主張した．同法はその関連部分において次のように規定する．

「契約中に当事者に既存の関係を一方的に終了させる権限を与える条項が存在している場合であっても，本人又は譲与者は，直接的にせよ間接的にせよ，正当な理由なくして，既存の関係を破壊するなんらかの行為

any act detrimental to the established relationship or refuse to renew said contract on its normal expiration, except for just cause."

Defendant does not dispute that its agreement with plaintiff was a "dealer's contract" as defined in the Act. Although it contends it did have "just cause" for the cancellation, its position on this motion for summary judgment is that the Dealers' Contracts Act does not apply because the parties agreed that Indiana law would govern their contract's interpretation, and Indiana would give effect to the clause allowing unilateral termination. Plaintiff argues that, upon all the circumstances surrounding the execution and performance of the contract, Puerto Rican law applies despite the provision that Indiana law governs its interpretation. The court agrees with plaintiff and denies the motion for summary judgment.

Since this is a diversity case, New York state choice of law principles apply on the issue of whether the law of Indiana or Puerto Rico governs. There are, as defendant notes, a number of New York cases that hold the parties' choice of law to control where their contract has a reasonable relation to the jurisdiction whose law they choose. It cannot seriously be challenged that the contract at issue bore a reasonable relation to Indiana. Defendant has its headquarters and facilities there, and it shipped, processed, and did the paperwork in Indiana on Southern's orders for merchandise. But this begins rather than ends inquiry. There is also authority from the New York Court of Appeals suggesting that the parties' intention and stipulation as to the law governing their contract is but one factor, albeit a weighty one, in deciding the ultimate question-namely, which jurisdiction has the most significant contacts with the matter at issue. Under this analysis the significance of the parties' choice of Indiana law would pale when viewed against the facts that almost all of the equipment sold by Southern on defendant's behalf was sold in Puerto Rico, for Puerto Rican accounts and for use in Puerto Rico; the solicitation of customers occurred in Puerto Rico; and plaintiff signed the contract there. More to the point, the application of Indiana law would frustrate the

をしたり,通常の満了に基づく契約の更新を拒否してはならない.」

被告は原告との合意が同法で定義された「代理店契約」に該当することは争っていない.被告は,破棄の「正当事由」を有していると主張しているけれども,略式判決を求める本件申立についての立場は,当事者は契約の解釈についてはインディアナ法が適用されることに合意したのであるから,プエルトリコ代理店契約法は適用されず,インディアナは一方的終了を認める契約条項を有効とするというにあった.原告は,契約の締結と履行を取り巻くあらゆる事情を考慮すれば,インディアナ法がその解釈に適用されるという条項にもかかわらず,プエルトリコ法が適用されると主張する.当裁判所は原告に同意し,略式判決の申立を否認する.

本件は州籍の相違に基づく事件であるから,ニューヨーク州の法選択原則が,インディアナかプエルトリコのいずれの法が適用されるかの争点に適用される.被告が指摘するように,当事者が選択した州に契約が相当な関係を有する場合に,当事者の法選択を支持する多くのニューヨークの判例がある.本件の契約がインディアナと相当な関係を有していることに本気で異論を唱えることはできない.被告は,そこに本拠地と設備を有し,原告の商品注文に応じて,インディアナにおいて発送,加工及びペーパーワークを行った.しかしこれは探求の始まりであり,終わりではない.また当事者の意思とその契約を規律する法についての条項は,どの法域が問題となっている争点に最も重要な関連を有するかという,最終的な問題を決定するにあたって考慮すべき,有力なものではあるが1つの要素にすぎないとするニューヨーク最高裁の先例がある.この分析に従えば,当事者のインディアナ法の選択は,次の事実を考慮すればあまり重要なものでなくなる.すなわち,Southernが被告のために売った設備はほとんどすべて,プエルトリコの得意先のために,プエルトリコで使用されるためにそこで売られたし,顧客の勧誘もそこでなされ,原告は契約をそこで署名した.より重要なのは,インディアナ法の適用がプエルトリコ代理店契約法の基本的法目的を侵害することである.この

fundamental policy expressed in the Puerto Rican Dealers' Contracts Act. According to the Statement of Motives that accompanied the Act:

"The Commonwealth of Puerto Rico can not remain indifferent to the growing number of cases in which domestic and foreign enterprises, without just cause, eliminate their dealers, or without fully eliminating them, such enterprises gradually reduce and impair the extent of their previously established relationships, as soon as these dealers, concessionaires or agents have created a favorable market and without taking into account their legitimate interests.

"The Legislative Assembly of Puerto Rico declares that the reasonable stability in the dealer's relationship in Puerto Rico is vital to the general economy of the country, to the public interest and to the general welfare, and in the exercise of its police power, it deems it necessary to regulate, insofar as pertinent, the field of said relationship, so as to avoid the abuse caused by certain practices."

This strong legislative policy could easily be circumvented were the court to announce a rule that would allow a manufacturer, by wielding its economic might against a distributor, to exact a stipulation as to governing law compelling the distributor to forsake the protection afforded him by the Puerto Rican legislature. The facts presented here fit squarely within the rule of section 187 of the *Second Restatement of Conflict of Laws*, which provides in part:

"The law of the state chosen by the parties to govern their contractual rights and duties will be applied, even if the particular issue is one which the parties could not have resolved by an explicit provision in their agreement directed to that issue, unless ......

......

(b) application of the law of the chosen state would be contrary to a fundamental policy of a state which has a materially greater interest than the chosen state in the determination of the particular issue and which, under the rule of §188, would be the state of the applicable law in the absence of an effective choice of law by the parties."

法律の立法趣旨の説明によると，次のように述べられている．

「プエルトリコ・コモンウエルスは，内外の企業が正当な理由なく，そのディーラーを排除し，あるいはこのような企業がそれらを完全には排除しないまでも，これらのディーラーや代理店などが有利な市場を開発するとすぐに，その利益を無視してすでに確立した関係の程度を徐々に削減し，害するような，増大しつつある事態をそのまま放置できない．

「プエルトリコの立法府は，プエルトリコにおいてはディーラー関係の合理的な安定性は，国の経済一般，公的利益およびその一般的福利にとって必須のものであり，その警察権能を行使して，いくつかの慣行により引き起こされた濫用を避けるために，適切な限りにおいてこの関係の分野を規律することが必要であると考えることを宣言する．」

　この強い立法目的は，生産者がディストリビューターに対する経済力を用いてディストリビューターにプエルトリコ法が彼に与える保護を放棄することを強いる結果となるような準拠法に関する合意を強要することを認める規則を裁判所が宣言することによって損なわれるであろう．本件で提示されている事実はまさしく抵触法第2リステイトメント第187条の規則の適用範囲に入る．その一部分は以下のように規定する．

「当事者の契約上の権利及び義務を規律するために当事者により選択された邦の法は，問題となっている争点が，その争点に関する当事者の合意における明示の条項により，当事者が約定できなかった場合においても，これを適用する．但し，次のいずれかの場合はこの限りではない．
……

(b)　選択された邦の法の適用が，問題となっている争点の決定につき選択された邦よりも著しく大きな利害関係を有する邦であって，かつ第188条の規則によれば当事者による有効な法選択のない場合に準拠法邦となるべき邦の基本的法目的に反するとき．」

Section 188 of the *Second Restatement* applies in the absence of an effective choice of law by the parties, and calls for the application of the law of the state that "has the most significant relationship to the transaction and the parties" in light of the policy factors that shape choice of law.

Whether one applies the "most significant relation" test expressed in section 188 and in *Auten v. Auten* or the more recent "governmental interest" analysis of *Intercontinental Planning, Ltd. v. Daystrom, Inc.*, Puerto Rican law would plainly govern the validity of the contract in the absence of the parties' stipulation. As noted above, plaintiff is a Puerto Rican company and the contract's essential purpose was to create a means by which defendant could distribute its products to the Puerto Rican market. Puerto Rico's contacts with the parties and the transaction, and its substantial interest in seeing that its local distributors are not exploited by foreign manufacturers, far outweigh the contacts with Indiana or Indiana's interest, if any, in the validity of the unilateral termination clause of the contract at issue.

Under the circumstances, the general rule giving effect to the parties' choice of law must bow to the exception stated in section 187 of the *Second Restatement*. While the New York courts have yet to rule on the exact issue here presented, there is every reason to believe that they would follow the *Restatement* approach. It has found support in other courts, and in a case decided in this district and applying New York law. Moreover, the New York courts have cited section 187 of the *Second Restatement* with approval. ......While the failure to enforce the parties' choice of law does invalidate their contract to some extent, "[fulfillment] of the parties' expectations is not the only value in contract law; regard must also be had for state interests and for state regulation. The chosen law should not be applied without regard for the interests of the state which would be the state of the applicable law with respect to the particular issue involved in the absence of an effective choice by the parties."

第2リステイトメント第188条は，当事者による有効な法選択がなかった場合に適用され，法選択を形成する政策的要素に照らして「取引及び当事者と最も重要な関係を有する」邦の法の適用を指示する．

　第188条と *Auten v. Auten* 判決の「最も重要な関係」の基準によろうと，*Intercontinental Planning, Ltd. v. Daystrom, Inc.* 判決におけるもっと最近の「統治利益」分析論によろうと，プエルトリコ法が当事者による選択のない場合に契約の有効性を明らかに規律する．上に述べたように，原告はプエルトリコ会社であり，契約の最も重要な目的は被告がその製品をプエルトリコの市場に流通させる手段を創設することであった．プエルトリコが取引と当事者に対して有する関連と，プエルトリコのディストリビューターが他州の生産者から搾取されないよう見守ることに対して有する実質的利益は，インディアナの関連と，問題の契約の一方的終了条項の有効性に対して有するインディアナの利益――もしあれば――をはるかに凌駕する．

　このような状況の下では，当事者の法選択を有効とする一般規則は，第2リステイトメント第187条の例外に従わなくてはならない．ニューヨークの裁判所は本件で提示されている正確な争点について判断していないけれども，同裁判所が第2リステイトメントのアプローチに従うであろうと信じる十分な理由がある．それは他の裁判所や当裁判所で決定され，ニューヨーク法を適用した判決において支持されている．さらにニューヨーク裁判所は，第2リステイトメント第187条を支持して引用している．……当事者の法選択を執行しないことは，ある程度まで契約を無効とするものであるけれども，「当事者の期待の［達成］は契約法における唯一の価値ではない．邦の利益及び邦の立法もまた顧慮されなければならない．選択された法は，当事者による有効な選択がない場合において，当該争点につき準拠法邦となるべき邦の利害関係を考慮することなくして，適用されるべきではない．」

Since Puerto Rican law governs this controversy, the factual question whether Potter & Brumfield had "just cause" as defined in the Dealers' Contracts Act for the termination of its contract with Southern presents an issue of fact which is in dispute. Thus, defendant's motion for summary judgment is denied.

【解 説】

　本件は，米国インディアナ会社とプエルトリコ会社との間に締結された代理店契約において，契約に指定されたインディアナ法（契約の一方的終了は有効とする）の適用を否定し，正当事由のない限り，契約の一方的終了を禁止するプエルトリコ法が適用されるとした事例である．

1　代理店契約と法の抵触

　代理店契約については，1960年代以降，経済的に従属する立場にある代理店を保護するために，各種の代理店保護のための強行法規が制定されるに至った．これらの中には，本件で問題となったプエルトリコ法のように，代理店の不利な立場が表面化するのは，とくに契約終了時であることを考慮して，契約終了の正当事由を要求するなどの代理店保護措置を定めるとともに，代理店の側からの権利放棄を認めないことを内容とするものなどが多い．そこでこのような代理店契約において，当事者による法選択とこれらの強行法規の適用関係が問題となる．

　本件では，米国インディアナ会社とプエルトリコ会社との間に締結された代理店契約において，契約に指定されたインディアナ法（これによると契約の一方的終了は有効とする）が適用されるか，それとも正当事由のない限り，契約の一方的終了を禁止するプエルトリコ法が適用されるかが問題となった．裁判所は，抵触法第2リステイトメント第187条を適用し，契約に指定され

8 代理店契約の準拠法：Southern International Sales Co., Inc. v. Potter & Brumfield Div.

　本件の紛争にはプエルトリコ法が適用されるのであるから，Potter & Brumfield が Southern との契約について，代理店契約法で定義された終了の「正当事由」を有していたかという事実の問題が，争いとなっている事実についての争点を提示している．したがって被告の略式判決の申立は認められない．

たインディアナ法の適用を否定し，プエルトリコ法が適用されるとし，正当事由がない限り，一方的終了は許されないと判示した．

2　抵触法第2リステイトメント第187条第2項b号

　第2リステイトメント第187条は契約準拠法の一般原則として，一定の制限の下で当事者による法選択を承認する（アメリカ国際私法のおける当事者自治の原則については，松岡博『アメリカ国際私法の基礎理論』（大阪大学出版会，2007）1頁以下参照）．

　本件で主として問題となっているのは，その第187条第2項b号である．同号は，当事者の選択した法の適用が，当事者の選択がない場合に当該争点に適用される法の所属する邦の基本的な法目的に反する場合には，当事者の法選択は有効と認められないとする．

　同条の第2項b号についての説明（注釈g）の要約を以下に掲げる．

　　「……当事者の期待の達成は，契約法における唯一の価値ではない．邦の利益及び邦の立法もまた顧慮されなければならない．選択された法は，当事者による有効な選択がない場合において，当該争点につき準拠法邦となるべき邦の利害関係を考慮することなくして，適用されるべきではない．……選択された法律の適用が拒否されるのは，1　第188条の規則によれば当事者の選択がない場合に準拠法邦となるべき邦の基本的法目的を保護するためであって，かつ，2　この邦が個々の争点の決定につき選択された法の邦よりも著しく大きな利害関係を有する場合に限ら

れるべきである．……
　当事者の選択がなければ準拠法邦となるべき邦の「基本的」法目的がどのような場合に存在するとみなされるか……．考慮されるべき重要な要素の1つは，重要な連結素がどの程度この邦に集中しているかということである．……
　もう1つの考慮すべき重要な要素は，重要な連結素がどの程度選択された邦に集中しているかである．この邦が契約と当事者に密接に関連していればいるだけ，法選択条項の効力を否認することを正当化するためには，選択がない場合に準拠法邦となるべき法の法目的は一層基本的なものでなければならない．
　法目的が「基本的」であるためには，……それは実質的なものでなければならない．……基本的法目的は，ある種の契約を不法なものとする制定法に，あるいは優位な交渉力を威圧的に用いることから人を保護することを目的とする制定法に含まれることがある」(Restatement, Second, Conflict of Laws, §187, comment g)．

　上のリステイトメントの立場は，当事者の選択した法の適用を排除するために必要な要件を次の3つの要件，つまり，(a)当事者の法選択を排除してその適用が問題となっている邦が，当事者による有効な法選択がなかった場合に適用されるべき法の邦であること，(b)その邦が問題となっている争点の決定について選択された邦よりも著しく大きな利害関係を有する邦であること，(c)選択された邦の法の適用が，その邦の「基本的法目的」に反することに整理することができる．

3　本件への適用

　上の立場を本件に適用するとどうなるか．
　本件は，当事者の選択したインディアナ法の適用が排除され，(a)当事者による選択がなかった場合の準拠法であるプエルトリコ法の適用が認められた事件である．当事者の選択した法は，契約関係において優位な地位にある当事者の本拠の所在地法（インディアナ法）であり，その適用の結果は弱者であ

る代理店にとって不利であり，他方，当事者の法選択がない場合の準拠法（プエルトリコ法）の適用は，代理店にとって有利となるべき場合であった．

ただ結果が違うというだけで当事者の選択した法の適用を排除したわけではなく，裁判所の論理によれば，(c)代理店の保護がプエルトリコの基本的な法目的であること，(b)プエルトリコが事件と当事者に強い実質的な関連を有し（重要な連結点はかなり集中しているが，最も重要なのは代理店がプエルトリコの代理店であるという点であろう），プエルトリコの代理店を保護する強い利害関係をもっていることが，当事者の選択したインデイアナ（被告の本店のほか，ある程度の連結点が存在しており，決して偶然的なものではない）法の適用を排除した理由であると考えられる．

さらに注意すべきは，選択されたインデイアナ法に代わって適用されたのは，当事者の選択した法でもなく，また法廷地（ニューヨーク）法でもない，プエルトリコ法であった．

このように考えると，本判決は第2リステイトメントの規定を適切に適用しており，またこのことは第187条第2項b号が当事者の法選択を制限する一般理論としてもうまく機能しうる方法論であることを示しているものといえようか．

4 第2リステイトメント第188条

本件では有効な法選択のない場合の準拠法について第2リステイトメント第188条に依拠している．第188条は以下のように規定している（第188条について詳しくは松岡博『国際取引と国際私法』（晃洋書房，1993）205頁以下参照）．

「第188条　当事者による有効な法選択がない場合の準拠法

(1) 契約についての争点に関する当事者の権利及び義務は，第6条の原則に従い，その争点との関連で取引及び当事者と最も重要な関係を有する邦の法により，これを定める．

(2) 当事者による有効な選択のない場合において，第6条に定める原則に従って争点に適用すべき法を決定するに当たり斟酌すべき連結素には次のものがある．

Ⅱ　法選択（準拠法）

　　　(a)　契約締結地
　　　(b)　契約交渉地
　　　(c)　履行地
　　　(d)　契約の目的物の所在地
　　　(e)　当事者の住所・居所・国籍，法人の場合はその設立地，当事者の事業所の所在地
　　上に掲げる連結素は個々の争点との関連でその各々が有する重要性の程度に応じてその軽重を判定すべきものとする．
　(3)　契約交渉地と履行地が同一の邦にあるときは，通常はこの邦の法が適用される．但し第189条-199条及び第203条に別段の定めのある場合はこの限りでない．」

　本件判旨は，上の第188条をどのように適用したのであろうか．判旨は，「プエルトリコ法が当事者による選択のない場合に契約の有効性を明らかに規律する．……原告はプエルトリコ会社であり，契約の最も重要な目的は被告がその製品をプエルトリコの市場に流通させる手段を創設することであった．プエルトリコが取引と当事者に対して有する関連と，プエルトリコのディストリビューターが他州の生産者から搾取されないよう見守ることに対して有する実質的利益は，インディアナの関連と，問題の契約の一方的終了条項の有効性に対して有するインディアナの利益……をはるかに凌駕する」と述べている．

　ここで強調されているのは，代理店がプエルトリコ会社であり，代理店契約の最も重要な目的は，被告の製品をプエルトリコ市場に流通させることであるから，自州の代理店を保護するプエルトリコの関連と実質的利益は，インディアナの利益をはるかに上回るという点にある．これが法選択のない場合にプエルトリコ法が準拠法とされたポイントであろう．

5　*Wood Bros. Homes Inc. v. Walker Adj. Bureau*, 198 Colo. 444, 601 P.2d 1369（1979）．

　第2リステイトメント第188条を適用した注目すべき判決として *Wood*

Bros. Homes Inc. 判決がある.

　訴外カルフォルニア住民であるAが，被告であるデラウェア法人で，コロラドに本拠を有する会社と，被告がニューメキシコに有する共同住宅団地での大工仕事をする契約を締結した．契約の交渉は，カルフォルニア，コロラド，ニューメキシコで行われ，署名はニューメキシコでなされた．Aが仕事を始めてしばらくした後，ニューメキシコ当局が，Aはニューメキシコの工事請負人の許可を得ていないから，建設を止めるよう命令した．被告は，直ちに契約を破棄し，Aの従業員には27,000ドルを支払ったが，Aには支払いを拒否した．原告はこのAから，その債権の譲渡を受け，コロラド州裁判所に訴訟を提起した．コロラド法によれば，被告は有責とされるが，ニューメキシコ法によれば，建設産業許可立法により許可を受けていない工事請負人は，許可を必要とする行為の履行に基づく損失の補償を請求する訴訟を提起することができない．コロラド州最高裁は次のように判示して，ニューメキシコ法が適用されるとした．

　われわれは，不法行為同様，契約でも第2リステイトメントを採用する．抵触法問題において第2リステイトメントによれば，問題となっている争点に最も重要な関係を有する州を決定することが必要である．どの州が最も重要な関係を有するかは，第6条，第188条の原則を考慮しなければならない．

　このような一般原則に加えて，第2リステイトメントは，特定のタイプの契約に適用される規定を設けている．本件に関するものとしては，第196条の役務の提供のための契約がこれに当たる．これによると，役務が提供される地の州が契約の有効性の争点について最も重要な関係の州と推定されるが，他の州がより重要な関係を有するときはこの限りでない．控訴審は，コロラドが最も重要な関係の州と考えた．同裁判所は，契約を有効視し，当事者の期待を保護することに対して有するコロラドの利益が契約法の基礎にある基本的法目的と考えた．たしかにこの利益は強いものではあるが，他のすべてのものを凌駕するわけではない．

　ニューメキシコの工事請負人法は，ニューメキシコで建設業を営んでいる人に許可を与える包括的，強行規定である．この法律は，標準以下ないしは

Ⅱ　法選択（準拠法）

危険な建設と，建設業に従事する者の財政的無責任からニューメキシコの住民を守ることを目的とするものである．そして許可なく工事した者は，刑罰を科せられ，契約の司法的救済又は履行した役務の相当額の請求を禁じられる．このような状況の下では，契約を有効視し，当事者の正当な期待を保護するという価値よりも，ニューメキシコの契約を無効とするニューメキシコの利益がより重要である．したがってニューメキシコ法が適用されるという推定は覆されない．この結論はまた，第2リステイトメント第202条第2項の，履行が履行地で違法であるときは，契約は通常，その執行を否定されるであろうという規定にも合致するとして，ニューメキシコ法を適用した．

6　Summary Judgment

本件 *Southern International Sales* 判決では略式判決（summary judgment）の申立が問題となった．略式判決とは，正式の事実審理を経ないでなされる判決のことをいう．重要な事実について真正の争点がなく，法律問題だけで判決できる場合に，申立によりなされる判決である．陪審の審理を経ない点に大きな意味がある．本件ではその申立が認められなかった．

8　代理店契約の準拠法：Southern International Sales Co., Inc. v. Potter & Brumfield Div.

【設　問】

1　事実の概要を説明せよ．
2　インディアナとプエルトリコが当事者と事件に対して有する関連を整理せよ．
3　代理店契約とはどのようなものか．2つの法域の代理店法の内容を比較せよ．
4　本件の国際私法上の争点はなにか．本件判旨の結論はどうか．
5　判旨の主要な部分を要約せよ．
6　本件が依拠する抵触法第2リステイトメント第187条，とくに第2項bについて説明せよ．
7　第187条第2項bによれば，当事者による法選択が否定されるために必要とされる要件とはなにか．
8　上の立場を本件に適用するとどうなるか．判旨を主要部分について説明せよ．
9　競業禁止約款に関する *Nordson* 判決（本書7事件）と比較せよ．
10　本件はどのような事件か．判旨の結論，理論構成に賛成か．

9 契約能力の準拠法：
Lilienthal v. Kaufman,
239 Or.1, 395 P.2d 543 (1964)

DENECKE, Justice.

This is an action to collect two promissory notes. The defense is that the defendant maker has previously been declared a spendthrift by an Oregon court and placed under a guardianship and that the guardian has declared the obligations void. The plaintiff's counter is that the notes were executed and delivered in California, that the law of California does not recognize the disability of a spendthrift, and that the Oregon court is bound to apply the law of the place of the making of the contract. The trial court rejected plaintiff's argument and held for the defendant.

This same defendant spendthrift was the prevailing party in our recent decision in *Olshen v. Kaufman*, 235 Or. 423, 385 P.2d 161 (1963). In that case the spendthrift and the plaintiff, an Oregon resident, had gone into a joint venture to purchase binoculars for resale. For this purpose plaintiff had advanced moneys to the spendthrift. The spendthrift had repaid plaintiff by his personal check for the amount advanced and for plaintiff's share of the profits of such venture. The check had not been paid because the spendthrift had had insufficient funds in his account. The action was for the unpaid balance of the check.

The evidence in that case showed that the plaintiff had been unaware that Kaufman was under a spendthrift guardianship. The guardian testified that he knew Kaufman was engaging in some business and had bank accounts and that he had admonished him to cease these practices; but he

> 契約能力の準拠法について，いわゆる利益分析論を採用し，行為者の住所地（法廷地）であるオレゴン法を適用し，浪費者であるオレゴン住民の契約能力を否定した事例

DENECKE 裁判官

　本件は，2通の約束手形を取り立てる訴訟である．被告である振出人の抗弁は，被告がさきにオレゴンの裁判所で浪費者の宣告を受けて後見人の監督の下に置かれており，後見人が債務を無効とする旨の宣言をしたという点にある．これに対する原告の反論は，手形はカルフォルニアで作成・交付され，カルフォルニア法が浪費者の無能力を認めていないこと，オレゴン裁判所は，契約締結地法を適用しなければならないというにある．事実審裁判所はこの原告の主張を退けて被告勝訴の判決を下した．

　本件の同一被告は，われわれの最近の判決 *Olshen v. Kaufman*, 235 Or. 423, 385 P.2d 161（1963）の勝訴当事者であった．その事件では浪費者とオレゴンの住民である原告は，双眼鏡を転売用に購入するジョイント・ベンチャーを始めた．このために原告は浪費者に前渡金を支払った．これに対し浪費者は原告に前払いを受けた全額と，このベンチャー事業利益に対する原告の分け前とを個人小切手で返済した．この小切手は，浪費者が口座に十分な資金をもっていなかったために支払われなかった．訴訟はこの小切手の未払残高の請求であった．

　さきの事件での証拠によれば，原告は Kaufman が浪費者後見に服していることを知らなかった．後見人は，Kaufman がなにか事業を営んでおり，かつ，銀行口座を開設していることを知っており，これをやめるよう警告した．しかし後見人は浪費者をコントロールすることはできなかった．

could not control the spendthrift.

The statute applicable in that case and in this one is ORS 126.335:

"After the appointment of a guardian for the spendthrift, all contracts, except for necessaries, and all gifts, sales and transfers of real or personal estate made by such spendthrift thereafter and before the termination of the guardianship are voidable." (Repealed 1961, ch 344, §109, now ORS 126.280)

We held in that case that the voiding of the contract by the guardian precluded recovery by the plaintiff and that the spendthrift and the guardian were not estopped to deny the validity of plaintiff's claim. Plaintiff does not seek to overturn the principle of that decision but contends it has no application because the law of California governs, and under California law the plaintiff's claim is valid.

The facts here are identical to those in *Olshen v. Kaufman*, supra, except for the California locale for portions of the transaction. The notes were for the repayment of advances to finance another joint venture to sell binoculars. The plaintiff was unaware that defendant had been declared a spendthrift and placed under guardianship. The guardian, upon demand for payment by the plaintiff, declared the notes void. The issue is solely one involving the principles of conflict of laws.

……

Before entering the choice-of-law area of the general field of conflict of laws, we must determine whether the laws of the states having a connection with the controversy are in conflict. Defendant did not expressly concede that under the law of California the defendant's obligation would be enforceable, but his counsel did state that if this proceeding were in the courts of California, the plaintiff probably would recover. We agree.

同事件及び本件に適用される制定法は ORS 126.335 である．

「浪費者に対して後見人が任命された後において浪費者により，後見終了以前になされた，必需品契約を除くすべての契約，すべての贈与，売買及び物的，人的財産の譲渡は取り消しうるものとする．」（Repealed 1961, ch 344, §109, now ORS 126.280）

さきの事件においてわれわれは，後見人による契約の取消によって原告の損害賠償請求は排除されること，ならびに浪費者と後見人は，原告の請求を否認することを禁反言により禁じられるものではない，と判示した．原告は，この判決の原則を覆えそうとするのではなく，本件ではカルフォルニア法が適用されるのであるから，さきの判決の原則が適用されず，また，カルフォルニア法によれば原告の請求は有効である，と主張しているのである．

本件の事実は，取引が主としてカルフォルニアで行われたという点を除けば，前掲 *Olshen v. Kaufman* 事件と同一である．手形が発行されたのは，同じく双眼鏡を販売する別のジョイント・ベンチャーに融資する前渡金の支払いのためであった．また，原告は，被告が浪費者の宣告を受け，後見に服していることを知らなかった．原告による支払いの請求に対して，後見人が手形を無効とする宣言をした．したがって本件で問題となっている争点は，抵触法の原則だけである．

……

抵触法の一般分野における法選択問題に入る前に，紛争に関連を有する州の法が抵触しているかどうかを決定しなければならない．被告は，カルフォルニア法によれば被告の債務が執行されるとはっきりとは認めていないが，代理人はもし本件訴訟がカルフォルニアの裁判所で行われたならば，原告は多分その請求が認められるであろうと述べている．われわれも同意見である．

Ⅱ 法選択（準拠法）

　　At common law a spendthrift was not considered incapable of contracting. *Taylor v. Koenigstein*, 128 Neb. 809, 260 N.W. 544, 546 (1935). Incapacity of a spendthrift to contract is a disability created by the legislature. California has no such legislation. In addition, the Civil Code of California provides that all persons are capable of contracting except minors, persons judicially determined to be of unsound mind, and persons deprived of civil rights. §1556. ......

　　Defendant contends that the law of California should not be applied in this case by the Oregon court because the invalidity of the contract is a matter of remedy, rather than one of substance. Matters of remedy, procedure, are governed by the law of the forum. What is a matter of substance and what is a matter of procedure are sometimes difficult questions to decide. Stumberg states the distinction as follows: "...... procedural rules should be classified as those which concern methods of presenting to a court the operative facts upon which legal relations depend; substantive rules, those which concern the legal effect of those facts after they have been established." Stumberg, Principles of Conflict of Laws (3d ed), 133. Based upon this conventional statement of the distinction, it is obvious that we are not concerned with a procedural issue, but with a matter of substantive law.

　　Plaintiff contends that the substantive issue of whether or not an obligation is valid and binding is governed by the law of the place of making, California. This court has repeatedly stated that the law of the place of contract "must govern as to the validity, interpretation, and construction of the contract." *Jamieson v. Potts*, 55 Or. 292, 300, 105 P. 93, 25 L.R.A. (N.S.,) 24 (1910). Restatement 408, Conflict of Laws, §332, so announced and specifically stated that "capacity to make the contract" was to be determined by the law of the place of contract.

　　This principle, that *lex loci contractus* must govern, however, has been under heavy attack for years. For example, see Lorenzen, *Validity and*

コモンローでは，浪費者は契約能力を有しないとは考えられていなかった．*Taylor v. Koenigstein*, 128 Neb. 809, 260 N.W. 544, 546（1935）．浪費者の契約無能力は，制定法上のものであり，カルフォルニアはそのような制定法を有していない．加えて，カルフォルニアの民法は，未成年者，精神に障害があると裁判によって宣言された者及び市民権を剥奪された者を除くすべての者は契約能力があると規定している．§1556. ……

被告の主張によれば，契約の有効性の問題は実体の問題ではなく，救済の問題であるから，本件ではカルフォルニア法はオレゴンの裁判所によって適用されるべきでないという．救済ないしは手続に関する事項は法廷地法によって決定される．なにが実体に関する事項であるか，そして，なにが手続に関する事項であるかは，ときとして決定することが困難な問題である．Stumbergはその区別を次のように述べている．すなわち，「……手続規則とは，法律関係を左右する主要事実を裁判所に提出する方法に関する規則と性質づけられるべきであり，実体に関する規則とはこれらの事実が立証された後の，これらの事実の法的効果にかかわる規則と性質づけられるべきである．」Stumberg, Principles of Conflict of Laws（3d ed）, 133. この伝統的な区別の考え方によれば，本件においてわれわれがかかわっているのは，手続上の争点ではなく，実体法上の問題であることは明らかである．

原告は，債務が有効で拘束力があるかどうかという実体の問題は，契約締結地の法，つまり，カルフォルニア法によって規律される，と主張する．当裁判所は繰り返し，契約締結地法が「契約の有効性，解釈について適用されなければならない．」と述べてきた．*Jamieson v. Potts*, 55 Or. 292, 300, 105 P. 93, 25 L.R.A.（N.S.,）24（1910）．抵触法リステイトメント408頁，第332条もその旨を宣言し，とくに「契約を締結する能力」は，契約地法によって決定されると述べている．

しかしながら，*契約締結地法が適用されなければならないという原則は*，久しく激しい批判にさらされてきた．たとえば，Lorenzen, *Validity and*

213

Effects of Contracts in the Conflict of Laws, 30 Yale L. J. 565, 655 (1921); 31 Yale L. J. 53 (1921). The strongest criticism has been that the place of making frequently is completely fortuitous and that on occasion the state of making has no interest in the parties to the contract or in the performance of the contract. *Stumberg*, supra, at 231. The principle is undermined when it is observed that in many of the decisions, the state of the place of making had other associations with the contract, e.g., it was also the place of performance and the domicile of one of the parties. In our decisions stating this principle, the state whose law was applied had connections with the contract in addition to being the place of making. *Jamieson v. Potts*, supra (55 Or 292); *McGirl v. Brewer*, 132 Or. 422, 443, 280 P.508, 285 P.208 (1930). As a result of this long and powerful assault, the principle is no longer a cornerstone of the law of conflicts. Tentative Draft No. 6, p3, Restatement (Second), Conflict of Laws, comments on the new contracts chapter: "First, it no longer says dogmatically that the validity of a contract is governed by the law of the place of contracting."

There is no need to decide that our previous statements that the law of the place of contract governs were in error. Our purpose is to state that this portion of our decision is not founded upon that principle because of our doubt that it is correct if the *only* connection of the state whose law would govern is that it was the place of making.

In this case California had more connection with the transaction than being merely the place where the contract was executed. The defendant went to San Francisco to ask the plaintiff, a California resident, for money for the defendant's venture. The money was loaned to defendant in San Francisco, and by the terms of the note, it was to be repaid to plaintiff in San Francisco.

Effects of Contracts in the Conflict of Laws, 30 Yale L. J. 565, 655 (1921); 31 Yale L. J. 53 (1921) 参照. 最大の批判は, 締結地はしばしば全く偶然的であり, ときとして締結地州は契約当事者と契約の履行に対しなんらの利害関係を有しないという点にあった. *Stumberg*, 前掲 231 頁. さらに多くの判決において締結地は契約と他の関連を有していたこと, たとえば, 締結地は同時に履行地や当事者一方の住所地でもあったことが認められるときには, この原則の基礎が危うくなる. この原則を述べたわれわれの判決では, その法が適用された州は, 締結地であることに加えて, 契約と関連を有していた. *Jamieson v. Potts*, 前掲 (55 Or. 292); *McGirl v. Brewer*, 132 Or. 422, 443, 280 P.508, 285 P.208 (1930). これらの長期にわたる強力な批判の結果として, この原則はもはや抵触法のコーナーストーンではない. 抵触法第2リステイトメント試案 No.6 の3頁は, 新しい契約の章について,「まず, 第1に契約の有効性は契約地の法によって規律されるとは独断的に述べられてはいない.」とコメントする.

契約地法が適用されるとした, われわれの前の判示が誤っていたと決定する必要はない. われわれの目的は, われわれの判決のこの部分は, その原則に立脚するものではないということを明らかにすることにあるのである. というのは, 準拠法州と事件との唯一の関連が, その州が締結地であるにすぎない場合にも, この原則が正しいのだとすることに対してわれわれが疑念を抱いているからである.

本件においてカルフォルニアは, 単に契約が行われた場所であるという以上の取引との関連を有していた. 被告は, カルフォルニアの住民である原告に被告の事業のための資金を頼みにサンフランシスコへ行った. 金銭はサンフランシスコで被告に貸し付けられ, 手形の文言によれば, サンフランシスコで原告に返済されることになっていた.

On these facts, apart from *lex loci contractus*, other accepted principles of conflict of laws lead to the conclusion that the law of California should be applied. *Sterrett v. Stoddard Lbr. Co.*, 150 Or. 491, 504, 46 P.2d 1023 (1935), rests, at least in part, on the proposition that the validity of a note is determined by the law of the place of payment. ...... The place of payment, unlike the place of making, is usually not determined fortuitously. The place is usually selected by the payee and the payee normally selects his place of business or the location of his bank. The parties at the time of contract normally do not have in mind the problem of what law should govern. If they did, it is our belief that the payee would intend the law of the place of payment to be governing.

There is another conflict principle calling for the application of California law. Stumberg terms it the application of the law which upholds the contract. Stumberg, supra, at 237. Ehrenzweig calls it the "Rule of Validation." Ehrenzweig, Conflict of Laws, 353 (1962)........The "rule" is that, if the contract is valid under the law of any jurisdiction having significant connection with the contract, i.e., place of making, place of performance, etc., the law of that jurisdiction validating the contract will be applied. This would also agree with the intention of the parties, if they had had any intentions in this regard. They must have intended their agreement to be valid.

......

Thus far all signs have pointed to applying the law of California and holding the contract enforceable. There is, however, an obstacle to cross before this end can be logically reached. In *Olshen v. Kaufman*, supra, we decided that the law of Oregon, at least as applied to persons domiciled in Oregon contracting in Oregon for performance in Oregon, is that spendthrifts' contracts are voidable. Are the choice-of-law principles of conflict of laws so superior that they overcome this principle of Oregon law?

これらの事実からすれば，*契約締結地法の原則*とは別に，他の一般に受け入れられた抵触法の原則によっても，カルフォルニア法が適用されるべきとの結論が導き出せる．*Sterrett v. Stoddard Lbr. Co.*, 150 Or. 491, 504, 46 P.2d 1023（1935）は，少なくとも手形の有効性は，支払地の法によって決定されるという原則に基づいている．……支払地は締結地とは異なり，通常，偶然的に定められることはない．支払地は，普通，支払人によって選択され，支払人は通常，自分の事業所所在地又は銀行所在地を選択する．契約時に当事者は普通，どの法が適用されるかの問題を考慮しないが，かりに考慮するとすれば，われわれの信ずるところでは支払人は支払地法が適用されると考えるであろう．

カルフォルニア法の適用を要求するさらに別の抵触法原則がある．Stumberg は，これを契約を有効とする法の適用と表現している．Stumberg, 前掲 237 頁．Ehrenzweig は，これを「有効視の原則」と呼んでいる．Ehrenzweig, Conflict of Laws, 353（1962）……この「原則」は，締結地や履行地などの契約と重要な関係を有するいずれかの法域の法によれば，契約が有効であれば，その契約を有効とする法域の法が適用されるとするものである．これはまた，当事者がこの点についてなんらかの意思を有していたとすれば，この当事者の意思と合致するであろう．当事者の意思は契約を有効とすることにあったに違いないからである．

……

このようにこれまでのところは，すべてカルフォルニア法を適用し，契約を有効と判示すべきとの徴候が示されている．しかし，この結論に不可避的に到達しうるには，乗り越えなければならない障害がある．前掲 *Olshen v. Kaufman* 判決では，少なくともオレゴンに住所を有し，オレゴンでの履行のためオレゴンで契約する者に適用される限りでは，オレゴン法によれば浪費者による契約は取り消しうる，とわれわれは決定したのである．抵触法の法選択原則はこのオレゴン法の原則を凌駕するほど優位なものなのであろうか．

To answer this question we must determine, upon some basis, whether the interests of Oregon are so basic and important that we should not apply California law despite its several intimate connections with the transaction. The traditional method used by this court and most others is framed in the terminology of "public policy." The court decides whether or not the public policy of the forum is so strong that the law of the forum must prevail although another jurisdiction, with different laws, has more and closer contacts with the transaction. Included in "public policy" we must consider the economic and social interests of Oregon. When these factors are included in a consideration of whether the law of the forum should be applied this traditional approach is very similar to that advocated by many legal scholars. This latter theory is "that choice-of-law rules should rationally advance the policies or interests of the several states (or of the nations in the world community)." Hill, *Governmental Interest and the Conflict of Laws-A Reply to Professor Currie*, 27 Chi. L. Rev. 463, 474 (1960); Currie, *Selected Essays on the Conflict of Laws*, 64 -72 (1963), reprint from 58 Col. L. Rev. 964 (1958).
......

Some of the interests of Oregon in this litigation are set forth in *Olshen v. Kaufman*, supra. The spendthrift's family which is to be protected by the establishment of the guardianship is presumably an Oregon family. The public authority which may be charged with the expense of supporting the spendthrift or his family, if he is permitted to go unrestrained upon his wasteful way, will probably be an Oregon public authority. These, obviously, are interests of some substance.

Oregon has other interests and policies regarding this matter which were not necessary to discuss in *Olshen*. As previously stated, Oregon, as well as all other states, has a strong policy favoring the validity and

この問いに答えるためには，カルフォルニアが取引といくつかの密接な関連を有するにもかかわらず，同州法を適用すべきでないとするほどまでオレゴンの利益が基本的に重要なものであるかどうかをなんらかの根拠に基づいて決定しなければならない．当裁判所を含めて，ほとんどの裁判所で使われてきた伝統的な方法は，「公序」の名で表現されている．裁判所は，法廷地の公序が，異なった法を有する他の法域が取引と一層多くの密接な関連を有する場合であっても，法廷地法を優先しなければならないほど強いものであるかどうかを決定する．われわれは，「公序」の中にオレゴンの経済的，社会的利益を含めて考えなければならない．これらの要素が法廷地法を適用すべきかの考慮の中に含まれているときは，この伝統的アプローチは多くの国際私法学者によって主張されているアプローチと非常によく似たものになる．後者の理論は，「法選択規則は，それぞれの州（又は国際社会における国家）の法目的又は利益を合理的にみて促進するものでなければならない．」とするものである．Hill, *Governmental Interest and the Conflict of Laws-A Reply to Professor Currie*, 27 Chi. L. Rev. 463, 474（1960）; Currie, *Selected Essays on the Conflict of Laws*, 64-72（1963）, reprint from 58 Col. L. Rev. 964（1958）.
……

　本件におけるオレゴンの利益のうち，いくつかは前掲 *Olshen v. Kaufman* で述べられている．後見の開始によって保護されるべき浪費者の家族は多分，オレゴンの家族である．浪費者が止められないままに浪費生活を続ければ，浪費者又はその家族を扶助しなければならないのは，オレゴンの公的機関であろう．これらは明らかに実質的な利益である．

　オレゴンはまた，*Olshen* 判決では論じる必要のなかった利益と法目的を有している．さきに述べたように，オレゴンは他のすべての州と同様に，契約の有効性と執行性を支持する強い法目的をもっている．この法目的は，契約

enforceability of contracts. This policy applies whether the contract is made and to be performed in Oregon or elsewhere.

The defendant's conduct, —— borrowing money with the belief that the repayment of such loan could be avoided —— is a species of fraud. Oregon and all other states have a strong policy of protecting innocent persons from fraud.......

It is in Oregon's commercial interest to encourage citizens of other states to conduct business with Oregonians. If Oregonians acquire a reputation for not honoring their agreements, commercial intercourse with Oregonians will be discouraged. If there are Oregon laws, somewhat unique to Oregon, which permit an Oregonian to escape his otherwise binding obligations, persons may well avoid commercial dealings with Oregonians.

The substance of these commercial considerations, however, is deflated by the recollection that the Oregon Legislature has determined, despite the weight of these considerations, that a spendthrift's contracts are voidable.

California's most direct interest in this transaction is having its citizen creditor paid. As previously noted, California's policy is that any creditor, in California or otherwise, should be paid even though the debtor is a spendthrift. California probably has another, although more intangible, interest involved. It is presumably to every state's benefit to have the reputation of being a jurisdiction in which contracts can be made and performance be promised with the certain knowledge that such contracts will be enforced. Both of these interests, particularly the former, are also of substance.

We have, then, two jurisdictions, each with several close connections with the transaction, and each with a substantial interest, which will be

9 契約能力の準拠法：Lilienthal v. Kaufman

が締結され，履行されるのがオレゴンであろうと，それ以外の地であろうと，適合するものである．

　被告の行為，——つまり，貸付金の返済は免れるだろうと信じて，借金することは，——一種の詐欺である．オレゴンと他のすべての州は，詐欺から罪のない人を保護することに対して強い法目的をもっている……

　他州の市民がオレゴン住民と取引をするように仕向けることは，オレゴンの商業上の利益である．もしオレゴン住民が合意を守らないという評判がたてば，オレゴン住民との商取引は水を差されるだろう．オレゴンにオレゴン特有の法律があり，それによって本来オレゴン住民が負うべき債務から免れさせることが許されるとすれば，人々はオレゴン住民との商取引を避けることになって当然かもしれない．
　しかしながら，上に述べたような商業上の考慮のもつ意義は，これらの考慮の重要性にもかかわらず，オレゴンの立法機関が浪費者の契約は取り消しうると決定したことを想起すれば，減少する．

　この取引におけるカルフォルニアの最も直接的な利益は，自州の住民が支払いを受けることである．前に指摘したように，カルフォルニアの法目的は，すべての債権者は，カルフォルニアにおいてであろうとなかろうと，債務者が浪費者であっても，支払いを受けるべきであるという点にある．カルフォルニアは，もっと目にみえないものであるけれども，別の利益をもつ．州内で契約が強制実現されるという確信をもって，契約が締結され，履行が約束されうる州であるとの評判を有することは，多分，すべての州にとって利益であろう．これらの利益はともに，とりわけ，前者は実質的なものである．

　したがって2つの法域，すなわち，それぞれ取引と密接な関連をもち，またいずれの法が適用されるかによって，それぞれの実質的な利益がかなえら

served or thwarted, depending upon which law is applied. The interests of neither jurisdiction are clearly more important than those of the other. We are of the opinion that in such a case the public policy of Oregon should prevail and the law of Oregon should be applied; we should apply that choice-of-law rule which will "advance the policies or interests of" Oregon. *Hill*, supra, 27 Chi. L. Rev. at 474.

Courts are instruments of state policy. The Oregon Legislature has adopted a policy to avoid possible hardship to an Oregon family of a spendthrift and to avoid possible expenditure of Oregon public funds which might occur if the spendthrift is required to pay his obligations. In litigation Oregon courts are the appropriate instrument to enforce this policy. The mechanical application of choice-of-law rules would be the only apparent reason for an Oregon court advancing the interests of California over the equally valid interests of Oregon. The present principles of conflict of laws are not favorable to such mechanical application.

We hold that the spendthrift law of Oregon is applicable and the plaintiff cannot recover.

Judgment affirmed.

O'CONNELL, J., specially concurring.

……

In the *Olshen* case we had to choose between two competing policies; on one hand the policy of protecting the interest of persons dealing with spendthrifts which, broadly, may be described as the interest in the security of transactions, and on the other hand the policy of protecting the interests of the spendthrift, his family and the county. It was decided that the Oregon Legislature adopted the latter policy in preference to the former.

The case at bar involves the same choice even though the contract was made in California and it was to be performed there. The fact that

れたり，脅かされたりすることになる2つの法域がある．いずれの法域の利益も他の法域の利益よりも明らかにより重要なものではない．このような場合には，オレゴンの公序が優先し，オレゴン法が適用されるべきだと考える．すなわち，オレゴンの「法目的又は利益を優先する」法選択規則を適用しなければならない．*Hill*, 前掲 27 Chi. L. Rev. at 474.

　裁判所は州の法目的を達成するための道具である．オレゴンの立法府は次のような法目的，すなわち，もし浪費者が債務を支払わなければならないとすれば，生じるかもしれないオレゴンの浪費者の家族の困窮とオレゴンの公的資金の出費の可能性を回避するための法目的を採用したのである．訴訟ではオレゴンの裁判所は，この法目的を実現させるための適切な道具である．オレゴンの裁判所が，オレゴンの利益を犠牲にして，カルフォルニアの利益を達成させる唯一の明白な根拠は，法選択規則の機械的な適用だけである．現在の抵触法の原則は，このような機械的適用に対して好意的ではない．
　われわれは，オレゴンの浪費者法が適用され，原告は損害賠償請求をなしえないと判示する．
　上訴棄却

O'CONNELL 裁判官の特別補足意見
……
　Olshen 判決において，われわれは2つの競合する法目的間の選択をしなければならなかった．一方は浪費者と取引をする人の利益保護という法目的であり，それはもっと広範には取引の安全に対する利益と表現することもできよう．他方は，浪費者，その家族及びカウンティの利益を保護する法目的である．オレゴンの立法府は後者の法目的を前者に優先して採択すると判断された．
　本件では，契約がカルフォルニアで締結され，そこで履行されることになっていたけれども，同じ選択が問題となっている．カルフォルニアが契約の

California was the setting for the making and performance of the contract is of no significance except that it requires us to consider California's interest in protecting its own citizens. That interest is an interest in the security of commercial transactions and was before this court in the *Olshen* case. To distinguish the *Olshen* case it would be necessary to assume that although the legislature intended to protect the interest of the spendthrift, his family and the county when local creditors were harmed, the same protection was not intended where the transaction adversely affected foreign creditors. I see no basis for making that assumption. There is no reason to believe that our legislature intended to protect California creditors to a greater extent than our own.

GOODWIN, J., dissenting.
I am unable to agree with the conclusion of the majority.

……

……I am aware of no compelling public reason for saving spendthrifts from the result of their folly at the expense of innocent merchants.

……

The plaintiff was a merchant in California who was approached in the ordinary course of business by a seemingly competent person and asked to enter into a business arrangement. The notes were executed, delivered, and made payable in California. If the parties gave any thought to law at all, which is unlikely, they would have assumed that California law would apply to their business. Consequently, if California law were to be applied, it would neither surprise the parties nor shock the conscience of the court. It would hardly violate any "fundamental principle of justice" or "prevalent conception of good morals."

……

締結と履行の舞台であるという事実は，それがわれわれにカルフォルニアが自州の住民を保護するというカルフォルニアの利益を考慮すべきことを要求することを除いては，なんら重要ではない．その利益は商取引の安全を図るという利益であり，*Olshen* 判決において当裁判所に提起されていたものである．*Olshen* 判決と区別するためには，立法府は自州の債権者が損害を被ったときには，浪費者，その家族及びカウンティの利益を保護することを意図したけれども，取引が州外の債権者に不利な影響を与えたときには，同様の保護は意図されていなかったと推量することが必要である．その推定をする根拠はないと私は考える．われわれの立法府が，自州民よりもカルフォルニアの債権者により大きな保護を与えようとしたことを信じる合理的な理由は存在しない．

GOODWIN 裁判官の反対意見

私は多数意見の結論に同意することはできない．

……

……私は，善意の商人を犠牲にしてまで浪費者の愚行の結果から浪費者を救済するための強い公的理由を知らない．

……

原告はカルフォルニアの商人であり，通常のビジネス・コースにおいて一見すると能力者とみられる者からアプローチされ，ビジネスに関する取決めを締結するよう求められた．手形はカルフォルニアで作成され，引き渡され，そして支払われることになっていた．かりに当事者が法律について思い及んだとすれば，それはありそうにないが，カルフォルニア法が彼らのビジネスに適用されるであろうと想定したであろう．したがってカルフォルニア法が適用されるとすれば，当事者にとって不意打ちとはならず，また裁判所の良心にショックを与えることはないであろう．それはなんら「正義の基本原則」や「広く認められている良い道徳観念」に反することはほとんどないであろう．

……

......The majority opinion virtually concedes that both the rule of validation and the center-of-gravity theory point to the application of California law. The majority says, however, that these established principles of conflict of laws should give way to the "public policy" of Oregon.

......

In the case before us, I believe that the policy of both states, Oregon and California, in favor of enforcing contracts, has been lost sight of in favor of a questionable policy in Oregon which gives special privileges to the rare spendthrift for whom a guardian has been appointed.

The majority view in the case at bar strikes me as a step backward toward the balkanization of the law of contracts. *Olshen v. Kaufman*, 235 Or. 423, 385 P.2d 161 (1963), held that there was a policy in this state to help keep spendthrifts out of the almshouse. I can see nothing, however, in Oregon's policy toward spendthrifts that warrants its extension to permit the taking of captives from other states down the road to insolvency.

I would enforce the contract.

……多数意見は，有効視の原則と重心理論はともにカルフォルニア法の適用を指示することを実際上は認めている．しかしながら，多数意見は，これらの確立された抵触法の原則は，オレゴンの「公序」に道を譲らなければならない，という．

……

本件においてはオレゴンとカルフォルニアの両州がともに共有する契約の強行を支持するという法目的が，オレゴンの後見人が任命されるまれな浪費者に特別の恩恵的利益を与えるというオレゴンにおける疑わしい法目的のために見失われていると，私は考える．

本件の多数意見は，私には契約法の分裂への後ろ向きのワンステップとの印象を受ける．*Olshen v. Kaufman*, 235 Or. 423, 385 P.2d 161（1963）は，この州には浪費者を救貧院に入れないように支援する法目的が存在すると判示した．しかしながら，浪費者に対するオレゴンの法目的の中には，その範囲を拡げて，破産への道をたどる他州からの捕虜をとらえることを許容することを正当化するものはなにも見出すことはできない．

私は本件契約の執行を認める．

Ⅱ　法選択（準拠法）

【解　説】

　本件の法選択における主要な争点は，浪費者の契約能力の準拠法は，カルフォルニア法かオレゴン法のいずれかという問題である．
　オレゴン州最高裁は，契約能力の準拠法についていわゆる Currie 流の利益分析論を採用し，契約締結地であり，取引の相手方の住所地法であるカルフォルニア法（浪費者を能力者とする）を適用せず，行為者の住所地であり，かつ法廷地であるオレゴン州の法を適用し，浪費者であるオレゴン州民の契約能力を否定した．

1　契約の準拠法

　契約の準拠法，とりわけ契約能力を含む契約の有効性に関するアメリカ国際私法の伝統的な解決は，契約締結地法主義であった．オレゴンの契約の準拠法に関する法選択規則もそうであった．これは，契約が締結された地の法が契約の有効性を決定するという．第1リステイトメントによれば，契約締結地とは契約を拘束力あらしめるに必要な最後の行為が行われた場所である．この規則は理論的には属地主義の当然の帰結として，また実際的にも確実性と予見可能性を確保する最善の規則として強力に主張，擁護された．
　しかし多くの有力な学者によって激しく論難された．この規則に対する批判は，その適用において2つの顕著な欠陥をもつという点にあった．すなわち，第1に契約が最終的に締結される場所を確定することは困難であり，したがってそれほど大きな確実性と予見可能性をもたらさないと批判され，第2にたとえそれが確定されたとしても，契約締結地は契約にとって偶然的であると批判された．
　契約締結地法主義以外には，判旨もいうように，当時は①履行地法主義，②重心理論，③契約有効視の原則などが主張されていた．
　①　履行地法が契約の有効性を支配する．履行は契約の本質的な目的であるから，履行地はつねに重要であり，当事者と契約に密接かつ現実の関連をもつと主張された．しかし，この規則に対しても，履行地の決定が困難であ

ること（履行が2以上の異なる州に分割されている通常の双務契約の場合とくに困難である），またかりに確定しえても，しばしば契約の有効性とほとんど実質的な関係をもたないという批判があった．

②　契約の有効性は契約と最も重要な関係を有する法域の法による．この規則は柔軟性に富み，かつ，最大の利害関係を有する地に個々の事実関係から生じる争点に対する最大の支配力を与えるという利点を有すると主張された（*Auten v. Auten*, 308 N.Y. 155, 124 N.E.2d 90（1954））．この理論によれば，どのようにして「最も重要な関係」又は「重心」を決定するかが問題となる．

③　契約を有効視する法の適用を指示する規則である．

以上のほか，当事者が明示又は黙示の意思により指定した法律が契約の有効性を支配する，いわゆる当事者自治の原則も有力になりつつあった．この点については，松岡博『アメリカ国際私法の基礎理論』1頁以下（2007）参照．

2　利益分析論

本判決は，以上のような状況下において，法選択理論としてCurrieの利益分析論（松岡・前掲アメリカ国際私法の基礎理論245-246頁）を契約の分野で採用したリーディング・ケースである．

Currieの利益分析論とはどのような理論か．Currieは，伝統的理論をすべて破棄し，それに代わるべき方法論を提示した．Currieの方法論の根底にあるのは，抵触法問題の解決は，州の実質法の基礎にある法目的と，その法目的を実現するためにその法を具体的事件に適用することに対して州が有する利益を考慮してなされなければならないとする認識であった．

Currieによれば，①　まず事件に関連を有する州の実質法の法目的と利益の分析の結果，事件に関連を有する州の法律の内容が異なっていても，1つの州のみが自州法を適用する利益を有するときはその法を適用する．この場合には法律の内容に抵触があっても，2つの州の間には法目的や利益の抵触は存在しない．これが「虚偽の抵触」である．

②　次に事件に関連を有する州法の法目的と利益の分析の結果，2州がと

II 法選択（準拠法）

もに自州法を適用する利益を有する場合であっても，これらの州の利益又は法目的に控え目の解釈をすることによって結局，1州のみが利益を有すると判断され，抵触を回避することができる場合がある．これが「表見上の抵触」である．

③ このようにしても抵触を回避できない，「真の抵触」の場合には，法廷地法が適用される．いずれの州も自州法を適用する利益を有しないときは，一定の要件の下で法廷地法を適用すべきとした．

3 不法行為事件における利益分析論

利益分析論が最初に採用されたのは，不法行為の分野におけるニューヨーク州最高裁判所の *Babcock* 判決である（*Babcock v. Jackson*, 12 N.Y.2d 473 (1963)）．ニューヨークの住民である原告と被告がカナダへ週末旅行にでかけ，オンタリオ州で被告の過失により原告が負傷した．オンタリオ法によれば，報酬を受けないでゲストを自動車に同乗させたときは，ホストは賠償責任を負わない．これに対してニューヨーク法はホストの過失の場合にゲストに損害賠償請求の権利を認めている．裁判所はニューヨーク法を適用して原告の請求を認容した．

裁判所は，オンタリオ法の基礎にある法目的は，ゲストとホストが保険会社に対して共謀することを防止することにあり，したがって，ニューヨークの被告が責任を課せられるか，あるいは，ニューヨークの保険会社がニューヨークの原告から保険金を詐取されるかどうかはオンタリオの立法の関心とはほとんどなりえない．他方，過失によってゲストに損害を与えた者に賠償責任を負わせるというニューヨーク法の目的はニューヨークの住民が州外で負傷した場合にも完全に適用されると判示した．

上の判決は，不法行為は不法行為地法によるという厳格で包括的な伝統的法選択規則を，それが不法行為地以外の州が特定の争点の決定に有する利害関係を無視しているとの理由で破棄して，事件に関連を有する州の実質法の目的と，事件の具体的関連を考慮して，準拠法を決定すべきであるとの革新的な理論を採用した（松岡博『国際私法における法選択規則構造論』（有斐閣，1987）

62-63頁).

同じく不法行為地法主義を破棄し利益分析論を採用した初期のカルフォルニア最高裁の判決としては，*Reich v. Purcell*, 67 Cal.2d 551, 432 P.2d 727（1967）がある．この判決で，裁判所は事件に関連を有する3つの州を確認し，これらの州の実質法の目的と事件に対して有する牽連関係からみて，それぞれの州が自州法を適用する利益を有するか否かを検討するという方法論を採用した．そして自州の住民に完全な補償を認めるカルフォルニアの関連は，事故発生当時においては被告のみが同州の住民であったのだから適切ではないとし，ついで原告の賠償請求に制限を加えるミズーリの利益は同州の住民でない当事者の事件では適用されないと判示する．最後に自州住民の遺族に完全な補償を認めるオハイオのみが自州法を適用する正当な利益を有するとして，オハイオ法を適用した．この判決については，松岡博『[新版]国際私法・国際取引法判例研究』(大阪大学出版会, 2003) 170-177頁参照.

4 本件における利益分析論

本件判旨は，Currie流の利益分析論を採用しているといえるであろうか．判旨の論理を要約してみよう（[ ] 内は，筆者のコメント）.

① 法選択規則は，それぞれの州又は国の法目的又は利益を合理的にみて促進するものでなければならない．[この点は利益分析論の基本的な考え方である]

② 本件におけるオレゴンの利益はなにか．まず，後見によって保護されるべき浪費者の家族はオレゴンの家族である．浪費者がそのまま浪費生活を続ければ，浪費者又はその家族を扶助するのは，オレゴン州である．これらは明らかに実質的な利益である．

次にオレゴンは，契約の有効性と執行性を支持するという別の強い法目的をもつ．貸付金の返済は免れるだろうと信じて，借金することは，一種の詐欺である．詐欺から罪のない人を保護することに対してオレゴンも他の州と同様に強い法目的をもつ．オレゴンに特有の法があり，オレゴン住民が負うべき債務から免れさせることが許されるとすれば，人々はオレゴン住民との

商取引を避けることになるかもしれない．しかしこのような商業上の考慮のもつ意義は，オレゴンの立法機関が浪費者の契約は取り消しうると決定したことを考えると，減少するであろう．

③ 次に，カルフォルニアの利益はどうか．この取引におけるカルフォルニアの最も直接的な利益は，自州の住民が支払いを受けることである．カルフォルニアは，別の利益をもつ．州内で契約が強制実現されることを確信をもって，契約が締結され，履行が約束されうる州であるとの評判を有することは，すべての州にとって利益であろう．これらの利益，とりわけ，前者は実質的なものである．

④ したがって2つの法域，すなわち，それぞれ取引と密接な関連をもち，またいずれの法が適用されるかによって，それぞれの実質的な利益がかなえられたり，脅かされたりすることになる2つの法域がある．［本件はその意味でCurrieのいう真の抵触の事例である］

⑤ このような場合には，オレゴンの公序が優先し，オレゴン法が適用されるべきだと考える．オレゴンの法目的又は利益を優先する法選択規則を適用しなければならない．裁判所は州の法目的を達成するための道具である．訴訟ではオレゴンの裁判所は，州の法目的を実現させるための道具である．［この解決は，Currieのいう真の抵触における法廷地法の優先を示している］

5 学説の対応

本件に対する学説の対応はどうか．評価は，賛成と反対に鋭く対立する．

まず，Kramerは，*Lilienthal*判決は正しく判決された，しかし判決理由は誤っているとする．Kramer, *Rethinking Choice of Law*, 90 Colum.L.Rev. 277, 323（1990）．また，Weinbergも*Lilienthal*判決は不当な判決ではないという．Weinberg, *On Departing From Forum Law*, 35 Mercer L. Rev. 595, 605（1984）．これらは本判決に好意的な立場であるといえよう．

これに対して，Caversは本判決の結論に批判的である．まず一般論としては，行為者の保護を否定し，合意を有効とする州に取引が集中しているときは，その法を適用することが州際取引の安全という多州間利益の観点から望

ましい．売主又は貸主が，州外からその市場にやってきてその市場で行われている法に適合する取引に従事しようとする顧客に物を売ったり，金銭を貸すときには，これらの法の利益を売主や貸主に許容する根拠は通常は強いであろうという．そしてこのような考えを否定した判決として *Lilienthal* 判決をあげている．David F. Cavers, Choice of Law Process (1965), 189.

Lilienthal 判決は，Currie が当初，展開した法選択方法論と一致する．しかしその結論に私は反対である．オレゴンの住民に取引の相手方が後見に服しているという危険にオレゴン住民をさらすということと，カルフォルニアにおいてカルフォルニア住民を同じ危険にさらすこととの間には，その公正さにおいて著しい差異がある．オレゴン住民は［カルフォルニアの住民よりも］，用心深くするより大きな理由と知りうるより大きな機会を有する．カルフォルニアの貸主が相当の注意をもって行動していたとすれば，本判決の結論は人の正義の観念を損なうであろう．州外で犠牲者を見つけて，欺こうとした自州の浪費者に逃げ場所を提供するという結果に無関心でいることをオレゴンの立法機関はオレゴンの裁判所に強いているものでない（D. Cavers, *supra*, at 191-192）．

Weintraub も次のように批判する．裁判所は *Olshen* 判決の存在のために，カルフォルニアの債権者をオレゴンの債権者よりも有利に扱うことに気が進まなかったのではないか．しかし抵触法の主たる目的は，州際事件がどのような場合に純粋な国内事件とは異なって扱われるべきかを決定することにある．異なった国内法の基礎にある法目的の真の抵触に直面した裁判所は，オレゴンの浪費者法は変わったものか（unusual），カルフォルニアの債権者は不公正に不意打ちを受けたか，事件を審理するいずれの裁判所にも受け入れられる好ましい全国的解決はなにかを探求すべきである．これらの質問に適切に対応することによって本件の結論は変わったであろうと，Russell J. Weintraub, Commentary on the Conflict of Laws (4th ed.2001), at 467.

Richman & Reynolds もオレゴン法の抑制された穏健な解釈によって，*Lilienthal* 判決は異なった結果になったであろうとする．原告には明らかに浪費者と取引をしていることを知る手だてはなかった．カルフォルニアには

II 法選択（準拠法）

そのような制定法の規定がないからである．無能力の可能性さえ知らなかった者は罰せられるべきではない．州外の契約当事者の正当な期待は，*Lilienthal* 判決における浪費者法の解釈において重要な考慮事項であるべきであったと批判している．William M. Richman & William L. Reynolds, Understanding Conflict of Laws（3rd ed. 2002），at 250-51.

以上のほか *Lilienthal* 判決については，*Recent Developments, Oregon Adopts Governmental Interest Approach to Choice of Law*, 17 Stan. L. Rev. 750（1965）; *Recent Cases*, 34 U. Cin. L. Rev. 390（1965）参照．

【設　問】

1　本件の争点はなにか．
2　オレゴン法とカルフォルニア法とはどのように異なるか．
3　事実の概要を述べよ．オレゴンとカルフォルニアが事件と当事者に対して有する関連を整理せよ．
4　*Olshen v. Kaufman* 判決を簡単に紹介せよ．本判決との違いはどのようなところにあるか．
5　判旨は，これまでのオレゴンの契約の準拠法に関する法選択規則はどのようなものかといっているか．またこの立場に対してどのような批判が加えられているか．
6　原告の主張を要約せよ．また原告の代理人としてはどのような主張が説得的か．
7　カルフォルニア法の適用を導くほかにどのような立場がある，と判旨はいっているか．
8　外国の適用を排除する「公序」とはどのようなものか．判旨はこの点についてどのようにいっているか．
9　本判決は，法選択理論としてCurrieの利益分析論を採用したといわれる．Currieの利益分析論とはどのような理論か．その特徴について説明せよ．また本件判旨は，この理論を採用しているか．
10　オレゴンの利益はどのようなところにあると判旨はいっているか．またカルフォルニアの利益はどうか．
11　判旨は，両州の利益のどちらが大きいかを比較考慮しているか．
12　判旨は，どのような理由でオレゴン法を適用したと考えられるか．
13　反対意見を要約し，多数意見との違いを要約せよ．
14　本件は要約すると，どのような判決か．

10 生産者責任の準拠法：
Tomlin v. Boeing Co., 650 F.2d 1065 (9th Cir. 1981)

BOOCHEVER, Circuit Judge:

The laws of four states and the Republic of South Vietnam are potentially involved in this case. The issue is whether the appellants' wrongful death action against the Boeing Company is time-barred. The answer turns on which statute of limitations governs. The district court, interpreting Washington conflicts law, concluded that a Washington court would not apply Washington's three year statute of limitation and dismissed the case as time-barred under the other states' shorter limitation periods. We conclude that a recent decision of the Washington Supreme Court indicates that it would apply Washington's three year statute and reverse.

The relevant facts are not disputed. Two servicemen, Barry Tomlin and Samuel Harrell, were killed in a helicopter crash in South Vietnam on May 10, 1972. The helicopter which they were piloting crashed because an aft rotor blade developed a crack and separated in mid-flight. Vetrol, a Pennsylvania based division of The Boeing Company, built the helicopter and rotor blade. The United States Army acquired the helicopter in 1965.

Tomlin and Harrell were each survived by a wife and two children. Tomlin's wife, Maria, and children lived in Alabama at the time of the accident. Maria Tomlin is the administratrix of Tomlin's estate which is being probated in Alabama. At the time she filed her complaint, she had

生産物責任訴訟において，不法行為による死亡に基づく訴訟が出訴期限を過ぎたものであるかどうかという点について，原告に有利な生産者の主たる営業所所在地法（ワシントン州法）を適用した事例

BOOCHEVER 巡回裁判官
　本件において4つの州と南ヴェトナム共和国の法律が潜在的に関係している．問題となっている争点は，上訴人による Boeing 社に対する，不法行為死亡に基づく訴訟が出訴期限経過により禁止されるかどうかである．その答えは，どの出訴期限法が適用されるかにかかっている．地方裁判所は，ワシントンの抵触法を解釈して，ワシントンの裁判所がワシントンの3年の出訴期限法を適用しないと結論し，他の州のより短い出訴期限法によれば期限経過により禁止されるとして事件を却下した．われわれは，ワシントン州最高裁の最近の判決によれば，同裁判所はワシントンの3年の出訴期限法を適用すると結論し，判決を破棄する．

　事実関係は争われていない．2人の軍人，Barry Tomlin と Samuel Harrell は，1972年5月10日，南ヴェトナムにおいてヘリコプターの墜落事故により死亡した．墜落の原因は，後部回転翼に徐々にひびが入り，飛行中にそれが分解したことによるものであった．ヘリコプターと回転翼は，Boeing 社の一部門で，ペンシルベニアに主たる営業所を有する Vetrol が製造した．合衆国陸軍はヘリコプターを1965年に取得した．

　Tomlin と Harrell には，それぞれ妻と2人の子どもが遺族として残された．Tomlin の妻 Maria と子どもは，事故当時アラバマに居住していた．Maria Tomlin は，アラバマで検認された Tomlin の遺産の遺産管理人である．本件申立時は，ジョージアに移住していた．Christine Harrell とその子どもは事

moved to Georgia. Christine Harrell and her children lived in Florida at the time of the accident and she is probating Harrell's estate there. She was still living in Florida when she filed her complaint.

Boeing's principal place of business is in the State of Washington.
Tomlin and Harrell brought this action for the wrongful deaths of their husbands in the Federal District Court for the Western District of Washington on May 9, 1975, a day short of Washington's three-year statute of limitation. .... Boeing moved for summary judgment on the ground that the action was barred by the statute of limitation. On May 14, 1979, Judge Voorhees granted Boeing's motion and this appeal followed.

No party contends that the law of Vietnam should be applied and we have not considered the possibility. Each of the four states, namely, Alabama, Florida, Pennsylvania and Washington, has a wrongful death statute and the only conflict with which this appeal is concerned relates to the applicable limitation period. Alabama and Florida both have two-year statutes of limitation applicable to wrongful deaths, Pennsylvania has a one-year statute, and Washington has a three-year statute. The case is thus time-barred unless Washington's statute applies.

This is a diversity case and Washington is the forum state. A federal court sitting in Washington will apply Washington law, including its conflicts law. Klaxon Co. v. Stentor Electric Manufacturing Co., 313 U.S. 487, 496, 61 S. Ct. 1020, 1021, 85 L. Ed. 1477 (1941).
Washington has rejected the doctrine of lex loci delicti which requires a forum state to apply the substantive law of the place of the injury. Instead it applies the law of the state with the most significant contacts and interest in having its law applied. Johnson v. Spider Staging Corp., 87 Wash.2d 577, 555 P.2d 997, 1000 (1976).

故当時フロリダの住民であり，妻はそこで Harrell の遺産の検認を受けているところである．彼女はその申立の当時，フロリダに住んでいた．

　Boeing 社の本拠地はワシントン州にある．
　Tomlin と Harrell は，不法行為による夫の死亡に基づく本件訴訟をワシントンの3年出訴期限法の期間満了の1日前の1975年5月9日に，ワシントン西部地区連邦地裁に提起した．……Boeing は，本件訴訟は出訴期限法により禁じられるとして，略式判決を求めた．1979年5月14日，Voorhees 裁判官が Boeing の申立を認めたので，本件上訴がなされた．

　いずれの当事者もヴェトナム法の適用を主張していないから，われわれはその可能性を考えない．4つの州，すなわち，アラバマ，フロリダ，ペンシルベニア及びワシントンはそれぞれ不法行為による死亡法を有しており，本件上訴で問題となっている唯一の法の抵触は適用される出訴期間の問題に関するものである．アラバマ，フロリダはともに不法行為による死亡に適用される2年の出訴期限法を有しており，ペンシルベニアは1年，ワシントンは3年の制定法を有している．したがってワシントン法が適用されるのでない限り，本件訴訟は出訴期限経過で禁止される．

　本件は州籍の相違に基づく事件であり，ワシントンが法廷地である．ワシントンに所在する連邦裁判所は抵触法を含めたワシントン法を適用する．Klaxon Co. v. Stentor Electric Manufacturing Co., 313 U.S. 487, 496, 61 S. Ct. 1020, 1021, 85 L. Ed. 1477 (1941).
　ワシントンは，損害発生地の法の実質法を適用することを要求する不法行為地法主義を拒否し，それに代えて最も重要な関連をもち，かつその法が適用される利益を有する州の法律を適用する．Johnson v. Spider Staging Corp., 87 Wash.2d 577, 555 P.2d 997, 1000 (1976).

In a thoughtful opinion, the district judge suggested that a Washington court might analyze a conflict in statutes of limitation using either of two approaches. Under the first approach (modified interest analysis), a Washington court would first decide which wrongful death act applied. If the court decided that a foreign state had the greatest interest in application of its wrongful death act, the court would next determine whether the applicable statute of limitation was substantive or procedural. Washington would apply the statute of limitation of the foreign state's wrongful death act if substantive, but its own statute of limitation if procedural.

Since the two plaintiffs were domiciliaries of Alabama and Florida at the time of the accident, the judge concluded that those two states were the most interested in having their wrongful death acts applied. He further concluded that the Alabama and Florida statutes of limitation relating to wrongful deaths were substantive. Thus he concluded that Washington would apply the two-year statute of limitation from those states rather than Washington's three-year statute.

The district judge considered it more likely that Washington would follow modified interest analysis and look to the applicable wrongful death act before examining the statute of limitation. Nevertheless, the judge alternatively examined how a Washington court applying "direct" interest analysis would approach a conflict in statutes of limitation. Under this approach, the judge analyzed the choice of law issue relating to the statute of limitation independently of the wrongful death act to be applied. The judge believed that Pennsylvania had the greatest interest in seeing its shorter statute of limitation applied, and concluded that a Washington court would dismiss the appellants' case under this approach as well.

地裁の裁判官は，よく考えられた意見において，ワシントンの裁判所が出訴期限法における抵触を2つのアプローチのいずれかを使って分析するであろうと示唆した．最初のアプローチ（修正利益分析論）によれば，ワシントンの裁判所は，最初にどの不法行為死亡法が適用されるかを決定しなければならない．裁判所が他の州がその不法行為死亡法の適用に最大の利害関係を有していると判断したら，裁判所は次に適用される不法行為死亡法が実体的か手続的かを決定するであろう．実体的であれば，ワシントンはその他州の不法行為死亡法の出訴期限法を適用し，手続的だとすれば，自州自身の出訴期限法を適用するであろう．

　2人の原告は，事故当時，アラバマとフロリダの住民であったから，裁判官はこれら2つの州がその不法行為死亡法が適用されることに最大の利害関係を有すると結論した．さらに彼は，不法行為死亡に関するアラバマとフロリダの出訴期限法が実体的であると結論した．かくして彼は，ワシントンがワシントンの3年の出訴期限法ではなく，これらの州の2年の出訴期限法を適用するであろうと結論した．

　地裁裁判官は，ワシントンが修正利益分析論に従い，出訴期限法を検討する前に，適用される不法行為死亡法を調査するであろうと考えた．それにもかかわらず，裁判官は，二者択一的に，「直接」利益分析論を採用するワシントン裁判所がどのように出訴期限法の抵触にアプローチするかを検討した．裁判官は，このアプローチに従って，適用されるべき不法行為死亡法とは別に，出訴期限に関する法選択問題を分析した．裁判官は，ペンシルベニアがその短期の出訴期限法を適用する最大の利害関係を有していると考え，ワシントン裁判所がこのアプローチの下でも，上訴人の訴訟を却下するであろうと結論した．

II 法選択（準拠法）

I APPLICATION OF MODIFIED INTEREST ANALYSIS

......

As discussed, the district court's primary approach used modified interest analysis. Under that analysis, the court first used interest analysis to determine which state's wrongful death act was applicable and then used a substantive-procedural test, rather than interest analysis, to determine whether that state's statute of limitation controlled....... [O]ur reading of Washington law convinces us that a Washington court would apply direct interest analysis to both aspects of the conflicts issue, rather than a modified interest analysis. We also believe that a Washington court applying direct interest analysis would apply its own statute of limitations.

......

Although the authorities certainly suggest that Washington would extend interest analysis to a conflict in statutes of limitation, the district court noted that no Washington case had done so. But the issue has never been addressed by a Washington court. We believe, though, that the Washington Supreme Court's decision in Johnson v. Spider Staging Corp., 87 Wash.2d 577, 555 P.2d 997 (1976), clearly portends what the result would be. There the Washington court applied an examination of state

10　生産者責任の準拠法：Tomlin v. Boeing Co.

I　修正利益分析論の適用

［この部分において，Boochever 巡回裁判官は，不法行為死亡に関する訴訟において，どの州の出訴期限法が適用されるかを決定するにあたって，ワシントンの裁判所はまずどの州の不法行為死亡法が適用されるかを決定するために直接に以下に紹介する利益分析論を使い，その後にどの州の出訴期限法を適用するかを決定するために実体＝手続の判断テストを使用するのではなく（地裁裁判官はこのような立場をとった），むしろ，前掲 *Johnson* 判決に従い，次に述べるように，この双方の抵触問題に直接に同州の採用する利益分析論を適用するであろう，と結論する．］（訳者注）

すでに論じたように，地裁の最初のアプローチは，修正利益分析論を使用した．このアプローチの下では，裁判所はまずどの州の不法行為死亡法が適用されるかどうかを決定するために利益分析論を用いた．そしてそれから，その州の出訴期限法を適用するかどうかを決定するために，利益分析論ではなく，実体＝手続テストを使用した．……われわれのワシントン法の読み方によれば，ワシントン裁判所は抵触法問題の双方の側面に修正利益分析論ではなく，直接利益分析論を適用するであろうと確信する．われわれはまた，直接利益分析論を適用するワシントン裁判所が自州自身の出訴期限法を適用するものと考える．
……

ワシントンが出訴期限法の抵触に関して利益分析論を拡大するであろうと先例は明らかに示唆するけれども，地裁はそのようなワシントンの事件はないと指摘した．たしかにこの争点はこれまでワシントンの裁判所で真正面から取り上げられたことはない．しかし，Johnson v. Spider Staging Corp., 87 Wash.2d 577, 555 P.2d 997（1976）におけるワシントン州最高裁判所の判決は，明らかにその結果がどうなるかを予兆しているとわれわれは信じる．その事件でワシントン裁判所は，2 つの不法行為死亡法の下での損害賠償金

contacts and governmental interest to resolve a conflict as to the limitation on recoverable damages under two wrongful death acts. After Johnson, we do not believe a Washington court would approach statutes of limitation conflicts differently because there is little, if any, basis for distinguishing between a time limitation and a damage limitation.
......

Consequently, we conclude that a Washington court would follow the Johnson choice-of-law analysis in resolving the statute of limitation conflict.

II INTEREST ANALYSIS APPLIED TO THE CONFLICT IN STATUTES OF LIMITATION

The purpose of a statute of limitation is to protect courts and defendants. By barring stale claims, such statutes conserve judicial resources and provide repose to defendants. Ruth v. Dight, 75 Wash.2d 660, 453 P.2d 631, 634-35 (1969); Milhollin, supra note 4 at 10-11. The district judge correctly concluded that there was no conflict between the interests of the four states with regard to conserving judicial resources. Washington has expressed a policy of not closing its courts to wrongful death actions for three years. If Washington chooses to allow a case to be brought in its courts that would be time-barred in Alabama, Florida, or Pennsylvania, the judicial resources of those states are unaffected.

The district judge also correctly determined that application of Washington's three year statute would not frustrate any policy of Alabama or Florida to protect in-state defendants. Although those states would have barred the action in their courts, they are not interested in denying a recovery to their own residents where it would not affect a resident defendant.

についての出訴期限法に関する抵触を解決するために，州の関連と統治利益を検討する方法を適用した．Johnson 判決後は，ワシントンの裁判所が出訴期限法の抵触について，時間の制限と損害の制限との間に，かりにあるにしても僅かしかない区別をする根拠があることを理由に，異なったアプローチを採用するであろうとはとても信じられない．
……

以上の結果として，われわれは，ワシントン裁判所が出訴期限法の抵触を解決するにあたって Johnson 判決の法選択分析を採用すると結論する．

II　出訴期限法の抵触に対する利益分析論の適用

　出訴期限法の法目的は，裁判所と被告の保護である．このような制定法は，古くなった請求権を禁止することによって裁判所の負担を軽減し，被告にその応訴の負担からの解放を与える．Ruth v. Dight, 75 Wash.2d 660, 453 P.2d 631, 634-35（1969）; Milhollin, supra note 4 at 10-11. 裁判所の負担の軽減という点では4つの州の利益の抵触は存在しない，と地裁裁判官が結論したのは正しかった．ワシントンは，不法行為による死亡訴訟に対して3年間は自州の裁判所を閉ざさないという政策を表明している．アラバマ，フロリダ，ペンシルベニアで許されない訴えの提起をワシントンが許容しても，アラバマ，フロリダ，ペンシルベニアの裁判所の労力はなんら影響を受けることはない．

　またワシントン法の3年の出訴期限法の適用は，アラバマ及びフロリダの自州被告の保護という法目的と抵触しないと地裁裁判官が判断したことも正しかった．これらの州は，自州の裁判所における訴訟を禁止したであろうけれども，自州の被告が影響を受けない場合において，自州の住民が賠償を否定されることになんらの利益をも有しないからである．

The conflict, then, is between Pennsylvania's former one year statute and Washington's more plaintiff oriented three year statute. Pennsylvania contacts include the location of a Boeing subdivision and the place of manufacture of the rotor blade. Washington is the forum and principal place of business of Boeing, one of the largest corporations in the state. We believe that these contacts present a fairly even balance between the two states and we would not hesitate to affirm the district court's decision as to how Washington would resolve the issue were it not for the guidance furnished by Washington's highest court.

In balancing the interests of the two states, we believe that the district court erred in failing to give adequate weight to the Washington Supreme Court's opinion in Johnson, supra. In that case the court considered the Kansas wrongful death act provision limiting damages to $50,000. The case involved faulty scaffolding manufactured in Washington. Although the decedent was a domiciliary of Kansas, the product was ordered from a Kansas City distributor, and the accident occurred there, the Washington court still rejected application of the Kansas wrongful death act in favor of Washington law because

> Washington's deterrent policy of full compensation is clearly advanced by the application of its own law.

Johnson, 555 P.2d at 1002. By providing for a longer period of limitation, Washington has in effect similarly expressed a policy of deterring the conduct of tort defendants.

As the district judge noted in his opinion, courts have generally applied the law of the state where a decedent's beneficiaries live because it is likely to be the state most interested in seeing that its residents are compensated. See, e. g., Sibley v. KLM Royal Dutch Airlines, 454 F. Supp. 425, 428 (S.D.N.Y.1978). We believe Johnson's departure from this general pattern to further Washington policy is a significant indication of

そこでペンシルベニアの前の1年の出訴期限と原告に有利なワシントンの3年の出訴期限法との抵触が問題となる．ペンシルベニアと本件の関連は，Boeing の部門の所在地，及び回転翼の製造地であったことである．ワシントンの関連は，法廷地であること，州における最大の会社である Boeing の事業活動の本拠地であることである．われわれは，両州の関連はほぼ対等であると考えて，ワシントンの最高裁判所によって提供されるガイダンスがなければ，どのようにワシントンがその争点を解決するであろうかについての地方裁判所の決定を支持することに躊躇しないであろう．

2州の利益を比較考慮するにあたって，地裁が前掲 Johnson 判決におけるワシントン最高裁の意見に適切な考慮を払わなかったのは誤りであるとわれわれは考える．この事件において裁判所は，不法行為死亡に基づく賠償額を5万ドルに制限するカンザス法を検討した．この事件は，ワシントンで製造された欠陥足場材に関する事件であった．故人はカンザスの住民であり，製品はカンザス市のディストリビューターから注文され，事故はそこで発生した．それでもワシントン裁判所は，カンザス不法行為死亡法の適用を否定し，ワシントン法を適用した．その理由は，

　　それ自身の法の適用により，ワシントンの完全な賠償による不法行為
　　の抑止という法目的が明らかに促進される，からである．
Johnson, 555 P.2d at 1002. ワシントンは，より長期の出訴期限を規定することで，実際上同様に被告による不法行為に対する抑止の法目的を表明している．

これまで裁判所は，地裁の裁判官がその意見で述べているように，故人の受益者の居住地州が，不法行為による死亡者の補償について最も強い利害関係を有するとの理由で，通常は適用されるとしてきたことは確かである．たとえば，Sibley v. KLM Royal Dutch Airlines, 454 F. Supp. 425, 428（S. D.N.Y. 1978）参照．Johnson 判決によりワシントンの利益を促進するために，この一般的なパターンから離脱したことは，ワシントンの裁判所がどの

how the Washington court would decide this case.

It is, as we have discussed in the previous section, a small step to conclude that the deterrent policy provided by a more liberal damage recovery advances interests similar to that provided by a longer statute of limitation.

The principal distinction between this case and Johnson, is that the manufacturing activity here actually took place in another state. We are not persuaded that this distinction should lead to a different result. In this case, as in Johnson, the defendant has its principal place of business in Washington and Washington is the forum. We believe Washington would be interested in deterring the wrongful conduct of its most prominent corporate citizen regardless of where the manufacturing is performed. This action is against the Boeing Company, not its Vertol division. Our attention has not been directed to any equally strong defendant protecting policy of Pennsylvania, other than what might be inferred from that state's shorter statute of limitations. Finally, Boeing can hardly claim unfamiliarity with Washington law or surprise that Washington law might be applied. See Allstate Insurance Co. v. Hague, 449 U.S. 302, 101 S. Ct. 633, 642-643, 66 L. Ed. 2d 521 (1981); Restatement (Second) of Conflicts §6, comment g (1971). When a corporation is sued at its principal place of business one would ordinarily expect that state's law to govern.

In applying the Washington statute, we are also guided by Washington's reliance on a more general principle of law favoring the decision of cases on their merits. This policy has been expressed by the Washington Supreme Court which has stated that where it is "questionable which of two statutes (of limitation) apply the rule is that the statute applying the longest period is generally used." Shew v. Coon Bay Loafers, Inc., 76 Wash.2d 40, 455 P.2d 359, 366 (1969). Recently, in reversing a district

ように本件を判断するかについて重要な示唆を与えると考える.

　それは, さきに述べたように, より寛大な損害賠償を認めることによる不法行為の抑止という法目的は, より長期の出訴期限を認めることによる不法行為の抑止と同様の利益を促進すると結論する小さな第一歩である.
　本件と Johnson 判決との主要な差異は, 本件では現実に生産行為が行われたのが他州であるということである. しかし, この差違は, そこから異なった結果を導き出すべきだという説得的な根拠とはならない. 本件においては, Johnson 判決と同様に, 被告はワシントンに本拠地を有し, ワシントンは法廷地である. ワシントンは, 製造行為がどこで行われたどうかにかかわりなく, その最も有名な自州企業による不法行為を抑止する利益をもつ, と考える. 本件訴訟は, Boeing の一部門である Vertol に対してではなく, Boeing 社自体に対するものである. 短い出訴期限から推察されるものとは別に, それと同様に強いペンシルベニアの被告保護の法目的で注目すべきものは認められない. また被告はワシントン法に熟知していないとか, 同法の適用が不意打ちであると主張することはできない. Allstate Insurance Co. v. Hague, 449 U.S. 302, 101 S. Ct. 633, 642-643, 66 L. Ed. 2d 521 (1981); Restatement (Second) of Conflicts §6, comment g (1971) 参照. というのは, 企業がその事業活動の本拠地で訴えられる場合には, 通常はその州法の適用は予測されるからである.

　ワシントンの制定法を適用するにあたって, われわれはまた, 本案に関する事件の決定をできる限り可能にするという, より一般的な法の原則をワシントンがとっていることによっても影響を受けた. この法目的は, 「2つの (出訴期限) 法のいずれが適用されるかが疑問である場合には, 最も長い出訴期限を定める制定法が一般的には使用されるのが原則である」として, ワシントン最高裁によって表明された. Shew v. Coon Bay Loafers, Inc., 76 Wash. 2d 40, 455 P.2d 359, 366 (1969). 最近, 適用されるカルフォルニア

court's interpretation of the applicable California statute of limitation, a panel of this court referred to this principle. Marshall v. Kleppe, 637 F.2d 1217, 1224 (9th Cir. 1980).

We therefore conclude that Washington would apply its three year statute of limitation and reverse the decision of the district court.

REVERSED.

【解　説】

　本件は，生産物責任訴訟において，不法行為による死亡に基づく訴訟が出訴期限を過ぎたものであるかどうかという点について，原告に有利な生産者の主たる営業所所在地法（ワシントン法）を適用した事例である．

1　生産物責任における法の抵触

　アメリカを中心として，生産物責任においてどのような法の抵触が問題となるか．

　各法域の実質法は，不法行為における生産者の責任の基礎について，のちにみるように，判例で最も問題となることの多いのは，厳格責任と過失責任の抵触である．アメリカの多くの州は不法行為第2リステイトメント第402A条の厳格責任の法理を採用するが，過失責任主義を依然として採用する法域との間に，さらにまた厳格責任の具体的内容についても法の抵触が生じ，準拠法の決定が必要となる．

　また，被害者が死亡した場合に損害賠償額にたとえば5万ドルの制限を設ける法とこのような制限を認めない法との抵触，あるいは懲罰的損害賠償を認める法とこれを否定する法との抵触も問題となる．さらに本件で問題となったように，生産物責任における出訴期限法や法定責任期間（statute of repose）

の出訴期限法に関する地裁の解釈を破棄するにあたって，当裁判所のパネルは，この原則に言及した．Marshall v. Kleppe, 637 F.2d 1217, 1224（9th Cir. 1980）.

以上によりわれわれはワシントンが出訴期限を3年とする自州の出訴期限法を適用すると結論し，原判決を破棄する．

破棄

の抵触のほか，保証責任を追求する場合に当事者間に契約関係の存在を要するかについての抵触も存在する．

そして上のような法の抵触は，結局は，特定の事件における事実関係と争点の下で考えると，原告に有利な（pro-claimant）法と，生産者に有利な（pro-producer）法とに分けて考えることができる．

2 生産物責任の準拠法に関する判例の法選択方法論

法選択方法論としては，伝統的理論，利益分析論，第2リステイトメントなど様々の理論が提唱され，判例においてもそれぞれのアプローチに追随するものがあり，もとより，決着がついたとはいえない．その中にあって，第2リステイトメントの立場——とりわけ利益分析論と融合したそれ——が有力になりつつあるといえるであろう．

また判例・学説において，一般的に原告に有利な法の優先的適用が有力であるが，最近の傾向は必ずしもそのようにはいえないとの指摘がある．高杉直「米国国際私法の現状と課題——製造物責任の準拠法問題を中心として」国際私法年報5号32頁（2003）．

3 *Reyno v. Piper Aircraft* 判決

利益分析論の立場から，原告に有利な生産地法を適用した事例としては，

Ⅱ　法選択（準拠法）

Reyno v. Piper Aircraft Co., 630 F.2d 149（3rd.Cir,1980）がある．
　スコットランドにおける航空機事故から生じたペンシルベニアの航空機製造者とオハイオのプロペラ製造者に対する不法行為死亡に基づく訴訟である．航空機はスコットランド会社が所有し，乗客と乗組員はすべてスコットランド人であった．訴訟は当初カルフォルニアで提起されたが，その後ペンシルベニアの連邦裁判所に移送された．第3巡回区控訴裁判所はペンシルベニア航空機製造者（パイパー社）に対してはカルフォルニアの法選択規則が適用されるとした上で次のように判示した．
　①　カルフォルニアはCurrie教授の統治利益分析論を採用したパイオニア州であった．
　アメリカの厳格責任とスコットランドの過失責任法との主張されている抵触は虚偽の抵触である．2つの基本的な法目的が不法行為責任の法理の基礎には存在する．つまり損害を生ぜしめる行為の阻止とその行為によって損害を受けた人に対する補償である．刑事責任ではなく，民事責任が課せられる不法行為法においては，阻止機能は原告に対する補償によって達成される．生産者を過失のある場合に限って有責とすることと，危険な製品又は設計に対して厳格な責任があるとすることとのいずれを選択するかは，実際には，有害な行為を阻止する最適な方法の探求と損害の費用を生産者か消費者のいずれに配分すべきかの問題なのである．概括的にいえば，過失の基準がより生産者保護的であり，厳格責任がより消費者のことを配慮している．
　②　本件における抵触は，生産者を保護し，消費者の損害賠償をより困難にすることによって産業の発展を奨励することに対してスコットランドの有する利益と，他方は厳格責任を採用することによって損害の負担を消費者から生産者へと移行させようとするペンシルベニアの利益との抵触である．ペンシルベニアはそうすることによって生産者が過失責任の基準のままに放置された場合よりも，その生産と設計により注意を払うことを求めているのである．
　③　ペンシルベニアの厳格責任基準をその住民である生産者に対して適用することは，その州が生産行為の規律に対して有する利益を促進する．スコ

ットランドがその領域内における産業を奨励することに対して有する利益は，スコットランドになんらの産業施設を有していない外国法人により厳格な注意の基準を課したとしても，損なわれることはない．さらにスコットランドは，外国法人に利益を与えるために自国の住民に完全な補償を否定することになんらの利益をも有しないであろう．最後に，被告に厳格責任を課することは被告にとって不公正とはいえない．被告がその製品を作るペンシルベニア及び，被告の航空機のほとんどが売られ，飛行するアメリカの大多数の法域が厳格責任を有し，それが被告の経営を計画する法的基準である限りはそうである．

④ 製品における欠陥を阻止することに対して有するペンシルベニアの有する利益は，スコットランドの利益をなんら損なうことなしに達成できる．スコットランドの過失責任法の適用は，自国の住民の利益を侵害するだけで，自国の産業経済に対してなんらの利益をも与えるものではない．したがってわれわれは，この争点に関するペンシルベニアとスコットランドの抵触については，カルフォルニアはペンシルベニアの厳格責任を適用すると結論する．

4 *Turcotte v. Ford Motor Company* 判決

Turcotte v. Ford Motor Company, 494 F.2d 173（1974）は，利益分析論により，原告に有利な原告の住所地法を適用した事例である．つまり，原告に有利な原告の住所地法であるロードアイランド法を適用し，生産者に有利な損害発生地法の適用を否定したロードアイランド連邦地裁の判決である（なお，生産地法も原告に有利な法を有している）．

問題となった争点は，不法行為による死亡に基づく損害賠償額の制限と厳格責任の2つである．裁判所はその2つの争点について，利益分析を行って，準拠法を決定している．

ロードアイランドの住民である原告Xの息子は，同じくロードアイランド州の住民である訴外Aの運転する車に同乗中，マサチューセッツ州において，車が他車と衝突，炎上し，死亡した．原告は，車（フォード製70年型マーベリック）の構造上の欠陥のために衝突の際に火災を引き起こし，それが原因で

Ⅱ 法選択（準拠法）

息子が死亡したと主張して，デラウエア法人である被告Ｙ（フォード自動車会社）に対して損害賠償を求める訴訟をロードアイランドの連邦地裁に提起した．

ロードアイランド州の不法行為死亡法は，賠償額に制限を設けず，また厳格責任法により厳格責任法理を採用する．これに対してマサチューセッツ州の不法行為死亡法は，全く懲罰的な基準により，現実の損失よりも単に被告の過失の程度により，損害を算定するとともに，賠償額を5万ドルに制限する（判決時は20万ドルに改正）．また同州の裁判所は厳格な生産物責任法理を認めていない，と本件裁判所は仮定する．車の生産地であるミシガン州の法律はロードアイランド州と同じである．原告勝訴の第1審判決に対して，被告が控訴し，マサチューセッツ州法が適用されると主張したのに対して，控訴審は原審がロードアイランド州の不法行為死亡法と厳格責任法を適用したのは正しかったとして，これを認めなかった．

① 利益衡量アプローチ

ロードアイランド州は，不法行為地法主義を放棄し，「利益衡量」アプローチを採用する．最高裁はこのアプローチの下で考慮すべき利益を次の5つのガイドラインに要約している．(1)結果の予測可能性，(2)州際的秩序の維持，(3)裁判業務の簡素化，(4)法廷地の統治利益の促進，(5)より良い法規則の適用．これらの利益を不法行為死亡法と不法行為法に分けて検討する．

② 不法行為による死亡に基づく訴訟における賠償額の制限

本件における抵触法問題にこの利益衡量理論を適用すると，第4の要因，すなわち法廷地利益の促進がロードアイランド法の適用をより適切なものとして強く指示する．法廷地はいかなる場合においても自州の住民を保護する利益を有しているが，個人の損傷あるいは死亡を含む不法行為においては，その利益はとくに強い．けだし，十分な補償が得られないと，原告がその州の負担となるであろうからである．次に第2の要因である州際的秩序の維持に関し，ロードアイランド法を適用することが他州の法目的を損なうかについて検討すると，被告はマサチューセッツ州の会社ではないから，マサチューセッツ州は直接的には5万ドルの賠償責任制限を適用する利益はない．ま

た，傷害の原因となった，車の設計がマサチューセッツ州外で行われたという事実を考慮すると，同州の懲罰的な性質は本件ではほとんど関連はない．さらにマサチューセッツ州が他州の企業の活動を奨励することについて有する利益は，ロードアイランド州が自州の住民を保護することに対して有する利益と比較すると弱い．残りの3つの利益は決定的なものでないか，又はロードアイランド法の適用を指示するものである．

③ 厳格責任法理

ロードアイランド州が厳格責任に関する自州法を適用する実質的な利益を有することは明らかである．ロードアイランド州の利益は，欠陥製品から自州の住民を保護することであるが，それには原告やその息子のほか，70年型マーベリックの購入者が含まれており，賠償を否定するマサチューセッツ法の適用は明らかにこのロードアイランド州の利益を侵害する．同時にロードアイランド法の適用はマサチューセッツ州の法目的を損なうとは思われない．マサチューセッツ州が厳格責任法理を採用しないことが自州の生産者の保護にあると仮定しても，被告はその保護の対象外にある．かりに，他州の企業がその製品をマサチューセッツ州内において売却することを促進することがマサチューセッツ州の利益であると仮定しても，本件のように製品がロードアイランド州住民に売られ，同州の住民がその結果として死亡した場合には，そのマサチューセッツ州の利益は実質的なものではない．また，マサチューセッツ州はその道路上の運転の仕方を規律することに否定することのできない利益を有することは確かであるが，本件では重要な考慮ではない．すなわち，原告がロードアイランド州の住民に売却された車についてミシガンにおいて生じた設計の欠陥を主張している場合には，衝突事故がマサチューセッツ州で発生したという事実は偶然的なことにすぎない．マサチューセッツ州における事故の原因が問題になっているのではなく，原告は，衝突の原因がどのようなものであろうと，車に存在していた欠陥が自分の息子の死亡を引き起こしたと主張しているのであって，マサチューセッツ州はこのような問題を決定する利益を有しない．その他の利益もロードアイランド州の適用を指示する．

5 Johnson v. Spider Staging Corporation 判決

次には判旨が引用する*Johnson v. Spider Staging Corp.*, 87 Wash.2d 577, 555 P.2d 997（1976）を紹介する．この事件は，建築足場の倒壊から生じた不法行為死亡訴訟事件である．足場は，ワシントンで製造販売され，原告の故人の居住地であるカンサスで倒壊した．実質的な争点は，不法行為死亡の損害賠償に関するカンサスの制限（5万ドル）が適用されるべきか，それとも無制限のワシントン法が適用されるべきかであった．

ワシントン裁判所は，第2リステイトメントの不法行為死亡に関する条文である第175条がその問題に最大の利益を有する州を指定し，そして関連している実質法規則が達成しようとする法目的の検討を要求する，と指摘した（Restatement（Second）of Conflict of Laws §175, comment d.）．

裁判所は，各州が取引に対して有したすべての連結点を列挙し，その任務が「単に連結点を勘定するというのではなく，むしろどの連結点が最も重要であるかを考慮することである」とする．そのためには，不法行為死亡の損害賠償に関する制限の基礎にある法目的分析を必要とする．そして裁判所はそれを，過剰な財産的負担と投機的な請求から被告を保護することと，困難な計算の回避の双方にあると判断した．これらの法目的のいずれもが本件には当てはまらない．というのは，制限州（カンサス）は，法廷地でもないし，被告の居住地でもないからである．したがってこれらの法目的は，カンサスの損害賠償制限を適用することによって促進されることはない．

さらに裁判所は，法廷地（ワシントン）の抑止の法目的が無制限の損害賠償によって促進されるであろうと判断した（本件は，それゆえに虚偽の抵触の事例である）．したがって，無制限のワシントン法が適用されるべきであると結論した．

Johnson 判決は，生産地の抑止的法目的を強調し，生産地がその法目的を実現するために自州法を適用することに対して有する利益に重点をおいてワシントン法の適用を正当化した．また，この判決は，「最も重要な関係」と実質法の法目的の分析＝原告に有利な法を適用した事例としても注目される．現在のアメリカ国際私法における不法行為の準拠法を決定する有力な方法の

1つは，この事例のように，実質法の法目的の分析をも考慮した上での，最も重要な関係の理論としての第2リステイトメントの立場にたつものであるといえよう．

本件 *Tomlin* 判決は，上に紹介した *Johnson* 判決の強調した生産地の抑止的法目的を，自州企業が州外で生産を行うときでも，そのまま同様に妥当するとして，原告に有利な主たる営業所所在地州法を適用したものである．本件は，判旨もいうように，基本的にはこの *Johnson* 判決の立場を踏襲したものといえるであろう．

Johnson 判決について詳しくは，松岡博『国際私法における法選択規則構造論』（有斐閣，1987）97-100頁を参照されたい．

6　第2リステイトメントの「最も重要な関係」のアプローチ

上に述べたように，最近における判例の注目すべき傾向の1つは，第2リステイトメントの「最も重要な関係」の理論を採用する判決が多いことである．不法行為に関する一般原則を定めた第145条は次のように規定する．

「第145条　一般原則

(1)　不法行為についての争点に関する当事者の権利及び義務は，第6条の原則に従い，その争点との関連で事実及び当事者と最も重要な関係を有する邦の法により，これを定める．

(2)　第6条に定める原則に従って争点に適用すべき法を決定するにあたり斟酌すべき連結素には次のものがある．

　(a)　損害の生じた地

　(b)　損害を生ぜしめた行為の行われた地

　(c)　当事者の住所，居所，国籍，法人の場合はその設立地，当事者の事業所の所在地

　(d)　当事者間に関係が存するときはその関係の中心のある地

　上に掲げる連結素は個々の争点との関連でその各々が有する重要性の程度に応じてその軽重を判定すべきものとする．」

Ⅱ　法選択（準拠法）

なお，第2リステトメントの不法行為については，William M. Richman & William L. Reynolds, Understanding Conflict of Laws, 218-223（3rd ed. 2002）参照.

7　生産物責任の準拠法に関するハーグ条約

1973年の「生産物責任の準拠法に関するハーグ条約」は，被害者の常居所，生産者の主たる営業所所在地，生産物の取得地，損害発生地の連結点を組み合わせて段階的に準拠法を決定するとともに，一定の限られた範囲で原告の選択を認めている.

① まず，直接の被害者の常居所地が，同時に責任を問われている者の主たる営業所所在地であるか，又は直接の被害者が生産物を取得した地であれば，この被害者の常居所地法が適用される（第5条）.

② 次に損害の発生地が同時に，直接の被害者の常居所地であるか，生産物の取得地であるか，又は責任を問われている者の主たる営業所所在地であれば，その損害発生地法が適用される（第4条）.

③ 以上のような連結点の組合せが存在しないときは，責任を問われている者の主たる営業所所在地法を適用する．ただし，責任を問う者が損害発生地法の適用を主張しているときは，この限りでない（第6条）．責任を問われている者が，損害発生地法または被害者の常居所地法の適用を予見しえないときは，これらの法によってその者に責任を課することはできず，責任を問われている者の主たる営業所所在地法による（第7条）.

【本件参考文献】

松岡博『国際取引と国際私法』（晃洋書房，1993）288頁以下.

10 生産者責任の準拠法：Tomlin v. Boeing Co.

【設　問】

1　本件の争点はなにか．本件ではどのような法の抵触が問題となっているか．ほかに生産物責任ではどのような法の抵触が問題となるか．

2　事実の概要を説明せよ．事件と当事者との関連を整理せよ．

3　裁判所の判旨を要約せよ．

4　本件は，法選択方法論としては，どのような方法論を採用しているか．

5　*Reyno v. Piper Aircraft Co.*, 630 F.2d 149（3rd. Cir, 1980）を紹介せよ．

6　*Turcotte v. Ford Motor Company*, 494 F.2d 173（1974）を紹介せよ．

7　*Johnson v. Spider Staging Corp.*, 87 Wash.2d 577, 555 P.2d 997（1976）を紹介せよ．

8　不法行為の準拠法決定の一般原則を定めた抵触法第2リステイトメント第145条の規定を説明せよ．

9　生産物責任の準拠法に関するハーグ条約の概要を説明し，本件ではどうなるかについて説明せよ．

10　通則法の規定を適用すると，本件はどうなるか．

11　本件の結論，理論構成に賛成か．

11 著作権の準拠法：
Itar-Tass Rusian Agency v. Rusian Kurier, Inc., 153 F.3d 82 (2d Cir.1998)

JON O. NEWMAN, Circuit Judge:

This appeal primarily presents issues concerning the choice of law in international copyright cases and the substantive meaning of Russian copyright law as to the respective rights of newspaper reporters and newspaper publishers. The conflicts issue is which country's law applies to issues of copyright ownership and to issues of infringement. The primary substantive issue under Russian copyright law is whether a newspaper publishing company has an interest sufficient to give it standing to sue for copying the text of individual articles appearing in its newspapers, or whether complaint about such copying may be made only by the reporters who authored the articles. Defendants-appellants Russian Kurier, Inc. ("Kurier") and Oleg Pogrebnoy (collectively "the Kurier defendants") appeal from the March 25, 1997, judgment of the District Court for the Southern District of New York (John G. Koeltl, Judge) enjoining them from copying articles that have appeared or will appear in publications of the plaintiffs-appellees, mainly Russian newspapers and a Russian news agency, and awarding the appellees substantial damages for copyright infringement.

On the conflicts issue, we conclude that, with respect to the Russian plaintiffs, Russian law determines the ownership and essential nature of the copyrights alleged to have been infringed and that United States law determines whether those copyrights have been infringed in the United States and, if so, what remedies are available. We also conclude that

ロシア国民によりロシアで発行された新聞雑誌などの米国における著作権侵害につき，著作権の所有権についてはロシア著作権法を適用し，侵害の問題には合衆国著作権法を適用すべきとした事例

JON O. NEWMAN 巡回区裁判官

本件控訴では，主として国際的著作権事件における法選択に関する争点と，新聞記者及び新聞社のそれぞれの権利をめぐるロシア著作権法の実体的な意味についての争点が提起されている．法選択に関する争点とは，著作権の所有権問題と侵害問題にどこの国の法律が適用されるかである．ロシア著作権法上の主要な実体的な争点とは，新聞社が，新聞に掲載された記事の本文の複製に対して訴訟を提起する当事者適格を付与されるに十分な利益を有しているか，それとも複製に対して訴訟を提起することができるのは記事を書いた記者のみであるかである．被告・上訴人 Russian Kurier, Inc.（「Kurier」）と Oleg Pogrebnoy（一括して「Kurier 被告」という）は，主にロシアの新聞各社とロシア通信社からなる原告・被上訴人らの発行物に掲載され，又はこれから掲載される記事の複製を被告らに差し止めるとともに，被上訴人らに著作権侵害の賠償を認めた 1997 年 3 月 25 日のニューヨーク南部地区地方裁判所（John G. Koeltl 裁判官）の判決に対して控訴裁判所に上訴した．

法選択問題についてわれわれは，次のように結論する．すなわち，ロシアの原告に関して，侵害があったと主張される著作権の所有権とその本質的な性質については，ロシア法が適用される．これに対し，合衆国法は，著作権が合衆国国内で侵害されたかどうか，そしてもし侵害されたとすればどのような救済が利用できるかを決定する．われわれはまた，ロシア法が，職務著

II 法選択（準拠法）

Russian law, which explicitly excludes newspapers from a work-for-hire doctrine, vests exclusive ownership interests in newspaper articles in the journalists who wrote the articles, not in the newspaper employers who compile their writings. We further conclude that to the extent that Russian law accords newspaper publishers an interest distinct from the copyright of the newspaper reporters, the publishers' interest, like the usual ownership interest in a compilation, extends to the publishers' original selection and arrangement of the articles, and does not entitle the publishers to damages for copying the texts of articles contained in a newspaper compilation. We therefore reverse the judgment to the extent that it granted the newspapers relief for copying the texts of the articles. However, because one non-newspaper plaintiff-appellee is entitled to some injunctive relief and damages and other plaintiffs-appellees may be entitled to some, perhaps considerable, relief, we also remand for further consideration of this lawsuit.

Background

The lawsuit concerns *Kurier*, a Russian language weekly newspaper with a circulation in the New York area of about 20,000. It is published in New York City by defendant Kurier. Defendant Pogrebnoy is president and sole shareholder of Kurier and editor-in-chief of *Kurier*. The plaintiffs include corporations that publish, daily or weekly, major Russian language newspapers in Russia and Russian language magazines in Russia or Israel; Itar-Tass Russian News Agency ("Itar-Tass"), formerly known as the Telegraph Agency of the Soviet Union (TASS), a wire service and news gathering company centered in Moscow, functioning similarly to the Associated Press; and the Union of Journalists of Russia ("UJR"), the professional writers union of accredited print and broadcast journalists of the Russian Federation.

The Kurier defendants do not dispute that *Kurier* has copied about 500 articles that first appeared in the plaintiffs' publications or were distributed

11 著作権の準拠法：Itar-Tass Rusian Agency v. Rusian Kurier, Inc.

作の法理から新聞社を明示的に排除して，新聞記事に対する排他的所有権を記者の記事を編集した新聞社である使用者ではなく，記事を書いた記者に付与していると，結論する．さらに，われわれは，ロシア法が新聞記者の著作権とは異なる利益を新聞社に認める限りにおいて，編集に対する通常の所有権のような新聞社の法的利益は，新聞社による記事の独創的な選択や配列には及ぶが，編集された新聞に含まれる記事本文が複製されたことに対する損害賠償の権利を新聞社に与えるものではない，と結論する．したがって，判決が記事の本文を複製することに対する救済を新聞社に認めた限りにおいてこれを破棄する．しかし新聞社でない原告・被上訴人 1 社は差止めの救済と損害賠償が認められ，他の原告・被上訴人もいくらかの，多分相当の救済が与えられるであろうから，われわれはまた，本件訴訟のさらなる検討のため差し戻す．

背景

本件訴訟は，ニューヨーク地域で約 2 万部を発行するロシア語週刊新聞，*Kurier* に関する事件である．この新聞は被告 Kurier によってニューヨーク市で発行されている．被告 Pogrebnoy は，*Kurier* の社長兼唯一の株主であり，Kurier の編集長でもある．原告には，ロシアにおいて日刊又は週刊の主要なロシア語新聞を発行する法人と，ロシア又はイスラエルでロシア語の雑誌を発行する複数の法人，さらに以前には Telegraph Agency of the Soviet Union（TASS）として知られ，連合プレスと類似の機能を有するモスクワに本拠を有する電信サービスとニュース収集の会社である Itar-Tass Russian News Agency（「Itar-Tass」），及びロシアの公認されたプロの新聞雑誌・放送記者からなる，ロシア・ジャーナリスト組合（「UJR」）が含まれている．

Kurier 被告は，*Kurier* が原告の発行物に最初に掲載され，又は Itar-Tass によって頒布された約 500 件の記事を複製したことを争っていない．複製さ

by Itar-Tass. The copied material, though extensive, was a small percentage of the total number of articles published in *Kurier*. ...... The Kurier defendants also do not dispute how the copying occurred: articles from the plaintiffs' publications, sometimes containing headlines, pictures, bylines, and graphics, in addition to text, were cut out, pasted on layout sheets, and sent to *Kurier's* printer for photographic reproduction and printing in the pages of *Kurier*.

Most significantly, the Kurier defendants also do not dispute that, with one exception, they had not obtained permission from any of the plaintiffs to copy the articles that appeared in *Kurier*. Pogrebnoy claimed at trial to have received permission from the publisher of one newspaper, but his claim was rejected by the District Court at trial. ....
......

Discussion

I Choice of Law

The threshold issue concerns the choice of law for resolution of this dispute. That issue was not initially considered by the parties, all of whom turned directly to Russian law for resolution of the case. Believing that the conflicts issue merited consideration, we requested supplemental briefs from the parties and appointed Professor William F. Patry as Amicus Curiae. Prof. Patry has submitted an extremely helpful brief on the choice of law issue.

Choice of law issues in international copyright cases have been largely ignored in the reported decisions and dealt with rather cursorily by most commentators. Examples pertinent to the pending appeal are those decisions involving a work created by the employee of a foreign corporation. Several courts have applied the United States work-for-hire doctrine, *see*

11 著作権の準拠法：Itar-Tass Rusian Agency v. Rusian Kurier, Inc.

れた資料は多数に上るけれども，Kurier において発行された全体の記事からすればその割合は少なかった．……Kurier 被告は，複製がどのように行われたかを争っていない．原告の発行物からの記事，ときには記事に加えてヘッドライン，写真，記事執筆者欄及びグラフィクスを含めて，それらが切り出され，レイアウト・シートにのり付けされ，Kurier の頁への写真複製と印刷のために Kurier のプリンターに送られた．

　最も重要なことには，Kurier 被告は，1 つの例外を除いて，Kurier に掲載された記事を複製する許諾を原告の誰からも得ていなかったことを争っていない．Pogrebnoy は，事実審において 1 新聞の発行者から許諾を得たことを主張したが，審理において地方裁判所によって彼の主張は拒絶された．…………

検討

I 法選択

　最初の争点は，この紛争を解決するための法選択に関するものである．その争点は当初は当事者によって考慮されず，誰もが，事件の解決のために直接にロシア法に向かった．抵触の争点が考慮に値すると確信して，われわれは当事者から補足の準備書面を要求し，法廷の友として，William F. Patry 教授を選んだ．Patry 教授は，法選択問題についてきわめて有用なブリーフを提出した．

　国際著作権事件における法選択問題は，これまでの判決では大部分は無視され，またほとんどの学者によってもなおざりに取り扱われてきた．係争中の控訴に関連する例は，外国会社の従業員によって創作された著作物に関する判決である．いくつかの裁判所は，抵触法の争点を明確に考慮することなく，合衆国の職務著作法理（17 U.S.C. §201(b)参照）を適用してきた．……

17 U.S.C. §201(b), without explicit consideration of the conflicts issue....... Other courts have applied foreign law. ......In none of these cases, however, was the issue of choice of law explicitly adjudicated.......

The Nimmer treatise briefly (and perhaps optimistically) suggests that conflicts issues "have rarely proved troublesome in the law of copyright." *Nimmer on Copyright* §17.05 (1998) (*"Nimmer"*) .... Relying on the "national treatment" principle of the Berne Convention and the Universal Copyright Convention ("U.C.C."), *Nimmer* asserts, correctly in our view, that "an author who is a national of one of the member states of either Berne or the U.C.C., or one who first publishes his work in any such member state, is entitled to the same copyright protection in each other member state as such other state accords to its own nationals." *Id.* (footnotes omitted). *Nimmer* then somewhat overstates the national treatment principle: "The applicable law is the copyright law of the state in which the infringement occurred, not that of the state of which the author is a national, or in which the work is first published." .... The difficulty with this broad statement is that it subsumes under the phrase "applicable law" the law concerning two distinct issues — ownership and substantive rights, *i.e.*, scope of protection. Another commentator has also broadly stated the principle of national treatment, but described its application in a way that does not necessarily cover issues of ownership. "The principle of national treatment also means that both the question of whether the right exists and the question of the scope of the right are to be answered in accordance with the law of the country where the protection is claimed." S.M. Stewart, *International Copyright and Neighboring Rights* §3.17 (2d ed. 1989). We agree with the view of the Amicus that the Convention's principle of national treatment simply assures that if the law of the country of infringement applies to the scope of substantive copyright protection, that law will be applied uniformly to foreign and domestic authors. *See Murray v. British Broadcasting Corp.*, 906 F. Supp. 858 (S.D.N.Y. 1995), aff'd, 81 F.3d 287 (1996).

11 著作権の準拠法：Itar-Tass Rusian Agency v. Rusian Kurier, Inc.

他の裁判所は，外国法を適用してきた．……しかしながらこれらのいずれの判決においても法選択の争点は，明示には判断されていない．……

　Nimmer の書物は，簡潔に（そしてたぶん楽観的に）法選択の問題は，「著作権法においては，めったにやっかいな問題とはならない」と示唆している．*Nimmer on Copyright* §17.05（1998）(「*Nimmer*」) 参照……ベルヌ条約と万国著作権条約（「U.C.C.」）の「内国民待遇」の原則に依拠して，Nimmer が，「ベルヌ条約又は U.C.C. の加盟国の国民である著者，又はいずれの加盟国においてであれ，その著作物を最初に公表した者は，それぞれの加盟国において，当該他国が自国の国民に与えるのと同じ保護を与えられる」同上（脚注略）と指摘するのは，われわれの見解では正しい．ついで Nimmer は，内国民待遇原則をいくぶん強調しすぎて次のようにいう．「準拠法は，侵害が生じた国の著作権法であって，著者が国民であるか，又著作物が最初に公表された国の著作権法ではない．」……このような広範な陳述をすることに伴う困難は，「準拠法」という表現には 2 つの明確に異なった争点――所有権と実体的な権利つまり保護の範囲――が含まれるという点にある．他の注釈者もまた，内国民待遇原則を広く解釈しているが，彼はその適用範囲を必ずしも所有権の争点をカバーしないやり方で述べている．「内国民待遇原則は，権利が存在するかどうかという問題と，その権利の適用範囲の問題が，ともに保護が主張される国の法に従って答えられるべきであることを意味する．」S.M. Stewart, *International Copyright and Neighboring Rights* §3.17（2d ed. 1989）．われわれが賛成するのは，条約の内国民待遇原則は侵害国の法が実体的な著作権の保護の範囲に適用されるとすれば，その法が外国人の著者にも内国人の著者にも統一的に適用されるであろうことを単に確保するにあるという法廷の友の見解である．*Murray v. British Broadcasting Corp.*, 906 F. Supp. 858（S.D.N.Y. 1995），aff'd, 81 F.3d 287（1996）参照．

Source of conflicts rules. Our analysis of the conflicts issue begins with consideration of the source of law for selecting a conflicts rule. Though *Nimmer* turns directly to the Berne Convention and the U.C.C., we think that step moves too quickly past the Berne Convention Implementation Act of 1988, Pub L. 100-568, 102 Stat. 2853, 17 U.S.C.A. §101 note. Section 4(a)(3) of the Act amends Title 17 to provide: "No right or interest in a work eligible for protection under this title may be claimed by virtue of ... the provisions of the Berne Convention .... Any rights in a work eligible for protection under this title that derive from this title ... shall not be expanded or reduced by virtue of the provisions of the Berne Convention." 17 U.S.C. §104(c).

We start our analysis with the Copyrights Act itself, which contains no provision relevant to the pending case concerning conflicts issues. We therefore fill the interstices of the Act by developing federal common law on the conflicts issue........ In doing so, we are entitled to consider and apply principles of private international law, which are "'part of our law.'" *Maxwell Communications Corp. v. Societe Generale*, 93 F.3d 1036, 1047 (2d Cir. 1996) (quoting *Hilton v. Guyot*, 159 U.S. 113, 143, 40 L. Ed. 95, 16 S. Ct. 139 (1985)).

The choice of law applicable to the pending case is not necessarily the same for all issues. *See* Restatement (Second) of Conflict of Laws §222 ("The courts have long recognized that they are not bound to decide all issues under the local law of a single state."). We consider first the law applicable to the issue of copyright ownership.

Conflicts rule for issues of ownership. Copyright is a form of property, and the usual rule is that the interests of the parties in property are determined by the law of the state with "the most significant relationship" to the property and the parties. *See id.* The Restatement recognizes the appli-

11 著作権の準拠法：Itar-Tass Rusian Agency v. Rusian Kurier, Inc.

抵触規則の法源　われわれは抵触法問題の分析を抵触規則を選定するための法源を検討することから始める．*Nimmer* は，直接にベルヌ条約とU.C.C.へと向かうが，われわれは，そのやり方は1988年のBerne Convention Implementation Act of 1988, Pub. L. 100-568, 102 stat. 2853, 17 U.S.C. A.§101 note を安易に取り扱っていると考える．同法のSection 4(a)(3)は，17編を改正し，次のように定める．「本編において保護されるべき著作物に関するいかなる権利又は利益もベルヌ条約の規定によって……請求することはできない．……本編から引き出される本編上の保護されるべき著作物におけるいかなる権利も……ベルヌ条約の規定によって拡張され，縮小されることはない．」17U.S.C. §104(c).

われわれの分析を著作権法自体から始めるが，この法には本件に適切な抵触問題に関する規定がない．そこで，本件の争点に関する連邦コモンローを発展させることによって同法の隙間を埋めることにする．……そうするに際して，われわれは，「われわれの法の部分である」国際私法の原則を考慮し，適用することができる．*Maxwell Communications Corp. v. Societe Generale*, 93 F.3d 1036, 1047（2d Cir. 1996）(*Hilton v. Guyot*, 159 U.S. 113, 143, 40 L. Ed. 95, 16 S. Ct. 139（1985）を引用).

本件に適用される法の選択は，必ずしもすべての争点について同じではない．Restatement (Second) of Conflict of Laws §222 参照（「裁判所は，すべての争点を単一の邦の地域法に基づいて決定することに拘束されるものではないことを久しく認めてきた.」．われわれはまず，著作権の所有権の問題に適用される法について検討する．

著作権の所有権問題に関する抵触規則　著作権は財産権の一形態であり，それに関して適用される通常のルールは，財産に対する当事者の利益がその財産及び当事者に「最も重要な関係」を有する邦の法律によって決定される．同上参照．リステイトメントは，「文学的アイデア」などの無体財産に対して

cability of this principle to intangibles such as "a literary idea." *Id.* Since the works at issue were created by Russian nationals and first published in Russia, Russian law is the appropriate source of law to determine issues of ownership of rights. That is the well-reasoned conclusion of the Amicus Curiae, Prof. Patry, and the parties in their supplemental briefs are in agreement on this point. In terms of the United States Copyrights Act and its reference to the Berne Convention, Russia is the "country of origin" of these works, *see* 17 U.S.C. §101 (definition of "country of origin" of Berne Convention work); Berne Convention, Art. 5(4), although "country of origin" might not always be the appropriate country for purposes of choice of law concerning ownership.

To whatever extent we look to the Berne Convention itself as guidance in the development of federal common law on the conflicts issue, we find nothing to alter our conclusion. The Convention does not purport to settle issues of ownership, with one exception not relevant to this case. *See* Jane C. Ginsburg, *Ownership of Electronic Rights and the Private International Law of Copyright*, 22 Colum. -VLA J.L. & Arts 165, 167-68 (1998) (The Berne Convention "provides that the law of the country where protection is claimed defines what rights are protected, the scope of the protection, and the available remedies; the treaty does not supply a choice of law rule for determining ownership.") (footnote concerning Art. 14*bis*(2)(a) omitted).

Selection of Russian law to determine copyright ownership is, however, subject to one procedural qualification. Under United States law, an owner (including one determined according to foreign law) may sue for infringement in a United States court only if it meets the standing test of 17 U.S.C. §501(b), which accords standing only to the legal or beneficial owner of an "exclusive right."

11 著作権の準拠法：Itar-Tass Rusian Agency v. Rusian Kurier, Inc.

　この原則が適用できることを認めている．同上．本件において，問題の著作物はロシア国民によって創作され，ロシア国内で最初に発行されたので，ロシア法が所有権の問題を決定するための適切な法源である．このことは，法廷の友であるPatry教授のよく根拠づけられた結論であり，この点に関しては，当事者もその補足的な準備書面において意見が一致している．合衆国著作権法とそれによるベルヌ条約への言及の文言によれば，ロシアはこれらの著作物の「本源国」である．17 U.S.C. §101（ベルヌ条約著作物の「本源国」定義）とベルヌ条約第5条(4)参照．もっとも「本源国」はつねに所有権に関する法選択の目的のためには必ずしも適当な国であるとは限らない．

　抵触法問題に関する連邦コモン・ローを展開していく上で，ベルヌ条約自体をどの程度まで手引きとして参考にするかにかかわらず，われわれの結論を変更すべきものはなにも見出せない．条約は，本件に関係のない1つの例外を除いて，所有権の問題を解決しようとはしていない．Jane C. Ginsburg, *Ownership of Electronic Rights and the Private International Law of Copyright,* 22 Colum. -VLA J.L. & Arts 165, 167-68（1998）（ベルヌ条約は，「保護が求められる国の法が，どのような権利が保護されるか，保護の範囲及び利用できる救済を定義する．条約は所有権を決定する法選択規則を提供していない．」）参照（第14条 *bis*(2)(a)に関する脚注略）．

　しかしながら著作権の所有権問題にロシア法が適用されることには1つの手続的な制限がある．合衆国法によれば，著作権の所有者は（外国法に基づいて決定される場合を含めて），「排他的権利」を有する法律上の又は利益を受けるべき所有者に対してしか当事者適格を付与しないと定めている17 U.S.C. §501(b)の規定の当事者適格基準に適合する場合に限って，合衆国の裁判所において侵害訴訟を提起することができるとされている．

II 法選択（準拠法）

Conflicts rule for infringement issues. On infringement issues, the governing conflicts principle is usually *lex loci delicti*, the doctrine generally applicable to torts. See *Lauritzen v. Larsen*, 345 U.S. 571, 583, 97 L. Ed. 1254, 73 S. Ct. 921 (1953). We have implicitly adopted that approach to infringement claims, applying United States copyright law to a work that was unprotected in its country of origin. See *Hasbro Bradley, Inc. v. Sparkle Toys, Inc.*, 780 F.2d 189, 192-93 (2d Cir. 1985). In the pending case, the place of the tort is plainly the United States. To whatever extent *lex loci delicti* is to be considered only one part of a broader "interest" approach, *see Carbotrade S.p.A. v. Bureau Veritas*, 99 F.3d 86, 89-90 (2d Cir. 1996), United States law would still apply to infringement issues, since not only is this country the place of the tort, but also the defendant is a United States corporation.

The division of issues, for conflicts purposes, between ownership and infringement issues will not always be as easily made as the above discussion implies. If the issue is the relatively straightforward one of which of two contending parties owns a copyright, the issue is unquestionably an ownership issue, and the law of the country with the closest relationship to the work will apply to settle the ownership dispute. But in some cases, including the pending one, the issue is not simply who owns the copyright but also what is the nature of the ownership interest. Yet as a court considers the nature of an ownership interest, there is some risk that it will too readily shift the inquiry over to the issue of whether an alleged copy has infringed the asserted copyright. Whether a copy infringes depends in part on the scope of the interest of the copyright owner. Nevertheless, though the issues are related, the nature of a copyright interest is an issue distinct from the issue of whether the copyright has been infringed, ... The pending case is one that requires consideration not simply of who owns an interest, but, as to the newspapers, the nature of the interest that is owned.

11 著作権の準拠法：Itar-Tass Rusian Agency v. Rusian Kurier, Inc.

侵害問題に関する抵触規則 侵害の問題に関する抵触法の原則は，通常，不法行為一般に適用することができる*不法行為地法*である．*Lauritzen v. Larsen*, 345 U.S. 571, 583, 97 L. Ed. 1254, 73 S. Ct. 921（1953）参照．われわれは，本源国で保護されない著作物に合衆国著作権法を適用することを通じて，暗黙のうちに侵害請求にそのアプローチを採用してきた．*Hasbro Bradley, Inc. v. Sparkle Toys, Inc.*, 780 F.2d 189, 192-93（2d Cir. 1985）参照．本件においても不法行為地は明らかに合衆国である．*不法行為地法が*より広範な「利益」分析論（*Carbotrade S.p.A. v. Bureau Veritas*, 99 F.3d 86, 89-90（2d Cir. 1996）参照）の一部としてどの程度まで考慮されるかはともかくとして，不法行為地が合衆国であると同時に被告も合衆国の法人であることから，やはり合衆国法が侵害問題に適用されるであろう．

　所有権問題と侵害問題の区別は上の議論が示しているようにつねに簡単に分割できるとは限らない．もし争点が相対立する2当事者のいずれが著作権を有するかという比較的単純なものであるならば，それは疑いもなく所有権の問題であり，その場合には著作物に最も密接な関連がある国の法が適用されることになる．しかしながら本件のような事例では，争点となっているのは，単に著作権の所有者が誰であるかということだけでなく，所有権に基づく利益の性質はなにか［排他的なものであるかどうか（訳者注）］という点が問題となっている．さらに裁判所が所有権に基づく利益の性質を検討する際，その複製が主張されている著作権を侵害したかどうかという問題の検討に直ちに移ってしまうという危険がある．というのは複製が権利を侵害したかどうかは，著作権所有者の利益の範囲いかんに部分的にかかっているからである．このように2つの争点は相互に関連しあっている．しかしそれにもかかわらず著作権に基づく利益の性質の問題は，当該著作権が侵害されたかどうかの問題とは区別されるのである．……本件は，単に誰が利益を所有するかといった点だけでなく，新聞社との関連では，所有される利益の性質をも考慮しなければならない事例である．

II Determination of Ownership Rights Under Russian Law

Since United States law permits suit only by owners of "an exclusive right under a copyright," 17 U.S.C. §501(b), we must first determine whether any of the plaintiffs own an exclusive right. That issue of ownership, as we have indicated, is to be determined by Russian law.

.....

Determination of a foreign country's law is an issue of law. *See* Fed. R. Civ. P. 44.1; *Bassis v. Universal Line, S.A.*, 436 F.2d 64, 68 (2d Cir. 1970). Even though the District Court heard live testimony from experts from both sides, that Court's opportunity to assess the witness's demeanor provides no basis for a reviewing court to defer to the trier's ruling on the content of foreign law. In cases of this sort, it is not the credibility of the experts that is at issue, it is the persuasive force of the opinions they expressed. *See Curley v. AMR Corp.*, 153 F.3d 5, 12 (2d Cir. 1998) ("[A]ppellate courts, as well as trial courts, may find and apply foreign law.").

Under Article 14 of the Russian Copyright Law, Itar-Tass is the owner of the copyright interests in the articles written by its employees. However, Article 14(4) excludes newspapers from the Russian version of the work-for-hire doctrine. The newspaper plaintiffs, therefore, must locate their ownership rights, if any, in some other source of law. They rely on Article 11. The District Court upheld their position, apparently recognizing in the newspaper publishers "exclusive" rights *to the articles*, even though, by virtue of Article 11(2), the reporters also retained "exclusive" rights to these articles.

Having considered all of the views presented by the expert witnesses, we conclude that the defendants' experts are far more persuasive as to the meaning of Article 11. In the first place, once Article 14 of the Russian

II ロシア法に基づく所有権の決定

　合衆国法は「著作権に基づく排他的権利」を有する所有者による訴訟だけを認めている．17 U.S.C. §501(b). したがってわれわれはまず，原告のうち誰が排他的権利を有するかどうかを決定しなければならない．この所有権の問題は，すでに指摘したようにロシア法に基づいて決定される．

……

　外国法の決定は法律上の争点である．Fed. R. Civ. P. 44.1; *Bassis v. Universal Line, S.A.*, 436 F.2d 64, 68（2d Cir. 1970）参照．地方裁判所は，双方の専門家から生の証言を聞いたが，同裁判所の証人の態度を評価する機会があるからといって，再審理裁判所が外国法の内容に関するその判定者の判断に従うべきとの根拠をなんら提供するものではない．この種の事件において問題となるのは，専門家の信用性ではなく，専門家の表明した意見の説得力である．*Curley v. AMR Corp.*, 153 F.3d 5, 12（2d Cir. 1998）参照（「控訴審は，事実審と同様に，外国法を調査し，適用することができる．」）．

　ロシア著作権法第 14 条によれば，Itar-Tass はその従業員が書いた記事の著作権上の利益の所有者である．しかし原告である新聞社については，第 14 条(4)は，ロシア版職務著作法理から新聞社を除外している．そのため，新聞社はその所有権の制定法上の根拠を，もしあるとすれば，別のところに求めなければならない．新聞社は，第 11 条を根拠として主張した．地方裁判所は，その立場を支持して，第 11 条(2)により記者が当該記事に対する「排他的」権利を保持するとしても，新聞の発行者にも記事に対する「排他的」権利を明白に承認している，という立場をとった．

　われわれは，鑑定人によって提出されたすべての意見を検討した結果，被告の鑑定人の方が第 11 条の意味に関してはるかに説得的であると結論する．第 1 にロシア著作権法第 14 条がいったん明示的に職務著作の法理の利益，そ

Copyright Law explicitly denies newspapers the benefit of a work-for-hire doctrine, which, if available, would accord them rights to individual articles written by their employees, it is highly unlikely that Article 11 would confer on newspapers the very right that Article 14 has denied them. Moreover, Article 11 has an entirely reasonable scope if confined, as its caption suggests, to defining the "Copyright of Compilers of Collections and Other Works." That article accords compilers copyright "in the selection and arrangement of subject matter that he has made insofar as that selection or arrangement is the result of a creative effort of compilation." Russian Copyright Law, Art. 11(1). Article 11(2) accords publishers of compilations the right to exploit such works, including the right to insist on having its name mentioned, while expressly reserving to "authors of the works included" in compilations the "exclusive rights to exploit their works independently of the publication of the whole work." *Id.* Art. 11(2). As the defendants' experts testified, Article 11 lets *authors* of newspaper articles sue for infringement of their rights in the text of their articles, and lets *newspaper publishers* sue for wholesale copying of all of the newspaper or for copying any portions of the newspaper that embody their selection, arrangement, and presentation of articles (including headlines) — copying that infringes their ownership interest in the compilation.

……

Relief. Our disagreement with the District Court's interpretation of Article 11 does not mean, however, that the defendants may continue copying with impunity. In the first place, Itar-Tass, as a press agency, is within the scope of Article 14, and, unlike the excluded newspapers, enjoys the benefit of the Russian version of the work-for-hire doctrine. Itar-Tass is therefore entitled to injunctive relief to prevent unauthorized copying of its articles and to damages for such copying, and the judgment is affirmed as to this plaintiff.

れはもし利用できるなら新聞社にその被用者が書いた個々の記事に対する権利を付与することになるが，その権利を新聞社に否定したのに，第14条が新聞社に否定したまさにその権利を，第11条が新聞社に与えることはきわめてありそうにない．さらに第11条は，その見出しが示すように，「集合物と他の著作物に関する編集者の著作権」を定義することに限られていると解すれば，全体として合理的な適用範囲を有していることになる．その条文は，編集者に「彼がなした対象事項の選定と配列において，その選定又は配列が編集の創造的な努力の結果である限りは，それに関する」著作権を与えている．ロシア著作権法第11条(1)．第11条(2)は，編集物の発行者に，その著作物を利用する権利を，その名前が言及されることを主張する権利を含めて，与えている．一方，編集物中に「含まれた著作物の著者」には「その著作物を全体の著作物の公表とは独立して，利用する排他的な権利を留保している．」同上第11条(2)．被告側の鑑定人が証言するように，ロシア著作権法第11条は，新聞記事の*著作者*にはその記事本文に対する権利の侵害があった場合に訴訟を提起することを認めるとともに，*新聞発行者*には新聞全体の大規模な複製あるいは（見出しを含む）記事の選択，配列及び表示を含む新聞の一部が複製された場合，――つまり編集に対する所有者利益を侵害するような複製の場合に，訴訟を提起することを認めているのである．
……

救済 　地方裁判所の第11条の解釈に同意しないからといって，被告らが免責されて，複製をそのまま継続できることにはならない．まず，Itar-Tass は，通信社として第14条の対象範囲に入るので，その対象から除外される新聞社とは異なり，職務著作法理のロシア版の利益を受ける．したがって Itar-Tass は，その記事の不正な複製を阻止する差止命令による救済を受ける権原を有するとともに，複製によって被った損害の賠償を請求することができる．したがってこの原告に関しては原判決は維持される．

Furthermore, the newspaper plaintiffs, though not entitled to relief for the copying of the text of the articles they published, may well be entitled to injunctive relief and damages if they can show that *Kurier* infringed the publishers' ownership interests in the newspaper compilations. Because the District Court upheld the newspapers' right to relief for copying the text of the articles, it had no occasion to consider what relief the newspapers might be entitled to by reason of *Kurier's* copying of the newspapers' creative efforts in the selection, arrangement, or display of the articles. Since *Kurier's* photocopying reproduced not only the text of articles but also headlines and graphic materials as they originally appeared in the plaintiffs' publication, it is likely that on remand the newspaper plaintiffs will be able to obtain some form of injunctive relief and some damages. On these infringement issues, as we have indicated, United States law will apply.

Finally, there remains for consideration what relief, if any, might be awarded to UJR, acting on behalf of any of its members whose articles have been copied.......

In view of our conclusion that the newspaper plaintiffs may not secure relief for the copying of the text of any articles as such, it will now become appropriate for the District Court on remand to revisit the issue of whether relief might be fashioned in favor of UJR on behalf of the authors.......

Conclusion

Accordingly, we affirm the judgment to the extent that it granted relief to Itar-Tass, we reverse to the extent that the judgment granted relief to the other plaintiffs, and we remand for further proceedings. ......

さらに原告たる新聞社は，発行した記事本文の複製については救済を受けることはできないが，Kurierが新聞記事の編集に関する発行者の所有権上の利益を侵害したことを証明できれば，おそらく差止命令による救済と損害賠償請求が認められるであろう．しかしながら，地方裁判所は，記事本文の複製に対して救済を受ける権利を新聞社に認めたため，記事の選択，配列又は表示に関する新聞社の創造的努力の結果をKurierが複製したことを理由に新聞社がどのような救済を受けることができるかについて，地方裁判所にはそれを検討する機会がなかった．Kurierのコピー行為は記事本文のみならず，それらが原告の発行物にもともと表示されていた見出しやグラフィック資料も含めて複製しているので，新聞社である原告らは，差戻し審理によってなんらかの形の差止命令による救済と一定の損害賠償を受けられる可能性が高い．この侵害問題に適用される法は，すでに指摘したように，合衆国法である．

　最後に，記事が複製された構成員のために行動しているUJRにどのような救済を与えるかという問題が残っている．……
　新聞社に記事本文の複製に対する救済は認められないというわれわれの結論からすると，地方裁判所が差し戻し審において，著作者の代わりにUJRにどのような救済を工夫するかという問題を再審理するのが適切であろう……

結論
　以上の理由から，われわれは，Itar-Tassに救済を認めた部分については原判決を維持する．また，その他の原告に救済を認めた部分については原判決を破棄し，さらなる審理のためにこれを差し戻すこととする．……

Ⅱ 法選択（準拠法）

【解　説】

　本件は，著作権の準拠法につき，ロシア国民によりロシアで発行された新聞雑誌などの米国における著作権侵害につき，著作権の所有権とその性質についてはロシア著作権法を適用し，侵害の問題には合衆国著作権法を適用すべきとした1998年の合衆国第2巡回区控訴裁判所の判決である．
　原告は，合衆国法が所有権の問題に適用されると主張し，被告はロシア法が適用されると主張した．合衆国法とロシア法の相違は，合衆国法の職務著作の規定によれば，新聞社を含むすべての原告が著作権者となり，原告適格を有するが，ロシア法によれば，原告のうち，Itar-Tass のみが原告適格を有する．William Patry, *Choice of Law and International Copyright,* 48 Am. J. Comp. L.383, 412-13（2000）．地方裁判所は，所有権と侵害の双方にロシア法を適用し，広い原告適格と合衆国法で許容される範囲を超えた救済を集合著作物権者に認めたのに対し，被告らが控訴裁判所に上訴したのが本件である．

1　著作権の準拠法

　本件は，著作権の準拠法について最も詳細な分析を行った判決であるといわれる．Grame B. Dinwoodie, *International Property Litigation: A Vehicle for Resurgent Comparativist Thought,* 49 Am. J. Comp. L. 429, 440 (2001)．とりわけ最近まで外国の知的財産法に基づく侵害請求について判断することにきわめて消極的であった合衆国の裁判所が著作権の所有者は誰かという問題について，外国法であるロシア法を適用したという点からみてきわめて注目される．Patry, *supra* at 412.

2　著作権の所有権問題と侵害問題との区別

　まず本件は，著作権の所有権の問題と侵害の問題とを区別し，所有権（その性質の問題を含めて）についてはロシア法を適用し，侵害については合衆国法を準拠法とした点で注目される．この点で本判決は，いわゆる depéçage（争点ごとの準拠法決定）を容認する．抵触法第2リステイトメントは，不法行為（第145

条), 契約 (第188条), 財産 (第222条) でこの原則を採用するが, 本判決も明示的にそれに従っている. Daniel C.K. Choe & Edward Lee, International Intellectual Property, 54 (2006).

3 著作権の所有権

著作権の所有権問題については, 本件判旨は, 財産権 (物権) 準拠法の一般原則を適用し, 著作物と当事者に「最も重要な関係」を有する国の法が適用されるとする. この点でも第2リステイトメントの立場を採用するといってよい.

財産権の一般原則について定めた第2リステイトメント第222条は,「物に関する当事者の利益は, 個々の争点につき第6条の原則に従い, 物と当事者に最も重要な関係を有する邦の法又は地域法によって決定される.」と規定する. Restatement Second Conflict of Laws §222 (1971). また判旨も指摘するように, 第2リステイトメントでは, ここにいう「物」の中には, 文学的アイデアなどの無体物も入るとされているから, 著作権についても第222条の財産権の一般原則が適用されると考えられている. Restatement Second Conflict of Laws §222 (1971).

本件で「最も重要な関係」の理論を適用するに際して, 問題の著作物はロシア人によって創作され, ロシアで最初に発行されたから,「最も重要な関係」を有する国はロシアであり, 準拠法はロシア法であると判示されている. 本件ではさらに創作地もロシアであり,「最も重要な関係」の国の決定にとっては比較的簡単な事件であった.

一般に著作権者の決定という争点にとって, 関連がある連結点としては, 創作者の国籍, 住所, 創作地, 最初の発行地が重要であろうが, これらが複数の国に分散するときには, その決定はそれほど簡単ではない. 本件判旨はその点を十分に考慮し, 単一の連結点のみを強調して一律に「最も重要な関係」を有する国を決定しようとはしていない (国籍と最初の発行地のどちらがより重要かについても言及していない) ことにも注意すべきであろう.

このような観点からすると, 判旨が国際的な著作権紛争を処理するに際し

Ⅱ 法選択（準拠法）

て，その所有権問題に関する法選択規則として「最も重要な関係」の理論を採用したことは，厳格な属地主義からの自由を裁判所に与えることになったとみることができる．

さらに判旨の立場をとることの実際的な利点は，単一の著作物に対して同じ著作権者を決定できるという点で結果の統一性を達成することができることにある．つまり，この立場によれば，「最も重要な関係」を有する唯一の国の法が同一の著作物に対するすべての著作権者を決定することができることとなる．これは，属地主義を採用し，著作権者を各国法により判断し，たとえば同一の著作物についてロシアでは従業員（記者）が著作権者であり，合衆国では使用者（新聞社）であるといった事態を回避することができるという観点からも正当化されることになろう．

4 著作権侵害

次に著作権侵害については，判旨は不法行為の準拠法の一般原則が適用されるとする．アメリカ国際私法の不法行為に関する伝統的な原則は，不法行為地法主義であったが，近時における抵触法革命により大きな修正を受けている．第2リステイトメントも「最も重要な関係」の理論を採用し，伝統的な不法行為地法主義には従っていない．

利益分析論や第2リステイトメントなどの新しい法選択方法論に共通する特徴は，①不法行為の種類・争点のいかんを問わず，一律的に不法行為地法を適用するのは妥当ではなく，当事者の住所などをも複数の連結点を考慮する必要がある．②法は一定の法目的を実現するためのものであるから，ある法が適用されるかどうかを決定するにあたっては，問題となっている争点に関して関連している国の法の内容とその法目的を考慮しなければならないという認識である．松岡博『国際私法における法選択規則構造論』（有斐閣，1987）57-60頁．

このような観点からすると，判旨による分析は，必ずしもは十分とはいえない．判旨は，単に利益分析論を採用しても，不法行為地が合衆国であり，被告が合衆国の法人であるから，不法行為の準拠法は合衆国法であると述べて

いるにすぎない．その分析が不法行為準拠法の決定における最近のアメリカ国際私法の動向からみて妥当であるかは，おそらく議論のあるところであろう．

5　法選択アプローチか域外適用か

本件が法選択アプローチを採用したことも注目すべき点である．最近まで合衆国の裁判所は，外国の知的財産法に基づく侵害請求について判断することにきわめて消極的であったことを考えると，本件の立場はきわめて注目すべきである．そして本件 *Itar-Tass* 判決に触発されて，複数の外国著作権法の適用を認めるいくつかの判決が下されている．

これに対して本件のような法選択アプローチをとらず，合衆国著作権法の域外適用のアプローチを採用し，侵害行為が全体として外国で発生したときには，合衆国著作権法の域外適用を否定した注目すべき判決としては，*Subafilms, Ltd. v. MGM-Pathe Communications Co.* 24 F.3d 1088（9th Cir. 1994）がある．この判決では，映画を国際的に配給することの許諾が合衆国内でなされても，主張されている侵害がすべて外国で発生した場合には，合衆国の著作権法を域外適用することはできないと判示された．この判決については，前田美紀「アメリカにおける知的財産法の域外適用」帝塚山法学19号12頁以下（2009）参照．

6　ALI 原則

最近の知的財産権に関する国際私法の立法提案として注目されるのは，アメリカ法律協会（American Law Institute）による提案（ALI 原則）であり，2007年3月の Proposed Final Draft が公表されている．*Itar-Tass* 判決に関連のある部分について紹介する．

①　ALI 原則は，知的財産権の準拠法決定における一般原則として属地主義（Territoriality）を採用する．

すなわち，第301条第1項によれば，第302条，第321-323条に定める場合を除き，知的財産権の存在，侵害，保護期間，属性（attributes）及び侵害の救済方法に適用される法は，(a)特許権などの登録から生じる権利につい

ては，それぞれの登録国法であり，(b)著作権等の登録から生じない権利については，その国に向けて保護が求められるそれぞれの国の法（the law of each State for which protection is sought）である．

ここでいう保護国とは，具体的には，許諾されていない利用が行われた国（the State in which unauthorized use has occured）を指す．「知的創作物が利用される地の法」（law of the place where the intellectual creation is used）といわれることもある．*Itar-Tass* 判決に即していえば，許諾を受けていない記事をコピーして利用したのは合衆国であるから，保護国法は合衆国法ということになろう．

複数の国で著作物の利用行為が行われた場合，たとえばかりに *Itar-Tass* 判決で合衆国のみでなく，カナダやメキシコでも同様の行為がなされたと仮定した場合には，それぞれの国（合衆国，カナダ，メキシコ）が保護国となり，それぞれの国の法が準拠法となる．このように複数の国での行為について，それぞれの国の法が適用されるところに着目して，属地主義の原則が採用されているといわれるものと推測される．

② 次に登録から生じないその他の権利の最初の権利帰属について，第313条が重要である．

著作権は創作行為により世界中で発生するのが一般的である．所有権の問題を異なった国の異なった法に規律させるのは，権利の行使に不安定を引き起こすことになろう．というのは権利の使用を許可しようとする者が実際にその権利をもっているかどうかが明らかではないからである．そこで，最初に世界中を通じて知的財産の所有者と考えられる者を所有者と指定することが望ましい．そして権利の帰属の始点が確認されると，その後をトレースし，事後の許可を有効とすることが可能となる．

そこで第313条第1項は，登録から生じないその他の権利［著作権等］の最初の権利帰属は，次の法によるとしている．(a)創作者が1人の著作物については創作時における創作者の常居所地法，(b)共同著作物については，共同著作者間の契約で指定された法，それがない場合には，創作者の多数が創作時に居住していた国の法，それもないときは，その著作が最も密接な関連を

有する国の法，(c)創作物が雇用関係に従って創作されたときは，その関係を規律する国の法，(d)著作物が法選択条項を含む大量市場契約に従って創作されたときは，契約中に指定された法，但しその条項が第 302 条第 5 項により有効な場合に限る．そして第 1 項により準拠法国となる国が著作物を保護しないときは，最初の権利帰属は権利が最初に開発され，承認された国の法により規律されるとする（第 313 条第 2 項）．

【本件参考文献】

松岡博「国際著作権事件の準拠法」（松岡博編『国際知的財産法の潮流』）28 頁以下（帝塚山大学出版会，2008）．

【設　問】

1　本件の争点はなにか．
2　ロシア法と合衆国の著作権法の内容について簡単に説明せよ．
3　事実の概要を述べよ．ロシアと合衆国が事件と当事者に対して有する関連を整理せよ．
4　判旨の結論を要約せよ．
5　判旨は，著作権の所有権の準拠法についてどのように判示しているか．またその根拠をどのように説明しているか．
6　判旨は，著作権の侵害の準拠法についてどのように判示しているか．またその根拠をどのように説明しているか．
7　アメリカ法律協会の ALI 原則を説明し，これを適用すると本件はどうなるか．
8　本件は要約すると，どのような判決か．
9　本件は国際的著作権事件について，法選択アプローチを採用するが，合衆国著作権法の域外適用の立場にたつ判決もある．この点について説明せよ．
10　本件の判旨に賛成か．理由を付して答えよ．

Ⅲ 域外適用

12 独占禁止法の域外適用：
Timberlane Lumber Co.
v. Bank of America N.T.& S.A.,
549 F.2d 597 (9th Cir.1976)

CHOY, Circuit Judge:

Four separate actions, arising from the same series of events, were dismissed by the same district court and are consolidated here on appeal. The principal action is *Timberlane Lumber Co. v. Bank of America* (Timberlane action), an antitrust suit alleging violations of sections 1 and 2 of the Sherman Act (15 U.S.C. §§1, 2) and the Wilson Tariff Act (15 U.S.C. §8). This action raises important questions concerning the application of American antitrust laws to activities in another country, including actions of foreign government officials. The district court dismissed the Timberlane action under the act of state doctrine and for lack of subject matter jurisdiction. The other three are diversity tort suits brought by employees of one of the Timberlane plaintiffs for individual injuries allegedly suffered in the course of the extended anti-Timberlane drama. Having dismissed the Timberlane action, the district court dismissed these three suits on the ground of forum non conveniens. We vacate the dismissals of all four actions and remand.

I The Timberlane Action

The basic allegation of the Timberlane plaintiffs is that officials of the Bank of America and others located in both the United States and Honduras conspired to prevent Timberlane, through its Honduras subsidiaries, from milling lumber in Honduras and exporting it to the United States, thus maintaining control of the Honduran lumber export business

独占禁止法の域外適用問題につき，管轄権に関する相当性の理論又はバランシング・テストを採用した事例

CHOY 巡回裁判官：

同じ一連の事実から生じた4件の別々の訴訟が同じ地方裁判所によって却下され，上訴で当裁判所で併合された．主要な訴訟は，シャーマン法第1条と第2条（15 U.S.C §§1, 2）及びウイルソン・タリフ法第8条（15 U.S.C. §8）の違反を主張する独占禁止法事件たる *Timberlane Lumber Co. v. Bank of America*（Timberlane 訴訟）である．本件訴訟は，外国政府の官吏の行為を含む外国での行為に対してアメリカの独占禁止法の適用に関する重要な争点を提起している．地方裁判所は，Timberlane 訴訟を国家行為理論と事物管轄権の欠如を理由に却下した．他の3件は，Timberlane 原告の従業員によって，長期にわたる反 Timberlane ドラマの過程において蒙ったと主張される個人的な損害に対して提起された州籍の相違に基づく不法行為訴訟である．Timberlane 訴訟を却下した後に，地方裁判所はこれらの3つの訴訟をフォーラム・ノン・コンヴィニエンスを理由に却下した．われわれは4件のすべての事件の却下を取消し，差し戻す．

I Timberlane 訴訟

Timberlane 原告らの基本的な主張は，合衆国及びホンジュラスに所在する Bank of America の役員とその他の者が，ホンジュラスの子会社を通じて，共謀して Timberlane をホンジュラスにおける木材の製造とその合衆国への輸出を阻止し，それによってホンジュラスにおける木材輸出事業を Bank から融資を受け，支配される少数の選ばれた個人の手にコントロール

in the hands of a few select individuals financed and controlled by the Bank. The intent and result of the conspiracy, they contend, was to interfere with the exportation to the United States, including Puerto Rico, of Honduran lumber for sale or use there by the plaintiffs, thus directly and substantially affecting the foreign commerce of the United States.
......

Cast of Characters

There are three affiliated plaintiffs in the Timberlane action. Timberlane Lumber Company is an Oregon partnership principally involved in the purchase and distribution of lumber at wholesale in the United States and the importation of lumber into the United States for sale and use. Danli Industrial, S. A., and Maya Lumber Company, S. de R. L., are both Honduras corporations, incorporated and principally owned by the general partners of Timberlane. Danli held contracts to purchase timber in Honduras, and Maya was to conduct the milling operations to produce the lumber for export. (Timberlane, Danli, and Maya will be collectively referred to as "Timberlane.")

The primary defendants are Bank of America Corporation, a California corporation, and its wholly-owned subsidiary, Bank of America National Trust and Savings Association, which operates a branch in Tegucigalpa, Honduras. Several employees of the Bank have also been named and served as defendants: ....
......

Facts Alleged

The conspiracy sketched by Timberlane actually started before the plaintiffs entered the scene. At that time, the Lima family operated a lumber mill in Honduras, competing with Lamas and Casanova, in both of which the Bank had significant financial interests. The Lima enterprise was also indebted to the Bank. By 1971, however, the Lima business was

することを維持しようとするところにあった．その共謀の意図と結果は，原告らによる合衆国での販売と使用のために，ホンジュラスの木材をプエルトリコを含む合衆国へ輸出することを妨害し，それによって合衆国の外国通商に直接かつ実質的な影響を与えることにあったと原告らは主張する．
……

登場人物

　Timberlane訴訟には3人の関連する原告がいる．Timberlane Lumber Companyは，オレゴンのパートナーシップであり，主として合衆国における木材の購入と販売の卸業及び販売と使用のために合衆国への木材の輸入業務に従事している．Danli Industrial, S. A., 及びMaya Lumber Company, S. de R. L. はともに，Timberlaneの無限責任パートナーによって設立され，主として所有されているホンジュラス法人である．Danliは，ホンジュラスにおいて木材を購入する契約を締結しており，Mayaは輸出用に木材を製造する事業を営むことになっていた（Timberlane, Danli, Mayaを一括して，「Timberlane」という）．

　主要な被告は，カルフォルニア法人であるBank of America Corporationとその完全所有子会社で，ホンジュラスのTegucigalpaで支店を経営するBank of America National Trust and Savings Associationである．またBankの数人の従業員が被告として名指され，送達された……
……

主張されている事実

　Timberlaneが概略述べたところによると，共謀は原告らが登場する以前から実際はスタートしていた．当時，Limaファミリーは，ホンジュラスで木材工場を操業し，ともにBankが重要な財政的利害関係を有していたLamasとCasanovaと競争していた．Lima企業もBankから借財があった．しかしながら1971年までには，Limaの事業は財政的な危機の状況に陥っていた．

in financial trouble. Timberlane alleges that driving Lima under was the first step in the conspiracy which eventually crippled Timberlane's efforts, but the particulars do not matter for this appeal. What does matter is that various interests in the Lima assets, including its milling plant, passed to Lima's creditors: Casanova, the Bank, and the group of Lima employees who had not been paid the wages and severance pay due them. Under Honduran law, the employees' claim had priority.

Enter Timberlane, with a long history in the lumber business, in search of alternative sources of lumber for delivery to its distribution system on the East Coast of the United States. After study, it decided to try Honduras. In 1971, Danli was formed, tracts of forest land were acquired, plans for a modern log processing plant prepared, and equipment purchased and assembled for shipment from the United States to Danli in Honduras. Timberlane became aware that the Lima plant might be available and began negotiating for its acquisition. Maya was formed, purchased the Lima employees' interest in the machinery and equipment in January 1972, despite opposition from the conspirators, and re-activated the Lima mill.

Realizing that they were faced with better-financed and more-vigorous competition from Timberlane and its Honduran subsidiaries, the defendants and others extended the anti-Lima conspiracy to disrupt Timberlane's efforts. The primary weapons employed by the conspirators were the claim still held by the Bank in the remaining assets of the Lima enterprise under the all-inclusive mortgage Lima had been forced to sign and another claim held by Casanova. Maya made a substantial cash offer for the Bank's interest in an effort to clear its title, but the Bank refused to sell. Instead, the Bank surreptitiously conveyed the mortgage to Casanova for questionable consideration, Casanova paying nothing and agreeing only to pay the Bank a portion of what it collected. Casanova immedi-

Timberlaneが主張するところによると，Limaを追い込むことは，やがてTimberlaneの努力を無に期せしめる謀議の第一段階であったが，その詳細な事実は本件控訴にとって重要ではない．重要なのは，Limaの木材プラントを含む資産に対する様々な権利が，Limaの債権者たち，つまりCasanova, Bank, Limaのグループ及び支払われるべき賃金，退職金の支払いを受けなかった従業員にわたったことである．ホンジュラス法によれば，従業員の請求権に優先権があった．

木材事業に長い経験をもつTimberlaneは，合衆国の東海岸における自社の流通システムに対する出荷用木材の代替的供給源を求めて登場する．Timberlaneは調査の後，ホンジュラスへの進出を決めた．1971年にDanliが設立され，森林地帯が取得され，近代的な丸太加工プラントの計画が準備された．そして機器類が合衆国からホンジュラスのDanliへ船積するために，購入され，組み立てられた．Timberlaneは，Limaのプラントを利用できるかもしれないことを知るようになって，その取得のための交渉を開始した．Mayaが設立され，共謀者の反対にもかかわらず，1972年1月にはLimaの従業員が有する，機器類と備品に対する権利を購入した．そして，Limaの工場を再開した．

被告らとその他の者は，Timberlaneとそのホンジュラスの子会社からの資金調達力の高い，もっと強力な競争に直面したことを知って，Timberlaneの取組みを妨害するために，反Limaの謀議を拡大した．共謀者たちが利用した主な武器は，Limaが署名せざるを得なかった包括的な抵当権に基づき，Lima企業の残余財産に対してBankがなお保持していた請求権とCasanovaが保持していた請求権であった．Mayaは，その権原を清算しようとして，Bankの権利を購入するために相当の現金を提示したが，Bankはその売却を拒否した．そのかわりにBankは，ひそかに疑わしい約因と引き換えに抵当権をCasanovaに譲渡した．Casanovaは，対価を払わずに，自己が集めた部分についてだけBankに支払うことを合意し，直ちにBankの請求権と自己

ately assigned the Bank's claim and its own on similar terms to Caminals, who promptly set out to disrupt the Timberlane operation.

Caminals is characterized as the "front man" in the campaign to drive Timberlane out of Honduras, ... Having acquired the claims of Casanova and the Bank, Caminals went to court to enforce them, ignoring throughout Timberlane's offers to purchase or settle them. Under the laws of Honduras, an "embargo" on property is a court-ordered attachment, registered with the Public Registry, which precludes the sale of that property without a court order. Honduran law provides, upon embargo, that the court appoint a judicial officer, called an "interventor" to ensure against any diminution in the value of the property. In order to paralyze the Timberlane operation, Caminals obtained embargoes against Maya and Danli. Acting through the interventor, since accused of being on the payroll of the Bank, guards and troops were used to cripple and, for a time, completely shut down Timberlane's milling operation. The harassment took other forms as well: the conspirators caused the manager of Timberlane's Honduras operations, Gordon Sloan Smith, to be falsely arrested and imprisoned and were responsible for the publication of several defamatory articles about Timberlane in the Honduran press.

As a result of the conspiracy, Timberlane's complaint claimed damages then estimated in excess of $5,000,000. Plaintiffs also allege that there has been a direct and substantial effect on United States foreign commerce, and that defendants intended the results of the conspiracy, including the impact on United States commerce.

......

Extraterritorial Reach of the United States Antitrust Laws

There is no doubt that American antitrust laws extend over some conduct in other nations. There was language in the first Supreme Court case in point, *American Banana Co. v. United Fruit Co.*, 213 U.S. 347,

の請求権を同じような条件でCaminalsに譲渡した．Caminalsはすぐに Timberlaneの操業を妨害しようと決心した．

　Caminalsは，Timberlaneをホンジュラスから追い出そうとするキャンペーンにおいて「隠れみの的な存在」であった．……Caminalsは，CasanovaとBankの請求権を取得した後に，Timberlaneがそれらを買い取るか，清算しようという申し込みを続けたにもかかわらず，それらの権利を執行するために裁判所に行った．ホンジュラス法によれば，財産に対する「出港禁止令」は，裁判所が命じる差押えであり，公共登録簿に登録され，裁判所の命令がなければ，当該財産の売却はできない．ホンジュラス法は，出港禁止令について，財産価値の減少から守るために「調停者」と呼ばれる裁判所の官吏を任命すると規定する．Timberlaneの事業を活動させなくするために，Caminalsは，MayaとDanliに対する出港禁止令状を取得した．Bankの従業員名簿に掲載されていると批判されたので，衛兵と軍隊が，調停者を通じて行動し，Timberlaneの工場の事業を駄目にし，しばらくの間，完全に閉鎖させるために利用された．ハラスメントは別の作戦をとることもあった．すなわち，共謀者たちは，Timberlaneのホンジュラス事業のマネージャーであるGordon Sloan Smithを不正に逮捕，投獄させ，そしてホンジュラスのプレスにTimberlaneについての名誉毀損記事の公表にも責任があった．

　このような共謀の結果として，Timberlaneは，その申立において，当時の5,000,000ドルを超える損害賠償金を請求した．原告の主張によれば，合衆国対外通商に対する直接かつ実質的な効果が存在し，また被告らは合衆国通商に対する影響を含む共謀の結果を意図していた．

……
合衆国独占禁止法の域外適用
　アメリカの独占禁止法が他の国家におけるなんらかの行為に対して拡張して適用されることには疑問の余地はない．この点に関する最初の連邦最高裁判決である*American Banana Co. v. United Fruit Co.*, 213 U.S. 347, 29 S.

29 S. Ct. 511, 53 L. Ed. 826 (1909), casting doubt on the extension of the Sherman Act to acts outside United States territory. But subsequent cases have limited *American Banana* to its particular facts, and the Sherman Act —and with it other antitrust laws— has been applied to extraterritorial conduct. *See, e.g., Continental Ore Co. v. Union Carbide & Carbon Corp.*, 370 U.S. 690, 82 S. Ct. 1404, 8 L. Ed. 2d 777 (1962); *United States v. Sisal Sales Corp.*, 274 U.S. 268, 47 S. Ct. 592, 71 L. Ed. 1042 (1927); *United States v. Aluminum Co. of America*, 148 F.2d 416, (2d Cir. 1945) (the *"Alcoa"* case). The act may encompass the foreign activities of aliens as well as American citizens. *Alcoa, supra; Swiss Watch*, 1963 Trade Cases P 70,600; *United States v. General Electric Co.*, 82 F. Supp. 753 (D.N.J.1949), *judgment implementing decree*, 115 F. Supp. 835 (D.N.J.1953).

That American law covers some conduct beyond this nation's borders does not mean that it embraces all, however. Extraterritorial application is understandably a matter of concern for the other countries involved. Those nations have sometimes resented and protested, as excessive intrusions into their own spheres, broad assertions of authority by American courts. *See* A. Neale, The Antitrust Laws of the United States of America 365-72 (2d ed. 1970); Assn. of the Bar of the City of New York, National Security and Foreign Policy in the Application of American Antitrust Laws to Commerce with Foreign Nations 7-18 (1957); Zwarensteyn, The Foreign Reach of the American Antitrust Laws, 3 Am.Bus.L.J. 163, 165-69 (1965). Our courts have recognized this concern and have, at times, responded to it, even if not always enough to satisfy all the foreign critics. *See Alcoa*, 148 F.2d at 443; *Swiss Watch*, 1965 Trade Cases P 71,352 (modification of order); *General Electric*, 115 F. Supp. at 878 (implementation of decree). In any event, it is evident that at some point the interests of the United States are too weak and the foreign harmony incentive for restraint too strong to justify an extraterritorial assertion of jurisdiction.

Ct. 511, 53 L. Ed. 826（1909）の中には，合衆国の領域外の行為に対してシャーマン法を拡張することについて疑問を呈する文言がある．しかしその後の事件は，*American Banana* 判決をその特殊な事実関係に制限し，シャーマン法――及びその他の独占禁止法は，――領域外の行為に適用されてきた．たとえば，*Continental Ore Co. v. Union Carbide & Carbon Corp.*, 370 U.S. 690, 82 S. Ct. 1404, 8 L. Ed. 2d 777（1962）; *United States v. Sisal Sales Corp.*, 274 U.S. 268, 47 S. Ct. 592, 71 L. Ed. 1042（1927）; *United States v. Aluminum Co. of America*, 148 F.2d 416,（2d Cir. 1945）．(「アルコア」事件) を参照．行為には，アメリカ人だけでなく，外国人の外国における活動をも含むものである．*Alcoa, supra; Swiss Watch*, 1963 Trade Cases P 70,600; *United States v. General Electric Co.*, 82 F. Supp. 753（D.N.J. 1949），*judgment implementing decree*, 115 F. Supp. 835（D.N.J.1953）．

しかしながら，アメリカ法がこの国の領域を越えたなんらかの行為を対象とするということは，そのすべてを包含するということを意味するものではない．よく理解できるように，域外適用は，関連している他の国家にとっても関心事である．これらの国は，ときにアメリカ裁判所による広い権限の主張を彼ら自身の領域への過剰な侵入であるとして憤慨し，抗議してきた．A. Neale, The Antitrust Laws of the United States of America 365-72（2d ed. 1970）; Assn. of the Bar of the City of New York, National Security and Foreign Policy in the Application of American Antitrust Laws to Commerce with Foreign Nations 7-18（1957）; Zwarensteyn, The Foreign Reach of the American Antitrust Laws, 3 Am. Bus. L. J. 163, 165-69（1965）参照．われわれの裁判所は，この関心を認めて，たとえすべての外国の批判者をつねに満足させるに十分でなかったにしても，それに対応してきた．*Alcoa* 判決, 148 F.2d at 443; *Swiss Watch*, 1965 Trade Cases P 71, 352（命令の修正）参照 ; *General Electric*, 115 F. Supp. at 878（判決の履行）参照．いずれにしても管轄権の域外的行使を正当化するに合衆国の利益があまりに弱く，そして外国との調和のために抑制への誘因がきわめて強くなる地点がど

What that point is or how it is determined is not defined by international law. Miller, Extraterritorial Effects of Trade Regulation, 111 U.Pa. L. Rev. 1092, 1094 (1963). Nor does the Sherman Act limit itself. In the domestic field the Sherman Act extends to the full reach of the commerce power. *United States v. South-Eastern Underwriters Assn.*, 322 U. S. 533, 558, 64 S. Ct. 1162, 88 L. Ed. 1440 (1944). To define it somewhat more modestly in the foreign commerce area courts have generally, and logically, fallen back on a narrower construction of congressional intent, such as expressed in Judge Learned Hand's oft-cited opinion in *Alcoa*, 148 F.2d at 443: ......

......

It is the effect on American foreign commerce which is usually cited to support extraterritorial jurisdiction. *Alcoa* set the course, when Judge Hand declared, *id*.:

It is setttled law...... that any state may impose liabilities, even upon persons not within its allegiance for conduct outside its borders that has consequences whithin its borders which the state reprehends; and these liabilities other state will ordinarily recognize.

......

Even among American courts and commentators, however, there is no consensus on how far the jurisdiction should extend. The district court here concluded that a "direct and substantial effect" on United States foreign commerce was a prerequisite, without stating whether other factors were relevant or considered. The same formula was employed, to some extent, by the district courts in the *Swiss Watch* case, 1963 Trade Cases P $ 70,600, in *United States v. R. P. Oldham Co.*, 152 F. Supp. 818,

こかにあることは明らかである．

　そこがどこであり，どのように決定されるかは，国際法によって定められてはいない．Miller, Extraterritorial Effects of Trade Regulation, 111 U.Pa. L. Rev. 1092, 1094（1963）．またシャーマン法自身もなんら制限はしていない．国内分野ではシャーマン法は，通商権限が及ぶ範囲一杯まで及ぶ．*United States v. South-Eastern Underwriters Assn.*, 322 U.S. 533, 558, 64 S. Ct. 1162, 88 L. Ed. 1440（1944）．対外通商の分野ではそれをいくぶんもっと穏やかに定義するために，裁判所は，*Alcoa* 判決の Learned Hand 裁判官のよく引用される意見に表明されている 148 F.2d at 443 ような，議会の意図のもっと狭い解釈に一般的に，そして論理的にやむを得ず頼ってきた．……
……

　域外的管轄権を支持するものとして普通よく引用されるのは，アメリカの外国との通商に対する効果である．*Alcoa* 判決において，Hand 裁判官がつぎのように宣言したときに，その路線が決まった．同上．
　　いかなる国家も，その忠誠の下にない者に対してさえ，自国の領域外でなされた行為がその国家が違法とする結果をその領域内にもたらす場合には，その行為に対する責任を追求できることは，……確立した法原則である．そして他の国家は，この責任を通常，承認するであろう．
……

　しかしながらアメリカの裁判所と学者の間においてさえ，管轄権がどこまで及ぶかについての合意は存在していない．本件の地方裁判所は，他の要素が関連しているか又は考慮されるかに言及することなく，合衆国の外国通商に対する「直接かつ実質的な効果」が不可欠であると結論した．同じ原則がある程度までつぎの事件の地方裁判所によって採用された．*Swiss Watch* case, 1963 Trade Cases P $ 70,600, in *United States v. R. P. Oldham Co.*, 152 F. Supp. 818, 822（N.D.Cal.1957）, and in *General Electric*, 82 F. Supp. at

822 (N. D. Cal. 1957), and in *General Electric*, 82 F. Supp. at 891. It has been identified and advocated by several commentators. *See, e.g.*, W. Fugate, Foreign Commerce and the Antitrust Laws 30, 174 (2d ed. 1973); J. Van Cise, Understanding the Antitrust Laws 204 (1973 ed.). Similarly, *see* Report of the Attorney General's National Committee to Study the Antitrust Laws 76 (1955)("substantial anticompetitive effects"); Restatement (Second) of the Foreign Relations Law of the United States Restatement §18.
......

......in several of the cases and commentaries employing the "effects" test, is the suggestion that factors other than simply the effect on the United States are weighed, and rightly so. As former Attorney General (then Professor) Katzenbach observed, the effect on American commerce is not, by itself, sufficient information on which to base a decision that the United States is the nation primarily interested in the activity causing the effect. "Anything that affects the external trade and commerce of the United States also affects the trade and commerce of other nations, and may have far greater consequences for others than for the United States." Katzenbach, Conflicts on Unruly Horse, 65 Yale L. J. 1087, 1150 (1956).

The effects test by itself is incomplete because it fails to consider the other nation's interests. Nor does it expressly take into account the full nature of the relationship between the actors and this country. Whether the alleged offender is an American citizen, for instance, may make a big difference; applying American laws to American citizens raises fewer problems than application to foreigners. ......

American courts have, in fact, often displayed a regard for comity and the prerogatives of other nations and considered their interests as well as other parts of the factual circumstances, even when professing to apply an

891. それは若干の学者により確認され，主張されてきた．たとえば，W. Fugate, Foreign Commerce and the Antitrust Laws 30, 174 (2d ed. 1973); J. Van Cise, Understanding the Antitrust Laws 204 (1973 ed.) 参照．同じく，Report of the Attorney General's National Committee to Study the Antitrust Laws 76 (1955)(「実質的な反競争的効果」), Restatement (Second) of the Foreign Relations Law of the United States Restatement §18 参照．
……

……「効果」基準を採用する判決と学説の中には，単に合衆国に対する効果以外の要素も考量すべきだとの主張がなされており，それはまさにそのとおりである．前の司法長官（当時は教授）の Katzenbach は，アメリカ通商に対する効果はそれだけでは合衆国がその効果を発生させた活動に主たる利害関係を有する国であるとの決定を下す基礎となる十分な情報ではないと述べた．「合衆国の対外貿易と通商に影響を与えるものはすべて，他の国家の貿易と通商にも影響を与えるのであり，ときには合衆国に対してよりもはるかに大きな結果をもたらすことがあるかも知れない．」Katzenbach, Conflicts on an Unruly Horse, 65 Yale L. J. 1087, 1150 (1956).

効果基準自体は，不完全なものである．なぜなら，それは，他国の利益を考慮することに失敗しているからである．それは，また，行為者と合衆国との関係の性質を十分明確には考慮していない．違反者と名指されている者がたとえば，合衆国の市民であるかどうかは大きな相違をもたらすであろう．なぜならアメリカの市民にアメリカ法を適用することは外国人に対する適用よりも僅かの問題しか発生させないであろうからである．……

アメリカの裁判所は，効果基準を適用すると宣言しているときでも，実際には，礼譲と他国の特権に対する顧慮をしばしば示し，事実的な状況と同様に他国の利益を考慮してきた．「実質的な」効果という要件は，ある程度まで

effects test. To some degree, the requirement for a "substantial" effect may silently incorporate these additional considerations, with "substantial" as a flexible standard that varies with other factors. The intent requirement suggested by *Alcoa*, 148 F.2d at 443-44, is one example of an attempt to broaden the court's perspective, as is drawing a distinction between American citizens and non-citizens.

The failure to articulate these other elements in addition to the standard effects analysis is costly, however, for it is more likely that they will be overlooked or slighted in interpretating past decisions and reaching new ones. Placing emphasis on the qualification that effects be "substantial" is also risky, for the term has a meaning in the interstate antitrust context which does not encompass all the factors relevant to the foreign trade case.

A tripartite analysis seems to be indicated. As acknowledged above, the antitrust laws require in the first instance that there be *some* effect-actual or intended-on American foreign commerce before the federal courts may legitimately exercise subject matter jurisdiction under those statutes. Second, a greater showing of burden or restraint may be necessary to demonstrate that the effect is sufficiently large to present a cognizable injury to the plaintiffs and, therefore, a civil *violation* of the antitrust laws. *Occidental Petroleum*, 331 F. Supp. at 102-03; Beausang, The Extraterritorial Jurisdiction of the Sherman Act, 70 Dick. L. Rev. 187, 191 (1966). Third, there is the additional question which is unique to the international setting of whether the interests of, and links to, the United States-including the magnitude of the effect on American foreign commerce-are sufficiently strong, vis-a-vis those of other nations, to justify an assertion of extraterritorial authority.

これらの付加的な考慮事項を，他の要素とともに変化する柔軟な基準としての「実質的な」の中に暗黙のうちに組み込んでいるのである．*Alcoa* 判決，148 F.2d at 443-44 によって示唆された意図の要件は，アメリカ人と外国人を区別しようとするのと同じように，裁判所の視点を広げようとする試みの1つの例である．

しかしながら，標準的な効果の分析に加えて，これらの付加的な要素をはっきりと表現しないことは，高い代価を支払うことになる．というのは，過去の判決を解釈し，新しいものに到達するのに，これらの付加的な要素が見過ごされたり，無視されることになりそうだからである．効果が「実質的」でなければならないという制限を強調することもまた危険を伴う．というのは，この言葉は，外国通商の事件に関連のあるすべての要素を包含しない州際反競争的なコンテキストにおける意味をもっているからである．

3つの部分からなる分析が示されているように思われる．上に述べたように，独占禁止法は，第1に，これらの制定法に基づいて，連邦裁判所が事物管轄権を正当に行使しうる前に，アメリカの外国通商に――現実の又は意図されたなんらかの効果が，存在することを要求している．第2に，その効果が，原告に対する認識することができる損害と，そしてそれゆえに独占禁止法の民事上の侵害を生じさせるに十分に大きいことを示すためには，負担または制限の存在をより明確に立証することが必要である．*Occidental Petroleum*, 331 F. Supp. at 102-03; Beausang, The Extraterritorial Jurisdiction of the Sherman Act, 70 Dick.L.Rev. 187, 191（1966）. 第3に，――アメリカの外国通商に対する効果の大きさを含めて――合衆国の利益及び合衆国への関連が，他国のそれと比較して域外的権限の主張を正当化するほど十分に強いものであるかどうかという，国際的な場面に特有の付加的な問題がある．

It is this final issue which is both obscured by undue reliance on the "substantiality" test and complicated to resolve. An effect on United States commerce, although necessary to the exercise of jurisdiction under the antitrust laws, is alone not a sufficient basis on which to determine whether American authority *should* be asserted in a given case as a matter of international comity and fairness. In some cases, the application of the direct and substantial test in the international context might open the door too widely by sanctioning jurisdiction over an action when these considerations would indicate dismissal. At other times, it may fail in the other direction, dismissing a case for which comity and fairness do not require forbearance, thus closing the jurisdictional door too tightly-for the Sherman Act does reach some restraints which do not have both a direct and substantial effect on the foreign commerce of the United States. A more comprehensive inquiry is necessary. We believe that the field of conflict of laws presents the proper approach, as was suggested, if not specifically employed, in *Alcoa* in expressing the basic limitation on application of American laws: ......

What we prefer is an evaluation and balancing of the relevant considerations in each case-in the words of Kingman Brewster, a "jurisdictional rule of reason." Balancing of the foreign interests involved was the approach taken by the Supreme Court in *Continental Ore Co. v. Union Carbide & Carbon Corp.*, 370 U.S. 690, 82 S. Ct. 1404, 8 L. Ed. 2d 777 (1962), where the involvement of the Canadian government in the alleged monopolization was held not to require dismissal. The Court stressed that there was no indication that the Canadian authorities approved or would have approved of the monopolization, meaning that the Canadian interest, if any, was slight and was outweighed by the American interest in condemning the restraint. Similarly, *see Lauritzen v. Larsen*, 345 U.S. 571, 73 S. Ct. 921, 97 L. Ed. 1254 (1953), where the Court used a like approach in declining to apply the Jones Act to a Danish seaman, injured

12 独占禁止法の域外適用：Timberlane Lumber Co. v. Bank of America N.T.& S.A.

　この最後の争点が，「実質性」の基準に過度に依存することによって曖昧にされ，またその解決を複雑にしたものなのである．合衆国の通商に対する効果は，独占禁止法に基づく管轄権の行使に必要なものではあるけれども，それだけでは，アメリカの権限がある特定の事件において国際礼譲と公正に関するものとして，主張されるべきかを決定する十分な基礎ではない．国際的なコンテキストにおいて直接かつ実質的な効果の基準を適用することは，これらの考慮事項からすれば却下となるであろうときに訴訟を是認することによってあまりに広くドアを開きすぎるという場合があるであろう．また別の場合には，逆の方向でうまくいかないことになるかも知れない．つまり，礼譲と公正さからすれば，自制が要求されない事件を却下し，かくして管轄権のドアを堅く閉めすぎることになるかも知れない．――というのはシャーマン法は，合衆国の対外通商に直接かつ実質的な効果を及ぼさない制限条項についても及ぶものだからである．もっと包括的な探求が必要である．われわれは，アメリカ法の適用に対する基本的な制限を表現するにあたって*Alcoa*判決においてとくに採用されたものではないが，そこで示唆された，抵触法の分野が適切なアプローチを提供すると考える．

　われわれがよいと考えるのは，各々の事件において関係する要因の評価と衡量――Kingman Brewsterの言葉によれば，「管轄権に関する相当性の原則」である．関連する外国の利益の衡量は，最高裁判所の*Continental Ore Co. v. Union Carbide & Carbon Corp.*, 370 U.S. 690, 82 S. Ct. 1404, 8 L. Ed. 2d 777（1962）によって採用されたものである．この事件では，主張されている独占におけるカナダ政府の関与は，却下を要求するものではないと判示された．裁判所は，カナダの官憲が独占を是認したか，是認したであろうことを示すものはなにも存在しないことを強調した．それは，カナダの利益が，かりにあるにしても僅かであり，制限を糾弾するアメリカの利益が優越することを意味するものであった．同様に，*Lauritzen v. Larsen*, 345 U.S. 571, 73 S. Ct. 921, 97 L. Ed. 1254（1953）を参照．この事件では，裁判所は同じようなアプローチを使い，デンマーク船舶上，ハバナで負傷し

in Havana on a Danish ship, although he had signed on to the ship in New York.

The elements to be weighed include the degree of conflict with foreign law or policy, the nationality or allegiance of the parties and the locations or principal places of business or corporations, the extent to which enforcement by either state can be expected to achieve compliance, the relative significance of effects on the United States as compared with those elsewhere, the extent to which there is explicit purpose to harm or affect American commerce, the foreseeability of such effect, and the relative importance to the violations charged of conduct within the United States as compared with conduct abroad. A court evaluating these factors should identify the potential degree of conflict if American authority is asserted. A difference in law or policy is one likely sore spot, though one which may not always be present. Nationality is another; though foreign governments may have some concern for the treatment of American citizens and business residing there, they primarily care about their own nationals. Having assessed the conflict, the court should then determine whether in the face of it the contacts and interests of the United States are sufficient to support the exercise of extraterritorial jurisdiction.

We conclude, then, that the problem should be approached in three parts: Does the alleged restraint affect, or was it intended to affect, the foreign commerce of the United States? Is it of such a type and magnitude so as to be cognizable as a violation of the Sherman Act? As a matter of international comity and fairness, should the extraterritorial jurisdiction of the United States be asserted to cover it? The district court's judgment found only that the restraint involved in the instant suit did not produce a direct and substantial effect on American foreign commerce. That holding does not satisfy any of these inquiries.

The Sherman Act is not limited to trade restraints which have both a

たデンマーク船員に対して，船員がニューヨークで乗船する契約に署名したけれども，Jones Act を適用することを否定した．

　衡量されるべき要素としてはつぎのものがある．外国の法又は政策との抵触，当事者の国籍又は忠誠及び事業又は会社の所在地又は主たる事業地，一方の国家による強制が遵守を達成するために期待される程度，他の場所への効果と比較した合衆国への効果の相対的重要性，米国の商業を害する又はそれに影響を及ぼす明白な目的が存在する程度，そのような効果の予測可能性，及び申し立てられた違反に対する合衆国内の行為の，国外行為と比較した相対的重要性である．これらの要素を評価する裁判所は，アメリカの権限が主張された場合に生じる抵触の可能性の程度を確認すべきである．法又は政策の相違は，常に存在するとは限らないけれども，おそらく触れると痛いところであろう．国籍ももう1つの例である．外国政府はその国に居住するアメリカ市民と事業の処遇にいくらかの関心をもっているけれども，主たる関心は自国の国民にある．このような抵触を評価したのち，つぎに裁判所は当該抵触を前にして合衆国の関連及び利益が域外管轄権の行使を支持するのに十分であるかどうかを決定すべきである．

　そこでわれわれは結論する．問題は3つの部分に分けて解決すべきである．主張されている制限は，合衆国の対外通商に与えたか，又は与えることを意図されていたか．それはシャーマン法の違反として認識できるほどの型と大きさのものであるか．合衆国の域外管轄権は，国際礼譲と公正さに関するものとして，それをカバーすべく主張されるべきか．地方裁判所の判決は，単に本件訴訟に関わる制限がアメリカの対外通商に直接かつ実質的な効果を生じていないとのみ認定した．そのような判示はこれらの調査のいずれをも充足するものではない．

　シャーマン法はわれわれの外国通商に対する直接かつ実質的な効果を有す

direct and substantial effect on our foreign commerce. Timberlane has alleged that the complained of activities were intended to, and did, affect the export of lumber from Honduras to the United States-the flow of United States foreign commerce, and as such they are within the jurisdiction of the federal courts under the Sherman Act. Moreover, the magnitude of the effect alleged would appear to be sufficient to state a claim.

The comity question is more complicated. From Timberlane's complaint it is evident that there are grounds for concern as to at least a few of the defendants, for some are identified as foreign citizens: Laureano Gutierrez Falla, Michael Casanova and the Casanova firms, of Honduras, and Patrick Byrne, of Canada. Moreover, it is clear that most of the activity took place in Honduras, though the conspiracy may have been directed from San Francisco, and that the most direct economic effect was probably on Honduras. However, there has been no indication of any conflict with the law or policy of the Honduran government, nor any comprehensive analysis of the relative connections and interests of Honduras and the United States. Under these circumstances, the dismissal by the district court cannot be sustained on jurisdictional grounds.

We, therefore, reverse and remand the Timberlane action.
……

る貿易制限に限られるわけではない．Timberlane が主張したのは，申し立てられている活動は，ホンジュラスから合衆国への木材の輸出に——合衆国の外国通商の流れに影響を与えることを意図し，そして現に影響を与えたこと，そしてそれはシャーマン法上，そのようなものとして連邦裁判所の管轄権内にあるという点にあった．さらに主張されている効果の大きさは請求を申し立てるのに十分であるようにみえる．

　礼譲の問題はもっと複雑である．Timberlane の申立からすると，少なくとも数人の被告については，外国人と認められるものがいるから，［礼譲との］関連が存在することは明らかである．つまり Laureano Gutierrez Falla, Michael Casanova 及び Casanova 社はホンジュラスの，そして Patrick Byrne はカナダの者である．さらに共謀はサンフランシスコから指示されたかも知れないけれども，ほとんどの活動はホンジュラスで発生したことは明らかである．また，直接的な経済的効果のほとんどは多分ホンジュラスに対するものであったであろう．しかしながら，ホンジュラス政府の法と政策とのなんらの抵触についてはなんらの言及もないし，ホンジュラスと合衆国との相対的な結びつきや利益についてのなんらの包括的な検討も行われていない．このような状況の下では，地方裁判所による却下は，管轄権上の理由で支持することはできない．

　したがってわれわれは，Timberlane 訴訟を破棄し，差し戻す．
……

III 域外適用

【解 説】

本件は，独占禁止法の域外適用問題につき，管轄権に関する相当性の理論又はバランシング・テストを採用した事例である．

1 *American Banana Co. v. United Fruit Co.* における属地主義

独占禁止法の分野で厳格な属地主義の原則を採用し，域外適用を否定した連邦最高裁の注目すべき判決は，*American Banana* 判決，213 U.S. 347（1909）である．この事件は，原告アラバマ会社 American Banana が，被告ニュージャージー会社 United Fruit に対し，被告がパナマ又はコスタリカにおいて，原告をバナナ貿易から排除し，市場を独占しようとした行為がシャーマン法違反となるとして3倍賠償を請求した事例である．

連邦最高裁の Holmes 判事は，「原告の主張は，いくつかの驚くべき命題に立脚していることは明らかである．すなわち，まず第1に，みた限りでは，損害を引き起こした行為は，合衆国の管轄外で，つまり他国の管轄権内で行われた．そのような行為が合衆国の法律により規律されるべきであるとの議論を聞くのは，驚くべきことである」と述べる．そして，一定の例外はあるにせよ，「一般的で，普遍的なルールは，行為の性質が適法か，不適法であるかは，その行為がなされた国の法律によってすべて決定されなければならない」，「被告がパナマ又はコスタリカでしたことは，本件訴訟に関するかぎりでは，その制定法の適用範囲にないことは明らかであると考える」と判示し，厳格な属地主義の理論を明確に宣言した．

2 *United States v. Aluminum Co. of America*, 148 F.2d 416（2d Cir. 1945）における効果理論の採用

これに対して，独占禁止法の分野で，*American Banana* 判決の厳格な属地主義の立場を否定し，合衆国独占禁止法の域外適用についての新しいアプローチを採用したのが，*United States v. Aluminum Co. of America*（以下 *Alcoa* 判決という）である．この事件において，連邦第2巡回区控訴裁判所の

Learned Hand 裁判官は，属地主義を放棄し，いわゆる効果主義（理論）を採用した．

　Alcoa 事件では外国のアルミメーカーによる生産制限のカルテルが問題となった．カルテル参加企業はすべて外国で，これが実行された場所もすべて外国であった．参加企業は協定を結び，共同でスイスに子会社を設立し，この子会社が親会社各社の生産数量を決定し，これを割り当てた．このようにして生産制限を実行したのであるが，この割当数量を超えて生産した企業は子会社にペナルティを支払わなければならなかった．この割当数量の中に，各企業が米国に輸出した分を含めることになっていたので，各企業が米国に輸出すると，それだけ早く割当量に達してしまうこととなった．この協定は参加各企業が米国に輸出しないという効果を有するものであった．

　米国政府は，この国際カルテルが米国独占禁止法に違反するとして提訴した．裁判所は以下のように判示して，米国政府を勝訴させた．裁判所がかかわっているのは，連邦議会が外国人が合衆国外でなした行為に対して責任を課すことを選択したかどうかである．外国企業が外国において行った行為であっても，これが米国市場に「効果」をあたえる「意図」を以てなされ，これが現実に効果をあたえる場合には，合衆国の独占禁止法はこの行為に対して適用することができるのである．

　裁判所は，国家は，外国人の外国における行為が国内に違法な結果をもたらす場合には，その責任を追求できるのであり，これは確立した法原則である，と判示する．そして，もし，供給制限の「効果」が合衆国市場に及び，かつ，その効果が「意図」されている場合には外国人が外国で締結したカルテル協定であっても，シャーマン法の適用範囲に入ることを認めた．

　Alcoa 判決の上の原則は，国内における「効果」があれば，自国の独占禁止法を適用できるとするところから，「効果理論」（effect doctrine）と呼ばれる．そして *Alcoa* 判決によって米国独占禁止法の域外適用の理論が確立したといわれており，この効果理論に基づいて，米国独占禁止法の域外適用が広く行われるようになった．

3 Timberlane 判決

　本件 Timberlane 判決は，単に「効果」の点だけから，アメリカの管轄権を判断するのではなく，外国で行われた行為がどの国と最も密接にかかわっているかを，外国の法律・政策との関係，行為者の国籍などの諸要素を考慮した上で決定すべきであるとした．

　すなわち，裁判所によれば，「効果基準自体は，不完全なものである．なぜなら，それは，他国の利益を考慮することに失敗しているからである．それは，また，行為者と合衆国との関係の性質を十分に明確には考慮していない．」．われわれがよいと考えるのは，各々の事件において関係する要因の評価と衡量──「管轄権に関する相当性の原則」──であるとし，様々な利益や要因を評価し，衡量する，いわゆるバランシング・テストを提唱する．

　そして，このような観点からすると，効果基準が満たされている場合であっても，バランシング・テストに従い，国際的な礼譲，公正の観点から不適切とされる管轄権の行使は認められないこととなる．

　その意味で，本判決は効果理論による過大な域外適用に対する抑制と制限の論理を示した判決であるといえよう．

4　アメリカ対外関係法第 3 リステイトメント

　Timberlane 判決の管轄権に関する相当性の原則またはバランシング・テストは，法適用問題の一般理論としても重要な意義を有し，その基本的な方法論は，1987 年に公刊されたアメリカ法律協会のアメリカ対外関係法第 3 リステイトメントにも大きな影響をあたえた（翻訳は，アメリカ対外関係法リステイトメント研究会（訳）「アメリカ対外関係法第三リステイトメント㈡」国際法外交雑誌 88 巻 6 号 60-61 頁（1990）（松岡博）によったが，一部修正部分を変更した．この点については，松岡博「多国籍企業の法的規制──総論」国際経済法 4 号 22 頁（1995）の注（23）を参照）．

　アメリカ対外関係法第 3 リステイトメント第 402 条・403 条

　そこでつぎには，Timberlane 判決を法典化したといわれる（Gary B. Born, International Civil Litigation In United States Courts: Commentary & Materials

588 (3d ed. 1996), 対外関係法第3リステイトメントの関連規定を紹介検討しておきたい.

とくに第402条, 第403条の規定が重要であり, 民事刑事をも含めた国際事件における法適用の国際法上の基本原則を宣言したものといわれる.

第402条　規律管轄権の基礎

「国家は, 第403条の制限の下で, 次の事項につき規律する (to prescribe law) 管轄権を有する.

(1)(a)　すべての又は主要な部分が領域内でなされる行為

　(b)　領域内に所在する人の身分又は領域内に所在する物に対する利益

　(c)　領域外でなされる行為であって, 領域内でその実質的効果を生じているもの, 又はそのような効果の生じることを意図したもの

(2)　領域内外における自国民の行為, 利益, 身分又は関係

(3)　自国民以外の者による領域外の行為で, 自国の安全又はその他の限られた種類の国家利益の侵害に向けられたもの」

(翻訳は, アメリカ対外関係法リステイトメント研究会 (訳)「アメリカ対外関係法第三リステイトメント㈠」国際法外交雑誌88巻5号80頁 (1989) (野村美明) によった.)

本条第1項(a)の規定は, いわゆる属地主義の原則を宣言したものであり,「すべての又は主要な部分が領域内でなされる行為」について, 国家の規律管轄権 (それには国家が自国法を適用することを含む) を認める. (c)が, 効果主義を認めた規定であり,「領域外でなされる行為であって, 領域内でその実質的効果を生じているもの, 又はそのような効果の生じることを意図したもの」について, 国家が自国法を適用することを肯定する.

第2項は, 国籍主義をとり, 自国民の行為については外国で行われた行為であっても, 国家は自国法を適用することができる.

第3項は, 規律管轄権の特別の基礎となる保護主義を述べたものである. 国際法は, 国家がその領域外で外国人によってなされた, たとえば, 通貨の偽造のような限られた種類の違法行為を罰することを認めている.

つぎの第403条は, 第402条によって認められた規律管轄権の行使に対す

る制限を定めたものである．

第403条　規律管轄権に対する制限

「(1)　第402条の管轄権の基礎の1つが存在している場合であっても，国家は，他国と関連を有する人又は行為につき規律管轄権を行使することが相当で（reasonable）ないときは，管轄権を行使することができない．

(2)　人又は行為に対する管轄権の行使が相当であるかどうかは，次に掲げるものを含むすべての関連する要素を，事案に応じて斟酌することにより決定するものとする．

　(a)　行為と，それを規制する国家の領域との結びつき，すなわち，行為が国家の領域内でなされる程度，又は行為が領域に対し，若しくは領域内で実質的，直接的かつ予見可能な効果を生ぜしめる程度

　(b)　国籍，居所又は経済的活動のような，規制する国家と規制される行為に主として責任を負う人との関連，又は国家とその規制により保護されるべき人との関連

　(c)　規制される行為の性格，規制する国家にとってその規制が有する重要性，他国がその行為を規制する程度，及びその規制が一般に望ましいとして受け入れられる程度

　(d)　その規制によって保護され，又は損なわれる正当な期待の存在

　(e)　その規制が政治的，法的又は経済的な国際秩序にとって有する重要性

　(f)　その規制が国際秩序の伝統と一致している程度

　(g)　他国がその行為を規制することに対して有する利害関係の程度

　(h)　他国の規制と抵触する蓋然性

(3)　2つの国家がともに人又は行為に対して管轄権を行使することが不相当とはいえない場合において，これらの国家による規律が互いに抵触するときは，いずれの国家も，前項に掲げるものを含むすべての関連する要素を考慮して，管轄権を行使することに対して有する自国の利益を他国の利益と同様に斟酌する義務を負う．国家は他国の利益が明らかに大きいときは他国に譲歩しなければならない．」

本条は，国家による管轄権の行使が第402条に列挙された管轄権の基礎のいずれかに基づくものであっても，その行使が相当でないときは，その管轄権の行使は違法であるとの原則を国際法上確立したものとして宣言したものであり，相当性の原則と呼ばれる．

本条第2項の考慮すべき要素のリストは，限定的なものではなく，列挙されている順序も重要性の順序を意味するものでもない．また複数の国家による管轄権の行使が相当とされる場合がある．たとえばある国家は属地主義の原則に基づいて管轄権を行使し，他の国家は国籍を基礎に管轄権を行使する場合がそうである．この場合には第2項の要素は双方の国家にともに適用される．

第3項が適用されるのは，2つの国家の管轄権の行使が不当ではないが，その規制が抵触するときである．この場合には，いずれの国家も管轄権を行使することに対して有する自国の利益と他国の利益を斟酌しなければならない．もし一方の国家が明らかにより大きな利益を有するときは，他方の国家は譲歩すべきである．

上に掲げた第402条と第403条の原則は，法適用の柔軟な一般原則を述べたものであり，具体的事件への適用は容易ではない面があることはたしかである．しかし経済的な規制立法の適用範囲を考える際に考慮すべき要素を列挙し，その解決方法を考える点からみて，重要な視点を提供するものといえよう．

5 Hartford 判決

その後の最高裁の判決としては，*Hartford Fire Insurance Co. v. California*, 509 U.S. 764（1993）が重要である．本判決の紹介としては，野村美明「域外適用の法と理論——国際法と国内法の交錯」阪大法学47巻971頁以下（1997），平覚・ジュリスト国際法判例百選24事件51頁（2001）がある．

裁判所は，「合衆国においてなんらかの実質的効果を生じるよう意図され，現実にそのような効果が生じた外国の行為に対してシャーマン法が適用される」と判示し，効果理論を支持する．ついで本件における唯一の実質的な問

題は，外国法と内国法との間に現実の抵触が存在するかどうかである．行為地において当該行為が合法であるという事実それ自体は，合衆国の独占禁止法の適用を妨げない．外国が，その行為を許容ないし推奨する強力な政策を有する場合であっても同じである．2国による規制に服する者が，両国の法律を遵守できる場合には，なんらの抵触も存在しないのである，として，バランシング・テストが適用できる範囲を制限する．言い換えると，当事者が外国法と米国法のいずれか一方を遵守すれば，他方から現実に制裁を課せられる場合に，現実の抵触が生じ，バランシング・テストが機能する．

上の判決の立場をリステイトメント第403条と比較すると，外国の政策や利益との比較考量は後退したか，米国独禁法の拡大適用傾向は収まったといえるであろうかが問題となるであろう．

6 *Empagran* 判決

独禁法の域外適用に関する，その後の最高裁判決としては，*Empagran S. A. v. F. Hoffman-La Roche, Ltd.*, 124 S.Ct 2359（2004）が重要である．この事件は，シャーマン法の外国取引への域外適用を制限しようとする「外国取引反トラスト改善法」（Forein Trade Antitrust Improvement Act）（FTAIA）の解釈が問題となった事件である．

合衆国司法省，EC委員会をはじめとする世界各国の競争当局は，ビタミンの国際カルテルを摘発し，多額の罰金その他の制裁措置をとった．*Empagran* 事件は，合衆国以外のビタミンの購買者がカルテルの参加企業に対して合衆国反トラスト法に基づいて，合衆国裁判所に提起した3倍賠償請求のクラスアクションである．ここでは，シャーマン法に違反する行為が外国において効果を生じ，これにより損害を受けた外国企業が合衆国裁判所に損害賠償を請求することができるかどうかが問題となった．

第1審は，シャーマン法の外国取引に対する適用を原則として禁止するFTAIAの例外に該当しないとして，シャーマン法の域外適用を否定した．これに対して控訴審は，例外に該当するとして第1審判決を取り消した．そこで被告であるビタミンメーカーが上訴した．連邦最高裁は，本件の価格協定

12　独占禁止法の域外適用：Timberlane Lumber Co. v. Bank of America N.T.& S.A.

には FTAIA の例外は適用されず，したがってシャーマン法は適用されないとした．（*Empagran* 判決については，白石忠志「*Empagran* 判決と日本独禁法」NBL796 号 42 頁以下（2004），松下満雄「エムバグラン事件米最高裁判決」国際商事法務 32 巻 10 号 1295 頁以下（2004）を参照．）

【設　問】

1　本件の争点はなにか．
2　事実の概要を述べよ．
3　判旨を（域外適用の部分を中心に）要約せよ．
4　独占禁止法の分野で，最初に効果理論を採用した *Alcoa* 判決を紹介し，本判決と比較せよ．
5　商標法の域外適用に関する *Star-Kist* 判決（松岡博『アメリカ国際私法の基礎理論』（大阪大学出版会，2007）228 頁以下）と本件を比較せよ．
6　アメリカ対外関係法第 3 リステイトメント第 402 条，第 403 条の立場と本判決の立場を比較せよ．
7　本判決を踏襲した *Mannington Mills* 判決（松岡・前掲 240 頁以下）を紹介し，本判決と比較せよ．
8　*Hartford* 判決と *Empagran* 判決を紹介せよ．
9　本判決はどのような判決か．
10　本件の判旨に賛成か．理由を付して答えよ．

13 商標法の域外適用：
Steele v. Bulova Watch Co., 344 U.S. 280 (1952)

MR. JUSTICE CLARK delivered the opinion of the Court.

The issue is whether a United States District Court has jurisdiction to award relief to an American corporation against acts of trade-mark infringement and unfair competition consummated in a foreign country by a citizen and resident of the United States. Bulova Watch Company, Inc., a New York corporation, sued Steele, petitioner here, in the United States District Court for the Western District of Texas. The gist of its complaint charged that "Bulova," a trade-mark properly registered under the laws of the United States, had long designated the watches produced and nationally advertised and sold by the Bulova Watch Company; and that petitioner, a United States citizen residing in San Antonio, Texas, conducted a watch business in Mexico City where, without Bulova's authorization and with the purpose of deceiving the buying public, he stamped the name "Bulova" on watches there assembled and sold. Basing its prayer on these asserted violations of the trade-mark laws of the United States, Bulova requested injunctive and monetary relief. Personally served with process in San Antonio, petitioner answered by challenging the court's jurisdiction over the subject matter of the suit and by interposing several defenses, including his due registration in Mexico of the mark "Bulova" and the pendency of Mexican legal proceedings thereon, to the merits of Bulova's claim. The trial judge, having initially reserved disposition of the jurisdictional issue until a hearing on the merits, interrupted the presentation of evidence and dismissed the complaint "with prejudice," on the ground that the court lacked jurisdiction over the cause. This decision rested on the

> アメリカに居住し，メキシコで事業を営むアメリカ人がメキシコで行った商標侵害と不正競争行為に基づいて，アメリカ会社が提起した訴訟において，アメリカ商標法の適用を肯定した事例

　CLARK 裁判官が法廷意見を述べた．
　本件の争点は，合衆国の市民，住民である者によって，外国で完成された商標侵害と不正競争の行為に対して，合衆国の地方裁判所がアメリカ会社に救済を与える管轄権を有するかどうかである．ニューヨーク会社である Bulova 時計会社は，本件上訴人 Steele に対する訴訟を合衆国テキサス西部地区地方裁判所に提起した．申立の主旨は，つぎのことを主張するにあった．すなわち，合衆国の法律の下で適切に登録された商標である「Bulova」は，長い間，Bulova 時計会社により，生産され，全国的に宣伝され，販売される時計を表示してきた．そして，テキサスのサン・アントニオに居住する合衆国の市民である上訴人が，メキシコ・シティーで時計業を営み，そこで Bulova の許可を得ることなく，購買する一般公衆を欺く目的で，そこで組み立て，販売する時計に「Bulova」の名前を刻印した．Bulova は，その請求趣旨申立をこれらの主張されている合衆国商標法違反にその根拠をおいて，差止命令と金銭的救済を求めた．サン・アントニオで直接訴状の送達を受けた上訴人はその答弁において，裁判所の事物管轄に異議を申し立てるとともに，いくつかの抗弁を主張しているが，それには「Bulova」商標のメキシコにおける自らの正当な登録と，Bulova の請求の争点に関するメキシコにおける法的手続の係属が含まれていた．事実審裁判官は，当初は，本案の審理まで管轄権の争点の処理を留保したが，その後，証拠の提出を中断し，裁判所が訴訟に対して管轄権を有しないという理由で「実体的効果をもつことなく，」訴えを却下した．この判決は，上訴人が合衆国ではなんらの違法な行為をしていないという裁判所の認定に基づくものであった．控訴審は，1人の裁判官の

court's findings that petitioner had committed no illegal acts within the United States. With one judge dissenting, the Court of Appeals reversed; it held that the pleadings and evidence disclosed a cause of action within the reach of the Lanham Trade-Mark Act of 1946, 15 U. S. C. §1051 *et seq.* The dissenting judge thought that "since the conduct complained of substantially related solely to acts done and trade carried on under full authority of Mexican law, and were confined to and affected only that Nation's internal commerce, [the District Court] was without jurisdiction to enjoin such conduct." We granted certiorari, 343 U.S. 962.

Petitioner concedes, as he must, that Congress in prescribing standards of conduct for American citizens may project the impact of its laws beyond the territorial boundaries of the United States. Cf. *Foley Bros., Inc.* v. *Filardo*, 336 U.S. 281, 284-285 (1949); *Blackmer* v. *United States*, 284 U.S. 421, 436-437 (1932); *Branch* v. *Federal Trade Commission*, 141 F.2d 31 (1944). Resolution of the jurisdictional issue in this case therefore depends on construction of exercised congressional power, not the limitations upon that power itself. And since we do not pass on the merits of Bulova's claim, we need not now explore every facet of this complex and controversial Act.

The Lanham Act, on which Bulova posited its claims to relief, confers broad jurisdictional powers upon the courts of the United States. The statute's expressed intent is "to regulate commerce within the control of Congress by making actionable the deceptive and misleading use of marks in such commerce; to protect registered marks used in such commerce from interference by State, or territorial legislation; to protect persons engaged in such commerce against unfair competition; to prevent fraud and deception in such commerce by the use of reproductions, copies, counterfeits, or colorable imitations of registered marks; and to provide rights and remedies stipulated by treaties and conventions respecting trade-marks, trade names, and unfair competition entered into between the

13 商標法の域外適用：Steele v. Bulova Watch Co.

反対意見があったが，これを破棄した．控訴審は，訴答手続と証拠からみて，訴訟原因が 1946 年のランハム商標法 15 U.S.C. §1051 以下の適用範囲にあることは明らかであると判示した．反対意見を述べた裁判官は，「申し立てられている行為は，実質的にはメキシコ法の完全な支配の下でなされた行為と，そこでの取引にかかわるものであり，その国の内国通商のみにかかわり，影響を与えるものであるから，〔地方裁判所は〕管轄権を欠く」と考えた．われわれは，裁量的上訴を認めた．343 U.S. 962.

上訴人は，もとより，連邦議会が合衆国市民に対して行為の基準を規律するにあたって，その法律の効果を合衆国の領域を越えて及ぼしうることは認める．Cf. *Foley Bros., Inc. v. Filardo*, 336 U.S. 281, 284-285 (1949); *Blackmer v. United States*, 284 U.S. 421, 436-437 (1932); *Branch v. Federal Trade Commission*, 141 F.2d 31 (1944). したがって本件における管轄権の争点に関する決定は，行使された連邦議会の権限の解釈いかんによるのであって，その権限自体に対する制限のいかんによるのではない．そして，われわれは，Bulova の請求の本案について判決を下すのではないから，ここでこの複雑で議論の多い法律のすべての面を調査する必要はない．

Bulova 時計会社が救済を求める上で根拠とした法律であるランハム法は，合衆国の裁判所に広範な管轄権を与えている．この法律が明確に示している立法の趣旨は，「他人を欺き，また誤解を招くような方法で商標を使用することに対し訴訟を提起できるようにすることによって，通商を連邦議会の統制の下で規律すること，このような通商で使用される登録商標を州や準州の法律の干渉から保護すること，このような通商に従事する者を不当な競争から保護すること，このような通商において，登録商標の複製品・コピー品・偽造品・模造品の使用による詐欺行為を防止すること，合衆国及びその他海外諸国との間に締結された商標・商業上の名称・不当競争に関する条約及び協定において，定められた権利と救済方法を付与することにある．」(§45, 15

Ⅲ 域外適用

United States and foreign nations." §45, 15 U. S. C. §1127. To that end, § 32 (1) holds liable in a civil action by a trade-mark registrant "any person who shall, in commerce," infringe a registered trade-mark in a manner there detailed. "Commerce" is defined as "all commerce which may lawfully be regulated by Congress." §45, 15 U. S. C. §1127. The district courts of the United States are granted jurisdiction over all actions "arising under" the Act, §39, 15 U. S. C. §1121, and can award relief which may include injunctions, "according to the principles of equity," to prevent the violation of any registrant's rights. §34, 15 U. S. C. §1116.

The record reveals the following significant facts which for purposes of a dismissal must be taken as true: Bulova Watch Company, one of the largest watch manufacturers in the world, advertised and distributed "Bulova" watches in the United States and foreign countries. Since 1929, its aural and visual advertising, in Spanish and English, has penetrated Mexico. Petitioner, long a resident of San Antonio, first entered the watch business there in 1922, and in 1926 learned of the trade-mark "Bulova." He subsequently transferred his business to Mexico City and, discovering that "Bulova" had not been registered in Mexico, in 1933 procured the Mexican registration of that mark. Assembling Swiss watch movements and dials and cases imported from that country and the United States, petitioner in Mexico City stamped his watches with "Bulova" and sold them as such. As a result of the distribution of spurious "Bulovas," Bulova Watch Company's Texas sales representative received numerous complaints from retail jewelers in the Mexican border area whose customers brought in for repair defective "Bulovas" which upon inspection often turned out not to be products of that company. Moreover, subsequent to our grant of certiorari in this case the prolonged litigation in the courts of Mexico has come to an end.On October 6, 1952, the Supreme Court of Mexico rendered a judgment upholding an administrative ruling which had nullified petitioner's Mexican registration of "Bulova."

U.S.C. §1127). このような目的のため，§32(1)は，同法に詳細を示す方法により，「通商において」登録商標を侵害する「者はすべて」，商標の登録者による民事訴訟において有責とされる，としている．「通商」とは，「議会が法律の下で規律するすべての通商」と定義されている．§45, 15 U.S.C. §1127. 合衆国の地方裁判所は，同法§39, 15 U.S.C. §1121 に「基づき，発生する」すべての訴訟について管轄権が与えられており，いかなる商標登録者の権利も，これが侵害されないよう，「エクイティの原則により」，差止命令をはじめとする救済を裁定することができる．§34, 15 U.S.C. §1116.

　記録によって明らかにされたところによれば，つぎに挙げる重要な事実が，上訴を棄却する目的上，真実なものとみなされなければならない．Bulova 時計会社は，世界有数の規模の時計製造業者であり，合衆国及び諸外国において，「Bulova」ブランドの時計を広告販売していた．1929 年以降，同社が行った英語及びスペイン語の両方による視覚的及び聴覚的宣伝は，メキシコに浸透している．長年にわたってサン・アントニオに居住している上訴人は，1922 年に同地において，初めて時計ビジネスに参入し，1926 年に「Bulova」の商標を知ることとなった．後に，上訴人は，事業をメキシコ・シティーに移し，メキシコでは「Bulova」の商標が登録されていない事実を知り，1933 年，メキシコにおける「Bulova」の商標登録を取得した．上訴人は，スイス製時計のムーブメント，文字盤及びケースをスイスや合衆国より輸入し，組み立てた上で，メキシコにおいて，作成した時計に「Bulova」の刻印をし，その名で販売した．「Bulova」の偽造品が流通した結果，Bulova 時計会社のテキサスの販売代理店は，メキシコ国境にある小売宝石業者から，多数のクレームを受けることとなった．これら小売業者の顧客が，「Bulova」の欠陥品を修理のため小売業者に持ち込み，点検が行われた結果，多くの場合，これらの商品が実際は Bulova 時計会社の商品ではないことが判明した．さらにわれわれが本件について裁量的上訴を認めたのちになって，メキシコの裁判所で長期にわたり行われた訴訟が終結した．1952 年 10 月 6 日，メキシコ最高裁は，上訴人による「Bulova」のメキシコ登録を無効とした行政決定を支持する判決を下した．

On the facts in the record we agree with the Court of Appeals that petitioner's activities, when viewed as a whole, fall within the jurisdictional scope of the Lanham Act. This Court has often stated that the legislation of Congress will not extend beyond the boundaries of the United States unless a contrary legislative intent appears. *E. g., Blackmer* v. *United States*, 284 U.S. 421, 437 (1932); *Foley Bros., Inc.* v. *Filardo*, 336 U.S. 281, 285 (1949). The question thus is "whether Congress intended to make the law applicable" to the facts of this case. *Ibid.* For "the United States is not debarred by any rule of international law from governing the conduct of its own citizens upon the high seas or even in foreign countries when the rights of other nations or their nationals are not infringed. With respect to such an exercise of authority there is no question of international law, but solely of the purport of the municipal law which establishes the duty of the citizen in relation to his own government." *Skiriotes* v. *Florida*, 313 U.S. 69, 73 (1941). As MR. JUSTICE MINTON, then sitting on the Court of Appeals, applied the principle in a case involving unfair methods of competition: "Congress has the power to prevent unfair trade practices in foreign commerce by citizens of the United States, although some of the acts are done outside the territorial limits of the United States." *Branch* v. *Federal Trade Commission*, 141 F.2d 31, 35 (1944). Nor has this Court in tracing the commerce scope of statutes differentiated between enforcement of legislative policy by the Government itself or by private litigants proceeding under a statutory right. *Thomsen* v. *Cayser*, 243 U.S. 66 (1917); *Mandeville Island Farms* v. *American Crystal Sugar Co.*, 334 U.S. 219 (1948); cf. *Vermilya-Brown Co.* v. *Connell*, 335 U.S. 377 (1948); *Foley Bros., Inc.* v. *Filardo, supra.* The public policy subserved is the same in each case.

In the light of the broad jurisdictional grant in the Lanham Act, we deem its scope to encompass petitioner's activities here. His operations and their effects were not confined within the territorial limits of a foreign nation. He bought component parts of his wares in the United States, and spurious "Bulovas" filtered through the Mexican border into this country; his competing goods could well reflect adversely on Bulova Watch

記録にあらわれた事実によれば，上訴人の活動を全体としてみると，ランハム法の管轄権内にあるという控訴審裁判所と，当裁判所は意見を同じくしている．当裁判所がたびたび言及するとおり，議会の立法対象範囲は，異なる意図が議会にない限り，合衆国外には及ばない．たとえば *Blackmer v. United States*, 284 U.S. 421, 437（1932）; *Foley Bros., Inc. v. Filardo*, 336 U.S. 281, 285（1949）．したがって，問題は，「議会が」本件事実に「その法を適用することを意図していたかどうかである．」同上．なぜなら，「他国の権利やその国民が有する権利が侵害されない限り，合衆国が公海上，又は諸外国における合衆国国民の活動についてさえ，これを規律することは，国際法のいかなる規則によっても禁止されていない．このような権限の行使については，国際法上の問題はなんら存在せず，唯一問題となりうるのは，国民が自国政府に対して負うべき義務を定めた国内法の立法趣旨の問題だけだ」からである．*Skiriotes v. Florida*, 313 U.S. 69, 73（1941）．当時，控訴裁判所の一員だった MINTON 裁判官が，この原則を不正競争に関する事件に適用したように，「活動の一部が合衆国の領域制限外で行われる場合であっても，連邦議会は，合衆国国民によってなされる外国通商における不正な取引慣行を防止する権限を有する．」*Branch v. Federal Trade Commission*, 141 F.2d 31, 35（1944）．さらに，制定法の通商の範囲を明確化するにあたって，当裁判所は，政府自身による立法政策の執行と，制定法上の権利に基づく私人である訴訟当事者による手続とを区別してこなかった．*Thomsen* v. *Cayser*, 243 U.S. 66（1917）; *Mandeville Island Farms* v. *American Crystal Sugar Co.*, 334 U.S. 219（1948）; cf. *Vermilya-Brown Co. v. Connell*, 335 U.S. 377（1948）; 前掲 *Foley Bros., Inc.* v. *Filardo*. どちらの場合においても，促進されるべき公の政策は，同じである．

ランハム法が広範囲にわたる管轄権を認めている事実に鑑みると，当裁判所は，その範囲に本件における上訴人の活動が包含されるものと判断する．上訴人の活動及び当該活動が与える効果は，外国国家の領域的制限内にとどまってはいなかった．上訴人は，合衆国において上訴人の商品に使用する部品を購入しており，「Bulova」の模造品は，メキシコ国境を越えて，この国

Company's trade reputation in markets cultivated by advertising here as well as abroad. Under similar factual circumstances, courts of the United States have awarded relief to registered trademark owners, even prior to the advent of the broadened commerce provisions of the Lanham Act. *George W. Luft Co.* v. *Zande Cosmetic Co.*, 142 F.2d 536 (1944); *Hecker H-O Co.* v. *Holland Food Corp.*, 36 F.2d 767 (1929); *Vacuum Oil Co.* v. *Eagle Oil Co.*, 154 F. 867 (1907), aff'd, 162 F. 671 (1908). Cf. *Morris* v. *Altstedter*, 93 Misc. 329, 156 N. Y. S. 1103, aff'd, 173 App. Div. 932, 158 N. Y. S. 1123 (1916). Even when most jealously read, that Act's sweeping reach into "all commerce which may lawfully be regulated by Congress" does not constrict prior law or deprive courts of jurisdiction previously exercised. We do not deem material that petitioner affixed the mark "Bulova" in Mexico City rather than here, or that his purchases in the United States when viewed in isolation do not violate any of our laws. They were essential steps in the course of business consummated abroad; acts in themselves legal lose that character when they become part of an unlawful scheme. *United States* v. *Bausch & Lomb Optical Co.*, 321 U.S. 707, 720 (1944); *United States* v. *Univis Lens Co.*, 316 U.S. 241, 254 (1942). "In such a case it is not material that the source of the forbidden effects upon ... commerce arises in one phase or another of that program." *Mandeville Island Farms* v. *American Crystal Sugar Co.*, 334 U.S. 219, 237 (1948). Cf. *United States* v. *Frankfort Distilleries*, 324 U.S. 293, 297 –298 (1945). In sum, we do not think that petitioner by so simple a device can evade the thrust of the laws of the United States in a privileged sanctuary beyond our borders.

の中に入り込んだ．上訴人の競合商品は，Bulova 時計会社が国内外で宣伝を行い，開拓した市場において，同社の取引上の評判を貶めかねなかった．ほぼ同様の事実関係の下で，ランハム法による広範な通商規定が立法として出現する以前であったにもかかわらず，合衆国の裁判所は，登録商標の所有者に対する救済を認めてきた．*George W. Luft Co.* v. *Zande Cosmetic Co.*, 142 F.2d 536（1944）; *Hecker H-O Co.* v. *Holland Food Corp.*, 36 F.2d 767（1929）; *Vacuum Oil Co.* v. *Eagle Oil Co.*, 154 F. 867（1907）, aff'd, 162 F. 671（1908）. Cf. *Morris* v. *Altstedter*, 93 Misc. 329, 156 N. Y. S. 1103, aff'd, 173 App. Div. 932, 158 N. Y. S. 1123（1916）．最も用心深く解釈したとしても，「連邦議会によって合法的に規律されるすべての通商」に対する，同法が及ぶ広範な範囲は，それ以前に制定された法律に制限を加えるものではないし，また，以前に行使していた管轄権を裁判所から取り上げるものでもない．また，当裁判所は，上訴人が自分の商品に，合衆国においてではなく，メキシコ・シティーで「Bulova」の商標をつけたこと，また，上訴人は合衆国内で部品を購入したこと，これをそれだけでみた場合には，合衆国の法律になんら違反していないということは，重要だとは思わない．これらの行為は，外国で完成されたビジネスの過程において重要なステップであり，それ自体が合法な行為であっても，違法な企ての一部となれば，合法性を失う．*United States* v. *Bausch & Lomb Optical Co.*, 321 U.S. 707, 720（1944）; *United States* v. *Univis Lens Co.*, 316 U.S. 241, 254（1942）．このような場合，…通商に与える違法な効果が，その計画のどの段階で生じたかは重要ではない．*Mandeville Island Farms* v. *American Crystal Sugar Co.*, 334 U.S. 219, 237（1948）. Cf. *United States* v. *Frankfort Distilleries*, 324 U.S. 293, 297-298（1945）．要するに，当裁判所は，われわれの境界を越えた特権を受けた聖域において，上訴人がこのような単純な仕組みによって，合衆国の法律の主眼とするところを回避することはできないと考える．

American Banana Co. v. *United Fruit Co.*, 213 U.S. 347 (1909), compels nothing to the contrary. This Court there upheld a Court of Appeals' affirmance of the trial court's dismissal of a private damage action predicated on alleged violations of the Sherman Act. The complaint, in substance, charged United Fruit Company with monopolization of the banana import trade between Central America and the United States, and with the instigation of Costa Rican governmental authorities to seize plaintiff's plantation and produce in Panama. The Court of Appeals reasoned that plaintiff had shown no damage from the asserted monopoly and could not found liability on the seizure, a sovereign act of another nation. This Court agreed that a violation of American laws could not be grounded on a foreign nation's sovereign acts. Viewed in its context, the holding in that case was not meant to confer blanket immunity on trade practices which radiate unlawful consequences here, merely because they were initiated or consummated outside the territorial limits of the United States. Unlawful effects in this country, absent in the posture of the *Banana* case before us, are often decisive; this Court held as much in *Thomsen* v. *Cayser*, 243 U.S. 66 (1917), and *United States* v. *Sisal Sales Corp.*, 274 U.S. 268 (1927). As in *Sisal*, the crux of the complaint here is "not merely of something done by another government at the instigation of private parties;" petitioner by his "own deliberate acts, here and elsewhere, ... brought about forbidden results within the United States." 274 U.S., at 276. And, unlike the *Banana* case, whatever rights Mexico once conferred on petitioner its courts now have decided to take away.

Nor do we doubt the District Court's jurisdiction to award appropriate injunctive relief if warranted by the facts after trial. 15 U. S. C. §§1116, 1121. Mexico's courts have nullified the Mexican registration of "Bulova"; there is thus no conflict which might afford petitioner a pretext

13 商標法の域外適用:Steele v. Bulova Watch Co.

　American Banana Co. v. United Fruit Co., 213 U.S. 347 (1909) は,なんら反対の結論を強いるものではない.そこでは,シャーマン法違反との主張に基づく私人による損害賠償訴訟を事実審が却下したことに対して,控訴審裁判所が上訴を棄却したことを,当裁判所は支持した.申立は,実質的には United Fruit を,中央アメリカと合衆国とのバナナ輸入貿易を独占したことと,パナマにおける原告の農園及び農産物を没収するように,コスタリカ政府当局を扇動したかどで,告発するものであった.控訴審裁判所は,原告が主張されている独占から生じた損害を立証しなかったことと,外国の主権的行為である没収に責任を基礎づけることはできないことをその根拠とした.当裁判所は,米国法の違反は外国国家の主権的行為に基礎づけることはできないという点で同意した.この観点からみると,その事件における判示は,ここでの違法な結果を発生させる貿易取引に対して,単にそれらが合衆国の領域的制限の外で始められたか,または完成されたという理由だけで,白紙の免責を与えることを意味するものではなかった.この国において違法な効果が発生すること——それが当裁判所の *Banana* 判決の状況にはなかった——がしばしば決定的な意味をもつ.当裁判所は,*Thomsen v. Cayser*, 243 U.S. 66 (1917) と,*United States v. Sisal Sales Corp.*, 274 U.S. 268 (1927) において,同じように判示した.*Sisal* 判決と同様に,本件における申立の核心は,「単に,私的当事者の教唆に基づく外国国家によってなされたことのなにかにあるのではない」,上訴人が彼「自身の,わが国及び他の国での故意の行為」により,「禁じられた結果を……合衆国内において生ぜしめた.」274 U.S., at 276, ことにある.そして,*Banana* 判決とは異なり,メキシコがかつて上訴人に与えた権利がどのようなものであろうと,メキシコの裁判所はその権利を奪うことを決定したのである.

　われわれは,事実審の審理後の事実によって正当だと認められるならば,地方裁判所が適切な差止命令による救済を与える管轄権を否定しない.15 U. S. C. §§1116, 1121. メキシコの裁判所は,「Bulova」のメキシコ登録を無効とした.かくしてそのような救済を認めることが外国法を排除することにな

that such relief would impugn foreign law. The question, therefore, whether a valid foreign registration would affect either the power to enjoin or the propriety of its exercise is not before us. Where, as here, there can be no interference with the sovereignty of another nation, the District Court in exercising its equity powers may command persons properly before it to cease or perform acts outside its territorial jurisdiction. *New Jersey* v. *New York*, 283 U.S. 473 (1931); *Massie* v. *Watts*, 6 Cranch 148 (1810); *The Salton Sea Cases*, 172 F. 792 (1909); cf. *United States* v. *National Lead Co.*, 332 U.S. 319, 351-352, 363 (1947).

Affirmed.

MR. JUSTICE BLACK took no part in the decision of this case.

MR. JUSTICE REED, with whom MR. JUSTICE DOUGLAS joins, dissenting.

......

The Court's opinion bases jurisdiction on the Lanham Act. In the instant case the only alleged acts of infringement occurred in Mexico. The acts complained of were the stamping of the name "Bulova" on watches and the subsequent sale of the watches. There were purchases of assembly material in this country by petitioners. Purchasers from petitioners in Mexico brought the assembled watches into the United States. Assuming that Congress has the power to control acts of our citizens throughout the world, the question presented is one of statutory construction: Whether Congress intended the Act to apply to the conduct here exposed.

......

...... Petitioner's buying of unfinished watches in the United States is not an illegal commercial act. Nor can it be said that petitioners were

るとの口実を上訴人に与えるかもしれないという抵触の問題は存在しない．したがって有効な外国での登録が，禁止する権限又はその行使の適切さに影響を与えるかどうかという問題は，われわれの前に提起されていない．本件のように，他の国家の主権との衝突が存在し得ない場合には，地方裁判所は，その衡平法上の権限を行使するにあたって，その面前の者に対して適切に，その領域的管轄権外での行為を禁じたり，履行するように命じることができるのである．*New Jersey v. New York*, 283 U.S. 473（1931）; *Massie v. Watts*, 6 Cranch 148（1810）; *The Salton Sea Cases*, 172 F. 792（1909）; cf. *United States v. National Lead Co.*, 332 U.S. 319, 351-352, 363（1947）.

上訴棄却

　BLACK 裁判官は，本件の判決に参加しなかった．

REED 裁判官の反対意見（DOUGLAS 裁判官同調）

　……

　当裁判所の法廷意見は，ランハム法に管轄権の基礎をおいている．本件において唯一の侵害行為といわれているものは，メキシコで発生した．申し立てられている行為は，時計に「Bulova」という名前を刻印することと，その後にその時計を販売することであった．この国では，上訴人の組立て部品の購入があった．メキシコでの上訴人からの［時計の］購入者は，組み立てられた時計を合衆国へ持ち込んだ．連邦議会がわが市民の世界中の行為を規制する権限を有していることを認めるとしても，ここで提起されている問題は，制定法の解釈の問題，すなわち，連邦議会が，その法律が本件で明らかにされた行為に適用されることを意図していたかどうかである．

　……

　……上訴人が合衆国で未完成の時計を購入したことは，違法な商業的行為ではない．また，メキシコの商標をつけた時計の完成品が上訴人から購入さ

engaging in illegal acts in commerce when the finished watches bearing the Mexican trade-mark were purchased from them and brought into the United States by such purchasers, all without collusion between petitioner and the purchaser. The stamping of the Bulova trade-mark, done in Mexico, is not an act "within the control of Congress." It should not be utilized as a basis for action against petitioner. The Lanham Act, like the Sherman Act, should be construed to apply only to acts done within the sovereignty of the United States. While we do not condone the piratic use of trade-marks, neither do we believe that Congress intended to make such use actionable irrespective of the place it occurred. Such extensions of power bring our legislation into conflict with the laws and practices of other nations, fully capable of punishing infractions of their own laws, and should require specific words to reach acts done within the territorial limits of other sovereignties.

【解　説】

　本件は，アメリカに居住し，メキシコで事業を営む合衆国市民がメキシコで行った商標侵害と不正競争行為に基づいて，アメリカ会社が差止命令と金銭的救済を請求した訴訟において，アメリカ商標法（ランハム法）の域外適用を肯定した事例である。ランハム法の域外適用に関する連邦最高裁の最初で，唯一の判決である。（Brebdan J. Witherell, Note: TRADEMARK LAW-The Extraterritorial Application of the Lanham Act: The First Circuit Cuts the Fat from the Vanity Fair Test, 29 W. Eng. L. Rev. 193, at 205 (2006)).

１　商標法の域外適用と属地主義

　本件における主たる争点は，合衆国の市民，住民である者によってなされ

れ、その購入者によって合衆国に持ち込まれたときに、これらすべてのことは上訴人と購入者との間の共謀なしに行われたから、上訴人が通商において違法な行為に従事していたとはいえない。Bulova の商標を刻印することは、メキシコでなされたのであって、「議会の規制内の」行為ではない。それは上訴人に対する訴訟を根拠づけるものとして用いられてはならない。ランハム法は、シャーマン法と同様に、合衆国の主権の範囲内でなされた行為に対してのみ適用される。われわれは、商標の海賊的利用を見逃すものではないし、また議会がそのような利用をそれがどこで生じたかにかかわりなく、それに対して訴訟を提起できるものとすることを意図したとはとても思われない。そのような権限の拡張は、われわれの立法を、自国の法律違反として十分に制裁を課することができる他の国家の立法と実行との間に抵触を生ぜしめるものである。他の主権者の領域の制限内でなされた行為にまで及びうるためには、明文の文言を必要とするというべきである。

た外国における商標侵害と不正競争行為に対して、内国の商標法を適用できるかどうかであり、この点をめぐって法廷意見と反対意見は鋭く対立する。

　Reed 裁判官の反対意見は、第1審判決と同様に、「ランハム法は、シャーマン法と同様に、合衆国の主権の範囲内でなされた行為に対してのみ適用される」べきであるとの厳格な属地主義の理論をとる。これは、シャーマン法の域外適用を否定した 1909 年の連邦最高裁の *American Banana Co. v. United Fruit Co.*, 213 U.S. 347（1909）と同様の立場を商標法の分野で採用するものである。そして、この理論によれば、本件では商標侵害といわれている行為、すなわち、上訴人が時計に Bulova の商標を付し、その時計を売却した行為はメキシコで行われたのであるから、ランハム法はこのような外国でなされた行為に対して適用されるべきではないということになる。もっとも、反対意見も「連邦議会がわが市民の世界中の行為を規制する権限を有

Ⅲ 域外適用

している」ことは否定しない．しかし，「他の主権者の領域の制限内でなされた行為にまで及びうるためには，明文の文言を必要とする」との立場をとり，ランハム法の適用が外国でなされた行為にまで及びうるには，それを認める明文の規定が必要と考える．

　これに対して，法廷意見は，上のような厳格な属地主義の立場はとらない．むしろ外国でなされた行為に対しても，内国商標法が適用されることを肯定する．この点の判示が本件において最も重要である．もっとも法廷意見も「議会の立法対象範囲は，異なる意図が議会にない限り，合衆国外には及ばない」との立場をとる点では，反対意見と異ならない．したがって問題は，まさしくランハム法について，「議会が本件事実についてその法を適用することを意図していたかどうか」，つまりランハム法の解釈問題である．そしてこの点の判断が反対意見と鋭く対立する．

　法廷意見が，商標侵害行為がメキシコで行われたにもかかわらず，ランハム法が適用されるとした実質的な根拠は，どこに求められているとみるべきであろうか．上訴人の行為が合衆国の市場への効果を生ぜしめていること，上訴人が合衆国市民であること，メキシコの裁判所が上訴人の商標登録を無効としたことに求められているとみる立場が有力である．

2　*Vanity Fair Mills, Inc. v. T. Eaton Co.* 234 F.2d 633（2d Cir. 1956）判決

　本件の争点の1つもランハム法の域外適用問題である．原告は，ペンシルベニア会社で，「Vanity Fair」の商標で婦人用下着の製造，販売に従事しており，1914年に「Vanity Fair」商標を登録した．一方，被告は，カナダ会社であり，ニューヨークにも営業所を有していたが，1915年にカナダで「Vanity Fair」の商標登録の申請をし，カナダ当局はこの商標登録申請を認めた．

　原告は，ニューヨーク南部地区地方裁判所に提起した訴訟において，被告による合衆国とカナダにおける商標侵害と不正競争を主張した．これに対して被告は，カナダにおける商標侵害と不正競争に関する限りでは，地裁が事物管轄権を欠いているなどと主張した．地裁は，カナダの商標の争点から生

じる申立の部分については，地裁が事物管轄権を欠いていると判断した．

控訴審において，原告が依拠した点の1つは，メキシコで合衆国市民がなした行為に対してランハム法の域外適用を認めた最高裁の *Bulova* 判決であった．

(1) ランハム法§32(1)(a)は，登録商標の所有者を，その出所源に関して購入者に混同，錯誤又は欺罔を生ぜしめるような他人による使用から保護する．原告は，*Bulova* 判決に依拠して，この規定が域外適用されるべきであり，本件における被告のカナダにおける Vanity Fair の商標の使用が，通商に実質的な効果を有しているから，本規定の適用範囲に入ると主張する．

(2) 連邦議会は，被告による商標の使用が合衆国の外国又は州際通商に実質的な効果をもたらす限りにおいて，憲法上，侵害に対する救済を提供することができる．しかしわれわれは，連邦議会が，§32(1)(a)に規定されている侵害に対する救済が，外国人により，その本国で多分有効な商標に基づいて，本国でなされた行為に対して適用されるべきことを意図したとは思わない．

(3) *Bulova* 判決において，最高裁は，連邦地裁がメキシコにおける原告によるマークの不正な使用を阻止する管轄権を有すると判示した．その際，最高裁は，つぎの3つの要素を強調した．①被告の行為が合衆国の通商に実質的な効果を及ぼしたこと，②被告が合衆国の市民であり，合衆国が自国民の外国における行為を規律する広範な権限を有していること，③被告のメキシコでの登録がメキシコでの手続によって無効とされたために，外国法上，成立した商標権との抵触がなかったこと．本件では最初の要素だけが存在しているにすぎない．

(4) *Bulova* 判決が原告の主張を支持するとは思えない．むしろ反対に，最高裁の論理は，公海又は外国における合衆国市民の行為を規律する合衆国の権限に強く基礎づけられているから，上の要素の1つを欠いても決定的であり，2つを欠くことは致命的である．ランハム法によって与えられる救済は，外国において多分有効な商標に基づいて行為した外国人に対して，域外適用すべきではないと結論する．

Ⅲ　域外適用

　本件は，*Bulova* 判決を最初に解釈した控訴審判決であった．Witherell, *supra* at 206-207. *Vanity Fair* 判決では，*Bulova* 判決とは異なり，外国でなされた行為に対し，それが合衆国の通商に実質的影響を及ぼしたにもかかわらず，結局のところ内国商標法の適用が否認された．その限りで「内国法は内国で発生した行為に対してのみ適用され，外国で発生した行為には適用されない」という意味での属地主義の理論を採用した場合と結果的には一致するかのようにみえる．

　しかし，判旨は，被告が外国人であり，その行為がそれがなされた外国法上有効なものであるという点で，この事件が *Bulova* 判決とは異なっているところに，内国商標法不適用の根拠を求めているのであって，単なる行為の属地性を理由とするわけではない点に注目する必要がある．*Bulova* 判決の基本的立場はもとより維持されているのである．

3　*Wells Fargo & Co. v. Wells Fargo Express Co.* 556 F.2d 406（9th Cir. 1977）判決

　本件は，シャーマン法の域外適用に関する *Timberlane* 判決のバランシング・テストが，ランハム法の域外適用を決定するのに適用されると判示した連邦第9巡回区控訴裁判所の判決である．ネバダ連邦地方裁判所が，ランハム法の適用範囲は，一般的には米国から生じた訴訟原因に限られるが，外国における行為が *Vanity Fair* 判決の掲げる3つの要素が存在する場合に限って，これに及びうると判示するとともに，本件では外国での行為が合衆国の通商に実質的な効果を有しないこと，合衆国と外国との商標法に抵触が存在することを理由に管轄を否定した．

　控訴審は，3つの要素の1つが欠けていることが必ずしも決定的なものではなく，各要素は，*Timberlane* 判決で採用された礼譲と公正さの「管轄権に関する相当性の原則」において秤量される1つの要素に過ぎないと判示し，原判決を破棄し，*Timberlane* 判決のテストに管轄事実を適用する機会を与えるために差し戻した．この判決により，第9巡回区控訴裁判所は，第2巡回区控訴裁判所の *Vanity Fair* テストから離れ，バランシング・テストを採用

したといえるであろう．Witherell, *supra* at 207.（*Timberlane* 判決のバランシング・テスト及びこのテストを採用したその他の判決については，松岡博『アメリカ国際私法の基礎理論』（大阪大学出版会，2007）（以下「基礎理論」という）228-231頁を参照．)

4　*McBee v. Delica Co.*, 417 F.3d 197（1st Cir.2005）判決

　Vanity Fair 判決テストを採用した第1審の地裁判決を拒否し，実質的効果テストを採用した連邦第1巡回区控訴裁判所の判決である．裁判所は，外国の被告に対する管轄権を決定する唯一の基礎は，被告の行為が合衆国の通商に実質的な効果（substantial effect）を有するかどうかであるとした．域外適用問題を適切に分析するには，まず被告がアメリカ国民であるかどうかを問い，そして被告がそうでないなら，管轄権を決定する唯一の基礎として実質的効果のテストを用いることであるという．実質的効果テストでは，合衆国に訴訟における合理的にみて強い利益を与えるに十分な証拠が必要とされる．実質的効果のテストはまた，ランハム法の基礎にある中核的な法目的，つまり合衆国消費者の混同を防止し，商標権者の商標に対する財政的利益を保護するという目的に沿って適用されなければならない．管轄権を行使する合衆国通商に対する実質的効果が存在する場合であっても，裁判所は礼譲の分析に基づいて，管轄権の行使を拒否することができる．この判決については，Witherell, *supra* at 212-214, 225-229 を参照．

　上のように，ランハム法の域外適用については，連邦巡回区控訴裁判所間では，*Bulova* 判決以降，*Vanity Fair* テスト，バランシング・テスト，実質的効果テストの3つの立場があり，その帰趨は明らかではない．連邦最高裁の判断が待たれるところである．

【本件参考文献】

　松岡博『アメリカ国際私法の基礎理論』（大阪大学出版会，2007）207頁以下．

Ⅲ　域外適用

【設　問】

1　本件の争点はなにか．
2　事実の概要を述べよ．事件と当事者が米国のテキサスとメキシコに対して有する関連を整理せよ．
3　本件判旨を要約せよ．
4　法廷意見と反対意見の対立点について説明せよ．
5　域外適用とはどのようなものか，本件を例にとって説明せよ．
6　域外適用に厳格な立場を採用した *American Banana* 判決について説明せよ．
7　本件の法廷意見が商標法の域外適用を肯定した根拠はどのようなところに求められるか．
8　*Vanity Fair* 判決について説明せよ．この判決は，*Bulova* 判決をどのように読んだか．この2つの判決は矛盾するか．
　　また *Vanity Fair* 判決と，*Wells* 判決，*McBee* 判決とを比較せよ．
9　本件は厳格な属地主義を否定した判決と読むことができるか．
10　本件判旨の結論及びその理論構成に賛成か．
11　要約すると本件はどのような判決か．

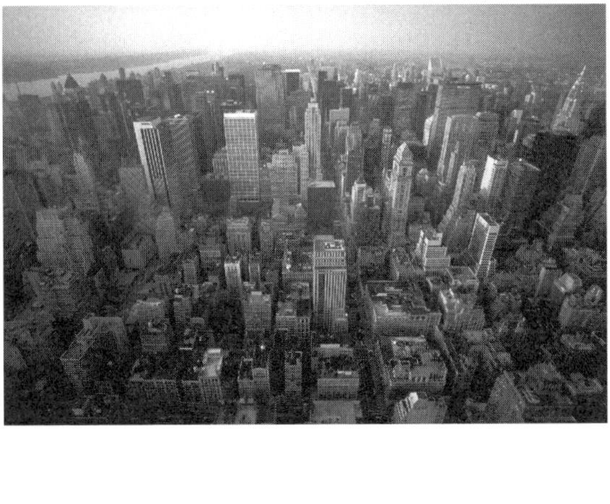

14 証券法の域外適用：
Zoelsch v. Arthur Andersen & Co., 824 F.2d 27 (D.C. Cir.1987)

BORK, Circuit Judge:

Klaus Zoelsch brought this action against Arthur Andersen & Co. in federal court in the District of Columbia on behalf of himself and at least thirty-one others, all citizens of the Federal Republic of Germany. In the complaint, he stated two claims under the United States securities laws and four common law claims. He alleged federal court jurisdiction on the basis of the federal claims and diversity of citizenship. The district court dismissed the action for want of subject matter jurisdiction. Zoelsch appeals only the district court's refusal of jurisdiction over the federal claims. We affirm.

I The transactions that led to this lawsuit involved four principal participants. Dr. Loescher und Co. KG ("Loescher") is a West German limited partnership. First American International Real Estate Limited Partnership ("FAIR") is an American limited partnership based in Miami, Florida. Arthur Andersen & Co. GmbH ("GmbH") is a West German limited liability corporation. Arthur Andersen & Co. ("AA-USA"), the sole defendant in this case, is an American general partnership organized under the laws of Illinois.

Zoelsch and the other West Germans invested in an intricate investment and tax shelter plan. Under the plan, their funds were placed either directly with Loescher, or indirectly with another West German entity that is a limited partner of Loescher. In either case, the investors understood that their funds would be channeled through these entities to FAIR. FAIR,

> 外国（西ドイツ）で行われた証券取引につき，アメリカになんらの効果も生じていない場合において，その取引に関連してアメリカ国内で準備的な行為をしたアメリカのパートナーシップに対する証券法上の請求について，アメリカ証券取引所法の適用が否定された事例

BORK 巡回区裁判官

　Klaus Zoelsch は，彼自身と少なくとも他の31人（すべてドイツ連邦共和国の国民である）のために，コロンビア特別区の連邦地方裁判所に Arthur Andersen & Co. に対して本件訴訟を提起した．彼はその申立において，合衆国証券法に基づく2つの請求とコモンローに基づく4つの請求を主張した．彼は，連邦法上の請求と州籍の相違を基礎として連邦裁判所の管轄権を主張した．地方裁判所は事物管轄権を欠いていることを理由に訴訟を却下した．Zoelsch は連邦法上の請求に対する管轄権を地裁が拒絶したことのみについて上訴した．上訴棄却．

I　本件訴訟のもととなった取引には4人の主要な参加者が関連していた．Dr. Loescher und Co. KG（「Loescher」）は西ドイツのリミテッド・パートナーシップである．First American International Real Estate Limited Partnership（「FAIR」）は，フロリダのマイアミに本拠を有するアメリカのリミテッド・パートナーシップである．Arthur Andersen & Co. GmbH（「GmbH」）は，西ドイツの有限責任会社である．Arthur Andersen & Co.（「AA-USA」）は，本件の唯一の被告であるが，イリノイ法に基づいて設立されたアメリカのゼネラル・パートナーシップである．

　Zoelsch と他の西ドイツ人は，複雑な投資と租税回避プランに投資した．計画によると，彼らのファンドは，直接的に Loescher におかれるか，Loescher のリミテッド・パートナーである他の西ドイツの団体に間接的におかれるかのいずれかであった．どちらの場合でも，投資家たちは，彼らのファンドが

in turn, would invest the funds in property and condominium conversions in Memphis, Tennessee, and Atlanta, Georgia.

In April of 1981, Loescher and FAIR entered into an investment agreement. In September of 1981, Loescher commissioned GmbH to prepare an audit report on the entire plan, including an analysis of FAIR's written description of the American investments. Within the month, GmbH issued its report. Loescher then solicited investors by distributing a package of materials to them, which included GmbH's audit report and FAIR's materials. It is undisputed that FAIR's materials were prepared in the United States, that the audit report was prepared in West Germany, and that the package of materials was distributed only in West Germany to West German investors. The investments were not successful, and Zoelsch's complaint alleges that he and the other investors detrimentally relied on a number of false representations and material omissions in the audit report.

Zoelsch has brought a separate suit against GmbH in Munich, West Germany. He brings this suit, however, only against AA-USA, which was not directly involved in the solicitation of these investors or in the preparation of any of the documents that induced these purchases of securities. The sole link between AA-USA and the package of materials distributed by Loescher is one reference to AA-USA in the audit report prepared by GmbH. The reference is in German, and plaintiff's translation reads: "With respect to a number of data and particulars in the prospectus in conjunction with the economic fundamentals we have made inquiries thereabout by way of our branch-establishment Arthur Andersen & Co., Memphis." ......

Zoelsch's complaint alleged that AA-USA provided false and misleading information to GmbH with ample reason to know that this

14 証券法の域外適用：Zoelsch v. Arthur Andersen & Co.

これらの団体を通じて FAIR に送られるであろうと理解していた．つぎに FAIR は，そのファンドをテネシーのメンフィスとジョージアのアトランタにある不動産とコンドミニアムの改造に投資することになっていた．

　1981 年 4 月に，Loescher と FAIR は投資契約を締結した．1981 年 9 月には，Loescher は GmbH に全体プランについての，アメリカでの投資に関する FAIR の書面による記述の分析を含む監査報告を委託した．GmbH は，その月内に報告書を発行した．その後，Loescher は，投資家に資料のパッケージを配布して，投資家を勧誘した．その配布資料には，GmbH の監査報告書と FAIR の資料が含まれていた．FAIR の資料が合衆国で準備されたことと，監査報告書が西ドイツで準備され，資料のパッケージが西ドイツの投資家に西ドイツでのみ配布されたことは争われていない．投資は成功しなかった．そして Zoelsch の申立は，彼と他の投資家が監査報告書中の多くの虚偽の表示と重要な省略を信じて損害を受けた，と主張している．

　Zoelsch は，GmbH に対して西ドイツのミュンヘンで別の訴訟を提起した．しかし彼は，これらの投資家の勧誘又はこれらの証券の購入を誘導した報告書の準備に直接にはかかわっていない AA-USA に対してのみ本件訴訟を提起した．AA-USA と Loescher により準備され配布された資料のパッケージとの唯一の結びつきは，GmbH が準備した監査報告書において AA-USA に対する 1 カ所の言及があったことだけである．その言及は，ドイツ語で書かれ，原告による翻訳はつぎのとおりである．「経済ファンダメンタルに関連する多くの資料と詳しい情報については，われわれの部門会社である，メンフィスの Arthur Andersen & Co. を通じて照会した．」……

　Zoelsch の申立は，AA-USA が，虚偽で誤解を生じさせる情報を，それが GmbH の監査報告書に挿入され，Zoelsch のような投資家によって信頼され

information would be incorporated in GmbH's audit report and would be relied on by investors such as Zoelsch. *See* Complaint paras. 16-18, J.A. at 28-29. Zoelsch alleged fraud in connection with the sale of securities and the aiding and abetting of securities fraud in violation of section 10 (b) of the Securities Exchange Act of 1934 and its attendant Rule 10b-5. *See* 15 U.S.C. §78j (b) (1982); 17 C.F.R. §240.10b-5 (1985). The district court granted defendant's motion to dismiss for lack of subject matter jurisdiction.

II A

The issue, not previously addressed in this circuit, is American court jurisdiction over securities law claims against a defendant who acted in the United States when the securities transaction occurred abroad and there was no effect felt in this country.

Congress can, of course, prescribe the extent of federal jurisdiction over actions to enforce the federal securities laws, so long as it does not overstep the broad limits set by the due process clause. *See, e.g., Leasco Data Processing Equip. Corp. v. Maxwell*, 468 F.2d 1326, 1334 (2d Cir. 1972). But in the Securities Exchange Act of 1934, Congress said little that bears on this issue. The explicit purposes of the Act are:

> to remove impediments to and perfect the mechanisms of a national market system for securities and a national system for the clearance and settlement of securities transactions and the safeguarding of securities and funds related thereto, and to impose requirements necessary to make such regulation and control reasonably complete and effective, in order to protect interstate commerce, the national credit, the Federal taxing power, to protect and make more effective the national banking system and Federal Reserve System, and to insure the maintenance of fair and honest markets in

ることを知る十分な理由がありながら，提供したと主張した．訴状 paras. 16-18, J.A. at 28-29 参照．Zoelsch は，1934 年の証券取引所法第 10 条(b)とその付則第 10 条 b-5 に違反して，証券販売に関する詐欺と詐欺の幇助と教唆を主張した．15 U.S.C. §78j (b)(1982); 17 C.F.R. §240. 10b-5 (1985) 参照．地方裁判所は事物管轄権の欠如を理由とする被告による却下申立を認めた．

II A

本件の争点は，これまで本巡回区控訴裁判所で取り扱われたことのないものであるが，証券取引が外国で行われ，この国になんらの効果も生じていない場合において，合衆国内で行為した被告に対する証券法上の請求に関するアメリカ裁判所の管轄権である．

連邦議会はもとより，適正手続条項の広範な制限を踏み外さない限り，連邦証券法を執行する訴訟に対する連邦管轄権の限度を規律することができる．たとえば，*Leasco Data Processing Equip. Corp. v. Maxwell*, 468 F.2d 1326, 1334 (2d Cir. 1972) 参照．しかしながら，連邦議会は，1934 年の証券取引所法においてこの争点に関してほとんどなにも言っていない．この法の明示の法目的はつぎのとおりである．

> 証券の全国市場システムと証券取引の決済と精算のための全国システムのメカニズムと，証券とそれに関するファンドを保護することに対する障害を取り除き，改善すること，州際通商，国家信用，連邦徴税権限を保護するために，そのような規制とコントロールを完全で効果的ならしめるに必要な要件を課すること，そのような取引における公正で正直な市場の維持を確実にすることである．

15 U.S.C. §78b (1982)．第 10 条(b)の関連文言は，SEC により禁止された「いかなる証券の購入又は売却に関して…いかなる操作的又は欺瞞的方法

suchtransactions.

15 U.S.C. §78b (1982). The relevant language of section 10 (b) prohibits "any person, directly or indirectly, by the use of any means or instrumentality of interstate commerce or of the mails" from using "in connection with the purchase or sale of any security ... any manipulative or deceptive device or contrivance" proscribed by the SEC. *Id.* §78j (b). "Interstate commerce" is broadly defined to include "trade, commerce, transportation, or communication . . .between any foreign country and any State." *Id.* §78a. And the federal district courts are given exclusive jurisdiction of suits brought to enforce the securities laws. *See id.* §78aa. These provisions frame a fairly broad grant of jurisdiction, but they furnish no specific indications of when American federal courts have jurisdiction over securities law claims arising from extraterritorial transactions.

A single passage in the statute addresses this issue explicitly. Section 30 (b) states that the 1934 Act "shall not apply to any person insofar as he transacts a business in securities without the jurisdiction of the United States, unless he transacts such business in contravention of such rules and regulations as the Commission may prescribe as necessary or appropriate to prevent the evasion of this chapter." 15 U.S.C. §78dd (b)(1982). But AA-USA is not alleged to have transacted a business in securities anywhere. Nevertheless, as will be seen, ..., section 30 (b) gives some reinforcement to the conclusion that there is no jurisdiction to entertain Zoelsch's claims.

If the text of the 1934 Act is relatively barren, even more so is the legislative history. Fifty years ago, Congress did not consider how far American courts should have jurisdiction to decide cases involving predominantly foreign securities transactions with some link to the United States. The web of international connections in the securities market was

14 証券法の域外適用:Zoelsch v. Arthur Andersen & Co.

又は計略」を「いかなる者であろうと直接又は間接に州際通商のどのような手段,方法又は郵便を利用することによって」使うことを禁止する.同上 §78j(b).「州際通商」は,広く定義され,どの外国とどの州間の…「貿易,通商,運送,コミュニケーション」を含む.同上 §78a.そして連邦地方裁判所は,証券法を執行するために提起された訴訟の排他的な管轄権を有する.同上 §78aa 参照.これらの規定は,かなり広い管轄権の付与を認めているが,アメリカの連邦裁判所がどのような場合に域外的取引から生じる証券法上の請求に対する管轄権を有するかについてはなんら特定の指摘を提供していない.

その制定法の一文がこの争点について明示に取り上げている.第30条(b)は,1934年法は,「いかなる人であれ,その者が合衆国の管轄権の外で証券取引に従事する限り,その者に対しては適用されない.ただしその者が本章の回避を防止するために必要又は適切であると委員会が定める規則又は規制に反してそのような取引を行うときはその限りでない」と述べている.15 U.S.C. §78dd(b)(1982).しかし AA-USA は,どこにおいても証券業務に従事したとは主張されていない.それにもかかわらず,のちに見るように……,第30条(b)は,Zoelsch の請求を受理する管轄権は存在しないという結論をいくぶんかは補強するものを提供する.

1934年法のテキストが相対的にみて内容の乏しいものであるとすれば,その立法の歴史はもっとそうである.50年前,連邦議会は,アメリカの裁判所が合衆国にいくらかのリンクを有するが,主として外国の証券取引に関連する事件を決定する管轄権をどこまで有すべきかを考慮しなかった.証券市場における国際的なつながりの複雑に絡み合った関係は,当時は,いまの状況

then not nearly as extensive or complex as it has become. In this state of affairs, our inquiry becomes the dubious but apparently unavoidable task of discerning a purely hypothetical legislative intent. As Judge Friendly candidly put it in a very similar case: "We freely acknowledge that if we were asked to point to language in the statutes, or even in the legislative history, that compelled these conclusions, we would be unable to respond. The Congress that passed these extraordinary pieces of legislation in the midst of the depression could hardly have been expected to foresee the development of offshore funds thirty years later. ... Our conclusions rest on ... our best judgment as to what Congress would have wished if these problems had occurred to it." *Bersch v. Drexel Firestone, Inc.*, 519 F.2d 974, 993 (2d Cir.), *cert. denied*, 423 U.S. 1018, 96 S. Ct. 453, 46 L. Ed. 2d 389 (1975).

II B

The courts have not confined federal jurisdiction to securities transactions consummated in the United States. They have deviated from this position in two respects. First, they have asserted jurisdiction over extraterritorial conduct that produces substantial effects within the United States, such as effects on domestic markets or domestic investors. *See, e.g., Schoenbaum v. Firstbrook*, 405 F.2d 200, 206-08 (2d Cir.), *partially rev'd on other grounds*, 405 F.2d 215 (1968), *cert. denied*, 395 U.S. 906, 89 S. Ct. 1747, 23 L. Ed. 2d 219 (1969). Second, they have asserted jurisdiction in some cases over acts done in the United States that "directly caused" the losses suffered by investors outside this country. *See, e.g., Bersch*, 519 F.2d at 991-93.

Zoelsch concedes that jurisdiction in this case cannot be premised on domestic "effects" of predominantly foreign conduct, *see* Brief for Appellant at 5-6; *Zoelsch v. Arthur Andersen & Co.*, No. 85-2353, mem.

ほどには大規模でも複雑でもなかったといってよい．このような状況の下では，われわれの探求は，純粋に仮定的な立法的意思を見分けるという疑念のある，しかし明らかに避けることのできない仕事となる．Friendly 裁判官が本件と非常によく似た事件において率直に述べたように，「もしわれわれが，これらの結論を強要する文言を制定法中又は立法の歴史の中に指摘するよう求められたとすれば，われわれは答えることができないであろうことを率直に認める．不況のまっただ中にあって，驚くべき数の立法を通過させた連邦議会が 30 年後の海外ファンドの発展を予期することはほとんど期待されえなかったであろう．…われわれの結論は，…連邦議会がこれらの問題に思い及んでいたとすれば，なにをしようとしたであろうかについてのわれわれの最善の判断にかかっている．」*Bersch v. Drexel Firestone, Inc.*, 519 F.2d 974, 993 (2d Cir.), *cert. denied*, 423 U.S. 1018, 96 S. Ct. 453, 46 L. Ed. 2d 389 (1975).

II B

裁判所は証券取引に関する連邦の管轄権を合衆国で完成した取引に限定してこなかった．裁判所は 2 つの点でこの立場から逸脱した．第 1 に，裁判所は国内市場又は国内の投資家に対する効果のように，合衆国内に実質的な効果を発生させる域外的な行為に対して管轄権を行使してきた．たとえば *Schoenbaum v. Firstbrook*, 405 F.2d 200, 206-08 (2d Cir.), *partially rev'd on other grounds*, 405 F.2d 215 (1968), *cert. denied*, 395 U.S. 906, 89 S. Ct. 1747, 23 L. Ed. 2d 219 (1969) 参照．第 2 に，裁判所は，いくつかの事件において，投資家がこの国の外において被った損害を「直接に発生させた」合衆国内でなされた行為に対して，管轄権を行使してきた．たとえば *Bersch*, 519 F.2d at 991-93 参照．

Zoelsch は，本件の管轄権が主として外国でなされた行為の国内的「効果」に基礎づけることはできないことを認めている．上訴趣意書 5-6 頁；*Zoelsch v. Arthur Andersen & Co.*, No. 85-2353, mem. op. at 4 (D.D.C. Apr. 29,

op. at 4 (D.D.C. Apr. 29, 1986), and "jurisdiction may not be sustained on a theory that the plaintiff has not advanced." *Merrell Dow Pharmaceuticals Inc. v. Thompson*, 478 U.S. 804, 106 S. Ct. 3229, 3233 n.6, 92 L. Ed. 2d 650 (1986) Zoelsch relies on AA-USA's domestic conduct as the basis for jurisdiction.

Several tests have been devised for determining when American courts have jurisdiction over domestic conduct that is alleged to have played some part in the perpetration of a securities fraud on investors outside this country. The Second Circuit has set the most restrictive standard. It has declined jurisdiction over alleged violations of the securities laws based on conduct in the United States when the conduct here was "merely preparatory" to the alleged fraud, that is, when the conduct here did not "directly cause" the losses elsewhere. *See, e.g., Bersch*, 519 F.2d at 992-93; *IIT v. Vencap, Ltd.*, 519 F.2d 1001, 1018 (2d Cir. 1975). In later cases, the line between domestic conduct that is "merely preparatory" and conduct that "directly causes" the losses elsewhere has been significantly clarified. The Second Circuit's rule seems to be that jurisdiction will lie in American courts where the domestic conduct comprises all the elements of a defendant's conduct necessary to establish a violation of section 10 (b) and Rule 10b-5: the fraudulent statements or misrepresentations must originate in the United States, must be made with scienter and in connection with the sale or purchase of securities, and must cause the harm to those who claim to be defrauded, even though the actual reliance and damages may occur elsewhere. ......

The Third, Eighth, and Ninth Circuits appear to have relaxed the Second Circuit's test. They too have asserted jurisdiction only when the conduct in this country "directly causes" the losses elsewhere. *See SEC v. Kasser*, 548 F.2d 109, 115 (3d Cir.), *cert. denied*, 431 U.S. 938, 97 S. Ct.

1986）参照．そして「原告が主張していない理論に基づいて，管轄権を認めることはできないであろう．」*Merrell Dow Pharmaceuticals Inc. v. Thompson,* 478 U.S. 804, 106 S. Ct. 3229, 3233 n.6, 92 L. Ed. 2d 650（1986）．Zoelsch は，管轄権の基礎として，AA-USA の国内の行為に依拠している．

　アメリカの裁判所が，どのような場合に，この国の外での投資家に対する証券詐欺の悪事の幾分かを担ったと主張されている国内の行為に対して，管轄権を有するかを決定するために，いくつかのテストが考案されてきた．第2巡回区控訴裁判所が最も制限的な基準を設定した．同裁判所は，合衆国内における行為に基づいて，その国内での行為が主張されている詐欺に対して「単に準備的な」ものである，つまり，国内でのその行為が外国での損害を「直接に発生させ」なかったときには，主張されている証券法の違反に対して管轄権を否認してきた．たとえば *Bersch*, 519 F.2d at 992-93; *IIT v. Vencap, Ltd.*, 519 F.2d 1001, 1018（2d Cir. 1975）参照．後の事件において，「単に準備的な」国内の行為と，外国での損害を「直接に発生させる」行為との間の境界線がきわめて明確になった．第2巡回区控訴裁判所の規則は，国内での行為が第10条(b)と規則第10b-5の違反を立証するのに必要な被告の行為のすべての要素を含んでいるときには，管轄権はアメリカの裁判所に帰属するというもののように思われる．つまり，詐欺的な陳述又は不実表示は，実際の信頼と損害が外国で生じたとしても，合衆国に源を有するものでなければならず，故意でなされ，証券の販売又は購入と関連を有するものでなければならず，さらに詐欺を被ったと主張する者に害を発生させるものでなければならない．……

　第3，第8及び第9巡回区控訴裁判所は，第2巡回区控訴裁判所のテストを緩和したと思われる．これらの裁判所もまた，この国における行為が外国で損害を「直接に発生させた」ときに限って管轄権を行使してきた．*SEC v. Kasser*, 548 F.2d 109, 115（3d Cir.）, *cert. denied*, 431 U.S. 938, 97 S. Ct.

2649, 53 L. Ed. 2d 255 (1977); *Continental Grain (Australia) Pty. Ltd. v. Pacific Oilseeds, Inc.*, 592 F.2d 409, 418-20 (8th Cir. 1979); *Grunenthal GmbH v. Hotz*, 712 F.2d 421, 424 (9th Cir. 1983). But in *Continental Grain* the court explicitly repudiated the Second Circuit's requirement that "domestic conduct constitute the elements of a rule 10b-5 violation," 592 F.2d at 418, infavor of a test that would find jurisdiction whenever the domestic conduct "was in furtherance of a fraudulent scheme and was significant with respect to its accomplishment." *Id.* at 421. The Third Circuit's formulation seems more permissive, allowing subject matter jurisdiction "where at least some activity designed to further a fraudulent scheme occurs within this country." *Kasser*, 548 F.2d at 114. The consequence of these approaches has been a loosening of the jurisdictional requirements: any significant activity undertaken in this country – or perhaps any activity at all – that furthers a fraudulent scheme can provide the basis of American jurisdiction over the domestic actor.

II C

We believe that a more restrictive test, such as the Second Circuit's, provides the better approach to determining when American courts should assert jurisdiction in a case such as this. There is no doubt, of course, that Congress could confer jurisdiction over activity like that alleged to have been engaged in by AA-USA. Moreover, considerations of comity, which will often cause a court to stay its hand, appear to be minimal or nonexistent here. Appellants do not seek to have us assert jurisdiction over West German parties, nor would a judgment about AA-USA's conduct in the United States necessarily or even probably require a pronouncement on the propriety of the behavior of the West German parties. The case going forward in the Federal Republic would likely be unaffected by this case. Nevertheless, we think we should not assert jurisdiction.

2649, 53 L. Ed. 2d 255 (1977); *Continental Grain (Australia) Pty. Ltd. v. Pacific Oilseeds, Inc.*, 592 F.2d 409, 418-20 (8th Cir. 1979); *Grunenthal GmbH v. Hotz*, 712 F.2d 421, 424 (9th Cir. 1983) 参照．しかし，*Continental Grain* 判決において裁判所は，「国内における行為は規則第10b-5違反のすべてを含む」という第2巡回区控訴裁判所の要件をはっきりと拒絶し，592 F.2d at 418，国内でなされた行為が「詐欺的なスキームを増進させ，その完遂にとって重要である．」同上421頁ときは，いつでも管轄権を認めるというテストを支持した．第3巡回区控訴裁判所の定式は，「少なくとも詐欺的なスキームを増進させることを意図したなんらかの活動がこの国で生じた場合には」*Kasser*, 548 F.2d at 114，事物管轄権を認めるという，より緩やかなもののように思われる．これらのアプローチの結果，管轄権の要件が緩和されることとなった．つまり，詐欺的なスキームを増進することとなる，この国において取られたなんらかの重要な行為が——多分どんな行為でも——国内の行為者に対するアメリカの管轄権の基礎を提供しうることとなる．

II C

われわれは，第2巡回区控訴裁判所のようなより抑制的なテストが，アメリカの裁判所が，どのような場合に本件のような事件において管轄権を行使すべきかを決定するよりよいアプローチを提供するものと信じる．もとより連邦議会は，AA-USA が従事したと主張されている活動に対して管轄権を与えることができることは疑いない．さらに，礼譲への考慮，それは，しばしば裁判所の手を拘束しようとするものではあるが，ここではほんの僅かにすぎないか，又は存在しないようにみえる．上訴人は，西ドイツの当事者に対してわれわれが管轄権を行使することを求めていないし，合衆国における AA-USA の行為に関する判決は，必ずしも又は多分，西ドイツ当事者の行動が適切であったかどうかの宣言を要求するものではないであろう．連邦共和国で進められている事件は，本件によっておそらく影響を受けることはないであろう．それにもかかわらず，われわれは管轄権を行使すべきでないと考える．

We begin from the established canon of construction that "legislation of Congress, unless a contrary intent appears, is meant to apply only within the territorial jurisdiction of the United States," which "is based on the assumption that Congress is primarily concerned with domestic conditions." Rule 10b-5. See 15 U.S.C. §78j (b)(1982); 17 C.F.R. §240.10b-5 (1985). And even aside from this presumption, it is quite clear that the Securities Exchange Act of 1934 had as its purpose the protection of American investors and markets. See, e.g., H.R. Rep. No. 1383, 73d Cong., 2d Sess. 1-16 (1934); S. Rep. No. 792, 73d Cong., 2d Sess. 1-13 (1934). That is the inference to be drawn from section 30 (b) as well, for it states that the statute does not apply to persons transacting business in securities abroad unless the Securities and Exchange Commission issues rules and regulations making the statute applicable to such persons because that is "necessary or appropriate to prevent the evasion" of the statute. That rather clearly implies that Congress was concerned with extraterritorial transactions only if they were part of a plan to harm American investors or markets. The Commission has never issued such rules or regulations and there is no allegation in this case that AA-USA's conduct was engaged in to evade American law.

Courts have also been concerned to preserve American judicial resources for the adjudication of domestic disputes and the enforcement of domestic law. *Bersch*, 519 F.2d at 985 ("When, as here, a court is confronted with transactions that on any view are predominantly foreign, it must seek to determine whether Congress would have wished the precious resources of the United States courts and law enforcement agencies to be devoted to them rather than leave the problem to foreign countries."). It is far from clear that these resources would be well spent on all the potential disputes in which domestic conduct makes a relatively small contribution to securities fraud that occurs elsewhere.

14 証券法の域外適用:Zoelsch v. Arthur Andersen & Co.

　われわれは,解釈の確立したつぎの規範から始める.「連邦議会の立法は,反対の意図が見えない限り,合衆国の領域管轄権内においてのみ適用されることを意味するものであり」,それは「連邦議会は主として国内的状況のみに関心があるという前提に基礎をおいている.」規則第10条 b-5. 15 U.S.C. § 78j(b)(1982);17 C.F.R. § 240.10b-5(1985)参照.そしてこの前提から離れても,1934年証券取引所法がアメリカの投資家と市場の保護を主たる目的とするものであることは全く明らかである.たとえば,H.R. Rep. No. 1383, 73d Cong., 2d Sess. 1-16(1934);S. Rep. No. 792, 73d Cong., 2d Sess. 1-13(1934)参照.それが第30条(b)から同様に引き出される推論である.というのは,証券取引所法は,外国で証券事業に従事する者に対しては,証券取引委員会が,そのような者に対して,その法律を適用することがその法律の「回避を防止するのに必要又は適切である」と考えるために,そうすることを可能とする規則と規制を発するのでない限りは,適用されないと述べているからである.このことはむしろ明らかに,連邦議会は,域外取引がアメリカの投資家と市場に害を与える計画の一部を構成する場合に限って,域外取引に関心があることを意味している.委員会はそのような規則や規制を発していないし,またAA-USAの行為がアメリカ法を回避するために行われたとの主張は本件ではなされていない.

　裁判所もまた,国内の紛争と国内法の執行のために,アメリカの司法資源を保持することに関心があった.*Bersch*, 519 F.2d at 985(「本件のように,裁判所がどのような見解によっても圧倒的に外国的である取引に直面しているときには,裁判所は,連邦議会が,その問題を外国の裁判所に委せるよりも,合衆国の裁判所と法執行機関の貴重な資源をこれらの取引に費やされることを望んだかどうかを決定しなければならない.」).これらの資源が,国内での行為が外国で発生した証券詐欺に相対的にみて僅かの貢献しか有しないすべての可能性のある紛争に費やされてよいとは,まったく明らかではない.

355

Were it not for the Second Circuit's preeminence in the field of securities law, and our desire to avoid a multiplicity of jurisdictional tests, we might be inclined to doubt that an American court should ever assert jurisdiction over domestic conduct that causes loss to foreign investors. It is somewhat odd to say, as *Bersch* and some other opinions do, that courts must determine their jurisdiction by divining what "Congress would have wished" if it had addressed the problem. A more natural inquiry might be what jurisdiction Congress in fact thought about and conferred. Congress did not think about conduct here that contributes to losses abroad in enacting the Securities Exchange Act of 1934; it could easily provide such jurisdiction if that seemed desirable today. But, for the reasons just given, we defer to *Bersch* and the later Second Circuit cases and adopt the Second Circuit's approach. We are not persuaded by the reasoning of those circuits that have broadened federal court jurisdiction for reasons that are essentially legislative. In *Continental Grain*, the court said, "we frankly admit that the finding of subject matter jurisdiction in the present case is largely a policy decision." 592 F.2d at 421. Yet Congress is available to make any policy decisions that are required. In *Kasser*, similarly, the court justified its approach in part because "from a policy perspective, and it should be recognized that this case in a large measure calls for a policy decision, we believe that there are sound rationales for asserting jurisdiction." 548 F.2d at 116 (footnote omitted). Three rationales were offered. "First, to deny such jurisdiction may embolden those who wish to defraud foreign securities purchasers or sellers to use the United States as a base of operations." *Id.* Second, "by finding jurisdiction here, we may encourage other nations to take appropriate steps against parties who seek to perpetrate frauds in the United States." *Id.* Finally, the court's action "will enhance the ability of the SEC to police vigorously the conduct of securities dealings within the United States." *Id.; see also Continental Grain*, 592 F.2d at 421-22 (approving and employing these same policy rationales). *Kasser* concluded: "We are reluctant to conclude that Congress intended to allow the United States to become a 'Barbary Coast,' as it were, harboring international securities 'pirates.'" 548 F.2d at 116.

第2巡回区控訴裁判所が証券法の分野において傑出した存在であることと，管轄権テストの多様性を避けようとするわれわれの願望がなければ，外国の投資家に対して損害を発生させる国内行為に対する管轄権をアメリカの裁判所が行使すべきことを疑いたくなったかもしれない．もし連邦議会がその問題を扱ったとすれば，「連邦議会が望んだであろうこと」を推測することによって，裁判所がその管轄権を決定しなければならないということは，*Bersch*判決やその他の意見がいうように，少し奇妙なことである．もっと自然な探求方法は，どんな管轄権を連邦議会が実際に考え，そして与えたかということであろう．連邦議会は，1934年証券取引所法を制定するにあたって，国外での損害をもたらすような国内の行為のことを考えなかった．連邦議会は，今日，それが望ましいと思われるのならば，容易にそのような管轄権を規定することができた．しかし先に述べた理由で，われわれは，*Bersch*判決とその後の第2巡回区控訴裁判所の判決に従い，第2巡回区控訴裁判所のアプローチを採用する．われわれは，連邦裁判所の管轄権を拡大してきた巡回区控訴裁判所の理由づけ，それは本質的には立法論である，という議論には説得されない．*Continental Grain*判決において，裁判所は，「本件における事物管轄権に関する判断は，主として政策的な決定であることを率直に認める．」592 F.2d at 421 と言った．しかし連邦議会は要求されている政策決定をすることができる．同様に*Kasser*判決において，裁判所はそのアプローチを正当化するに際して，部分的に「政策的なパースペクティブからすると，そして本件ではかなりの程度，政策決定を必要とすることを認めなければならないが，われわれは管轄権を行使する確かな根拠が存在すると確信する．」548 F.2d at 116（脚注略）という理由を挙げた．3つの根拠があげられた．「第1に，そのような管轄権を否認することは，外国の証券購入者又は売主に対して，事業基地として合衆国を使って，詐欺を働こうとする者を奨励することとなる．」同上．第2に，「内国の管轄権を認めることによって，他の国家が合衆国における詐欺を永続させようとする当事者に対する適切な措置をとることを勇気づけることができる」．同上．最後に，裁判所の行動は，「SECが合衆国内における証券取引の行動を力強く監督することができる」同上．

357

We, too, are reluctant to conclude that Congress intended any such thing, but we are less reluctant to conclude that Congress in 1934 had no intention at all on the subject because it was concerned with United States investors and markets. That being so, *Kasser's* policy arguments may provide very good reasons why Congress should amend the statute but are less adequate as reasons why courts should do so. As the Supreme Court has said in another context, "the responsibilities forassessing the wisdom of such policy choices and resolving the struggle between competing views of the public interest are not judicial ones: 'Our Constitution vests such responsibilities in the political branches.'" *Chevron U. S. A. Inc. v. Natural Resources Defense Council, Inc.*, 467 U.S. 837, 866, 81 L. Ed. 2d 694, 104 S. Ct. 2778 (1984)(quoting *TV A v. Hill*, 437 U.S. 153, 195, 57 L. Ed. 2d 117, 98 S. Ct. 2279 (1978)). This is particularly the case since such an amendment providing jurisdiction over aspects of predominantly foreign transactions should take into account considerations of comity and foreign affairs. Those factors do not weigh heavily in this case but they may in others.

For these reasons we adopt what we understand to be the Second Circuit's test for finding jurisdiction based on domestic conduct: jurisdiction is appropriate when the fraudulent statements or misrepresentations originate in the United States, are made with scienter and in connection with the purchase or sale of securities, and "directly cause" the harm to

Continental Grain 592 F.2d at 421-22 も参照（これらの同じ政策的理由づけに賛成し，採用）．*Kasser*判決は「われわれは，連邦議会が，合衆国がいわば，国際的な証券『海賊』をかくまう，「バーバリー・コースト」［暗黒街］となることを許容することを意図したとは結論したくない．」と結論した．548 F.2d at 116.

われわれもまた，連邦議会がそのようなことを意図したと結論したくはない．しかしわれわれは，連邦議会が1934年にこの問題についてなんらの意図をもまったくもたなかったと結論することには，それほど気が進まないというわけではない．というのはそれは合衆国の投資家と市場にとっての関心事であったからである．そうであるから，*Kasser*判決の政策論はなぜ連邦議会がその法を改正すべきかの非常によい理由を提供するかもしれないが，裁判所がそうすべき理由としてはそれほど適切ではない．連邦最高裁が他のコンテキストで述べたように，「そのような政策選択が賢明であるかどうか評価することと，公的な利益の競合する見解間の争いを解決することの責任は，裁判所のものではない．つまり，『われわれの憲法は，そのような責任を政治的な部門に与えている』．」*Chevron U. S. A. Inc. v. Natural Resources Defense Council, Inc.*, 467 U.S. 837, 866, 81 L. Ed. 2d 694, 104 S. Ct. 2778 (1984)（*TV A v. Hill*, 437 U.S. 153, 195, 57 L. Ed. 2d 117, 98 S. Ct. 2279（1978）を引用）．本件はとくにそのような場合である．というのは，主として外国取引の側面に対する管轄権の規定を定める改正は，礼譲と外交事項への配慮を考慮に入れるべきだからである．これらの要素は本件では重いウエイトを有しないけれども，他の事件では有するかも知れない．

これらの理由により，われわれは，国内での行為に基礎をおく管轄権を判断するにあたって，第2巡回区控訴裁判所のテストと理解するものを採用する．合衆国で始められた詐欺的な陳述又は不実表示が，故意に，証券の購入又は販売に関連して行われており，そして騙されたと主張する者に対する損害を「直接に発生させる」ときには，信頼行為と損害が外国で生じたとして

those who claim to be defrauded, even if reliance and damages occur elsewhere. Indeed, we believe this test is only a slight recasting, if at all, of the traditional view that jurisdiction will lie in American courts only over proscribed acts done in this country.
......

III ......
These allegations, even if true, are insufficient to support jurisdiction under the test we have enunciated. At the most, they establish that AA-USA made misrepresentations to GmbH that GmbH credited in drawing up its audit report. AA-USA's statements were not themselves made for distribution to the public, and were not transmitted to the public. AA-USA was merely one of the sources GmbH consulted in conducting the investigations which culminated in its audit report. That report, which was circulated to investors as part of the larger package of materials distributed by Loescher, was prepared and certified by GmbH alone. ......

To put the matter in the Second Circuit's terminology, AA-USA's alleged misrepresentations to GmbH were "merely preparatory" to any fraud perpetrated on West German investors, and did not "directly cause" their losses. *Bersch*, 519 F.2d at 992-93......

WALD, Chief Judge, concurring in the judgment:
I agree with the majority that the District Court properly dismissed this action for lack of subject matter jurisdiction. In reaching that result, I find it unnecessary, however, to adopt the Second Circuit's restrictive test for determining the extent of federal jurisdiction over securities law claims

も，管轄権［の行使］は適切である．事実，われわれは，このテストが，管轄権は，禁止された行為がこの国でなされた場合に限って，アメリカの裁判所に存在するという伝統的な考え方を少し書き直したものにすぎないと確信している．
……

III
……
　これらの主張は，たとえ真実であるとしても，われわれの挙げたテストの下では，管轄権を認めるのに不十分である．それらは，せいぜいのところ，AA-USA が GmbH に対して不実表示を行い，GmbH がそれを監査報告書を作成するにあたって信頼したということを立証するに過ぎない．AA-USA の報告書は，一般の人々に対して配布するために作成されたものではなかったし，また一般の人々に伝達されたものでもなかった．AA-USA は単に，GmbH が最終的にはその監査報告書となった調査を行うにあたって参照した情報源の1つに過ぎなかった．その報告書は，投資家に Loescher によって配布されたより大きな資料のパッケージの1部として投資家に行きわたったものであるが，それは GmbH のみによって準備され，認定されたものであった．……

　この事態を第2巡回区控訴裁判所の言い方で表現すると，主張されている AA-USA の GmbH に対する不実表示は，西ドイツの投資家に対してなされた詐欺に対する「単なる準備的な」ものであり，かれらの損害を「直接に発生させる」ものではなかった．*Bersch*, 519 F.2d at 992-93. ……

WALD 主席裁判官の判決への補足意見
　私は，地方裁判所が事物管轄権を欠いているという理由で本件訴訟を却下したことに同意する．しかしながら，その結果に到達するに際して，国際取引に関する証券法上の請求に対する連邦管轄権の程度を決定するために，第2巡回区控訴裁判所の制限的なテストを採用することは不必要であると考え

involving international transactions. It seems clear that, even under the less strict approach adopted by the Third, Eighth, and Ninth Circuits, AA-USA's alleged misrepresentations or omissions of material fact were so insignificant and so indirectly related to the overall fraudulent scheme as set out in the complaint that no federal jurisdiction would exist over Zoelsch's claims.
......

【解　説】

　本件は，外国（西ドイツ）で行われた証券取引につき，アメリカになんらの効果も生じていない場合において，その取引に関連してアメリカ国内で準備的な行為をしたに過ぎないアメリカのパートーナーシップに対する証券法上の請求について，アメリカ証券取引所法の適用が否定された事例である．

1　証券取引所法第10条(b)

　本件で問題となっている1934年証券取引所法は，アメリカ合衆国における証券の流通市場を規制する連邦制定法であり，1934年6月6日に制定された．1933年の証券法と並んで，アメリカ合衆国における金融市場とその参加者に対する規制の中心をなしている．そしてこれらを運用する政府機関として，SEC（証券取引委員会）が置かれている．
　この1934年証券取引所法第10条(b)とそれに対応するSEC規則第10b-5が，不公正な証券取引に対する包括的な規制を設けている．すなわち，証券取引法第10条(b)は，いかなる者も，直接又は間接に，何らかの州際通商の手段若しくは方法，又は何らかの全国的証券取引所の設備を用いて，次の行為をすることを違法としている．全国的証券取引所に登録されたいかなる証券，若しくはその登録がされていないいかなる証券の売買に関しても，証券

る．第3，第8及び第9巡回区控訴裁判所が採用するもっと厳格でないテストによってさえも，AA-USA の主張されている不実表示又は重要事実の省略は，それほど重要ではなく，又申立において述べられている，全体としての詐欺的スキームに間接的にしか関連していないから，Zoelsch の請求に対する連邦管轄権が存在しないことは明らかである．
……

取引委員会が公益のため又は投資家の保護のために必要又は適切なものとして定めることができる法令及び規則に反するような，何らかの操縦的又は詐害的な計画又は仕組みを使用し，又は採用すること．

　証券関係訴訟における第10条(b)及び規則第10b-5の適用範囲は広く，その実際的意義は大きい．規則第10b-5は，価格操作，株価を上昇させるための偽の会社売却情報，さらには関連情報を投資家に提供しなかったケースにまで適用されてきた．したがって証券関係訴訟の原告は，個別的な証券取引所法の反詐欺条項違反のほかに，本法第10条(b)及び規則第10b-5違反を包括的な主張として述べる場合が多い．

2　証券法の域外適用における行為テストと効果テスト

　合衆国の裁判所は，証券取引における国境を越えた詐欺に対応するために，第10条(b)を含めた連邦証券法の規定を広く域外適用してきた．そしてこの域外適用の基準として，2つのテストが認められてきた．行為テストと効果テストである．行為テストの下では，損害を直接に引き起こした重要な詐欺的行為や詐欺と本質的に結びついた行為がアメリカ合衆国で発生した場合には，証券取引所法第10条(b)を国外で生じた外国の取引に適用してきた．ただし，合衆国内での行為が単に詐欺の準備的な行為である場合は事物管轄権は否定される．つぎに効果テストの下では，合衆国外での証券取引が，合衆

国内において実質的かつ予見可能で有害な効果をもたらす場合には，域外適用が認められてきた．たとえば，国外でなされた詐欺的行為が合衆国の取引所に上場されている株式の価値を減少させた場合には，連邦証券法の適用範囲内にあるとみなされた（マーク・I・スタインバーグ（著）小川宏幸（訳）『アメリカ証券法』（レキシスネクシス・ジャパン，2008）291頁参照）．

本件は，上の分類によれば，行為テストの事例であり，合衆国内での行為が単に詐欺の準備的な行為である場合には事物管轄権は否定されるとの第2巡回区控訴裁判所の厳格な立場を採用した．

3 第2巡回区控訴裁判所の関連判決

本件判旨が依拠した第2巡回区控訴裁判所の関連判決を簡単に紹介する．

① *Shoembaum v. Firstbrook*, 405F. 2d 200（2d Cir.1968）

証券取引所法第10条(b)と規則第10b-5の下での株主代表訴訟において，裁判所は事物管轄権を肯定し，証券取引所法の適用を肯定した．アメリカの株主がカナダ会社に対して訴訟を提起し，会社の金庫株が，被告である取締役が不当に安い価格であることを知りながら，他の外国会社に売却したと主張した．裁判所は，株式の下落は米国の通商に対する十分に重大な効果であり，アメリカ人投資家を保護するために管轄権を行使する（証券取引法を適用する）ことを正当化すると判示した（本件については，徳岡卓樹「民事責任に関する証券取引法の域外適用(1)」法学協会雑誌99巻2号313頁以下参照）．

② *Leasco Data Processing Equipment Corp. v. Maxwell*, 468 F.2d 1326（2d Cir.1972）

Leascoとその英国の子会社は，子会社がロンドンの証券市場で英国会社の株式を購入するよう詐欺的に勧誘されたと主張した．主張されている不実表示は，国外と合衆国内で発生したと主張された．Friendly裁判官は，実質的な不実表示が合衆国内でなされた場合には，合衆国の証券法の適用に有利なように傾くであろうと判示した．しかし，同裁判官は，ここで主張されているすべての不実表示が英国で行われたとすれば，合衆国の親会社に対する効果のみに基づいて管轄権が存在するかについての疑念を表明した（本件につ

き，徳岡・前掲315頁以下参照）．

③ *Bersch v. Drexel Firestone, Inc.*, 519 F.2d 974（2d Cir.1975）

本件は，カナダ会社の株式の売却において，外国で詐欺的行為が行われたことを理由とする証券取引所法に基づくクラスアクションである．裁判所は，合衆国の居住者か市民以外の購入者又は売却者を排除することを地方裁判所に命じた．Friendly裁判官は，すべての重要な詐欺的行為が外国で行われたときには，合衆国の規律管轄権が肯定されるのは，外国での行為の結果が合衆国が利害関係を有する購入者又は売却者であるときに限られるのであって，行為がアメリカの経済又はアメリカ人の投資家一般に対する有害な結果を有するときではないと判示した．このことは，詐欺的行為が外国で行われたときには，合衆国の利益に対する有害な効果が重要であることを示している（本件については，徳岡・前掲321頁以下参照．）．

4　アメリカ対外関係法第3リステイトメント第416条（証券に関する行為を規律する管轄権）

証券法の域外適用については，対外関係法第3リステイトメント第416条の規定も注目される．第416条は，域外適用を含む法適用の一般原則を述べた第3リステイトメント第402条，第403条を証券取引法の適用問題に応用した条文である．本件で特に問題となっているのは，第416条(1)dである．関連部分を以下に掲げる．

「第416条　証券に関する行為を規制する管轄権

(1) 合衆国は，一般に，次に掲げる事項につき規律管轄権を行使することができる．

(a)(i)　いかなる証券取引であれ，合衆国の国民又は居住者（resident）がその一方の当事者である取引であって，合衆国において実行されるもの．

(ii)　証券取引の締結のためのいかなる申込であれ，合衆国においてなされた申込であって，合衆国の国民若しくは居住者によるもの又はそれらの者に対するもの．

(b) いかなる証券取引であれ，つぎのいずれかに該当するもの．
　　(i) 合衆国における組織された証券市場で執行される取引又は執行が予定されている取引
　　(ii) 組織された証券市場において執行されるものでなくとも，主として合衆国で実行される取引又は実行が意図されている取引
　(c) どこで行われるかを問わず，本項(b)に掲げる取引と密接に関係する行為であって，合衆国において実質的な効果を生じているもの，又はそのような効果が生じることをいたしたもの．
　(d) 証券取引は合衆国外で行われる場合であっても，当該証券取引に関係する取引であって，主として合衆国において行われるもの．
　　　　　　　　　　　　　　　　　　　　　　　　　　(以下略)」

(翻訳は，アメリカ対外関係法第3リステイトメント研究会（訳）「アメリカ対外関係法第3リステイトメント(3)」国際法外交雑誌89巻1号100-101頁（1990）（川又良也担当）によった．)

5　その後の展開

本件以後の判決の中で注目すべき2つの判決を挙げておく．

① *Central Bank of Denver v. First Interstate Bank of Denver, N.A.*, 511 U.S. 164（1994）

私人である原告は，1934年証券取引所法10条(b)に基づく訴訟を「[他の被告の] 詐欺を幇助，教唆した行為のために第2次的に有責」と主張されている被告に対して，提起することはできないと判示した．この連邦最高裁の立場は，本件判旨が採用した域外適用の範囲を狭く限定する第2巡回区控訴裁判所の見解を補強するものであるといえようか. Russell Weintraub, International Litigation and Arbitration 394（3rd ed. 2001）．

② *Itoba, Ltd. v. Lep Group PLC*, 54 F.3d 118（2d Cir. 1995), cert. denied, 516 U.S. 1044（1996）

この判決は，証券取引委員会に虚偽の情報を提出したと主張されているロンドンに本拠を有する会社に対する証券取引所法に基づく管轄を肯定したも

のである．裁判所は，域外適用管轄を「行為」と「効果」の2つの基準に基づいて分析し，2つのテストの混合又はコンビネーションが，アメリカ裁判所による管轄権の行使を正当化するに十分な合衆国の関連が存在するかどうかという問題のよりよい像を提供する，と判示する．そして「行為テスト」は，合衆国における被告の行動が，国外で行われた証券詐欺にとって単なる準備的なものであるかどうか，これらの合衆国における行動が主張されている損害を直接に引き起こしたかどうかに焦点をあわせるものであるという．そして裁判所は，この継続的な非開示が多くの合衆国の株主に与えた有害な効果に鑑みると，合衆国において十分な効果があると判断した．

【設　問】

1　事実の概要を述べよ．
2　ドイツと米国が事件と当事者との間に有する関連を整理せよ．
3　本件の争点はなにか．
4　1934年証券取引所法とその第10条(b)について簡単に説明せよ．
5　判旨の主要な部分を要約せよ．
6　第2巡回区控訴裁判所と，第3，第8，第9巡回区控訴裁判所の立場の違いについて説明せよ．
7　対外関係法第3リステイトメント第416条(1)について説明し，それを本件に適用するとどうなるかについて述べよ．
8　法廷意見と補足意見を対比せよ．
9　本件はどのような判決かを要約せよ．
10　本件判旨に賛成か．
11　商標法の域外適用，独占禁止法の域外適用と証券法の域外適用とを比較せよ．

［事項索引］

あ 行

域外的管轄権　299
域外的取引　347
域外適用　283, 285, 297, 310, 312, 315-317,
　　332-338, 363-367
一般管轄権の基礎　20

か 行

解釈の統一　160
外国取引反トラスト改善法　316
外国の証券取引　347
過失責任　19, 250, 252, 253
合衆国著作権法　271, 273, 280, 283, 285
株主代表訴訟　364
管轄権拡大法　9, 27, 52, 53
管轄権に関する相当性の原則　305, 312, 336
企業秘密　183
基本的法目的　175, 177, 186-190, 195, 197,
　　201, 202, 205
規律管轄権　313, 314, 365
　　——に対する制限　314
　　——の基礎　313
求償請求　39
求償訴訟　27, 39, 48, 51-53
競業禁止約款　171, 173, 181-191, 207
　　——における法の抵触　183
　　——の準拠法　187
虚偽の抵触　229, 252, 256
継続的で組織的な活動　20
契約終了の正当事由　200
契約の一方の終了条項　199, 204
契約能力　213, 228
　　——の準拠法　228
契約の交渉地　189

契約の更新　195
契約の締結地　189
契約の目的物の所在地　189, 204
契約の有効性　141, 143, 145, 162, 199, 204,
　　205, 213, 215, 219, 228, 229, 231
結果の統一性　147, 282
結果の予測可能性　254
厳格責任　250, 252-255
厳格な属地主義　282, 310, 333, 334, 338
原告に有利な法　251, 253, 256
合意管轄　91
行為テスト　363, 364, 367
効果基準　301, 312
効果主義（理論）　311
効果テスト　363
効果理論　310-312, 315, 317
公序　65, 75, 79, 85, 87, 94, 151, 153, 155, 158,
　　173, 185, 219, 223, 227, 232, 235
国際曳航契約　90
国際カルテル　311, 316
国際仲裁　117, 119, 123, 125
国際仲裁廷　119
国際著作権事件　265, 285
国際旅客運送契約　156
国際礼譲　111, 123, 305, 307
国家行為理論　289
雇用関係　177, 179, 285
雇用契約　182
雇用者の主たる事務所の所在地　190
雇用者の法　188

さ 行

詐欺　63, 65, 83, 85, 94, 97, 115, 221, 231, 321,
　　351, 353, 357, 361, 363-366
　　——と本質的に結びついた行為　363
　　——の準備的な行為　363, 364
　　——的な陳述　351, 359
最小限テスト　53

[事項索引]

最小限の関連 25, 31, 35, 39, 43, 47, 49, 50, 53
最初の発行地 281
裁判業務の簡素化 254
裁量的上訴 3, 31, 71, 109, 321, 323
差止命令 165, 171, 181, 183, 277, 279, 319, 323, 329, 332
事物管轄 319
事物管轄権 289, 303, 334, 335, 341, 345, 353, 357, 361, 363, 364
実質的効果テスト 337
実質的な反競争的効果 301
実質法の法目的の分析 256, 257
シャーマン法 101, 105, 107, 111, 117, 123, 125, 126, 127, 289, 297, 299, 305, 307, 309-311, 315-317, 329, 333, 336
州際事件 52, 94, 188, 233
州際通商 335, 345, 347, 362
州際的秩序の維持 254
重心 160, 161, 229
——理論 161, 227, 228
修正利益分析論 241, 243
州籍の相違 133, 165, 173, 193, 195, 239, 289, 341
重要な詐欺的行為 363, 365
主権の行為 329
出港禁止令 295
出訴期限条項 159
出訴期限法 149, 237, 239, 241, 243, 245, 247, 250, 251
準拠法約款 157-162, 175, 182, 184-191
証券の購入 343, 345, 359
証券詐欺 351, 355, 367
証券市場 347, 364, 366
証券取引 98, 107, 126, 127, 345, 347, 349, 355, 357, 362-366
証券取引所法 107, 345, 355, 357, 362-367
——第10条(b) 345, 362-364
証券取引法上の請求 98, 126

証券販売に関する詐欺 345
証券法の域外適用 340, 363, 365, 367
商標侵害 319, 332-334
商標法 319, 321, 332-334, 336
——の域外適用 317, 318, 332, 338, 367
職務著作法理 265, 275, 277
真の抵触 230, 232, 233
生産者責任の準拠法 236
生産者の責任の基礎 250
生産制限のカルテル 311
生産地の抑止的法目的 256, 257
生産物責任訴訟 250
生産物責任における法の抵触 250
生産物責任の準拠法に関するハーグ条約 258, 259
製造物訴訟 57
専属管轄裁判所 90, 94
専属的販売代理店 193
創作者の国籍 281
創作者の常居所地法 284
創作地 281
争点ごとの準拠法決定 280
相当性 41, 51, 87, 96
——のテスト 181
——の原則 184, 315
——の理論 310
属地主義 228, 282-284, 310, 311, 313, 315, 332, 336
損害発生地 51, 239, 253, 258

た　行

対外関係法第3リステイトメント 312, 313, 365-367
——第402条 312, 317
対人管轄権 7, 9, 11, 13, 15, 18-20, 31, 33, 37, 39, 43, 47, 48, 52, 55, 57, 59, 61, 65-67
対人管轄権革命 48
代理店契約と法の抵触 200

369

代理店契約の準拠法　192
代理店契約法　193, 195, 201
代理店保護のための強行法規　200
大量契約　157
第1リステイトメント　156, 228
第2リステイトメント　20, 66, 92, 99, 156-159,
　　162, 184, 185, 187, 188, 190, 191, 197, 199
　　-201, 203, 205, 207, 215, 250, 251, 256, 257,
　　280-282
　　――の方法論　187
　　――第145条　259
　　――第187条第2項　157, 175, 184, 186
　　-188, 191, 201
　　――第188条　189, 199, 203, 204
　　――第202条第2項　206
　　――第222条　281
多国籍企業に対する裁判管轄権　66
単一の連結点　281
地理的制限　181, 183
仲裁合意　98, 107, 109, 111, 113, 115, 121, 123
仲裁条項　98, 101, 107, 109, 111, 113, 121, 126
　　-129
仲裁適格性　98, 100, 101, 107, 109, 121, 126,
　　127, 128, 129
懲罰的損害賠償　250
著作権侵害　261, 280, 282
著作権の準拠法　260, 280
著作権の所有権　261, 269, 271, 280, 281, 285
直接利益分析論　241, 243
通商の流れ　25, 31, 33, 35, 37, 39, 43, 45, 49,
　　50, 52, 53, 309
ディストリビューター　35, 57, 103, 105, 169,
　　171, 197, 199, 204, 247
ディラーズ法　109
適正手続条項　9, 15, 17-20, 27, 31, 33, 37, 45,
　　48, 55, 345
伝統的法選択規則　230
投資家の勧誘　343

投資契約　343
当事者自治　156, 157, 158, 184, 187, 201, 229
当事者による法選択　175, 177, 184, 188, 200,
　　201, 207
当事者の正当な期待の保護　156, 157
統治利益分析論　199, 252
登録国法　284
独占禁止法　105, 107, 109, 111, 113, 115, 117,
　　119, 121, 123, 126, 128, 289, 295, 297, 303,
　　305, 310, 311, 316, 317
　　――の域外適用　288, 295, 310, 311, 367
　　――上の請求　107, 111, 119, 126, 127, 128
特別管轄権　17, 19-21
トレード・シークレット　165, 169, 171

　　　　　　　　な　行
内国民待遇　267
2段階テスト　50, 53

　　　　　　　　は　行
バランシング・テスト　310, 312, 316, 336, 337
パリの国際商業会議所　98, 127
反致　155
秘密情報　165, 167, 169, 171, 173, 181, 183
表見上の抵触　230
標準約款　160
フェアネス　50, 51
フェアプレイと実質的正義　25, 43, 45, 47, 49
　　-51, 53
　　――という伝統的観念　37
フォーラム・ノン・コンヴィニエンス　77,
　　289
不公正な証券取引　362
附合契約　94, 113, 153, 155, 157-159, 161, 162
不実表示　147, 158, 351, 359, 361, 363, 364
不正競争　171, 319, 325, 334
不正競争行為　332, 333
船荷証券　91, 145

[事項索引]

不法行為死亡訴訟　7, 18, 256
不法行為死亡法　241, 243, 247, 254
不法行為地法　230, 273, 282
　——主義　231, 239, 254, 282
不法行為による死亡に基づく訴訟　250, 254
不法行為の準拠法　256, 259, 282
フランチャイズ契約　59, 185
ベルヌ条約　267, 269, 271
編集者の著作権　277
放棄　81, 107, 109, 141, 147, 149, 155–157, 197, 200, 254, 311
法人格否認　67
　——の法理　63, 65–68
法選択アプローチ　283, 285
法選択条項　75, 113, 157–160, 173, 202, 285
法選択方法論　187, 233, 251, 259, 282
法選択理論　187, 229, 235
法廷地　9, 11, 15, 17, 19–23, 25, 31, 33, 35, 37, 39, 41, 43, 45, 47, 49–52, 66, 73, 75, 77, 79, 81, 83, 85, 87, 89, 91–94, 97, 98, 113, 115, 125, 158, 203, 213, 219, 228, 230, 239, 247, 249, 254, 256
　——州に意図的に向けられた行為　37, 45
　——選択条項　71, 73, 75, 77, 79, 81, 83, 87, 90–97, 99, 113
　——の統治利益の促進　254
　——法の優先　232
保護が求められる国　271
保護国　284

ま 行

免責条項　73, 77, 89, 99
最も重要な関係　189, 199, 203, 205, 229, 256, 257, 269, 281, 282
　——の理論　257, 281, 282

や 行

有効視の原則　217, 227, 228

予見可能性　31, 33, 111, 156, 157, 160, 228
より良い法規則の適用　254

ら 行

ランハム法　321, 325, 327, 331–337
利益衡量アプローチ　254
利益分析論　228–231, 235, 243, 245, 251, 253, 282
略式判決　95, 135, 149, 159, 160, 193, 195, 201, 206, 239
旅客運送契約　132, 157
礼譲　123, 301, 305, 309, 312, 336, 337, 353, 359
連結点の集中　160
連邦コモンロー　269
連邦証券法　345, 363, 364
連邦仲裁法　101, 103, 111, 121, 126
連邦抵触法規則　143
労働者の競業行為　182
浪費者　209, 211, 213, 217, 219, 221, 223, 225, 227, 228, 231–234
　——の契約能力　228
　——後見　209
労務給付地　188–190
ロシア著作権法　261, 275, 277, 280

A–Z

ALI 原則　283, 285
amicus curie　22
Beale　142, 143, 157
Cavers　232, 233
certiorari　2, 30, 70, 107, 320, 322
Currie　157, 218, 219, 228, 229, 231, 232, 233, 235, 252
diversity action　164, 192
Due Process Clause　8, 14, 16, 18, 26, 30 ,32 34, 36, 44, 46, 54, 344
Ehrenzweig　154, 155, 216, 217

in personam jurisdiction 6, 8, 10, 12, 19, 54, 56, 60, 64
long arm statute 52
Lorenzen 212, 213
Patry 264, 265, 270, 271, 280
Reese 142, 143, 159
Restatement, Second, Conflict of Laws, §35 20
Restatement, Second, Conflict of laws, §80 92
Richman & Reynolds 156, 233, 234
Stumberg 212-217
summary judgment 134, 148, 192, 194, 200, 206, 238
Vanity Fair テスト 336, 337
von Mehren & Trautman 20
Weintraub 21, 51, 156, 233, 366

[判例索引]

Allstate Insurance Co. v. Hague 40, 41, 248, 249
American Safety Equipment Corp. v. J. P. Maguire & Co. 104, 105, 110
Asahi Metal Industry Co. Ltd. v. Superior Court of California 24
Bean Dredging Corp. v. Dredge Technology Corp. 32, 33
Bersch v. Drexel Firestone, Inc. 348, 349, 365
Bisso v. Inland Waterways Corp. 77, 78, 84, 85, 90, 91
Blackmer v. United States 320, 321, 324, 325
Blalock v. Perfect Subscription Co. 184
Branch v. Federal Trade Commission 320, 321, 324, 325
Burger King Corp. v. Rudzewicz 44, 45, 46, 47
Carbon Black Export, Inc. v. The Monrosa 74, 75
Carbotrade S.p.A. v. Bureau Veritas 272, 273
Carnival Cruise Lines, Inc. v. Shute 94
Central Bank of Denver v. First Interstate Bank of Denver 366
Chevron U. S. A. Inc. v. Natural Resources Defense Council, Inc. 358, 359
Commercial Credit Plan, Inc. v. Parker 176, 177
Continental Grain (Australia) Pty. Ltd. v. Pacific Oilseeds, Inc. 352, 353
Continental Ore Co. v. Union Carbide & Carbon Corp. 296, 297, 304, 305

[判例索引]

Curley v. AMR Corp.　274, 275
Dixilyn Drilling Corp. v. Crescent Towing & Salvage Co.　77, 78
Dothan Aviation Corp. v. Miller　172, 173
Erie R. R. Co. v. Tompkins　137
Foley Bros., Inc. v. Filardo
　320, 321, 324, 325
Foley Bros., Inc. v. Filardo.　325
Fricke v. Isbrandtsen Co.　159
Gaunt v. John Hancock Life Ins. Co.
　150, 151
George W. Luft Co. v. Zande Cosmetic Co.　326, 327
Grunenthal GmbH v. Hotz　352, 353
Gulf Oil Corp. v. Gilbert　74, 75
Hal Roach Studios, Inc. v. Film Classics　142, 143, 145
Hartford Fire Insurance Co. v. California　315
Hasbro Bradley, Inc. v. Sparkle Toys, Inc.　272, 273
Hedrick v. Daiko Shoji Co.　33, 51
Helicopteros Nacionales de Colombia, S.A. v. Hall　2
Howard Schultz & Assoc. v. Broniec
　172, 173
Howse v. Zimmer Manufacturing Co., Inc　54, 55, 58, 59
Humble v. Toyota Motor Co.　34, 35, 51
Hutson v. Fehr Bros., Inc.　34, 35
IIT v. Vencap, Ltd.　350, 351
Indussa Corp. v. S.S. Ranborg　93
Intercontinental Planning, Ltd. v. Daystrom, Inc.　199
International Shoe Co. v. Washington　10, 11, 24, 25, 36, 37, 44-48, 60, 61
Itar－Tass Rusian Agency v. Rusian Kurier, Inc.　260

Itoba, Ltd. v. Lep Group PLC　366
Jamieson v. Potts,　212-215
Johnson v. Spider Staging Corp.
　238, 239, 242, 243, 256, 259
Keeton v. Hustler Magazine, Inc.
　8, 9, 34, 35
Klaxon Co. v. Stentor Electric Manufacturing Co.　172, 173, 238, 239
Kotam Electronics v. JBL Consumer Products, Inc.　128
Kulukundis Shipping Co. v. Amtorg Trading Corp.　120, 121
Lauritzen v. Larsen　272, 273, 304, 305
Leasco Data Processing Equip. Corp. v. Maxwell　344, 345
Leasco Data Processing Equipment Corp. v. Maxwell　364
Mandeville Island Farms v. American Crystal Sugar Co.　324-327
Marshall v. Kleppe　250, 251
Massie v. Watts　330, 331
Max Daetwyler Corp. v. R. Meyer　34, 35
Maxwell Communications Corp. v. Societe Generale　268, 269
Merrell Dow Pharmaceuticals Inc. v. Thompson　350, 351
Miller v. Honda Motor Co.　54
Milliken v. Meyer　24, 25, 36, 37
Mitsubishi Motors Corporation v. Soler Chrysler-Plymouth, Inc.　100
Morris v. Altstedter　326, 327
Murray v. British Broadcasting Corp.
　266, 267
Nasco, Inc. v. Gimbert　172, 173, 176, 177
National Equipment Rental, Ltd. v. Szukhent　80, 81
New Jersey v. New York　330, 331

373

New York Life Insurance Co. v.
   Cravens   144, 145
Nordson Corp. v. Plasschaert   164, 176, 177
Olshen v. Kaufman   208–211, 216–219, 226,
   227, 235
Perkins v. Benguet Consolidated Mining
   Co.   8, 9, 20
Phillips Petroleum Co. v. Shutts   40, 41
Prima Paint Corp. v. Flood & Conklin Mfg.
   Co.   112, 113
Puritan/Churchill Chemical Co.   172, 173
Reich v. Purcell   231
Reyno v. Piper Aircraft Co.   252, 259
Rosenberg Bros.& Co. v. Curtis Brown
   Co.   13
Schoenbaum v. Firstbrook   348, 349
Shoembaum v. Firstbrook   364
Sibley v. KLM Royal Dutch Airlines
   246, 247
Siegelman v. Cunard White Star Ltd.   132
Skiriotes v. Florida   324, 325
Southern International Sales Co., Inc. v.
   Potter & Brumfield Div.   192
Sterrett v. Stoddard Lbr.   216, 217
The Bremen v. Zapata Off- Shore Co.   70
Thomsen v. Cayser   324, 325, 328, 329
Timberlane Lumber Co. v. Bank of
   America   288, 289
Tomlin v. Boeing Co.   236
Turcotte v. Ford Motor Company   253, 259

United Rope Distributors, Inc. v. Kimbely
   Line   22
United States v. Aluminum Co. of
   America   296, 297, 310
United States v. Bausch & Lomb Optical
   Co.   326, 327
United States v. First National City
   Bank   42, 43
United States v. Frankfort Distilleries
   326, 327
United States v. General Electric Co.
   296, 297
United States v. National Lead Co.
   330, 331
United States v. R. P. Oldham Co.   298, 299
United States v. Sisal Sales Corp.
   296, 297, 328, 329
United States v. Univis Lens Co.   326, 327
Vacuum Oil Co. v. Eagle Oil Co.   326, 327
Vanity Fair Mills, Inc. v. T. Eaton Co.   334
Vita Food Products, Inc. v. Unus Shipping
   Co., Ltd.   144, 145
Wells Fargo & Co. v. Wells Fargo Express
   Co.   336
Wilko v. Swan   104, 105, 118, 119, 126
Wood Bros. Homes Inc. v. Walker Adj.
   Bureau   204
Zoelsch v. Arthur Andersen & Co.
   340, 348, 349

著者紹介

松岡　博（まつおか　ひろし）

1939年 大阪市生まれ，1961年 大阪大学法学部卒業，1981年 大阪大学法学部助手・助教授・ハーバードロースクール客員研究員を経て大阪大学法学部教授，1987年 法学博士（大阪大学），1990年 大阪大学学生部長，1993年 大阪大学法学部長，1994年大阪大学副学長，2002年 帝塚山大学法政策学部教授，2003年 帝塚山大学法政策学部長，2005年 帝塚山大学学長、2008年 国際高等研究所フェロー

現　在	帝塚山大学法政策学部教授・国際ビジネス法務塾塾長／大阪大学名誉教授／国際高等研究所フェロー／弁護士（土居総合法律事務所）
専　攻	国際私法・国際取引法
学　会	国際私法学会（監事），国際法学会（名誉会員），国際経済法学会，国際法協会（日本支部理事），日米法学会，国際ビジネス法務研究会（会長）
主　著	『現代国際私法講義』法律文化社（2008年），『アメリカ国際私法の基礎理論』大阪大学出版会（2007年），『［新版］国際私法・国際取引法判例研究』大阪大学出版会（2003年），『国際家族法の理論』大阪大学出版会（2002年），『国際取引と国際私法』晃洋書房（1993年），『国際私法における法選択規則構造論』有斐閣（1987年），『国際私法講義要綱』玄文社（1984年），『国際関係私法入門（第2版）』有斐閣（2009年，編著），『国際私法概論（第5版）』有斐閣（2007年，共著），『現代国際取引法講義』法律文化社（1996年，編著），『基本法コンメンタール　国際私法』日本評論社（1994年，共編著），『アメリカ抵触法（上巻）』レクシスネクシス・ジャパン（2009年，共訳）

大阪大学新世紀レクチャー

アメリカ国際私法・国際取引法判例研究

2010年3月31日　初版第1刷発行　　　［検印廃止］

著者　松　岡　　　博

発行所　大阪大学出版会
代表者　鷲田清一

〒565-0871　吹田市山田丘2-7
　　　　　　大阪大学ウエストフロント
電話：06-6877-1614
FAX：06-6877-1617
URL：http://www.osaka-up.or.jp

印刷・製本所　　（株）遊文舎

ⓒHiroshi Matsuoka 2010　　　　　　Printed in Japan
ISBN978-4-87259-294-8 C3032

Ⓡ〈日本複写権センター委託出版物〉
本書を無断で複写複製（コピー）することは，著作権法上の例外を除き，禁じられています．本書をコピーされる場合は，事前に日本複写権センター（JRRC）の許諾を受けてください．

　　JRRC〈http://www.jrrc.or.jp　eメール：info@jrrc.or.jp　電話：03-3401-2382〉